California's
Wilderness Areas

THE COMPLETE GUIDE

VOLUME I
**MOUNTAINS AND
COASTAL RANGES**

TEXT AND
PHOTOGRAPHY BY
GEORGE WUERTHNER

WESTCLIFFE PUBLISHERS

Preface

I grew up in the eastern United States. Though I'd done a little car camping and a lot of day hiking as a teenager, I didn't start backpacking until I entered college at the University of Montana in Missoula in the early '70s. Immediately upon my arrival there, I began exploring the wildlands that surrounded the community, meeting other students who also loved hiking.

One of my new friends was an older student, John Wight of Orinda, California. At school, everyone knew him as "John of the Mountains," and indeed, the appellation was fitting. John had spent every summer since he was fifteen exploring the Sierra Nevada. He would work for a few weeks, long enough to afford a couple of big bags of oatmeal, some raisins, brown sugar, tea, noodles, and a few other basics, then head off to the mountains for two to three weeks at a time. After graduating from high school, John spent four years wandering around the western states, hiking and climbing for months at a time.

I was fascinated by John's tales of the Sierra, a mountain range he considered to be the finest in the West. His opinion wasn't based on a chauvinistic California homeboy pride—he had seen a considerable amount of the West's mountains. Thus it was with real excitement that I contemplated a trip we hatched that spring: a two-week long backpack in the Sierra Nevada. To be asked to join John on a hike was a major compliment. He usually preferred to go alone, since he considered most people a drag on his enthusiasm and time. I had somehow impressed on him that I was capable of keeping up with his pace and willing to consume oatmeal for breakfast, lunch, and dinner for weeks, if necessary. I wanted to be in the mountains at any cost, too.

At the end of the spring term, I hitchhiked from Montana to Yosemite, where I did a four-day solo trip through the park's backcountry and celebrated my nineteenth birthday before rendezvousing with John at the climber's camp in Yosemite Valley. From there, we hitched south to Big Pine and walked up Pine Creek to the Palisades, one of John's favorite haunts. Camped on the snowfields, we spent a number of days ascending peaks—my first Sierra climbs.

When I attained the summit of 13,891-foot Mount Agassiz, I was overwhelmed: I had never been on top of a major peak before, and I had never been in a mountain range like the Sierra. In every direction, snowy

Across Canyon Creek to Red Mountain, Marble Mountain Wilderness.

peak upon snowy peak unfolded to the distant edge of the horizon. And in all that my eye could behold, there was not a single road. I didn't know it then, but I was looking out on the second largest roadless area in the lower 48 states—a wilderness that stretched 177 miles from Tioga Pass south to Sherman Pass near Lake Isabella.

After several days in the Palisades area, we crossed 12,800-foot Agassiz Col and descended into Dusy Basin, then headed to Muir Pass. In over a week in the mountains, we had not seen another person until we hit the John Muir Trail, a major hiking thoroughfare in the middle of the Sierra. I had expected "crowds" in the California backcountry, where hikers were supposed to be "loving the wilderness to death." Yet I found plenty of solitude. Indeed, that has been my experience ever since. In most of the wilderness areas I've explored in California, I've seldom encountered more than a handful of people if I steered away from the popular destinations or trails. People may be "loving the wilderness to death" as some claim, but my experience suggests it's a tiny fraction of our wildlands most people are loving.

Since that first California hike, I've had the opportunity to visit and revisit many parts of the Golden State, as well as many other wildlands throughout the country. I've traveled throughout the Rockies —in western Canada, the Yukon, and all over Alaska. Yet I continue to return to California over and over again, and I can truly say after all these years that there are few places that rival its beauty. Nowhere in the United States will you find such diversity of landscapes and terrain nor a greater variety of wildlands so accessible to people of ordinary means, strength, and endurance. Many people immigrate to California because it's seen as a land with economic choices, but it is really a land of back-country opportunities unsurpassed anywhere else in the United States. This guide offers an introduction to those opportunities.

—*George Wuerthner*
Eugene Oregon

Shooting star and small tarn below Bishop Pass, John Muir Wilderness.

Table of Contents

ISBN: 1-56579-233-5

PHOTOGRAPHY AND TEXT COPYRIGHT: George Wuerthner, 1997. All rights reserved.

Tom Lorang Jones, 1997. All rights reserved.
Pages 24-27; adapted with permission.

PRODUCTION MANAGER: Harlene Finn, Westcliffe Publishers

EDITOR: Bonnie Beach

DESIGN AND PRODUCTION: Rebecca Finkel, F + P Graphic Design; Boulder, CO

PUBLISHED BY: Westcliffe Publishers, Inc.
2650 South Zuni Street
Englewood, Colorado 80110

H & Y Printing Limited
Hong Kong

LIBRARY OF CONGRESS CATALOGING-IN-PUBLICATION DATA

Wuerthner, George.
The complete guide to California's wilderness areas / text and photography by George Wuerthner.
p. cm.
Includes index.
Contents: v. 1. Mountains and coastal ranges
ISBN: 1-56579-233-5
1. Wilderness areas—California—Guidebooks.
2. Natural history—California—Guidebooks. 3. Trails —California—Guidebooks. 4. Hiking—California— Guidebooks. I. Title
QH76.5.C2W84 1997   97-6015
508.794—dc21   CIP

For more information about other fine books and calendars from Westcliffe Publishers, please contact your local bookstore or write, call (303) 935-0900, or fax (303) 935-0903 for our free catalogue.

COVER CAPTION:
Big Sur Coast on the edge of the Ventana Wilderness, Los Padres National Forest.

PLEASE NOTE:
Risk is always a factor in backcountry and high-mountain travel. Many of the activities described in this book can be dangerous, especially when weather is adverse or unpredictable, and when unforeseen events or conditions create a hazardous situation. The author has done his best to provide the reader with accurate information about backcountry travel, as well as to point out some of its potential hazards. It is the responsibility of the users of this guide to learn the necessary skills for safe backcountry travel, and to exercise caution in potentially hazardous areas, especially on glaciers and avalanche-prone terrain. The author and publisher disclaim any liability for injury or other damage caused by backcountry traveling, mountain biking, or performing any other activity described in this book.

Acknowledgments

Many people assisted me in my research on California
wilderness areas, in particular, the staff of the various agencies
that manage our public lands who were very generous with
their time and knowledge. In far too many instances, I did
not note or even ask their names as they answered ques-
tions and provided reports, maps, or literature about the
areas under their care. In general, these employees who are
responsible for our public lands are doing an extraordinary
job in an era of growing pressure for greater exploitation
by commercial users and declining budgets for staff and
monitoring purposes. In particular, I want to recognize
the often unnamed seasonal workers—the naturalists,
biological technicians, wilderness rangers, trail crews,
and others—who do much of the public contact and
field work for low pay and with little thanks from the
population at large.

In addition, our wildlands would not exist today
if it were not for the often thankless efforts of dedicated
citizens and environmental organizations who have struggled
for decades to generate public support for wilderness values.
All such organizations deserve the financial, emotional, and
active participation of all those who value and visit natural
landscapes.

Finally, I want to thank some individuals whose
names I do know who assisted in widening my knowledge
and appreciation for California's wildlands. They include
Jim Eaton and Ryan Hanson at the California Wilderness
Coalition, Felice Pace of the Klamath Forest Alliance, Jim
Carlson of High Sierra Hikers Association, Eric Gerstrung
of the California Department of Fish and Game, Eric
Beckwith of the Sierra Biodiversity Project, and Tony
Caprico, research ecologist at Sequoia National Park.

California Wilderness Areas

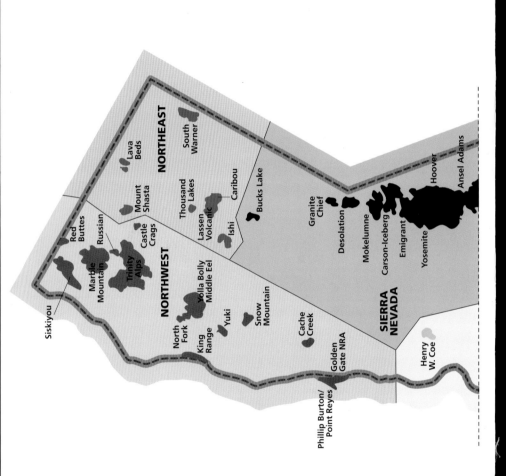

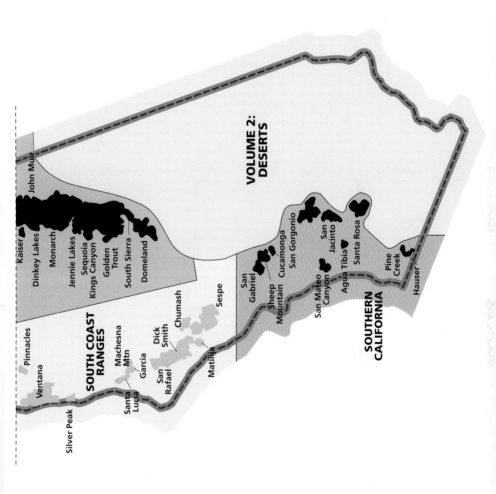

VOLUME 2:
DESERTS

SOUTH COAST RANGES

SOUTHERN CALIFORNIA

Kaiser
John Muir
Dinkey Lakes
Monarch
Jennie Lakes
Sequoia
Kings Canyon
Golden Trout
South Sierra
Domeland

Pinnacles
Ventana
Silver Peak
Santa Lucia
Machesna Mtn
Garcia
San Rafael
Dick Smith
Chumash
Matilija
Sespe

San Gabriel
Sheep Mountain
Cucamonga
San Gorgonio
San Mateo Canyon
San Jacinto
Agua Tibia
Santa Rosa
Pine Creek
Hauser

🚏🚏 Border	TH Trailhead
--- Trail	🔺 Campground
—— Access Road	○ Point of Interest
—— River	S Ranger Station
🌊 Lake	P Parking Lot
	🏕 Picnic Area

About California

Some say that California is as close to paradise as one can get without dying and going to heaven. And in many ways, they are correct. There are few places on Earth with such an overwhelmingly pleasant climate, diverse and inspiring landscape, and rich cultural heritage. Scenically, the state offers something for almost any taste. There are 1,200 miles of coastline, 32 million acres of forest, 21 million acres of desert, and mountains almost everywhere except the 400-mile-long Central Valley. The highest point in the lower 48 states (Mount Whitney) as well as the lowest point (Death Valley) are within its bounds. California has the continent's highest waterfall (Yosemite), tallest trees (coast redwood), oldest trees (bristlecone pine), and largest trees (sequoia). And it has a surprising amount of wildlands left, despite the fact that it is also the most populous state in the nation.

Since the gold rush sparked the first mass migration to California in 1849, people have been descending on the "Golden State." The population is now pushing 32 million, more than the entire country of Canada. Although this influx of humanity has dramatically altered much of California's landscape, most of it is still essentially undeveloped, leading to the idea that California's moniker could well be the "Wilderness State." This may sound incongruous to anyone caught in a Los Angeles traffic jam or trying to find a place to sit on a crowded summer beach, but it is these concentrations of humanity that leave the rest of the state largely uninhabited. Alpine County, for example, in the central Sierra Nevada, has fewer than 2,000 residents. The population density of the Klamath Mountain Province located in northwest California, an area as large as many states, has fewer than five people per square mile—less than the average density found in Montana, Idaho, Oregon, Colorado, and most of the remaining western states.

California also has the most federally designated wildlands—as well as the largest number of undesignated roadless areas of 100,000 acres or greater—in the United States outside of Alaska! And the state includes a wildlands roadless complex, the High Sierra, which encompasses 2.8 million acres—approximately the size of the state of Connecticut—making it the second largest unroaded area found in the lower 48 states! Only the Central Idaho complex that includes the Frank Church–River of No Return Wilderness is larger.

With the 1994 passage of the California Desert bill, the Golden State now has more than 13.8 million acres of federally designated wilderness. In addition, nearly a million acres of state lands are also managed primarily for wildlands values. Today, California's total acreage of federally designated wilderness nearly equals the combined acreage of designated wilderness found in the remaining western states, minus Washington!

What This Book Covers

Filled with a variety of trail descriptions and recreational opportunities, this guidebook also offers an exploration of California's wildlands heritage, a peek into the state's past, and a glimpse of the hope for its future. I have covered the existing federally designated non-desert mountain and coastal wilderness areas, as well as a few undesignated but significant roadless lands that could eventually be added to the wilderness

Lakes stud cirque basin below Bishop Pass, John Muir Wilderness.

system. Wildlands found within California's state park system are also covered. All the areas in this book, volume one, are located outside the desert region. Volume two features desert wildlands.

Given the scope of the subject, not all areas are equally treated. Emphasis is given to the larger wildlands complexes or areas that represent unique or special features.

Biodiversity and Wildlands

Although the main criteria for wilderness designation tends to be roadless character, California's wildlands system also protects at least a representative sample of every major ecoregion found in the state. This is fortunate, indeed, because within its 160,000 square miles California harbors more endemic and unique plant and animal life than any other state. More than one third of the state's plants and animals are endemic, which means they are found no place else. There are more than 750 native vertebrate animals, 6,800 plant species, and 25,000 native insect species, along with a recognized 380 natural communities—more than any other similar-sized temperate region in the world. Designated wilderness includes everything from the fog-shrouded bird colonies of the nearly inaccessible Farallon Islands and the prickly, arid, cactus forests of Joshua Tree National Monument to the old-growth Douglas fir of the Trinity Alps.

Thus far urbanization, including all freeways, roads, subdivisions, and cities, directly affects less than three to five percent of the state's landscape. While this growth increasingly poses a threat to California's native landscapes, urban development is still highly concentrated. If the only modern influence upon California's landscape were freeways and subdivisions, there would be huge parcels of the state that would still support native ecosystems and species, including grizzly bear, wolves, salmon, and large herds of elk and antelope. The reason the animals and ecosystems are no longer found in the state is due to a more pernicious and less obvious environmental degradation, which has resulted from logging and agricultural activities, including livestock grazing. These two occupations influence far more land use than all urban development combined, exerting a widespread but pervasive negative effect upon California's biological and physical integrity.

For example, more than 31 million acres of private land, or approximately one third of California, is directly impacted by farming or livestock grazing (and this figure does not include livestock grazing occurring on federal lands). Indeed, everything from alien plant and animal invasion to overuse of waterways for agricultural production (primarily forage for livestock) has contributed to an accelerating degradation of habitat, with a corresponding decline or diminishment in native species. In the past 200 years, nearly 900 native plant species have become rare or endangered, and 34 are already extinct.

Nevertheless, a surprising number of the state's natural landscapes remain relatively intact, with the potential for eventual ecological restoration. Wilderness protection and designation is a key element in any ecological recovery strategy. Unfortunately, the protective umbrella of wilderness designation is not evenly distributed over the landscape. Though the total acreage of legally protected wilderness is impressive by any standard, in the past most wildlands preservation efforts focused on scenically spectacular lands or landscapes that had little commercial extractive value. As a consequence, the majority of protected lands are alpine or subalpine landscapes. While recreationally valuable, such lands tend to be low in plant and animal community diversity. The ecologically important riparian lowlands, grasslands, oak savannas, low elevation old-growth forests, and other biologically critical landscapes are falling through the cracks of preservation efforts. For example, 90 percent of the state's old-growth redwood forests have been logged in the past 100 years, leaving only fragmented patches intact. This is one reason why almost half of the state's 380 natural communities are rare or imperiled, according to the California Department of Fish and Game. California also has more endangered species than any other state in the nation—in part because it has more endemic species with limited or very restricted habitat requirements—but also because many of these species are concentrated on the very lands least likely to receive protected status, such as lower elevation forests, grasslands, and riparian habitats.

As our understanding of the importance of maintaining biological diversity and functioning ecosystems grows, we can expect increasing attention to the protection of biological corridors—preservation of landscapes that include entire ecological units that are large enough to permit continued operation of ecological processes, such as wildfire, and restoration of wide-ranging predators, such as wolves. California's existing protected wilderness presents core areas to build on, but without expansion of protected habitat—along with modification or elimination of some existing land use practices on the remaining lands—the state's biological heritage will continue to erode.

Geography

California's remarkable biological diversity is in part the result of its unusual topographical and climatic geography. Mountains are a dominant feature: From Oregon in the north to Mexico in the south, the majority of the state is wrinkled with hills, ridges, and peaks. The Coast Range, as its name implies, follows the coast from Oregon south to Los Angeles. San Francisco Bay divides this range into a north and south component. A north to south gradient of decreasing moisture influences vegetation so that chaparral dominates southern ranges, while conifers, including coast redwood and Douglas fir, blanket the northern coast.

On the opposite side of the state, across the 400-mile-long Central Valley, lies the Sierra Nevada, the longest and highest mountain range in the lower 48 states (the Cascades and Appalachian Mountains are longer, but made up of several units). It is a single block of granite that runs halfway down the state with a gentle western slope and an abrupt eastern face. The northern portion of the range is characterized by deep, river-cut canyons, rolling terrain, and peaks that seldom exceed 9,000 feet. The southern portion of the range, often called the High Sierra, has more than 500 peaks topping 12,000 feet, culminating in sky-piercing 14,496-foot Mount Whitney.

Beyond the Sierra lies the Basin and Range province, which reaches across Nevada all the way to the Wasatch Range of Utah. The White Mountains on the California–Nevada border contain the highest summits in the province, including 14,246-foot White Mountain Peak. The province takes in most of the desert ranges of Southern California as well as some in the northeast corner of the state, including the Warner Mountains.

North of Los Angeles, the Coast Range and the Sierra Nevada run together to form the Transverse Ranges, including the San Bernardino Mountains, San Gabriel Mountains, Santa Monica Mountains, and Tehachapi Range. South of Banning Pass, where I–10 crosses from the Los Angeles Basin to the Mojave Desert, lies the Peninsula Ranges that include the Palomar Mountains, San Jacinto Mountains, and Santa Rosa Range.

The Cascade Range, volcanic in origin, extends from Mount Lassen north-ward into Oregon. It includes Mount Shasta, over 14,000 feet in elevation, which is one of the highest peaks in California.

Occupying the northwest corner of the state are the Siskiyou Mountains, Marble Mountains, Trinity Alps, Scott Mountains, and Scott Bar Mountains, collec-tively known as the Klamath Mountains.

These mountain uplands are separated by major valleys and basins. The largest of these is Central Valley, which is 400 miles long with a northern branch drained by the Sacramento River and a southern arm drained by the San Joaquin River. Both waterways flow into San Francisco Bay. Other major valleys include the Santa Clara and Napa, which extend south and north of San Francisco Bay, Salinas Valley by Monterey Bay, and Santa Ynez Valley by Santa Barbara. Nearly all of these valleys are devoted to agriculture and, increasingly, to urban centers as well. However, none matches the Los Angeles Basin in Southern California for urbanization.

Climate

California's climate is Mediterranean, one of only four locations in the world with weather patterns dominated by winter rainfall and summer drought. But because of the great elevational differences in the state, one encounters everything from sub-tropical to sub-arctic weather zones. California has the continental record for heat at 134 degrees recorded in Death Valley, but also experiences winter temperatures of 30 below in some higher Great Basin valleys. Due to cool off-shore currents, fog dominates the coast in spring and summer, but it is also a common occurrence in the Central Valley in winter. Annual precipitation is just as varied: Along the northwest coast, it may exceed 100 inches a year, while less than two inches may fall in some of the dry, low valleys of the Mojave Desert.

What is Wilderness?

The History of Wilderness Protection

Depending on how the word is used, wilderness can have several meanings. Throughout the book I will use the term "Wilderness" with a capital letter for congressionally designated wilderness areas, such as the John Muir Wilderness, Trinity Alps Wilderness, etc., while a lower case "wilderness" implies undeveloped landscapes that have no formal legislative protection, but have wildlands characteristics.

Formally designated wilderness or "Big W" is given congressional protection via the 1964 Wilderness Act. Congress passed the Wilderness Act to provide permanent protection for federal wildlands. Earlier preservation efforts were aimed toward protection of other resource values such as geological, biological, scenic oddities, or what one writer termed "freaks of nature." For example, the designation of Yellowstone as a national park in 1872 was done primarily to protect the region's abundance of hot springs and geysers, not for protection of the wilderness. Similarly, Yosemite was declared a park just to preserve its scenic grandeur. Although Sierra Club founder John Muir was primarily interested in advocating protection for the Sierra and elsewhere to preserve wildlands qualities, it was not the dominant philosophy guiding most early park designations.

Formal recognition for protection of large landscapes in a primitive and undeveloped condition did not occur until 1924, when the Forest Service set aside a half-million acres in New Mexico as the Gila Wilderness. This administrative decision signaled a change in the nation's collective philosophy. For more than 300 years it had been the country's goal to "tame" wilderness—to protect civilization, not wildlands. To be sure, even in 1924 the majority of people still considered "subduing" the wilderness as a major priority in American affairs, but at least a few were now asking that some scattered remnants of wildlands be preserved for future generations.

The philosophical roots of the wilderness protection concept can be traced back to Henry David Thoreau, who said, "A town is saved, no more by the men and women in it than the woods and swamps that surround it." John Muir continued this tradition, ceaselessly advocating for preservation of the Sierra Nevada and protection from logging, mining, and livestock grazing. In fact, Muir's major reason for proposing expansion of Yosemite's boundaries to include the watersheds of the Merced and Tuolumne Rivers was based primarily on his desire to eliminate livestock grazing from the high country. He also advocated park protection for the entire southern Sierra, encompassing much of what is now the John Muir Wilderness and Sequoia–Kings Canyon National Park Wilderness as a means of protecting the ranges from destructive timbering and grazing practices. But in the context of his day, Muir had to base most of his arguments for protection upon the grandeur of the scenery, rather than purely upon its wildlands values. However, there is no doubt that preservation of the philosophical concept of wilderness is what drove Muir's passions.

The first direct effort to set aside land from development to maintain its wildlands qualities occurred in 1919. Arthur Carhart, a Forest Service landscape architect, was sent to Trappers Lake in Colorado to survey the area for a proposed summer home recreational development. After seeing the site, Carhart decided that maintaining its natural condition was far more valuable than ringing the lake with cabins. In his memorandum to his superiors, Carhart advised against any development.

His original recommendation for Trappers Lake only involved a small amount of land, and it appears that initially Carhart did not have the vision to see the need for landscape-wide preservation. But within a few years he began to advocate that some natural areas should be protected for their wilderness qualities. As Carhart's vision began to grow, he came into increasing conflict with the Forest Service's development mandate. He quit only four years later.

Prior to his resignation, Carhart met with another early wilderness advocate— Aldo Leopold. At that time, Leopold was an assistant forester for the Forest Service in Albuquerque, New Mexico. Author of the now classic book, *A Sand County Almanac,* Leopold was thinking along similar lines as Carhart, but he had already acquired a landscape-wide vision. Very early in his career, Leopold recognized that preservation of large roadless areas was the only way to protect wildlands values. In 1921 he published his seminal essay, "The Wilderness and Its Place in Forest Recreation Policy," in the *Journal of Forestry.* Partly due to Leopold's vision and encouragement, the Forest Service set aside a half-million-acre New Mexico tract as the Gila Wilderness. However, as with Carhart, Leopold eventually became disenchanted with the agency and took a position as a professor at the University of Wisconsin, Madison.

Although merely a bureaucratic decision that carried no weight of law, the creation of the Gila Wilderness captured the imagination of others in the Forest Service. In 1926 an inventory of the agency's holdings revealed that there were 74 areas totaling 55 million acres where no roads existed, and none were as yet planned. This lead to the designation of Forest Service lands as "primitive areas" under the agency's L-20 regulations implemented in 1929. These ordinances allowed the chief of the Forest Service to withdraw roadless lands from development schemes. Eventually, 72 primitive areas were established within the ten western states. Their main purpose was "to maintain primitive conditions of transportation, subsistence, habitation, and environment to the fullest degree…with a view to conserving the values of such areas for purposes of public education and recreation."

Primitive area status offered no real long-term protection, since such designation was purely administrative in nature and could be reversed by any succeeding Forest Service chief. Nevertheless, many of California's currently designated wilderness areas were originally set aside as primitive areas or future incantations of the same concept. These include portions of what is now the San Rafael Wilderness, the John Muir Wilderness, Domeland Wilderness, Ventana Wilderness, Trinity Alps Wilderness, plus many others.

Throughout the 1930s, the Forest Service added to the acreage of lands that were to be protected in an undeveloped state, setting aside many additional "primitive areas." One of the most ardent proponents of primitive area establishment was an energetic Forest Service employee named Bob Marshall.

Marshall grew up in the East and dreamed of wilderness adventure as a boy. By the time he entered college, he, along with brother George, had become the first to climb all 46 peaks over 4,000 feet in the Adirondack Mountains where the Marshalls had a summer home. He went on to study forestry, eventually obtaining a Ph.D. in plant pathology from Johns Hopkins University. In his search for ultimate wilderness,

Marshall made four trips to Alaska's Brooks Range, which he helped to publicize, calling for preservation of everything north of the Yukon River as a huge wilderness area. Marshall liked to think big.

Like many other idealistic conservationists of the era, Marshall went to work for the Forest Service. In 1930 he wrote a seminal paper in *Scientific Monthly* outlining a justification for a nationwide wilderness preservation system. "There is just one hope of repulsing the tyrannical ambition of civilization to conquer every niche on the whole earth," Marshall wrote. "That hope is the organization of spirited people who will fight for the freedom of wilderness."

In 1936 Marshall published an article outlining the results of a study he had done of the remaining roadless lands left in the United States outside of Alaska. He found 48 forested roadless areas in excess of 300,000 acres, plus another 29 desert areas that were 500,000 acres or larger. The central Sierra was the fourth largest roadless area left in the country, with more than 2.3 million acres intact in one piece, according to his calculations. Other large California roadless areas included 600,000 acres north of Yosemite, 440,000 acres in the Marble Mountains, 410,000 acres in the Trinity Alps, and 400,000 acres south of Yosemite. An earlier preliminary list Marshall made in 1927 also included more than a million roadless acres just east of Santa Barbara. Anyone familiar with California's larger wilderness blocks of today will quickly recognize that in many cases, the amount of roadless country has been significantly reduced since the 1930s.

Marshall eventually rose through the ranks to become director of the Division of Recreation and Lands. In this capacity, Marshall restricted development on 14 million acres by implementing the more restrictive "U" regulations that superseded the "L" regulations. Although the U regulations still had no legal teeth, they nevertheless set the tone that wildlands protection would continue.

Realizing that outside political pressure was necessary to ensure protection of wildlands values, Marshall, along with other like-minded conservationists that included Aldo Leopold, Olaus Murie, Robert Sterling Yard, Harvey Broome, and Benton Mackaye, founded the Wilderness Society in 1935. The group's goal was to establish a nationwide system of federally protected wildlands. From its beginnings, Marshall not only provided great energy and enthusiasm for the organization, but also funded the fledgling group with his significant inherited wealth. It was a real blow to the Society and the wilderness movement when the 38-year-old Marshall died of a heart attack in 1939.

Nevertheless, the idea of a nationwide wilderness system prevailed. With the advent of the post-World War II housing boom, development continued to chip away at the remaining roadless areas. Howard Zahniser, who became executive director of the Wilderness Society in 1945, recognized that a systematic way of protecting wildlands that went beyond the Forest Service's U regulations was necessary. In 1956 he penned the first version of what would become the Wilderness Act. It called for establishment of a nationwide wilderness system on all suitable federal lands, including those managed by the National Park Service, U.S. Fish and Wildlife Service, and the Forest Service. It was to be a policy change, not establishment of a new agency, thus it needed no additional funds. The law would require that designated federal lands be managed to retain their primitive character. Consequently, activities such as motorized vehicle access, road building, and logging would not be permitted. Senator Hubert Humphrey of Minnesota introduced the bill into Congress in 1957.

Then, as now, western commercial extractive interests rallied against the bill, arguing that withdrawing even a tiny percentage of the West from potential development would destroy western economic opportunities. The bill was also opposed by the Forest Service and the Park Service; both agencies saw it as potentially hamstringing their own development designs and plans.

Opposition was strong, and the bill was revised 66 times before it finally passed both houses of Congress. President Lyndon Johnson signed it into law in September of 1964. However, in making its way through the political process, a number of concessions were made to ensure its passage. Mineral and oil exploration were given a twenty-year grace period to give ample opportunity for these industries to find and develop new deposits. In addition, livestock grazing was specifically permitted to continue in designated wilderness to reduce opposition from that quarter. These concessions would come back to haunt conservationists in the ensuing years. In particular, livestock grazing continues to be the single greatest source of environmental degradation on western lands, including those within the wilderness areas.

The Act immediately granted wilderness protection to 54 areas totaling 9.1 million acres. In California, this included the Hoover, John Muir, Marble Mountain, San Gorgonio, San Gabriel, South Warner, Domeland, Cucamonga, and Minarets (now Ansel Adams) areas. In addition, another five million acres of primitive areas were to be reviewed for potential permanent protection as designated wilderness.

After passage of the Act, the federal agencies were to recommend additional areas for inclusion within the National Wilderness Preservation System. A number of new wilderness areas in California came about in the years following passage of the Act, including the Ventana Wilderness, Desolation Wilderness, and San Rafael Wilderness—the latter established in 1968 and the first new addition to the National Wilderness Preservation System. However, designation of many of the larger wildlands was stalled by agency resistance to change.

In 1972, the Forest Service embarked upon its Roadless Area Review Evaluation, or what became known as "RARE I." The agency was supposed to determine which lands had wilderness qualities, but the results seemed to be more a review of which lands had little commercial value. Two years later, the agency released its results, calling for protection of 12.3 million acres out of a possible 56 million. This was disappointing to conservationists, who thought that too many areas deserving recognition were left out of the recommendations. The Sierra Club filed suit against the Forest Service, barring it from developing any roadless areas without first doing an Environmental Impact Statement as required by the National Environmental Protection Act (NEPA), passed by Congress in 1969.

To comply, the Forest Service went back to the drawing board and did a second roadless areas review, or RARE II. As before, a small percentage of the roadless lands—15 million acres—was recommended for wilderness. In California, six million acres were identified as roadless, but only 900,000 acres were recommended as suitable for addition to the Wilderness System. The State of California sued the Forest Service, claiming it had done a rushed and incomplete job.

View from Mount Linn toward Cottonwood Creek, Yolla Bolly–Middle Eel Wilderness.

In 1982, a federal court of appeals ruled in the state's favor in the case of *California v. Block,* saying that RARE II environmental impact statements were inadequate. Until a more detailed study of each area was conducted, the Forest Service could not develop or otherwise compromise the wildlands quality of RARE II lands, which effectively barred development of 47 California roadless areas.

In the meantime, public pressure to designate additional wilderness acres continued culminating in the California Wilderness Act of 1984. The bill established 23 new wilderness areas, including the Dick Smith, South Sierra, Trinity Alps, Siskiyou, and Carson–Iceberg. Additions to 15 other existing national forest wildernesses included expansion of the Domeland, Marble Mountain, Mokelumne, Ansel Adams, and Yolla Bolly–Middle Eel. In addition, two new national park wildernesses were established that covered major portions of Yosemite, Kings Canyon, and Sequoia National Parks. The bill also declared 83 miles of the Tuolumne River as Wild and Scenic, and established the Mono Basin National Scenic Area.

The next major wilderness designation occurred with the passage of the California Desert Bill in 1994. The bill established 69 new Bureau of Land Management (BLM) wilderness areas totaling 3.5 million acres and 95,000 acres of Forest Service wilderness; it designated four million acres of national park service wildernesses in three national parks, and 9,000 acres in two national wildlife refuges, altogether totaling 7.6 million acres of new wilderness protection in California. The bill also enlarged Joshua Tree and Death Valley National Monuments and upgraded them to national park status. In addition, the Mojave National Preserve was created. It was by far the most significant wilderness legislation since the passage of the 1980 Alaska Lands Act, bringing the total designated federal wilderness in the state to 13,971,548 acres, or approximately 13 percent of the entire state.

However, the bill not only released nearly one million acres of roadless lands with wildlands qualities from further protection, it also failed to address the fate of other roadless lands in the state. For example, there are millions of acres of national forest lands that remain open to development, including more than 200,000 acres in the White Mountains, and the BLM manages lands that could qualify as wilderness, particularly in northern California. In total, depending on how you draw the boundaries, an additional four million acres may qualify as wilderness. Clearly formal protection of California's wildlands base is not yet over.

Undoubtedly, even after the fate of most of the larger roadless areas is determined, new legislation will seek to preserve the ecological integrity of California's wildlands. The new science of conservation biology recognizes that habitat fragmentation poses one of the greatest threats to long-term preservation of biological and ecological processes. Biodiversity is more than protecting or sustaining a few token individuals of any species: Real biodiversity protection requires that there be long-term viability of breeding populations. In addition, the evolutionary processes that shape and influence species must be maintained. Thus, the reestablishment of wildfire and maintaining predation from large carnivores such as the mountain lion are as critical to biodiversity preservation as perpetuating populations of rare species such as the California condor or Stephen's kangaroo rat.

Increasingly, conservation reserve proposals are being developed that seek to link established designated wilderness areas with other protected areas via corridors and buffers. In some instances, wilderness recovery zones may even be established that attempt to restore wildlands values to previously developed landscapes. If you consider the fact that much of northern California as well as the desert regions have far fewer people than, say, the mountain valleys of western Montana or northern Idaho—both places where wolves, grizzly bears, and many other wildlands species still persist—it is not unreasonable to suggest that ecological recovery, and even restoration or expansion of populations of species, may someday be possible in the Golden State.

Eventually, California may become a state ribboned by roads and freeways, with islands of urban and agricultural development set within a sea of wildlands. Such a vision is not really impractical from a biological–ecological perspective, although mustering the needed political support for such a transformation may still be decades away. Hopefully, this book will act as both a guide and inspiration to those who wish to pursue such a vision.

What Does Wilderness Designation Do?

The passage of the Wilderness Act institutionalized an idea—that our natural land-scape in an undisturbed condition had a value to humanity equal to using that landscape for consumptive purposes. As written, the Act seeks to preserve for posterity an "endur-ing resource" of wilderness on those federal lands that are essentially "untrammeled" or undeveloped. As defined by the Act, these are lands that "generally appear to have been affected primarily by the forces of nature, with the imprint of man's work substantially unnoticeable." Thus, lands that are heavily logged, mined, and roaded usually do not qualify for wilderness. However, minor intrusions such as dams, fencing for livestock, cabins for administration or recreational users, and even previously developed areas damaged from mining or logging that have largely reverted to a more natural condi-tion, can be found in designated wilderness.

Besides the consideration of natural appearance, an area must include opportunities for solitude and unconfined recreation and be at least 5,000 acres in size. Wilderness areas may also preserve features that are of historic, geologic, or ecological significance.

In order to maintain these qualities, activities that are felt to be "high impact"—timber harvesting, road building, mining, motorized vehicle use, and even some modern recreational sports such as mountain biking—are not permitted. However, some existing commercial activities are still allowed, such as livestock grazing and outfitting. Unless prohibited by other agency mandates, recreational uses such as hunting, fishing, cross-country skiing, canoeing, hiking, and camping are felt to be "low impact" and are recognized as legitimate wilderness uses.

The most important purpose of wilderness is protection of watersheds, biological diversity, ecological processes, and scenic qualities. All these "ecological services" are accomplished at no additional "cost" to taxpayers and make wilderness protection extremely valuable, whether or not a single person ever hikes in the areas.

It's important to note that Congress does not "create" wilderness, any more than a weatherman creates a sunny day. All legislation can do is recognize the existing qualities of the landscape and decide to maintain those features in an undeveloped state. Wilderness designation is therefore a generous act, giving future generations the opportunity to know something of California's natural landscape. The California that first drew people to the state still exists, albeit in a reduced fashion. As Dave Foreman, author of *The Big Outside,* has noted, "California may no longer be paradise, but it ain't all a parking lot either."

Exploring the Wilderness

Permits

Be forewarned that many California wilderness areas now have some form of restricted entry for overnight camping through the use of permits, trailhead quotas, group size restrictions, or other limits. A few areas even have day hiking restrictions, and some are now experimenting with charging a daily permit fee. Since these regulations continuously change, I have not listed them in this book. It is best to contact the managing agency prior to your hike to determine what is necessary to be in compliance with bureaucratic policy.

Leave No Trace

The lands that contain the California wilderness areas belong to every American, and they are administered by the federal government through agencies such as the Forest Service. The growing popularity of these areas has begun to overtake this agency's ability to counteract the detrimental effects of overuse, so we are faced with a situation in which the responsibility of stewardship falls to every individual who uses and enjoys these last vestiges of American wilderness. When we set foot here, we should accept a simple creed—that we will respect these places in their natural state, and that we will strive to leave no trace of our passing. To this end, the Forest Service has developed the principle of Leave No Trace, which should govern the behavior of every visitor to the California backcountry. Please learn and practice the following trail ethics and Leave No Trace concepts.

TRAILS

Hiking single-file and staying on the trail helps to avoid trampling fragile plants and soft ground, which can result in wider trails or new trails altogether. Never cut switchbacks. Follow the trail through muddy or snowy sections instead of creating a new trail around such impediments.

In those places where there is no trail, or where it is necessary to leave the trail, choose the most durable surfaces to walk on, such as rocks, dry ground, or a carpet of pine needles. In the absence of a trail, groups should fan out to disperse their impact.

When meeting other trail users such as mountain bikers and horse packers, be courteous and give them room to pass. The current standard is that bikers and hikers yield to horses, and bikers yield to hikers, but the prudent hiker will make room for a mountain biker. When passing a horse party, calmly make your presence known and move off the trail on the lower side until everyone has passed. Do not make any sudden movements or loud noises that might spook the horses.

SELECTING A CAMPSITE: CONCENTRATE IMPACTS IN HIGH-USE AREAS

In well-traveled areas, it is best to select an established campsite that has already seen a lot of use. This reflects the philosophy that certain spots are sacrificed to be used again and again without the intention of restoring them to a natural state. Choose hard, dry ground with the least amount of vegetation for a tent site. Make sure your camp is at least 200 feet from streams, lakes, and trails, and be aware of "visual pollution"—how visible your tent and camp are to other visitors seeking a remote backcountry experience.

While moving about camp, be aware that each step is potentially harmful. If you are in a heavily used area, use existing trails instead of tromping down new ones. If you are in an area that has seen less human impact, try not to use the same route each time you travel around camp so that no single area becomes worn. Additionally, you can minimize the number of trips required to retrieve water by using water bags or other large-capacity containers. The cooking area should be situated on a durable surface, such as a large, flat rock. Wear light shoes instead of heavy, hard-soled hiking boots once you arrive at camp.

USE FIRE RESPONSIBLY

Campfires have long been a source of warmth and comfort, providing a sense of security in the vast darkness of the natural world. But they are an unnatural impact on the environment, leaving scars, gobbling nutrients, and sterilizing the soil. I encourage hikers to consider the rewards of experiencing the darkness of the forest on its own terms, as nature intended it, without the glaring interruption of a fire. A small backpacking stove provides a quick and efficient way to cook. Your eyes will see things they would have missed when blinded by the flames, and you will hear sounds otherwise drowned out. More exciting, you may have the opportunity to see nocturnal animals that stay well away from the crackle of a blazing fire.

If you must build a fire, make sure you are well below timberline and far from water sources or wetlands, in an area where there is an abundant supply of dead and downed wood. Use an existing fire ring or build a "mound fire" — **NEVER BUILD A NEW FIRE RING.** A mound fire is built by finding a source of mineral soil, such as a streambed during low water or the hole left by a tree that has blown over. Use a stuff sack to carry a large amount of this soil to the fire site, lay down a ground cloth, and use the soil to build a flat-topped mound 6 to 8 inches thick on top of the cloth. Build the fire on the mound. When it is time to break camp, scatter the few ashes, and then use the ground cloth to return the soil to its source. This is the fire-building method prescribed by the National Outdoor Leadership School in their Leave No Trace literature.

GARBAGE AND FOOD: PACK IT IN, PACK IT OUT

Nothing should be left in the woods that wasn't there before our passing, with the exception of human waste. Everything else, including toilet paper, personal hygiene items, and uneaten food, should be packed out. Most trash, even paper, will not burn completely in a camp fire, so it remains in the environment for a long time. Leaving food for animals or giving it to them directly habituates them to humans, alters their diet, and makes them less self-sufficient. It also gives them an appetite for human food, which can result in more aggressive behavior in these animals. Never feed a wild animal.

Long-distance hikers should not use food caches in their planning strategy. A food cache is a stash of food that is deposited somewhere along the trail before a hike begins. They are not allowed in many areas, and they are often dug up by animals or simply left behind when a hiker's plans change. Careful planning will eliminate the need to cache food.

HUMAN WASTE: PROPERLY DISPOSE OF WHAT YOU CAN'T PACK OUT

The best way to dispose of solid human waste is via the "cat hole" method, which entails digging a hole 6 to 8 inches deep and filling it in after use. Toilet paper should be packed out; a double plastic bag works well for this.

DOMESTIC ANIMALS

Pets are best left at home during a trip to the backcountry, but if you must have yours along, be sure to use a leash. Be aware that a dog can be loud and disturbing to other visitors who seek a tranquil wilderness experience, and most dogs chase any wildlife they see.

Horses are also an unnatural representative of the animal kingdom in our national forests, and, bound as they are to a party of humans, their impact can be very concentrated and destructive. At camp, horses should be hitched to a highline. Select access to water where they will cause the least amount of erosion to stream banks and lake shores. Avoid tethering horses in a small area, such as at the base of a tree, where the ground will be devastated and unable to sustain any vegetation in the future, even after just one instance of equine presence. Horse parties can also cause extensive damage to trails.

Water

Drinking clean water directly from a stream is one of the great pleasures of wilderness travel. Unfortunately, most water from streams is no longer safe to consume. In many areas, domestic livestock and pack stock foul the waters, but even where these animals aren't found, there's always the chance of getting the waterborne parasite *Giardia lamblia*, which can be carried by everything from deer to voles. *Giardia* causes severe intestinal distress with flu-like symptoms. Boiling all water is one way to avoid *Giardia* contamination; otherwise, the use of a good water filter is recommended.

How threatening *Giardia* really is to wilderness travelers is difficult to determine. *Giardia* cysts have been found in many areas, but I want to note that I have never used a water filter, nor do I boil my water. I always drink directly from streams other than those frequented by cattle, and I've never had a case of *Giardia;* nor have any of my friends, using similar practices, ever suffered from *Giardia.* I only mention this to make the point that the threat of *Giardia,* while real, may be like the threat of a grizzly mauling in Glacier National Park—something to be aware of, but don't let it keep you from enjoying the Big Outside.

Altitude Sickness

If you climb above 9,000 feet too rapidly, you may find yourself experiencing nausea, headache, or lack of appetite. If such symptoms are ignored, altitude sickness can quickly develop into complications that may be fatal. The best remedy is to retreat to lower elevations. If this is not possible, don't continue hiking to higher altitude; rest and acclimate your body, consuming plenty of water and quick energy foods such as candy bars or dried fruit. I have experienced altitude sickness several times, including one occasion when I was hiking up Mount Whitney. I drove from San Bernardino (elevation 1,000 feet) to the Whitney Portal, then hiked to Trail Crest at 13,200 feet—all in one day. By the time I camped that night on the pass, I was feeling the effects of altitude sickness. After a night's rest, my body had adjusted, and I was able to continue to the summit of Mount Whitney without further complications.

Sunburn

California's great climate encourages outdoor activity and excessive exposure to sun. Be aware that at higher elevations, the strength of the sun's ultraviolet rays are more intense. When combined with reflection from snow, the effect of solar radiation can be severe. Apply liberal amounts of sunscreen, wear sunglasses, and have a hat or other protective headgear.

Essentials

All wilderness travelers should have these items in their pack:

> matches or fire starter
> poncho or emergency blanket
> water bottle with fluid
> flashlight with extra batteries (handy for descending trails in the dark)
> sunscreen
> extra clothes, such as windbreaker and gloves
> map

A few other items that are nice to have, but not necessarily essential, include extra food, a knife, sunglasses, a compass, first-aid book, extra film, and mosquito dope.

Maps

The maps in this book are intended to provide general orientation. They are not detailed enough to permit exact route finding or for use in cross-country travel, and they won't be useful for finding your way from a major highway to the trailhead. It is recommended that hikers obtain either the appropriate topographical map for each area or a wilderness map where available, or—at the least—a map to the national forest, national park, BLM district, or state park being visited. Toward that end, I have listed the names of several maps at the beginning of each wilderness description and in Appendix 4 on page 318.

I seldom buy topo maps—they are expensive and several are required to adequately cover an area. I find that Forest Service and BLM maps serve most purposes, unless one is planning to do some cross-country exploration. The state-wide, two-volume topographical atlas put out by DeLorme Mapping Company of Freeport, Maine, is also a good resource for finding your way on backwoods logging roads and general route planning.

How to Use This Guide

I've divided the state into five regions: Northeast, Northwest, Sierra Nevada, South Coast Ranges, and Southern California. All desert wildernesses are discussed in volume two of this guide. Each region has a general introduction, with discussions of natural and human history, terrain, geology, and respective plant and animal life. The wilderness areas follow alphabetically, each with a brief introduction and a description that includes its location, size, elevation range, total trail miles, ecosystems, administrative agencies, and a list of the maps you can use to hike that wilderness. The 61 areas listed include three national parks and proposed wildernesses, and one national recreation area, state park, national monument, and national seashore. (See Appendix 1 on page 313 for "at-a-glance" information on each area and the name of the managing agency.)

Following the individual wilderness introductions are lists of day, overnight, and loop hikes, with additional information on other recreational opportunities where applicable. I recommended these hikes for a variety of reasons: Popularity of an area and scenic value were important, but I wanted to give families and those seeking a challenge or solitude some options. Each hike has a description of the route and terse directions to the trailhead. While these narratives will get you on the trail without mishap, I assume the reader will have a map to help with orientation and route finding. Furthermore, it is suggested that you always contact the managing agency listed in Appendix 2 on page 315 for updates and more detailed information.

For each hike I have provided a chart giving the distance (usually one way unless otherwise stated), approximate low and high elevation, and degree of difficulty. Defining difficulty is somewhat arbitrary, and my descriptions should be viewed as just a guideline. Estimates were based on such things as distance, slope, terrain, kind of trail, and other elements. A short day hike, if it climbs steeply up a mountain, could be considered difficult, while a longer overnight trek might be moderate or even easy if the trail is flat and wide. Most of the selected hikes fall somewhere in between—hence "moderate."

Although I sometimes mention potential hazards such as rattlesnakes, poison oak, difficult stream crossings, and avalanche chutes, most of these won't present a threat if prudent caution and judgment are exercised. Although fate may dictate otherwise, in general, wilderness travel is extremely safe. I do not make the usual admonishments about hiking alone and other cautionary messages most guidebook authors feel are necessary. Indeed, nearly all of the hikes made in this book I did alone. Wilderness travel should not be, in my mind, a handholding exercise, but an opportunity for individuals to use their own judgment without interference from others. It's a great opportunity for each of us to find out what we're made of—to exercise our own choices and self determination. I believe that wildlands provide us with the opportunity to make mistakes and learn from them. Despite a few hazards, hiking in most of California's wildlands is far safer than driving the freeway to access them. Use good judgment, don't over-extend yourself, take reasonable precautions, and you will likely have a great time.

Crest of the Warner Mountains from Warren Peak, South Warner Wilderness.

Northeast: The Cascades
to the Great Basin

This section of California lies east of the Sacramento River Valley and I-5 corridor and north of an arbitrary line that lies just south of Mount Lassen, where the Cascade Range officially begins. It is one of the least visited areas of California. Dominated by volcanic features from the impressive cone of Mount Shasta to the extensive lava fields at Lava Beds National Monument, this region, more than any other in California, appears to be born of fire.

The area is dominated by three sub-regions that all meet in this section. The Cascade Range is located on the west and the Basin and Range province on the east. In between lies the rolling expanse of the Modoc Plateau—the southern extension of the huge Columbia Plateau, often called "High Desert" for its dry, cold climate—that makes up most of eastern Oregon, eastern Washington, and adjacent parts of Idaho and northern Nevada. Despite its aridity, there are a number of large natural lakes such as Goose, Tule, Eagle, and others. And unlike other parts of the nearby Great Basin, the rivers of this region drain to the sea via the Pit–Sacramento River System.

Because the high coastal mountains that make up northwest California block the inward flow of moisture from the Pacific, the lower elevations of this section are relatively arid. Except for the western-most portions of the region lying in the snowy Cascades, the climate generally resembles other parts of the northern Basin and Range where winters are cold and summers are warm and usually dry. With low elevation areas such as the Ishi Wilderness as an exception, most of the vegetation in the region's wilderness areas consists of montane forests dominated by ponderosa pine, Jeffrey pine, incense cedar, white fir, red fir, aspen, and juniper, with sagebrush and bitterbrush understory.

This is one of the least populated sections of the state. Most of northeast California is part of Modoc County, which is home to fewer than 15,000 residents. Despite this low population, it is ironic that northeast California has little formally protected wilderness in comparison to the highly populated southern California. Much of the area is criss-crossed by roads built to expedite logging and livestock production. The paucity of designated wilderness may reflect the region's hostility to preservation efforts. I picked up a brochure in Alturis that proclaimed Modoc County

Sunset on Mount Shasta, Mount Shasta Wilderness.

as a place "where the West still lives." The irony of the brochure, which featured a number of photos of cows trampling stream banks and an antelope jumping a barbed wire fence, is the unfortunate fact that the traditional West does indeed still live in this corner of the state. One is more likely to hear the sound of a cow bellowing than the call of a coyote.

Despite these drawbacks, the northeast quarter is a place where you won't likely encounter competition for the best campsites, nor the need for reservations just to gain entry to public lands. It's a landscape of sweeping vistas, tall pine, and fragrant sage.

Caribou Wilderness

Gentle terrain, dozens of lakes, and a compact size make this a great family wilderness.

Near Hay Meadows in the heavily timbered and lake-studded Caribou Wilderness.

LOCATION: east of Lassen Volcanic National Park and 14 miles north of Chester

SIZE: 20,625 acres

ELEVATION RANGE: 6,000 to 8,370 feet

MILES OF TRAILS: 25.5

ECOSYSTEMS: mixed conifer, lodgepole pine

ADMINISTRATION: Lassen National Forest

MAP: Lassen National Forest Map

If the Thousand Lakes Wilderness is misnamed, there are at least a few lakes in it. There were, however, no caribou anyplace close to the 20,625-acre Caribou Wilderness. But unlike the Thousand Lakes Wilderness, the Caribou does have numerous lakes, albeit less than a thousand. The entire wilderness lies on what was the eastern slope of Mount Tehama, a volcano that at one time dominated Lassen Park. A huge glacier sliding off that mountain once overran most of what is today the Caribou Wilderness, scooping out numerous small lakes from the rolling terrain.

The Caribou Wilderness is a gently rolling, lake-dotted, forested plateau; its predominantly lodgepole pine woodland is somewhat reminiscent of the Yellowstone Plateau in Yellowstone National Park. The average elevation of nearly

7,000 feet means snow stays late—most trails aren't accessible until July. A few high points, such as Caribou Peaks and 8,370-foot Red Cinder, the loftiest of all, provide a little relief, but overall this area is nearly level. The dense forest and lack of relief make it easy to become disoriented, especially if you wander off the trail or they are buried under snow, as was the case when I visited the area once.

There are three major trailheads: Hay Meadows on the south, Caribou Lake on the east, and Cone Lake on the north. The compact size of the wilderness (only 9 miles long by 5 miles across), combined with the gentle terrain, make this a good place to introduce children to backcountry camping and hiking. Despite this advantage and the area's numerous lakes, the Caribou Wilderness receives little use.

> ### DAY HIKE: TRIANGLE LAKE
> One-way length: 1.8 miles
> Low and high elevations: 6,800 to 7,000 feet
> Difficulty: easy

This is an easy stroll to the largest lake in the Caribou Wilderness. You may reach the trailhead from Highway 44 by taking Forest Service Road 10 for 5.0 miles before turning onto Forest Service Road 32N09, which terminates at the Cone Lake Trailhead in 1.5 miles. It is almost 1.0 mile to the wilderness boundary, then about another 1.0 mile to the lake, which supports trout and lots of mosquitoes. There are good campsites at the lake for those inclined to spend the night.

> ### OVERNIGHT HIKE: CARIBOU LAKE–LONG LAKE
> One-way length: 6 miles
> Low and high elevations: 6,800 to 7,000 feet
> Difficulty: moderate

The hike from Caribou Lake to Long Lake is nearly level; it passes by a procession of ponds, kettles, and lakes, making a great overnight trek for a family with children. The hike begins at the Caribou Lake Trailhead, reachable from Chester on Highway 36 to Westwood, where A21 turns north. Go 14.0 miles to the junction for Silver Lake and head west 6.0 miles, following signs to the trailhead just beyond Silver Lake. From Caribou Lake, it's 0.8 mile to Cowboy Lake, and less than a mile further is Jewell Lake, followed by Eleanor Lake. At 2.0 miles from the trailhead, you will reach a junction. Go right (north) if you want to hike to Turnaround and Triangle Lakes, but to reach our goal of Long Lake, go left (south) to Black Lake, North Divide Lake, and South Divide Lake, where it's a downhill run—1.9 miles—to Long Lake. Long Lake has a good number of campsites and offers nice views of the glaciated North Caribou and South Caribou Peaks.

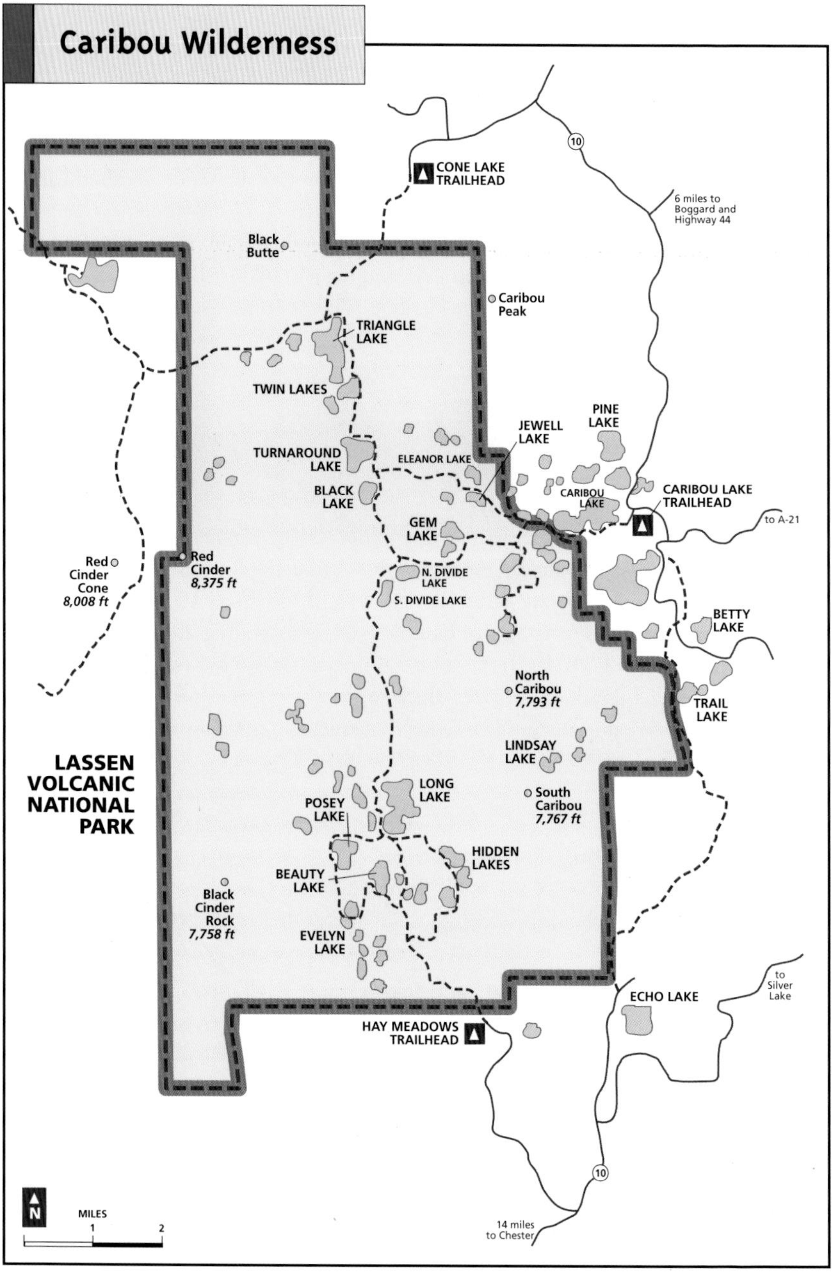

Caribou Wilderness

CONE LAKE
TRAILHEAD

6 miles to
Boggard and
Highway 44

Black
Butte

Caribou
Peak

TRIANGLE
LAKE

TWIN LAKES

TURNAROUND
LAKE

ELEANOR LAKE

JEWELL
LAKE

PINE
LAKE

BLACK
LAKE

CARIBOU
LAKE

CARIBOU LAKE
TRAILHEAD

to A-21

GEM
LAKE

Red
Cinder
Cone
8,008 ft

Red
Cinder
8,375 ft

N. DIVIDE
LAKE

S. DIVIDE LAKE

BETTY
LAKE

North
Caribou
7,793 ft

TRAIL
LAKE

LASSEN
VOLCANIC
NATIONAL
PARK

LINDSAY
LAKE

LONG
LAKE

POSEY
LAKE

South
Caribou
7,767 ft

HIDDEN
LAKES

BEAUTY
LAKE

Black
Cinder
Rock
7,758 ft

EVELYN
LAKE

ECHO LAKE

to
Silver
Lake

HAY MEADOWS
TRAILHEAD

14 miles
to Chester

N

MILES

1   2

Ishi Wilderness 2

*This is a gem of a wilderness, with oak woodlands,
flower-studded meadows, and beautiful, clear streams
containing some of the last chinook salmon runs in the
Sacramento River drainage.*

Oak savannas are common in the Ishi Wilderness.

A friend of mine says that in April, the Ishi Wilderness is
heaven on Earth. I'm inclined to agree with her assessment.
The Ishi is a rarity in the Cascades–Sierra, a wildlands that
protects a low elevation area. In spring, the 41,000-acre Ishi
Wilderness seems alive with the buzzing of bees, songs of
birds, and brightened by hillsides and meadows full of wildflowers. One can gain a sense of the kind of California John
Muir described when he first crossed the Central Valley
enroute to the Sierra Nevada.

The main drainage is Mill Creek, a clear, brawling,
icy stream, whose headwaters lie in Lassen Volcanic National
Park. Several other deep basalt canyons with streams,
including Deer Creek, make up the wilderness.

LOCATION: 25 miles
east of Red Bluff

SIZE: 41,000 acres

ELEVATION RANGE:
1,500 to 3,274 feet

MILES OF TRAILS: 33.3

ECOSYSTEMS:
oak-pine savanna, plus
riparian habitat

ADMINISTRATION:
Lassen National Forest

MAP: Lassen National
Forest Map

Chaparral dominates many of the drier slopes, but there are also lovely oak groves, including some of the best blue oak savannas in the state. Stately groves of digger pine and ponderosa pine, as well as dense riparian growth of cottonwood and California sycamore along the streams, adds to the vegetative mix. Black bear, mule deer, mountain lion, and bobcat are among the larger mammals, while some of the last remaining runs of steelhead and spring chinook salmon in the Sacramento River drainage spawn in Mill Creek and nearby Deer Creek. The Tehama deer herd, the largest migratory herd in California, winters in the area.

Ishi, for whom the wilderness is named, was the last surviving member of the Yahi Yana Native American tribe. Once whites entered the region after 1850, Ishi and a few others of his band lived for decades among the rough lava canyons of the Cascade foothills. One by one they all died, until there was no one left but Ishi, who then stumbled out of the mountains seeking food and companionship in August of 1911. He became a celebrity of sorts and eventually came to live with a University of California anthropology professor, who wrote a book about the Native American, using Ishi's name as the title. The book provides a remarkable insight to the way Ishi and his people had survived for generations in California before the advent of the white man. Interestingly enough, once Ishi had a chance to adjust to life in Berkeley, he had little desire to go camping back in his homeland.

Though only 41,000 acres of the lower Mill Creek area is protected, upper Mill Creek, east of the Ponderosa Way Road, is also roadless and could be added to the Ishi. There is a 13-mile-long trail accessible from the small community of Mill Creek that follows the stream up to a trailhead. Other roadless, but adjacent lands under state, private, and Forest Service management total more than 180,000 acres. This could be a significant low elevation wildlands if all currently roadless lands were protected as wilderness.

DAY HIKE: RANCHERIA–MILL CREEK TRAIL
One-way length: 2 miles
Low and high elevations: 1,500 to 2,500 feet
Difficulty: strenuous

The Rancheria Trail is the quick-and-dirty way to gain access to the main Mill Creek Canyon, but you have to pay a price in sweat. The road to the trailhead is not recommended for passenger cars, but if you've got a high clearance vehicle and want a challenge, give it a try. You reach the trailhead off Highway 36 and the Ponderosa Way Road. The access will just be the beginning of your endurance test. The trail, though short, is hot, steep, and dry. It first follows an old jeep road for about 1.0 mile, then drops more steeply through large basalt rock outcrops, descending 1,000 feet altogether to reach the clear waters of Mill Creek. There are great views along the descent that might take your mind off the fact that you have an even hotter, drier climb back out.

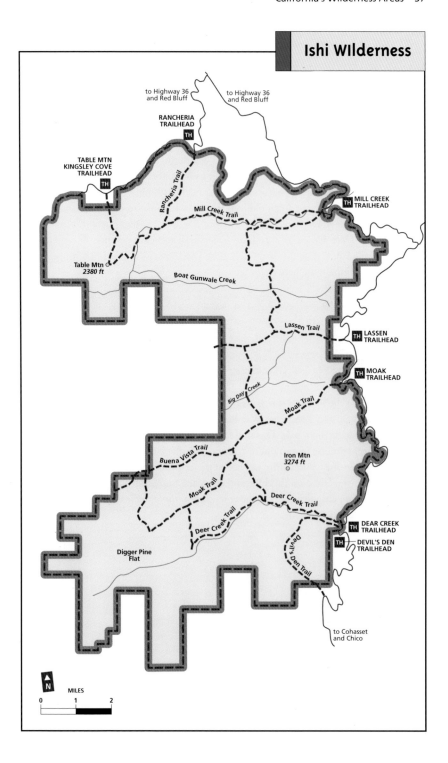

Ishi WIlderness

to Highway 36
and Red Bluff

to Highway 36
and Red Bluff

**RANCHERIA
TRAILHEAD**
TH

**TABLE MTN
KINGSLEY COVE
TRAILHEAD**
TH

Rancheria Trail

Mill Creek Trail

TH **MILL CREEK
TRAILHEAD**

Table Mtn
2380 ft

Boat Gunwale Creek

Lassen Trail

TH **LASSEN
TRAILHEAD**

TH **MOAK
TRAILHEAD**

Big Day Creek

Moak Trail

Buena Vista Trail

Iron Mtn
3274 ft

Moak Trail

Deer Creek Trail

Deer Creek Trail

TH **DEAR CREEK
TRAILHEAD**

TH **DEVIL'S DEN
TRAILHEAD**

Digger Pine
Flat

Devil's Den Trail

to Cohasset
and Chico

N

MILES

0   1   2

DAY HIKE: MOAK TRAIL
One-way length: up to 7 miles
Low and high elevations: 2,500 to 3,400 feet
Difficulty: moderate

The Moak Trail is a springtime hike. No shade. No water. No fun in the summer. But in spring, it's another story. Wildflowers and grassy slopes with great views of the Sacramento Valley beyond make this a wonderful early season hike. It's down-hill to Deep Hole Camp at 2,800 feet with its oaks, then about 1.0 mile further, the trail temporarily disappears in a boulder field. Assuming you can pick it up on the other side, you come to an old jeep trail that descends to Drennan Camp on the banks of Little Dry Creek, the turnaround point. Another possibility is to head south from Deep Hole Camp to Deer Creek Trail and back up that trail to Deer Creek Trailhead. Either walk back along the Ponderosa Way Road or arrange a shuttle—definitely the better choice.

OVERNIGHT HIKE: LOWER MILL CREEK
One-way length: 6.5 miles
Low and high elevations: 1,200 to 1,800 feet
Difficulty: moderate

This is one of the loveliest springtime hikes in California. You reach the trailhead via Highway 36 and Ponderosa Way Road; turn at Black Rock Campground and park in the shade of an oak. This trail follows the creek for its entire length to Papes Place, winding in and out of oak and pine flats, across wildflower-covered hillsides (in spring), and within earshot of the musical rushing waters of Mill Creek. Take your time on this hike and enjoy the numerous places to swim, fish, and camp. The only drawback is the cows that trample the landscape and spatter their waste across the wilderness.

Lassen Volcanic National Park Wilderness

Most of this park's terrain is gently rolling and heavily wooded.

Looking to Saddle Mountain in the rolling forested Lassen Wilderness.

Not more than a half-day's drive from the San Francisco and Sacramento metro areas lies Lassen Volcanic National Park. Lassen experiences far fewer visitors than the more popular areas in the Sierra Nevada, such as Yosemite, yet it provides countless hiking and camping options. Although a half million people pass through Lassen each year, most stay on the loop road that crosses the park.

Lassen Peak marks the southern end of the Cascade Range, a series of volcanic mountains that extend from northern California to British Columbia. A plug-dome volcano, the mountain rises to 10,457 feet. Except for a corridor along the Lassen Park Road that passes through the western third of the park and the areas around a few developed sites such as Butte Lake, Juniper Lake, and Manzanita Lake, most of

LOCATION: 45 miles east of Redding

SIZE: 78,982 acres

ELEVATION RANGE: 4,000 to 10,000 feet

MILES OF TRAILS: 150

ECOSYSTEMS: mixed conifer forest

ADMINISTRATION: Lassen Volcanic National Park

MAP: Lassen National Park Map

the 106,000-acre park is protected as wilderness. The majority of the designated 78,982-acre wilderness lies in the eastern two thirds of the park.

The centerpiece of the park is Lassen Peak, a volcano. The entire landscape consists of relatively recent volcanic flows, the oldest less than two million years in age and most quite a bit younger. Lassen Peak is a very recent feature, but volcanic activity has been centered on the region for some time. Predating Lassen Peak was another volcano, Mount Tehama, with Brokeoff Mountain, Mount Diller, Diamond Peak, and Mount Conard—all remnants of this great volcano. Following the appearance of Mount Tehama, other volcanos formed around the Warner Valley, and today Mount Harness, Prospect Peak, and Sifford Peak are all relics of these eruptions.

These volcanoes were preludes to the growth of Lassen Peak about 11,000 years ago. The peak is one of the world's largest dacite domes, formed by a thick, pasty lava poured out underneath glaciers that capped the entire region. Eventually, the mountain rose high enough to break the surface of the ice, which then scalloped the peak's surface, carving small cirques.

During the height of the Ice Age, glacial ice covered most of the uplands above 6,000 feet, and in some cases flowed to elevations as low as 4,500 feet. Ravines such as Warner Canyon in Lassen Park were carved by these glacial rivers. The Ice Age also left behind the legacy of lakes that dot the entire basin.

Although the eruption of Lassen Peak in 1915 led to the establishment of the park, volcanic activity has occurred repeatedly during the past 2,000 years. Chaos Crags erupted in the last 1,000 years, and more recently, in 1567, a lava flow filled the Butte Lake Valley, while cinder cones (small volcanoes) followed in the 1850s. The big event, though, was the catastrophic eruption that occurred on May 22, 1915, when a three-mile section now known as the "Devastated Area" was destroyed by volcanic flows. The volcano continued to rumble until 1917. It is now dormant, but could erupt any time in the future.

Due to the frequent lava flows and the effects of glaciation, which tends to round off prominent high points, most of the park's terrain is gently rolling and heavily wooded with beautiful forests of red fir, white fir, Jeffrey pine, western white pine, ponderosa pine, lodgepole pine, and stands of aspen. Wildlife is not abundant, but 50 species of mammals, 150 species of birds, and 12 amphibians and reptiles have been recorded for the park.

More than 50 backcountry lakes enhance the Lassen Park Wilderness and none is more than 5.5 miles from a trailhead. Like most destinations, two trails— Bumpass Hell and Lassen Peak, which are both outside of the designated wilderness boundaries and total less than three percent of the trail mileage—receive the majority of use, while the rest of the backcountry reaches are unpeopled.

Lassen Volcanic National Park Wilderness

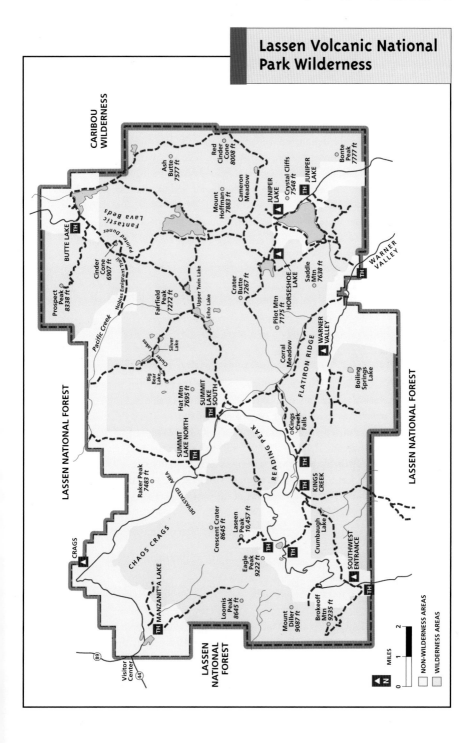

DAY HIKE: LASSEN PEAK
One-way length: 2.5 miles
Low and high elevations: 8,400 to 10,457 feet
Difficulty: moderate

This is one of the most popular hikes in the park, so don't expect to find solitude. Located outside of the designated wilderness, Lassen Peak is surrounded on all sides by official wilderness. The popularity of this hike is easy to understand: For a relatively small amount of effort, one is able to obtain extraordinary 100-mile views across northern California. The trailhead is located off the Park Loop Road, Highway 89, near Lake Helen. You switchback up 2,000 feet, passing through whitebark pine and mountain hemlock forest on a good, smooth, but 15-percent-grade trail. Snow often lingers until August, but the path is usually stomped out by the thousands who hike it each summer.

DAY HIKE: PROSPECT CRATER
One-way length: 3.5 miles
Low and high elevations: 6,000 to 8,338 feet
Difficulty: moderate

Prospect Crater is located in the northeast corner of the park near Butte Lake and gets less use than the other trails. Good views are available from the top of the crater, which was once the location of a fire lookout. To reach the trail, take the 6.0-mile road off Highway 44 to Butte Lake Ranger Station. Follow the Snag Lake–Nobles Emigrant Trail less than 0.5 mile to a turnoff to the west that leads the rest of the way up to the crater's summit. The trail climbs steadily, gaining more than 2,000 feet in three miles. From the top you can see Crater Butte, Lassen Peak, Mount Hoffman, and most of the western part of the park.

DAY HIKE: BROKEN TOP MOUNTAIN
One-way length: 3.6 miles
Low and high elevations: 6,500 to 9,235 feet
Difficulty: moderate

Broken Top Mountain is part of Mount Tehama, a volcano that once rose to 11,500 feet and preceded the development of Lassen Peak. Today Broken Top Mountain offers great in-your-face views of Lassen Peak, with far fewer hikers than found on the Lassen Peak Trail. The trailhead is located in the southwest corner of Lassen Park west of Highway 89, about 0.5 mile past the south entrance. The lower part of the trail follows Mill Creek and is forested, but once you pass Forest Lake, the countryside opens up to meadows and occasional groves of trees. On a clear day, it's possible to see the Coast Range, Trinity Alps, the northern parts of the Sierra Nevada, and Warner Mountains from the summit.

OVERNIGHT HIKE: CLUSTER LAKES–SILVER LAKE
One-way length: 5 miles
Low and high elevations: 6,800 to 7,300 feet
Difficulty: moderate

The eastern portion of Lassen Park has numerous lakes reachable by trail over gentle terrain. The hike to Silver Lake passes a half dozen lakes and small ponds, many of which are shallow and fun to swim. But heed this word of warning: The wet terrain supports "herds" of mosquitoes until things dry out in August. Nevertheless, the hike is a good way to gain easy access into Lassen's backcountry, and since the Cluster Lakes–Silver Lake Trail connects with a number of other major trails, it offers several longer potential loop trips.

The trailhead is located at the Summit Lake Campground and ranger station on Highway 89 Park Loop Road. About 1.0 mile into the hike, you will come to a trail junction where you stay left to reach Silver Lake. The right-hand trail takes you to Echo and the Twin Lakes, which is part of a loop described briefly below. The trail climbs to a plateau on the slope of Hat Mountain before descending to Little and Big Bear Lakes. Silver Lake, with a number of campsites, makes a good base for exploring the area, which has a number of other lakes within a short walking distance. If you wish to make this a loop, continue beyond Silver Lake to Feather Lake, which has good campsites, then to the Twin Lakes, which lie along the Pacific Crest Trail. It's only 3.2 miles across almost level ground from Upper Twin Lake back to the Summit Lake Trailhead.

OVERNIGHT HIKE: CINDER CONE–SNAG LAKE–
BUTTE LAKE LOOP
One-way length: 14 miles
Low and high elevations: 6,043 to 6,900 feet
Difficulty: moderate

This loop hike takes you through a recently created landscape with two of Lassen's largest lakes, plus it provides an opportunity to climb a volcanic butte with great views of the surrounding country. The trailhead lies on the northeast corner of the park, and it is reachable from Highway 44 by a 6.0-mile road that ends at the Butte Lake Campground and ranger station. The trail to Snag Lake lies just beyond the ranger station on Butte Lake's north shore. There are a number of side trails and routes diverging off this trail, so pay attention to your map and trail signs.

The first part of the hike follows the Nobles Trail, an early immigrant route to California's Central Valley. In a little less than 1.5 miles, you will come to a side trail that takes you to the top of 6,900-foot Cinder Cone, which last erupted in 1851. It's worth the climb, for the views from the top are fantastic. Whether you choose to do the climb or not, you will continue on to Snag Lake, formed 300 years ago when a lava flow from Cinder Cone blocked Grassy Creek. The trail circles the southern end of the lake before heading back (north) to the eastern shore of Butte Lake.

OTHER RECREATIONAL OPPORTUNITIES

The overall gentle and open terrain makes this a wonderful place to visit by skis or snowshoes in the winter. Snow cover usually closes most park roads by November until the following April or May. Although the Park Loop Road, Highway 89, is closed in winter, the highway is plowed to both the north and south entrances, permitting access for great cross-country skiing. Access to other parts of the park is more difficult, although it wouldn't be out of the question to ski the access roads to reach the wilderness boundary. For example, the road to Butte Lake is only 6.0 miles off Highway 44, and beyond the lake is a wonderland of rolling terrain that offers superb skiing.

Lava Beds National Monument Wilderness

4

Broken lava buttes and some of the best examples of native grasslands in northeast California are the highlights of the Lava Beds Wilderness.

Native bunchgrass near Black Butte, Lava Beds Wilderness.

Just south of the Oregon border lies Lava Beds National Monument, a land of sweeping vistas with big sky views. The monument has two formally designated wilderness parcels that total 28,460 acres, but these areas are contiguous to another 38,000 acres of adjacent roadless public lands on the Modoc National Forest, making the entire roadless acreage considerably larger. The designated wilderness within the monument consists primarily of rugged basalt flows with a scattering of juniper and ponderosa pine.

Located on the northern slope of a large shield volcano, the entire monument is made of a variety of volcanic rocks, including rhyolite, andesite, and basalt. Obsidian, commonly used by Native Americans for arrowheads, is one form of

LOCATION: 40 miles southeast of Klamath Falls, Oregon

SIZE: 28,460 acres

ELEVATION RANGE: 4,000 to 5,700 feet

MILES OF TRAILS: 22

ECOSYSTEMS: bunchgrass, ponderosa pine, juniper-sage

ADMINISTRATION: National Park Service

MAP: Lava Beds National Monument Map

rhyolite most people recognize. However, about 90 percent of the monument is covered by basalt, a relatively fluid lava that can flow for miles. As the outer surface cools, it forms a tube while the liquid lava inside continues to flow. Once the flow stops, these tubes are left behind, creating what we recognize today as caves. The most recent tubes were formed 30,000 years ago when Mammoth Crater erupted. There are about 300 in the monument, with more than 100 considered "wilderness" caves. Exploring them adds a unique dimension to any trip in this wilderness.

Many of the monument's features, however, predated the Mammoth Crater eruption. Schonchin Butte, Schonchin Flow, Eagle Nest Butte, Crescent Butte, the Three Sisters, and others existed before the Mammoth Crater flows. The most recent eruptions have taken place in the past 1,000 years, including Black Lava Flow, which erupted from Cinder Butte, just outside the monument's southwest corner.

The monument and region around Tule Lake have been occupied by various peoples for thousands of years. Hundreds of archaeological sites have been found within the monument, and in 1990 the area was designated the Modoc Lava Beds Archaeological District because of its wealth of archaeological material. More recently, the Lava Beds was home to the Modoc Indians. With the advent of white settlers in the 1850s, the Modoc were eventually forced onto a reservation, but a number of the tribe left to resume their old ways among the lava fields. In 1872, the U.S. Army was ordered to round them up. Initially, the Native Americans—under the leadership of Captain Jack, a Modoc—were able to hold off the Army by hiding among the rough lava flows that are now part of the monument. The standoff went on for five months. Because of dwindling food supplies and their suffering from the cold, the Modoc eventually surrendered in May of 1873. Captain Jack, along with three others, was hung, while the rest of the tribe was sent to a reservation in Oklahoma.

What may appear to be at first a relatively barren landscape has both a beauty and an ecological integrity not found in adjacent lands. The National Park Service, which manages Lava Beds National Monument, has conducted an active fire management program attempting to re-establish wildfire as a normal ecological process. Prior to the advent of modern fire suppression, fires occurred within the monument region on an average of every 15 to 30 years. Of course, like all averages, there were longer periods without fire, but there were also times when fires were more frequent. The fact is that fires did occur and with some regularity, not only in the drier grasslands of the northern end of the monument but also in the ponderosa pine forests as well. All these ecosystems are able to cope with fire.

The lush bunchgrass rangelands found in Lava Beds has occurred because of two factors—the restoration of fire to the ecosystem and the elimination of domestic livestock grazing. That these grasslands support sage grouse, jackrabbit, antelope, ground squirrels, and deer rather than domestic livestock adds to the beauty. Some of the healthiest native bunchgrass rangelands I've seen in California are located here.

Wild bighorn sheep were once common in the monument. Skull Ice Cave and Bighorn Cave are both named for the abundance of bighorn sheep remains found there. The last bighorn reported in the area died in 1915. Recently, California bighorn sheep were reintroduced into the monument and were thriving when they contracted a disease from domestic sheep that grazed on adjacent public lands, and the entire herd perished. It is hoped that in the future bighorn can be reestablished, but it is unlikely to occur as long as domestic animals continue to graze on lands surrounding the monument.

Pikas, small mammals that look like tiny rabbits, typically inhabit high, alpine regions, and are found among the lava tubes and broken rock of the monument. Although few mule deer are seen in summer, as many as 2,500 migrate from higher elevations during winter to spend the cold months there. An occasional antelope is sometimes seen in the northern portion of the monument as well.

The 25,300-acre Lavas Roadless Area (RA) and 12,900-acre Dobie Flat Roadless Area on the Modoc National Forest are separated from each other by a railroad line, but are otherwise continuous. The Lavas RA lies immediately east of Lava Beds National Monument. Both areas consist of expansive broken lava mixed with sagebrush, juniper, and grasses. They are used extensively as winter range for both deer and pronghorn antelope.

Although there are a number of trails within the monument, cross-country hiking, when not crossing a lava flow, is possible. However, be forewarned that what appears to be a level surface may, upon closer inspection, turn out to be extremely broken lava. All water must be carried as there is no surface water anywhere in the wilderness, although if you hike early in the spring it's possible to get snow or melt water in among the rocks and lava tubes.

The wilderness of Lava Beds National Monument is another one of those forgotten landscapes in California. If you want to get away from the crowds, this is the place to come.

DAY HIKE: BUNCHGRASS TRAIL
One-way length: 1 mile
Low and high elevations: 5,000 feet
Difficulty: easy

This short trail is not actually in the designated wilderness, but given the national park service protective mandate, hiking in non-wilderness is often the same experience. This trailhead is located near the Indian Well Campground and follows an old road around the side of Crescent Butte. The area has been rejuvenated by several recent fires and offers an excellent opportunity to see how native grasslands of the region could appear in the absence of domestic livestock.

DAY HIKE: SCHONCHIN BUTTE TRAIL
One-way length: 0.7 mile
Low and high elevations: 4,800 to 5,283 feet
Difficulty: moderate

Lava Beds National Monument Wilderness

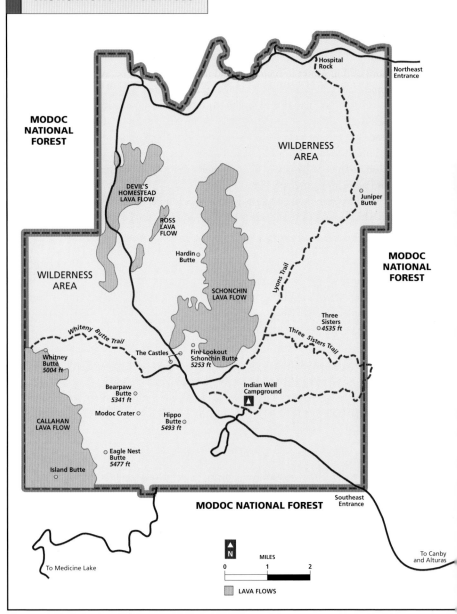

MODOC NATIONAL FOREST

WILDERNESS AREA

DEVIL'S HOMESTEAD LAVA FLOW

ROSS LAVA FLOW

Hardin Butte

Hospital Rock

Northeast Entrance

Juniper Butte

SCHONCHIN LAVA FLOW

Lyons Trail

MODOC NATIONAL FOREST

WILDERNESS AREA

Whiteny Butte Trail

The Castles

Fire Lookout Schonchin Butte 5253 ft

Whitney Butte 5004 ft

Three Sisters 4535 ft

Three Sisters Trail

Bearpaw Butte 5341 ft

Modoc Crater

Indian Well Campground

Hippo Butte 5493 ft

CALLAHAN LAVA FLOW

Eagle Nest Butte 5477 ft

Island Butte

MODOC NATIONAL FOREST

Southeast Entrance

To Medicine Lake

To Canby and Alturas

N

MILES

0   1   2

LAVA FLOWS

This trail is also outside of the official wilderness boundaries, nevertheless, it is immediately adjacent to the wilderness and provides a great viewpoint. The trail is short, but steep. It follows an old road that twists around Schonchin Butte—a volcanic cone—to a fire lookout. The 360-degree views from the top are easily worth the 500-foot climb. Along the way, note the excellent bluebunch wheatgrass grasslands that grow on the butte's slopes. The best time to make the climb is in evening when the views of Medicine Volcano, Tule Lake, and other nearby landmarks are glowing in the warm light of dusk.

DAY HIKE: WHITNEY BUTTE
One-way length: 3.4 miles
Low and high elevations: 5,000 feet
Difficulty: easy

This trail traverses the western part of the monument's officially designated wilderness, passing chunks of recently extruded basalt to the side of a small volcanic cone where terrific views of Mount Shasta are your reward. The trail leaves the Merrill Cave parking area near Bearpaw Butte and heads west toward Whitney Butte, where it extends around the butte's base to the monument boundary 3.4 miles out. Just beyond the monument boundary on Modoc National Forest lands lies the Black Lava Flow, a recent outpouring from the nearby Medicine Volcano. Most of the trail is through open sage, with an occasional mountain mahogany and juniper for shade.

DAY HIKE: LYONS TRAIL
One-way length: 9.4 miles
Low and high elevations: 4,700 to 5,000 feet
Difficulty: moderate

The only thing difficult about this trail is that you have to carry water the entire way. The trail is a gentle downhill grade through mostly open sage-bunchgrass country with almost no shade. I recommend doing this trip in the spring or fall, since it can be extremely hot on a summer afternoon. The trail, named for an early Modoc National Forest supervisor who lost his life near Juniper Butte in the 1920s, traverses a good portion of the eastern wilderness segment found in the monument. Lyons Trail begins at the Skull Cave parking area and ends at the Hospital Rock parking area near Tule Lake. Along the way you will pass Juniper Butte, which offers a potential vantage point from which to survey the wilderness.

5 Mount Shasta Wilderness

*The slopes of well-known Mount Shasta
are cloaked in beautiful forests.*

*Mount Shasta showing the cirque basin that contains the
popular Avalanche Gulch route to the summit.*

LOCATION:
10 miles east of Mount
Shasta City

SIZE: 38,200 acres

ELEVATION RANGE:
4,000 to 14,162 feet

MILES OF TRAILS: 15

ECOSYSTEMS:
Jeffrey pine and Shasta
red fir to tundra

ADMINISTRATION:
Shasta–Trinity National
Forests

MAPS: Shasta/Trinity
National Forest Map,
Mt. Shasta/Castle Crags
Wilderness Areas Map

Many believe there is something magical and spiritual about
Mount Shasta. Certainly, the mountain has a commanding
presence: With a base that is 17 miles in diameter and a rise
of more than 10,000 feet to an altitude of 14,162 feet, Shasta
is visible from throughout northern California and southern
Oregon. Some 7,000 feet of the mountain lies above timberline and is sheeted with snow and glaciers most of the year.

The first person to record seeing Shasta was Fray
Narcisco Duran, a Spanish explorer. He named the mountain
"Jesus Maria." The next reference to Shasta came from the 1841
Wilkes Expedition, which noted the presence of "Shasty Peak."
A few years later, legendary western explorer John Fremont
saw the mountain and called it "Shastl." The current name,
Shasta, was pinned on the mountain by Robert Williamson

(a river in southern Oregon bears his name), who was searching for a railroad route between the Columbia and Sacramento Rivers.

Shasta is still an active volcano. As a visible sign of this, a hot springs exists just 150 feet below its summit, and—although the mountain last erupted in 1786—whiffs of sulphur still emit from its peak. In the late 1800s, Sierra Club founder John Muir unexpectedly spent a night on Mount Shasta and survived by huddling next to one of the sulfur springs. Active magma movement continues today and has been recorded in 1978 and again in 1981. Indeed, in the past 20,000 years, there has been a major eruption approximately every 500 years.

In contrast to the hot springs, Shasta also sports seven named glaciers: Mud Creek, Watkinds, Bolan, Hotlum, Wintun, Konwakiton, and Whitney. These glaciers were in retreat, but recent evidence suggests that they are once again advancing.

The slopes of Shasta are cloaked in beautiful forests of sugar pine, Jeffrey pine, incense cedar, white fir, red fir, mountain hemlock, and near timberline, white-bark pine. Do not, however, expect unbroken expansive forest cover, since nearly all the lower forested slopes outside of the designated wilderness have been entered by logging operations. The most extensive forest patches are found on the northeast shoulder of the mountain between Diller Canyon and Whitney Falls, as well as on Red Fir Ridge on the mountain's southeast flank.

Wildlife is sparse, as most animal habitat lies outside of the wilderness boundaries. This is truly a "rocks and ice" preserve, but one may still see an occasional mule deer as well as black bear, red squirrels, and birds common to the region.

Most of the trails—which are sparse as well—start in the subalpine forest, climb a ridge or slope for a couple of miles, then dead-end beneath Shasta's glaciers. Going any further up the mountain, except by the southerly route described below, usually requires a lot of experience and climbing gear. Most people visit this wilderness to climb Shasta, the second highest peak in California; but there are great day hikes that offer fantastic vistas of the mountain and are particularly suitable to children, due to their relatively short distances. Even the climb to the top of Shasta can be accomplished in one long day. The distance from Bunny Flat Trailhead to the top of the mountain is a little more than six miles, but you climb 7,000 feet to get there! Bear in mind that altitude sickness can be a problem to those who ascend the mountain too rapidly.

> **DAY HIKE:** AVALANCHE GULCH–SHASTA SUMMIT
> One-way length: 6.5 miles
> Low and high elevations: 6,800 to 14,142 feet
> Difficulty: strenuous

There are numerous ways to climb to the top of Mount Shasta, but the most popular and safest routes all start on the south side of the mountain. The climb to the top of Shasta is mostly a long, steep slog—with a 7,000-foot elevation gain! However, with proper equipment, including an ice ax, most people in reasonably good shape can reach the summit when they give themselves adequate time. If you have doubts, there are guide services in Mount Shasta City as well as several stores that will rent climbing equipment.

Mount Shasta Wilderness

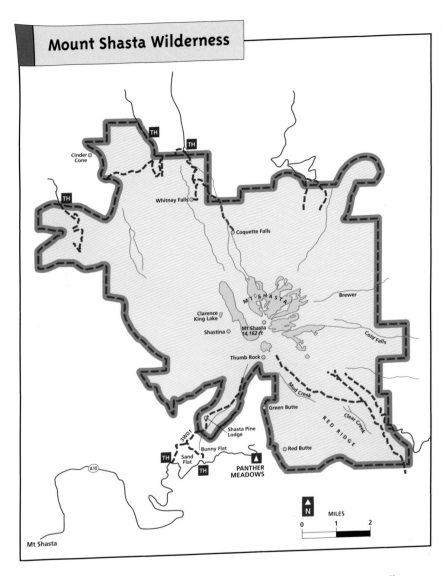

The best time for climbing Shasta is early summer when snow still covers the lower slopes. In late summer and fall after the snow has melted, the ash-covered slopes are more difficult to ascend. There is no real trail, but by early June the most popular path to the top is easily discernable in the snow.

Start your hike by 4:00 a.m., or even earlier, as you need to be on the summit long before afternoon thunderstorms may pose a danger. The entire climb takes 8 to 12 hours. Most summit baggers start their hike at either Sand Flat or Bunny Flat Trailheads. In either case, both trails converge on the stone hut at Horse Camp (mentioned in the Sand Flat day hike).

From the stone hut, you quickly move above timberline and follow the shoulder of a ridge, then hike up an ever-steepening bowl that is usually filled with snow. At 10,440 feet, there is a small tarn (typically frozen) named Helen Lake with a flat spot where some people camp for the night. This is a good spot to acclimate and put yourself in a better position to make the summit the following morning. Helen Lake is a popular campsite, and it is usually frozen, so all water must be obtained by melting snow with a stove (there is no wood at this elevation). Given the popularity of the site, be judicious about where you obtain your snow to melt for drinking water.

Beyond Helen Lake, the trail quickly steepens to a 35-degree slope as it climbs the headwall of a cirque. Without an ice ax, most people will turn back at this point. If properly equipped, you may continue up to 12,500 feet to a red volcanic outcrop known as the "Red Banks." Beyond Red Banks at 13,000 feet, you crawl up Misery Hill, so named because most people are feeling the effects of altitude and are disappointed when they top the hill to see that the final summit is another 0.25 mile and 500 feet higher! The end is the reward, as it provides tremendous views of all northern California.

Bear in mind that even on a warm summer day, the top of Shasta can be quite chilly. Its isolated location means that frequent and sometimes stiff winds are the rule, plus the temperature drops about five degrees for every 1,000 feet climbed. You could easily start your hike wearing shorts and a t-shirt and need a down parka and gloves by the time you reach the summit. Water is the other problem: Although there may be a lot of snow, finding running water once you pass Horse Camp can sometimes be a problem. Fill up canteens and take plenty of water with you.

DAY HIKE: BOLUM CREEK
One-way length: 1.6 miles
Low and high elevations: 5,600 to 7,000 feet
Difficulty: moderate

The north side of Mount Shasta receives little use, and one of the easier trails to the mountain, the Bolum Creek Trail, is accessed from this direction. The trailhead is 11.0 miles east of Weed off Highway 97 at the end of Forest Service Road 43N21. The trail, an old jeep road that has been closed, basically follows the creek, passing through red fir forest before petering out on a ridge with great views of Shasta. More adventurous types will want to continue another mile or so cross-country to Coquette Falls or beyond to Bolum Glacier.

DAY HIKE: SAND FLAT–HORSE CAMP
One-way length: 1.7 miles
Low and high elevations: 6,800 to 7,800 feet
Difficulty: moderate

This is probably the most popular trail in the Mount Shasta Wilderness. It offers quick and easy access to timberline and great views of Shasta, plus it is one of the most popular routes for ascending the mountain summit. The trailhead is accessible by the Everitt Memorial Highway about 10.0 miles east of Mount Shasta City. Once on the trail, you will pass through a beautiful red fir forest, ascending gradually at first, then climbing more steeply as you approach Horse Camp. The Sierra Club has a stone hut here, and you will find spring water coming from a piped source. Beyond Horse Camp you can connect to the main trail leading to Shasta's snowy summit.

DAY HIKE: CLEAR CREEK
One-way length: 1.5 miles
Low and high elevations: 6,800 to 8,800 feet
Difficulty: moderate

This hike follows the rim of Mud Creek Canyon to Clear Creek Springs with great views of the mountain. The trailhead is reachable from McCloud to the south via the Pilgrim Creek, Widow Springs, and McKenzie Butte roads. Once at the trailhead at 6,800 feet, the trail climbs steadily uphill along the rim of Mud Creek Canyon to Clear Creek Springs, where there are great views of the Konwakiton Glacier and Mud Canyon Falls.

OTHER RECREATIONAL OPPORTUNITIES

Mount Shasta's high elevation, open forests, and nearly year-round snow cover make it a fine destination for cross-country skiers and snowshoers. The Everitt Memorial Highway out of Mount Shasta City is plowed all winter, providing access to numerous ski trails.

South Warner Wilderness 6

The glacial lake basins, alpine tundra, aspen groves, terrific ridgeline views of northern Nevada, and sparse visitors make this one of the best-kept secrets in California.

Meadow in Pine Creek Basin, South Warner Wilderness.

Of all the wilderness areas in California, the South Warner is the most reminiscent of landforms and vegetation found in the Rocky Mountains, although the range is actually one of the westernmost fault-block mountains of the Great Basin. Nevertheless, open, sage-, and aspen-covered basins, alpine ridgelines, and a fault-block mountain uplift all replicate the features one sees in the Rockies.

Located in extreme northeastern California near the border with Oregon and Nevada, the Warner Mountains were named for Captain W. H. Warner of the United States Army Engineers, who was killed by Native Americans in 1849 while surveying a route from Nevada to California's Sacramento Valley. The Warner Mountain Range—approximately 80 miles long and 10 miles wide—is found on the

LOCATION: 20 miles east of Alturis

SIZE: 70,385 acres

ELEVATION RANGE: 5,800 to 9,900 feet

MILES OF TRAILS: 77

ECOSYSTEMS: sagebrush-aspen, mixed conifer forest, alpine tundra

ADMINISTRATION: Modoc National Forest

MAPS: Modoc National Forest Map, South Warner Wilderness Area Map

eastern portion of the Modoc National Forest. Highway 299 crosses the range at Cedar Pass, dividing it into two halves, North Warners and South Warners.

The South Warner Wilderness was originally set aside by the Forest Service as the South Warner Primitive Area in 1931. When the 1964 Wilderness Act passed Congress, the South Warners were one of the original Forest Service primitive areas to garner formal wilderness designation. The 1984 California Wilderness Bill enlarged the South Warner Wilderness to its present size of 18 miles long and 8 miles wide, totaling 70,385 acres.

The South Warners are a spectacular example of a fault-block mountain range. The eastern slope rises a very dramatic 5,000 feet above the adjacent valley, while the western slope is gentler with longer stream drainages. The range features the highest summits in northeastern California, which were lofty enough to support glaciers during the last Ice Age. Cirque lakes, U-shaped valleys, and glaciated basins all attest to this past natural event. Eagle Peak (9,892) is the highest summit, but Warren Peak (9,710) and Squaw Peak (8,646) are nearly as high. It's possible to see Mount Shasta, Mount Lassen, and much of northeast Nevada from one of these peaks on a clear day.

Although the steep eastern slope has sparse pockets of trees, the western side of the range supports a diverse forest of ponderosa pine, Jeffrey pine, western white pine, whitebark pine, lodgepole pine, white fir, western juniper, and aspen. Shrubs include bitterbrush, mountain mahogany, and sagebrush. One of the charms of the South Warner Wilderness is its abundance of aspen and meadows, as few other parts of California sport this type of growth or openness.

In keeping with the notion that wilderness areas should preserve natural evolutionary processes, wildfires are not always suppressed. Lightning-caused fires have rejuvenated portions of this forest's ecosystem. Some good places to see the restorative influence of fire include the Poison Flat area, which burned in 1981, and the Highrock Creek area, which hosted a blaze in 1987.

Wildlife common to northeast California is abundant in the wilderness, including mule deer, mountain lion, beaver, bobcat, coyote, marten, badger, and golden eagle. Although many of the higher mountain lakes are stocked with non-native fish such as brook trout and brown trout, a few of the streams in the Warner Mountains hold the rare redband trout, an early evolutionary form of rainbow trout.

I was not able to confirm the presence of elk in the South Warners, although these animals are currently expanding their range into the North Warners from Oregon, and it's only a matter of time before they spread southward into the wilderness. Restoration of another species, the wolf, may take a bit longer. Although the South Warners are not of sufficient size to support a viable breeding population of this predator, the abundance of public land in northeast California—coupled with sparse human population and adequate prey base—makes wolf restoration a future possibility.

Unfortunately, like many other wilderness areas, not all ecologically destructive practices have been eliminated. Domestic livestock—cattle and sheep—still graze the South Warners. The presence of livestock not only contributes to trampled meadows and stream banks, pollutes water, and introduces weeds into new areas, but it also has a detrimental effect upon wildlife.

In 1980, fourteen bighorn sheep were transplanted into Raider Canyon within the wilderness from Lava Beds National Monument and the Inyo National

Forest. By 1985, the herd had increased to 60 animals, but two years later the entire population died from bacterial pneumonia acquired from domestic sheep. According to Modoc Forest officials, the Warners could support up to 400 wild bighorn, but there will be no efforts at new reintroductions as long as domestic sheep grazing occurs in the range.

The Modoc Forest Plan says only 120,000 acres of its rangelands are in good to excellent condition, while more than 800,000 acres of rangelands are in fair to poor condition. "Fair condition" means that more than half of the plant species that should be found on a site are absent. The majority of the forest's riparian areas are also in fair to poor ecological condition. Astute observers will find abundant evidence of this type of damage in the South Warner Wilderness.

There are eight trailheads in the South Warners, most of them leading to streams or to the wilderness' seven lakes. The majority of recreational use focuses on Clear and Patterson Lakes, but this wilderness has so few visitors, even these areas are not crowded. There are 77 miles of maintained trails, but cross-country travel is relatively easy due to the open nature of the terrain.

> **DAY HIKE: PINE CREEK**
> One-way length: 3 miles
> Low and high elevations: 6,800 to 8,000 feet
> Difficulty: moderate

The Pine Creek Trail follows the South Fork of Pine Creek to Pine Creek Basin, one of the more attractive areas in the entire wilderness. Aspen groves intermixed with open, flowery slopes make the basin a particularly delightful destination in mid-summer or early fall. The trail climbs steadily 1,000 feet through forests of fir and pine, passing several small lakes enroute. One can continue another 1.5 miles beyond the bottom of the basin and ascend up a steep set of switchbacks to the Summit Trail, which offers spectacular views as well as access to popular glacier-carved Patterson Lake below Mount Warren.

> **DAY HIKE: CLEAR LAKE**
> One-way length: 0.5 mile
> Low and high elevations: nearly flat
> Difficulty: easy

The trail to Clear Lake begins at Mill Creek Falls Trailhead on the southwest corner of the wilderness. It is a short hike to Clear Lake, a beautiful water body that sits at 6,000 feet and is reputed to hold large trout. Backpackers might consider going beyond Clear Lake on the Poison Flat Trail, a little-used access that provides connections to other trails on the crest of the range.

South Warner Wilderness

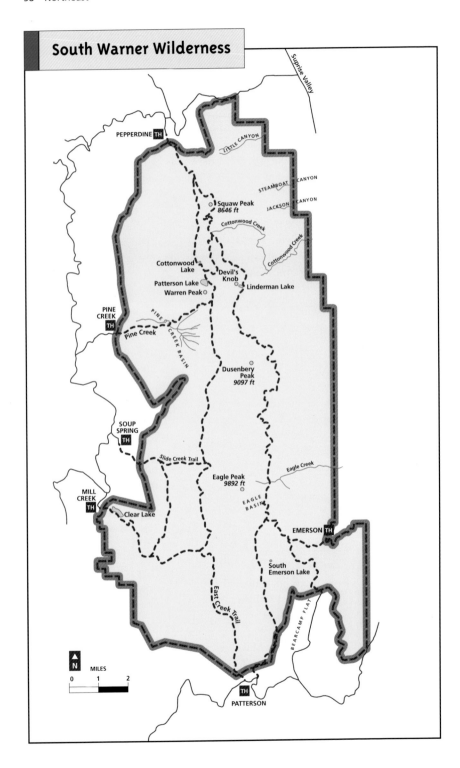

DAY HIKE: NORTH EMERSON LAKE
One-way length: 3.5 miles
Low and high elevations: 6,200 to 7,800 feet
Difficulty: moderate

The Emerson Trailhead, located on the southeast side of the wilderness accessible from Eagleville, is the most remote of the trails in the South Warners. The final few miles of the dirt access road are relatively steep and may be impassible in wet weather.

The trail is a continuation of the access road, steeply climbing 2,000 feet in just 3.5 miles, but it's worth the effort. North Emerson Lake lies in a rock-bound glacial cirque just below the summit rim. About 2.0 miles up the trail, you will reach the junction of the South Emerson Trail, which offers a poorly defined but potential alternative loop route back to the trailhead, adding another mile or so to the total distance. If you go this route, be sure to bear left at the Bear Camp Trail junction, approximately 1.5 miles from where you leave the North Emerson Trail.

Like most of the shorter day hikes in the Warners, it's possible to extend the North Emerson Lake hike by continuing another 0.5 mile past the lake to the North Owl Creek Trail, which runs north-south the length of the range. Once on the North Owl Creek Trail, you can hike north a few miles to the lovely Eagle Basin or scramble cross-country from the trail junction up 8,971-foot Cole Peak.

OVERNIGHT HIKE: EAST CREEK–PATTERSON MEADOW
One-way length: 15 miles
Low and high elevations: 7,000 to 8,400 feet
Difficulty: moderate

This loop is best done as an overnight backpack, although a strong hiker could complete it in one day. If you plan to camp overnight, be aware of the need for water. The first part of the trail angles down and follows East Creek, but once you're on the Summit Trail, there are few opportunities to obtain water without dropping down into basins to reach flowing streams.

The hike begins at the East Creek Trailhead, which lies at the southern end of the range. Follow Forest Service signs to Patterson Campground; the East Creek Trailhead and parking lot are a short distance off the main road to the campground. The trail angles down and follows the timbered canyon until you reach the Poison Flat Trail junction. The Poison Flat Trail climbs 800 feet in about 1.0 mile to connect with the Summit Trail. This trail passes through sparsely timbered country with spectacular views on the walk back (south) to Patterson Campground. The last few miles involve a relatively steep descent, then it's a short 0.5-mile walk on Forest Service roads back to the East Creek Trailhead.

OVERNIGHT HIKE: SUMMIT LOOP
One-way length: 22.4 miles
Low and high elevations: 7,200 to 9,200 feet
Difficulty: moderate to strenuous

This is the granddaddy of loop trips in the Warners. It would be best to allot at least four days to do the entire 45-mile trek, and it's better to have a few extra days if you like scrambling up peaks or fishing. It's also possible to make this a one-way, 26-mile jaunt along the length of the wilderness by hiking from Patterson Campground to Pepperdine Campground, but you need to arrange a shuttle. The loop hike, described here, starts and ends at Patterson Campground, which is located on the southern fringe of the wilderness reachable from Alturis via Jess Valley and South Warner Road. Summit Trail is relatively flat with large, open meadowlands and little available water, while the Owl Creek Trail has more elevation gains and drops as it dips in and out of water-ready glacial basins.

The trip starts at Patterson Campground, elevation 7,200 feet. Take Summit Trail, which climbs 1,000 feet to a rolling ridgeline with great views. Follow it north to the junction with Owl Creek Trail, which you will stay on for 15.25 miles, passing enroute Eagle Basin, Linderman Lake, and other lovely cirque basins that offer both water and campsites. Just south of Squaw Peak, the Owl Creek Trail intercepts the Squaw Peak Trail, which drops 2.74 miles into Patterson Lake on Summit Trail. Once you intercept Summit, turn south (left) and follow the trail as it winds through open country and meadows past Patterson Lake (a potential campsite), Pine Creek Basin, and the headwaters of Mill Creek to the Poison Flat–East Creek Trails, ending at East Creek Trailhead. From here, it is a short walk back on Forest Service roads to Patterson Campground.

OTHER RECREATIONAL OPPORTUNITIES

Cross-country skiing is almost unheard of in the South Warners Wilderness, but there's no lack of snow. The limiting factor seems to be the unplowed, snow-covered access roads. The best winter access is at Cedar Pass off Highway 299, where a small ski area operates in the winter months.

Thousand Lakes Wilderness

*This wilderness has 990 fewer lakes than a thousand,
but it's still rugged country, with the effects of glacial
and volcanic activity evident.*

*Whitebark pine on Magee Peak frame Mount Lassen,
Thousand Lakes Wilderness.*

Less than 10 percent of the heavily timbered, hence heavily
logged, Lassen National Forest remains in a wild, unroaded
condition. One of the areas spared from development is the
Thousand Lakes Wilderness northwest of Lassen Volcanic
National Park. The name of this wilderness conjures up
visions of a virtual "Boundary Waters" kind of place, such
as those found in northern Minnesota's lake-studded woodlands. With only 16,335 acres, however, it would be difficult
to fit one thousand lakes into this compact wilderness. The
glaciated landscape has somewhat fewer than the thousand
lakes its name implies—ten, to be exact, and only three
amount to much. The highest summit in the wilderness
and in the entire Lassen National Forest is 8,677-foot
Crater Peak, which is named for the glacial cirque carved

LOCATION: 55 miles
east of Redding

SIZE: 16,335 acres

ELEVATION RANGE:
5,540 to 8,677 feet

MILES OF TRAILS: 22

ECOSYSTEMS:
mixed conifer forest

ADMINISTRATION:
Lassen National Forest

MAP: Lassen National
Forest Map

into its flank. Glaciers also scoured out the lake basins that give the wilderness
its name.

This wilderness, like Lassen Volcanic National Park to its southeast, exhibits
many volcanic features. At least a dozen cinder cones erupted along a seven-mile stretch
of what is known today as Thousand Lakes Wilderness, some perhaps as recently as
the last few hundred years. And the Thousand Lakes Volcano once stood 9,000 to
10,000 feet in elevation, with the higher summits, such as Magee Peak, representing
the eroded rim of the former mountain. Hall Butte, a cinder cone, erupted within the
last 500 years.

There are 22 miles of trails within Thousand Lakes Wilderness, with four
trailhead access points—Cypress, Tamarack, Bunchgrass, and Magee—all reachable
off Highway 89. Tamarack Trailhead is the easiest to access and thus receives the
greatest use. Plan accordingly: You can walk across the entire wilderness in a day,
but this makes any overnight trek to one of the lakes an easy afternoon jaunt for most
people—even with a pack. Despite the ease of access, the Thousand Lakes Wilderness
receives relatively light use, and if you visit any place other than the most popular
destinations, you should have it to yourself. Mosquitoes are the most vicious wildlife
you'll likely encounter.

DAY HIKE: CYPRESS TRAILHEAD TO LAKE EILER
One-way length: 2.3 miles
Low and high elevations: 5,410 to 6,400 feet
Difficulty: easy

Lake Eiler is the largest lake in the wilderness and the most accessible. The relatively
moderate grade and short length makes this a good trail to bring children on for the
day or as an overnight camping trip. Bear in mind there are two access trails to the
lake: The 2.3-mile Cypress Trail is longer and steeper than the 2.0-mile Tamarack
Trail. If solitude is your goal, plan to take a different hike. Nevertheless, the 10.0-
mile drive required to reach the Cypress Trailhead does discourage a lot of potential
trail users. To find the trailhead, take Forest Road 26 (34N19) west off Highway 89.
Follow it 8.5 miles to road 34N22, then drive 1.5 miles to the trailhead.

The trail takes its name from some "cypress," or juniper trees, seen early in
the hike. It passes two intersections in the first 200 yards, crosses Eiler Creek, then
begins a 1,000-foot climb to the wilderness boundary before leveling off for the
remainder of the short trek to Eiler Lake. For those inclined to spend the night,
there are numerous good campsites along the lake shore and nearby. It's also possible
to continue on another 2.0 miles to the shallow Barrett Lake, which also has several
good campsites. From Barrett, it's 3.1 miles to the Cypress Trailhead.

DAY HIKE: MAGEE PEAK
One-way length: 3.7 miles
Low and high elevations: 6,050 to 8,549 feet
Difficulty: moderate

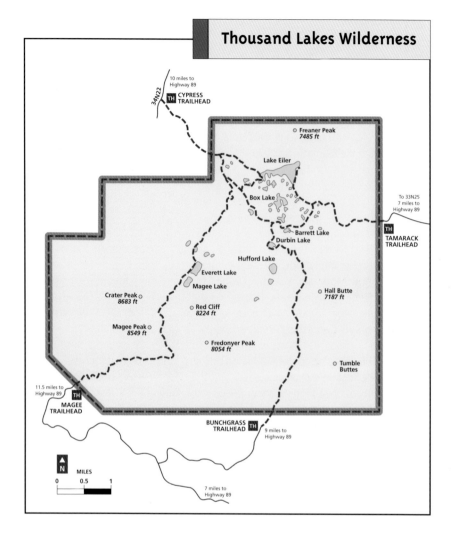

Thousand Lakes Wilderness

10 miles to Highway 89

34N22

CYPRESS TRAILHEAD

Freaner Peak 7485 ft

Lake Eiler

Box Lake

To 33N25 7 miles to Highway 89

Barrett Lake
Durbin Lake

TAMARACK TRAILHEAD

Hufford Lake

Everett Lake

Magee Lake

Crater Peak 8683 ft

Red Cliff 8224 ft

Hall Butte 7187 ft

Magee Peak 8549 ft

Fredonyer Peak 8054 ft

Tumble Buttes

11.5 miles to Highway 89

MAGEE TRAILHEAD

BUNCHGRASS TRAILHEAD   9 miles to Highway 89

N

MILES

0   0.5   1

7 miles to Highway 89

Magee Peak, although not the highest summit in the wilderness, is the site of a former lookout, and it offers superb views of the surrounding country, particularly Lassen Peak to the southeast. But the trail was built to accommodate supply mules, not hikers, and it tends to be direct, climbing steadily, with no available water, unless you can find some lingering snow patches. The first portion of the trail passes through forests of sugar pine, white fir, western white pine, and red fir. Eventually, you will reach the windswept ridgeline, which is cloaked primarily in twisted whitebark pine. About 0.25 mile from the top of Magee Peak, the main trail drops down into the glacial carved basin and continues for 2.0 miles to Magee and Everrett Lakes, which offer good overnight campsites. However, if you continue up the ridge, you will quickly reach the long, arching summit where the old lookout once stood. The views don't get any better than this, but if you're inclined, it's possible to work your way less than a mile along the crest northwest to Crater Peak. As the highest summit in the wilderness, Crater offers a different perspective on the surrounding countryside.

Northwest: The North Coast Ranges and the Klamath–Siskiyou Mountains

This region contains some of the least populated, most remote, and wildest landscapes in California. Encompassing the North Coast Ranges and the Klamath–Siskiyou Mountains, this mountainous region is virtually uninhabited. The largest population center in the entire region is the Eureka–Arcata complex, hardly a booming megalopolis. Population density is less than five people per square mile—less than Montana! Though the human population is sparse, the wildlands wealth is enormous. It has more federally designated Wild and Scenic Rivers than any other part of the United States, and it offers an abundance of designated wildlands, such as Trinity Alps, Marble Mountain, Yolla Bolly–Middle Eel, Russian, Snow Mountain, Siskiyou, Castle Crags, and more that make it one of the most wilderness-rich areas in California. *(Please note: This excludes the Fallon Islands Wilderness, located 30 miles from San Francisco, since no public access is permitted.)*

The area also contains a biologically rich landscape that has evolved over the past 40 million years. Northwest California is one of the major centers of plant biodiversity in the country. Among the forest giants, such as the venerable redwoods, live a minimum of 3,500 other plant species with new ones being discovered every year. Some 280 endemic plant species are found here, more than recorded for any place outside of the Southern Appalachians. The Klamath Mountains region supports 53 tree species, 33 of them conifers. Western North America has only 60 coniferous species in total! In 1992, the International Union for the Conservation of Nature identified the Klamath–Siskiyou region as one of seven areas in North America critical for conservation because of its "global botanical significance."

The region as defined for purposes of this book encompasses both the North Coast Ranges and the Klamath Mountains proper. Beginning at San Francisco Bay, the North Coast Ranges form a number of parallel mountain ranges aligned with the coast, eventually blending into the Klamath–Siskiyou Mountains region near the Oregon border. Most people traveling the area wouldn't discern any difference between the two, but for the most part, the Coast Ranges are less rugged and not as high as the Klamath–Siskiyou region. As a result, the Coast Ranges are more heavily roaded and logged. By default, then, the Klamath region contains larger wildlands complexes.

In outward expression both regions seem similar—dense forests on steep slopes. The South Fork Mountain Fault is generally considered to be the dividing line between the two areas. Both the North Coast Ranges and Klamath Mountains are composed primarily of sediments originally deposited on the ocean floor, but those in the Klamaths are older and have extensive intrusions of granitic bodies. The North Coast Ranges consist of sedimentary Franciscan rocks dominated by shales and sandstones. In all cases, the rocks are made up of separate terranes or slices of the earth's crust that were welded on to the edge of the North American continent. Each terrain had a different origin, so the rocks of the region are a complex mix of varying types, including metamorphosed marine sediments, such as marble, slate, and chert; ocean basin crusts, such as serpentine; and intrusions of igneous rock, such as granite.

Indian paintbrush on ridge by Kings Castle, Marble Mountain Wilderness.

The mountains of the Klamath province are very similar to those found in the Sierra Nevada. There is a near-perfect matchup of the rock strata in both places, so much so that geologists speculate that the two were joined some 130 million years ago and have since separated. According to current theory, the Klamath Mountains were transported via sliding faults north and west to their present position. As further evidence of this, foxtail pine, a California endemic, is found only in the southern Sierra and Klamath Mountains. The reason the Klamaths do not resemble the Sierra Nevada more is that they were not uplifted as high nor eroded to the same extent.

The Pacific Ocean bounds this area on the west and the Central Valley and I–5 largely define it on the east. Influenced by abundant precipitation, the area is heavily forested, with numerous rivers that have cut deep, rugged canyons through the maze of peaks and ridges that top out at 9,002 feet in the Trinity Alps. Salmon once filled these rivers with a silver throng. Most of the rivers in the region still host fish runs, but they are very much diminished.

Although not high enough to support extensive ice sheets, many of the higher peaks do display evidence of glaciation and some areas, such as the Trinity Alps, have extensively glaciated uplands and still host a few active glaciers today. Signs of glaciation are found in other wildernesses as well, including the Yolla Bolly, Snow Mountain, Siskiyou, Marble Mountain, Russian, and Red Buttes. However, it is the lack of glaciers at lower elevations that allowed the region to sustain its wealth of bio-logical treasures, since some plant communities have been able to persist and co-evolve together for millions of years.

The rainfall on the coastal side of the mountains is generous. More than 140 inches of annual precipitation has been reported for some stations. More than any other part of California, this area seems to be an outpost of the rainy Pacific Northwest. Yet the dry eastern slope of the Coast and Klamath Ranges support savannas of oak, chaparral, and other plant communities more typically associated with California.

The forests of the region are among the most diverse anywhere in the temperate world. Research has shown that these forests resemble the vegetation that was once widespread across North America as recently as one million years ago. The abundant rainfall and generally low eleva-tions support magnificent forests of Douglas fir, sugar pine, ponderosa pine, Jeffrey pine, bigleaf maple, tanoak, golden-cup oak, Oregon white oak, canyon live oak, western white pine, Pacific madrone, California laurel, Pacific dogwood, white fir, Pacific yew, mountain hemlock, whitebark pine, white alder, incense cedar, knobcone pine, lodgepole pine, and red fir. Locally common or even rare species include Brewer's spruce, foxtail pine, noble fir, Alaska cedar, subalpine fir, and Engelmann spruce.

The wildlife of the region is typical of that found throughout the forested Pacific Northwest, including birds such as the northern spotted owl, the blue grouse, varied thrush, chickadees, and pileated woodpeckers. Mammals include the red-backed vole, mountain beaver, northern flying squirrel, chickaree, porcupine, marten, fisher, river otter, wolverine, mule deer, black bear, and mountain lion. Black bear in particular are more abundant here than in any other part of California. It was a rare day that I didn't see at least one of these animals while hiking in the wildlands of the Northwest, and occasionally I would encounter as many as four or five in a single day! Fisher, once thought to be very rare, are abundant here. Unlike the marten, which appears to prefer mostly coniferous forests, the fisher seeks out a mixed woods of deciduous trees and conifers. Elk, extirpated in California by overhunting, are gradually moving south from populations in Oregon to recolonize the mountains of the region, including the Trinity Alps and Marble Mountain Wildernesses.

KLAMATH ECOSYSTEM RESTORATION

As spectacular as the Klamath region is, it is not untouched. Mining first opened up the region to development, resulting in numerous gold rushes to places such as the Scott Bar, Trinity Alps, and Salmon Mountains. Remains of these old mining camps still dot some of the backcountry. Since then, logging has riddled much of the area with roads, slicing up some of the larger areas into smaller units. Nevertheless, enough of its basic natural heritage remains intact for it to offer one of the best opportunities for wildlands restoration in California, perhaps even in the nation.

The closure and revegetation of old logging roads combined with the preservation of corridors—such as the Grider Creek area connecting existing wildlands of the Red Buttes Wilderness and Marble Mountain Wilderness, the Ukonom Creek area between the Marbles and Siskiyou Wilderness, Butler Creek between the Trinity Alps Wilderness and Marble Mountains, and elsewhere —could go a long way toward bringing about ecological restoration. Buffers in the already developed landscape could be managed for less destructive grazing, timber cutting, and roading practices. Within the present context of commercial use of the public lands, such a proposal offers a substantial change of direction.

However, even this may be a half-hearted solution. Employing the best timber harvest techniques isn't the same as no timber harvest at all. And domestic livestock grazing, although done with care, still places vegetation that would otherwise support native species into the belly of an exotic animal removed from the ecosystem. From what little we know about genetics, ecosystem function, and ecological processes, even a plan that calls for mitigation and buffers may not provide sufficient space for landscape-wide processes to really work. There are few places as biologically rich as the Klamath– Siskiyou, and few places that would respond as rapidly to restoration efforts. A more worthy goal would be to protect the entire Klamath–Siskiyou–North Coast Ranges, including the portions that lap into Oregon, as a national biological preserve. Instead of buffers, all commercial extractive industries on public lands would be phased out, including logging, mining, and livestock grazing.

This is not to suggest that all human use must halt or that communities must be removed and highways closed. A limited amount of access on major highways and roads could continue. Existing towns and communities would remain, although new growth on private lands would be controlled and zoned so as to minimize inappropriate uses or conflicts with biological preservation. Compatible recreational use could continue to function as part of the economic base, so long as it did not jeopardize ecological function and biological richness. Restoration projects, including road deconstruction, stream and fisheries restorations, and other work, could help to employ local people displaced from other industries.

The main goal of public lands management would be ecological restoration, not commercial exploitation. Runs of salmon and steelhead could be restored; wherever feasible, dams might even be removed; elk could be reestablished throughout their former range. Wildfire could once again assume its role as a natural process and burn tens of thousands of acres as it once did without risk to human habitation. Extinct species such as the wolf could even be reintroduced.

In particular, if most unnecessary spur roads were closed and a large wildlands complex could be more or less continuously reestablished, this region may be the best place in California for reintroduction of the grizzly. Rich in acorns, berries, and—potentially—salmon and elk, no place else in California has as great a capacity as the Klamath region for sustainable grizzly populations. Afterall, an area such as Admiralty Island in Alaska is no more than a million acres in size, yet it supports more than 1,500 bears due to its general resource richness—and Admiralty is not as rich as the Klamath region once was.

Such a bold plan will not be implemented overnight, and perhaps never. Yet, we have only a few such biologically diverse areas on the entire continent. If we are as rich a nation as we often like to claim we are, surely we can afford to set aside and restore at least a few large ecosystem regions such as the Klamath.

8 Cache Creek Proposed Wilderness

The Cache Creek area boasts the second largest Tule elk herd in California, a wintering bald eagle population, cross-country hiking, and whitewater rafting.

Hikers among oaks on the Judge Davis Trail, Cache Creek Proposed Wilderness.

LOCATION: 5 miles southeast of Clear Lake

SIZE: approximately 34,000 acres

ELEVATION RANGE: 200 to 2,000 feet

MILES OF TRAILS: 20

ECOSYSTEMS: riparian, oak woodlands, chaparral

ADMINISTRATION: Bureau of Land Management

MAP: Cache Creek Visitor's Map

Not more than an hour's drive from Davis and other population centers, the proposed Cache Creek Wilderness offers low elevation hiking options in winter, fall, and spring, when higher elevation areas are still buried under snow. The Cache Creek Roadless Area was first identified by the BLM in 1979 and was designated a Wilderness Study Area (WSA). The BLM ultimately recommended against wilderness designation for the area in 1986, but not because it didn't have wildlands value. Rather, a host of mining claims and other private properties made wilderness designation unattractive at the time. Nevertheless, the agency has continued to purchase private lands as it can, and eventually this obstacle may be overcome.

In the meantime, in recognition of its superb attributes, the BLM has designated part of the wilderness as a Research Natural Area. The 11,000-acre Northern California Chaparral Research Natural Area protects a representative example of the chaparral plant community. In addition, a half-mile corridor on either side of Cache Creek totaling another 8,204 acres was designated an ACEC, or Area of Critical Environmental Concern, to protect its important biological and other attributes.

One of the attractions of the proposed wilderness is the bald eagle. Up to 62 eagles have been counted in mid-winter using the area for perches, roots, and foraging, making it the second largest concentration of wintering bald eagles in California.

In addition to the eagles, there are over 500 Tule elk in the Cache Creek herd, making up 20 percent of all Tule elk in the state. The herd ranges over 100,000 acres of public and private lands. In recognition of the value of this area to elk, the California Department of Fish and Game has designated the Wilson Valley area of Cache Creek as an Area of Special Biological Importance. The valley is closed to public access in spring to protect elk calving grounds.

The best access to Cache Creek Proposed Wilderness is found along Highway 20 between Williams and Lake Clear.

DAY HIKE: JUDGE DAVIS TRAIL
One-way length: 5 miles
Low and high elevations: 1,000 to 1,500 feet
Difficulty: moderate

The Judge Davis Trail is the most direct way to Cache Creek and the popular Wilson Valley. To find the trailhead, which is located on the Lake and Colusa County line, drive west on Highway 20, 8.0 miles past the junction of Highway 16 and Highway 20, where you will round a sharp curve and see a sign, "Welcome to Lake County." The trailhead is located on the south side of the highway (left) by a corral. There is a trailhead sign at the parking area.

The first part of the trail takes hikers through oak woodlands at a moderate grade until you encounter a fire road; here you have a good view of the Cache Creek Valley. As you continue to follow the trail downhill to Cache Creek, you will notice the vegetation is now chaparral and grasslands. Wilson Valley, along Cache Creek, is a giant oak glade, wonderful in the spring when flowers are in bloom. Bear in mind that the California Department of Fish and Game closes Wilson Valley for part of the Tule elk calving season, so check with local officials if you are planning a trek at that time of year.

DAY HIKE: REDBUD TRAIL
One-way length: 7 miles
Low and high elevations: 1,000 to 1,500 feet
Difficulty: moderate

The Redbud Trail accesses Wilson Valley, with the trailhead at Highway 20 where the road crosses the North Fork of Cache Creek. The California Department of Fish and Game has a parking area and trailhead sign here. The hike is largely downhill through oak savanna, chaparral, and grasslands, and it offers a good place to see elk.

DAY HIKE: JUDGE DAVIS–WILSON VALLEY–HARLEY GULCH
Loop length: 13 miles
Low and high elevations: 1,000 to 1,500 feet
Difficulty: moderate

This hike offers a longer day hike or even an overnighter, passing along Cache Creek through rich oak woodlands. You start this trip following the Judge Davis Trail (see the previous description) to Cache Creek and Wilson Valley. From Wilson Valley, there is no trail, but if you walk up Cache Creek following the oak-covered benches to the first big drainage coming in from the northeast, you will be at Harley Gulch. Follow the gulch up to the highway and walk about 0.5 mile back to the parking area by the Judge Davis Trailhead.

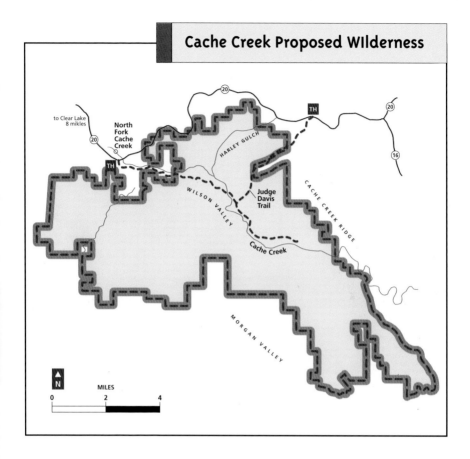

Cache Creek Proposed Wilderness

9 Castle Crags Wilderness

Rocky granite spires and a section of the Pacific Crest Trail grace this wilderness just off of the I–5 corridor.

Granite cliffs seen from the Pacific Crest Trail in Castle Crags Wilderness.

LOCATION: east of I–5 by Dunsmuir

SIZE: 10,500 acres

ELEVATION RANGE: 2,400 to 6,900 feet

MILES OF TRAILS: 14

ECOSYSTEMS: mixed conifer, chaparral, oak woodlands

ADMINISTRATION: Shasta–Trinity National Forest

MAPS: Shasta–Trinity National Forest Map, Mt. Shasta/Castle Crags Wilderness Areas Map

Although most of the Klamath province consists of sedimentary or metamorphic rocks, occasional plutons of granite have been intruded and in some instances exposed by erosion, and the Castle Crags represent a particularly dramatic example of this. The diminutive Castle Crags Wilderness packs a lot of striking scenery in a small area. Although no more than 6,900 feet in elevation, Ice Age glaciers scoured the granitic bedrock into fluted spires and cliffs that are visible from I–5 just south of Mount Shasta. The wilderness adjoins Castle Crags State Park, so the actual physical size of this preserve is somewhat larger than the acreage statistics might indicate. Besides cliffs and towers, there are five glacial lakes, waterfalls, a portion of the Pacific Crest Trail, and lovely forests of knobcone pine, ponderosa pine, Pacific dogwood, Brewer's spruce, bigleaf maple, white fir, red fir, incense cedar, sugar pine, lodgepole pine, Douglas fir, black oak, and other trees. Chaparral of manzanita, whitethorn, snow-brush, deerbrush, and ceanothus cloaks the lower, drier slopes. The Castle Crags hairbell is endemic to the wilderness.

The granite that makes up the Crags was formed some 170 to 225 million years ago, about the same time as the older western Cascades were forming. Molten magma rose toward the surface but did not erupt and flow out as in a volcano; instead, it remained buried and cooled in place. Gradually, the overlying rock formations were eroded away, exposing the granite we see today. Glaciers later carved out the basins and smoothed the rock.

Besides intrusions of granite, precious minerals were also locked in the Klamath province rocks. After gold was discovered in the foothills of the Sierra, miners spread out across California and the rest of the West, looking for more of the yellow metal. With the invasion of the Klamath region by miners in the 1850s, relations between the Native Americans and miners deteriorated to the point where warfare erupted. The Battle of Castle Crags occurred in 1855, beginning the Modoc War. The fight was located between what is now known as Castle Lake and Battle Rock. By 1886, the Southern Pacific Railroad had laid tracks up the Sacramento River, opening the region to additional pressure for mining and logging, plus a growing tourist trade. Resorts sprang up, as well as a bottled mineral water industry centered on springs located below Castle Rock. In the 1930s, citizen initiative managed to acquire lands in the area for a state park, but the adjoining Forest Service lands were not given protection until 1984, when the Castle Crags were included in the California Wilderness Act.

DAY HIKE: GRAY ROCK LAKE
One-way length: 0.75 mile
Low and high elevations: 5,600 to 6,400 feet
Difficulty: easy

Gray Rock Lake is the only lake basin in the Castle Crags Wilderness, and its hike is short and direct. To reach the trailhead, find the road to Lake Siskiyou west out of Mount Shasta City, take Forest Service Road 26 up the South Fork of the Sacramento to a wooden bridge 6.0 miles beyond Lake Siskiyou, then drive another 2.0 miles on a very poor, steep road to the trailhead. It's advisable to walk this stretch if you don't have 4WD.

Lower Gray Rock Lake, located in a wooded glacial basin, may be reached by a steep trail. If you hike another 0.5 mile beyond Lower Gray Rock Lake, you will come to Timber and Upper Gray Rock Lakes, both of which sit in spectacular glacial basins.

DAY HIKE: CASTLE DOME TRAIL
One-way length: 3 miles
Low and high elevations: 2,500 to 4,800 feet
Difficulty: strenuous

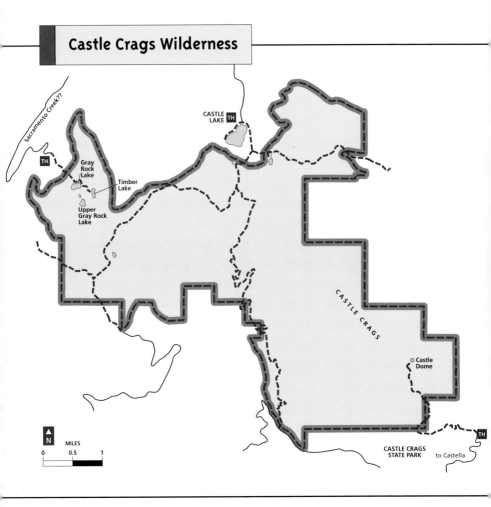

Castle Crags Wilderness

CASTLE DOME TRAIL: CONTINUED

When you drive I–5 north from Redding, the striking granite spires of the Castle Crags are visible just before you reach Dunsmuir. This hike brings you to the base of those peaks. Although 4,966-foot Castle Dome is within the Castle Crags Wilderness, the trailhead begins in Castle Crags State Park to the east of the wilderness boundary. Accessing the trailhead is easy: Get off I–5 at the Castle Crags State Park exit, enter the park, and go to the trailhead at 2,500 feet on Kettlebelly Ridge.

The first part of the hike follows Kettlebelly Ridge, passing through lovely forests of Jeffrey pine, black oak, and incense cedar. I found several confusing trail junctions, but if you continue uphill, you'll do alright. As you near Indian Springs at 3,600 feet, views of Castle Dome open up. Continue up the ridge, crossing from the state park to the Forest Service wilderness lands enroute. The final part of the trail offers wonderful views of the granite spires as you approach a saddle that lies at the foot of the crags.

Chanchelulla Wilderness

The Chanchelulla is little known and covered with small brush. It's a good place for solitude.

Lupine and poppies.

Managed by the Forest Service primarily as a trailless wilderness, the 8,200-acre Chanchelulla lies east of Red Bluff on the eastern side of the North Coast Ranges. The highest elevation, 6,399-foot Chanchelulla Peak, is steep and dry terrain, with the view from Chanchelulla Ridge below it open and spectacular. One maintained trail runs across a mile of the southwest corner, with several other "poor" trails criss-crossing the wilderness. Most of the area consists of brushfields.

The best access is Highway 36 from Platina. Go west past Harrison Gulch to Wildwood. Turn right (north) onto Forest Road 30N04, then right again on 30N016 to Midas Gap, where a trail to the southwest corner of the wilderness is located.

LOCATION: 30 miles west of Redding

SIZE: 8,200 acres

ELEVATION RANGE: 3,500 to 6,400 feet

MILES OF TRAILS: 10

ECOSYSTEMS: chaparral, mixed conifer

ADMINISTRATION: Shasta–Trinity National Forest

MAP: Shasta–Trinity National Forest Map

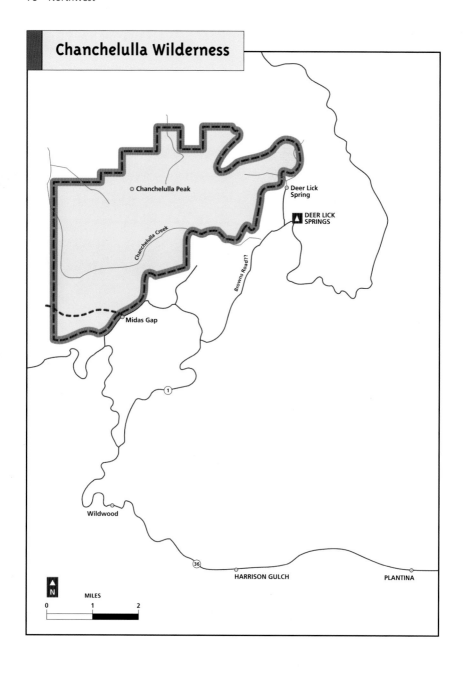

Chanchelulla Wilderness

Golden Gate National Recreation Area and Surrounding State Parks

These headlands, redwood forests, oak savannas, and grassy ridges are all within a few miles of California's second largest urban center.

View from Bolinas Ridge Trail, Golden Gate National Recreation Area.

Probably no other city in the United States has such a spectacular natural setting as San Francisco, and none has so much of its nearby landscape protected from development. Although these areas aren't officially designated wilderness, much of their landscape is undeveloped and could be restored to something approaching a natural wild state.

Beginning in downtown San Francisco, Golden Gate National Recreational Area (NRA) protects some of the urban landscape, including Baker and China Beaches. The recreation area, along with the adjacent state parks and the Marin County Water District lands, provides an extensive network of undeveloped land just across the Golden Gate Bridge. No part of the recreation area is more than an hour from downtown

LOCATION: San Francisco and headlands to the north of Golden Gate
SIZE: 76,000 acres
ELEVATION RANGE: sea level to 2,571 feet
MILES OF TRAILS: numerous interlocking trails
ECOSYSTEMS: redwood forest, grasslands, oak forests
ADMINISTRATION: National Park Service, California State Parks, and Marin Water District
MAP: Golden Gate National Recreation Area Map

San Francisco, and many of the hiking trails can be accessed via San Francisco Bay area mass transit system. The Marin Headlands and adjacent parklands north of the Golden Gate Bridge offer the best natural area hiking.

Golden Gate NRA was established in 1972. Most of the lands now part of the recreation area were once controlled by the military and were part of San Francisco's defensive rim. Fort Baker was established in 1850, just two years after California was annexed to the United States as part of the settlement of the Mexican War. Huge gun emplacements still exist on the Marin Headlands overlooking the entrance to San Francisco Bay.

Point Bonita Lighthouse was constructed in 1855. It was the first fog signal established on the California coast. A cannon was placed at the site, and a Sergeant Maloney was given responsibility for firing the gun every half hour during fogs. The sergeant resigned after failing at his responsibilities. According to Maloney, he was unable to get sufficient sleep since the nearly constant fogs made it impossible for him to have any time for more than a catnap.

Muir Woods National Monument is now part of Golden Gate NRA. The monument, set aside in 1908 by President Theodore Roosevelt, protects magnificent stands of coast redwoods, some of them more than 1,700 years old and 12 feet in diameter. The lands for the monument, which held one of the last uncut redwood stands in the San Francisco Bay area, were donated to the federal government by former U.S. Congressman William Kent. Kent urged that the monument be named in honor of conservationist and Sierra Club founder John Muir.

Adjacent to Golden Gate NRA is Mount Tamalpais State Park, a 6,300-acre preserve containing "Mount Tam," a well-known San Francisco Bay feature. Rising to more than 2,500 feet, Mount Tamalpais once was accessible by a railroad with more than 281 curves on its route. A fire took out most of the line in 1929, but the route is still used as a hiking trail.

Also filling out this natural area complex is Samuel P. Taylor State Park. With beautiful redwoods, a campground, and a number of trails, the 2,700-acre park cradles both sides of Papermill Creek, a salmon spawning stream.

Although none of Golden Gate NRA is currently managed as a designated wilderness, the NRA and the adjacent state and county lands offer plenty of opportunity for road closures and some minimal management changes that could result in a significant wilderness designation right at San Francisco's doorstep. With this in mind, I have included the NRA in this book in the hope of stimulating future wildlands protection and restoration.

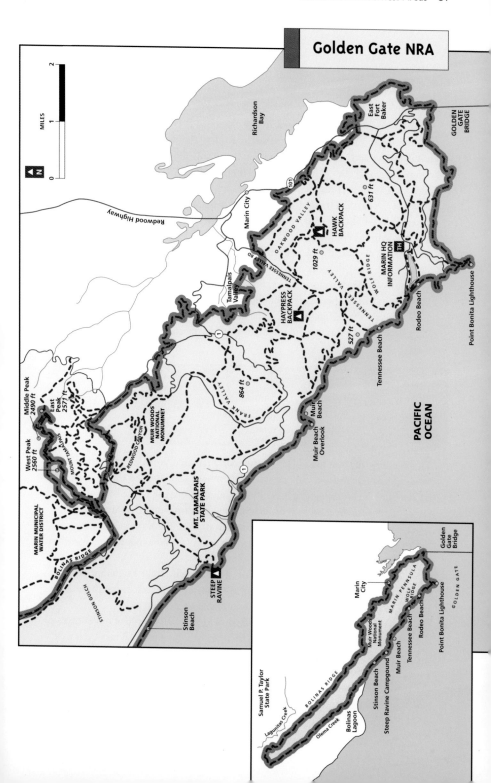

Golden Gate NRA

DAY HIKE: TENNESSEE VALLEY TRAIL
One-way length: 2.1 miles
Low and high elevations: 0 to 200 feet
Difficulty: easy

Though it's almost within earshot of San Francisco (I exaggerate only a little), the Tennessee Valley seems a world apart. Treeless—except for a small grove of Eucalyptus—and covered with flowers in the spring, this hike, with its views of the ocean, is a visual feast. The trail follows the Tennessee Valley, a canyon now part of the Marin Headlands section of the Golden Gate NRA, down to Tennessee Cove on the Pacific Ocean. It's a nice hike for the whole family to enjoy. To get to the trailhead, follow Highway 101, 5.0 miles north from the Golden Gate Bridge, turn off onto the Muir Woods highway exit, and within 0.5 mile turn onto the Tennessee Valley Road and go to the end.

The "trail" is more like a road at first, complete with pavement, but it soon turns into a gravel path, then finally a footpath as it winds down to a lagoon. The sunsets can be spectacular from here. A half mile before you hit the lagoon, the Tennessee Valley Trail intersects the Coast Trail, which leads eventually to Muir Beach. Long-distance hikers might consider this as an option.

DAY HIKE: BOLINAS RIDGE TRAIL
One-way length: 10.2 miles
Low and high elevations: 900 to 1,600 feet
Difficulty: moderate

This is one of the best long hikes close to San Francisco. It makes a great point-to-point hike, or you can walk partway then retrace your steps to the trailhead. As you glide across the rolling hills, you can almost imagine you're back in old California before the gold rush brought hordes of people into the state. I half expected to see elk and grizzly bears! Although none of these animals are here now (it's not unthinkable for the future), there are mountain lion and deer—all within sight of San Francisco.

The trailhead is on the south side of Sir Francis Drake Boulevard near the crest of a hill, just 3.5 miles past the Samuel P. Taylor State Park entrance station. Be sure to take plenty of water—none is available on the hike.

From the trailhead, it's an uphill stroll for the first couple of miles, then the terrain becomes more rolling as the trail (really a dirt fire road) takes you past oak savannas, grassy swales, groves of Douglas fir, and across green slopes dotted with poppies and lupine in the spring. Expansive views of Point Reyes Peninsula, the Marin Headlands, and even San Francisco are possible. Also a favorite mountain bike route, the trail ends at the Bolinas–Fairfax Road.

DAY HIKE: BOOTJACK–MUIR WOODS
Loop length: 6 miles
Low and high elevations: 100 to 1,400 feet
Difficulty: moderate

This hike gives you a chance to wander beneath giant redwoods in lush forests lined with ferns, bigleaf maple, and alder. To find your way to the Muir Woods Visitor Center from San Francisco, cross the Golden Gate Bridge and go 5.0 miles north on Highway 101, turn left (west) at the Stinson Beach exit and follow Highway 1 for 3.5 miles, then turn left on the Muir Woods Road and follow it to its end. The first 0.5 mile is a heavily used, nearly level path through magnificent redwoods adjacent to beautiful Redwood Creek. During the winter, the creek hosts runs of salmon and steelhead. Continue uphill 2.3 miles to Van Wyck Meadows, passing into the Mount Tamalpais State Park, and take the TCC Trail through shady, wooded canyons to the Stapelveldt Trail. This descends to join the Johnson Trail, which intersects the Hillside Trail at 5.2 miles and follows it back to Redwood Creek and the Muir Woods parking lot.

12 King Range Proposed Wilderness

This is the largest stretch of pristine beach on the Pacific Coast outside of Canada and Alaska.

Steep coastal mountains of the King Range proposed wilderness.

LOCATION: bordering the Pacific Ocean west of Gaberville

SIZE: 55,000 acres with 37,000 proposed as wilderness

ELEVATION RANGE: sea level to 4,087 feet

MILES OF TRAILS: 58

ECOSYSTEMS: old-growth Douglas fir, grasslands, coastal chaparral

ADMINISTRATION: BLM Ukiak District Office

MAP: King Range Conservation Area Map

Lying just 200 miles north of San Francisco, the King Range, often called the "Lost Coast," remains one of the most remote parts of the entire Pacific Coast outside of Alaska. There are just three access points: Shelter Cove on the south, Honeydew in the middle, and Petrolia on the north.

The rugged King Range is even more spectacular than the well-known Big Sur coastline to the south. King Peak, for example, rises more than 4,000 feet in just three miles from the Pacific Ocean. The extremely craggy terrain proved almost impenetrable by roads, hence development and settlement remained sparse. But there are miles of trails, including two designated national recreation trails: King Crest and Chemise Mountain. The highlight of the area is the 24-mile Lost Coast Trail, which many regard as one of the best beach hikes in

America. The 16-mile King Crest Trail offers fantastic views as well as potential for a multi-day trip.

The King Range is one of the most geologically active regions of the California Coast. Three different faults converge on the area, with rock shifts of up to 14 feet occurring every 1,000 years. The continuous uplift, combined with highly erodible rock, makes for a spectacular landscape.

It's coastal location means the area receives heavy rains in winter and frequent fog in summer. The town of Honeydew, just inland from the King Range, records an average of more than 100 inches of precipitation a year! Freezing temperatures at sea level are unknown, but snow is possible on the highest peaks.

The last Native American people to live here were the Mattole and Sinkyone. Shell mounds or middens, evidence of their past occupation, litter some of the beaches. Then, shortly after the California gold rush, Anglo settlers and their cattle moved into the area to take advantage of the lush grasslands. Oil was discovered at Petrolia, just north of the King Range, in 1865, but the product's low quality and the distance to market doomed the project. Logging of the region's Douglas fir forests began in the 1950s and 1960s, with much of the private land's forests completely cut down.

As early as 1929, the area's spectacular scenic and biological values were recognized; the public domain lands were withdrawn from sale, and in 1970, the King Range Conservation Area was created. Active acquisition of private property within the area has been ongoing, with more than 20,000 acres acquired thus far. Adding to the wildlands value of the area is the Sinkyone Wilderness, which protects some 17 additional miles of the Lost Coast south of the King Range.

The area is dominated by grasslands in the north and forests of Douglas fir mixed with sugar pine, madrone, and oak woodlands more common in the south. Open areas of chaparral are also common. Surprisingly, considering its location, there are almost no redwoods in this stretch of coastal mountains. It is unfortunate, as in many of the California wildlands, that livestock grazing still compromises the vegetation and biological integrity of the King Range Conservation Area.

Wildlife typical of the coast and coastal mountains abounds. This includes whales, seals, and sea lions along the coast, with black-tailed deer, black bear, mountain lion, and Roosevelt elk found inland.

DAY HIKE: CHEMISE MOUNTAIN TRAIL
One-way length: 1.5 miles
Low and high elevations: 2,000 to 2,596 feet
Difficulty: moderate

The Chemise Mountain Trail provides access to mountain views and the proposed Chemise Mountain Wilderness. The trailhead is off the Shelter Cove Road by the BLM's Wailaki Campground. The trail is steep, but short. The first part ascends through Douglas fir forest and eventually breaks out to chaparral near the summit. In no time at all you're at the top enjoying the great views of the Pacific, the Sinkyone State Wilderness to the south, and North Coast Ranges inland. The trail connects with the Lost Coast Trail that continues south to the Sinkyone Wilderness, run by the California State Parks.

DAY HIKE: KING PEAK
One-way length: 5 miles
Low and high elevations: 3,000 to 4,097 feet
Difficulty: moderate

The hike up King Peak offers spectacular coastal views on a clear day, and some say it's even possible to see all the way to Mount Lassen to the east. The hike begins off the Smith Etter Road, which is reachable from Honeydew.

The trail basically follows the top of the King Range Crest and is extremely narrow in many places. There are numerous views of the Pacific as well as inland. The hike dips in and out of forests of madrone, tan oak, and Douglas fir. There are several backpacker camps along the route, but water is scarce despite the heavy rainfall, so carry plenty. If you yearn to make this a longer hike, you can head beyond Kings Peak, following the Buck Creek Trail all the way to the beach, some 16 miles from your starting point.

OVERNIGHT HIKE: LOST COAST TRAIL
One-way length: 24 miles
Low and high elevations: sea level
Difficulty: moderate

One of the most popular attractions of the area is the Lost Coast Trail, a 24-mile trek along a remote beach. Although it's possible to hike the trail either way, north to south is generally recommended since the prevailing winds come from the north. The trailhead access is problematic for those covering the entire distance, since you need to have a shuttle. Most people begin at the Mattole Campground west of Petrolia and end at the Shelter Cove Campground. One way to get around the shuttling problem is to do the hike with another party, exchanging car keys enroute.

The trail basically follows the beach. High tides can be a problem in a few locations, and there are a few creek crossings, so plan accordingly. Camping is available just about anyplace you can find both water and a tent site. If poor weather or hiking on sand gets you down, there are several places where you can abort your trek via short routes—such as the Spanish Ridge, Buck Creek, and Telegraph Peak Trails—that provide access from the coast to roads.

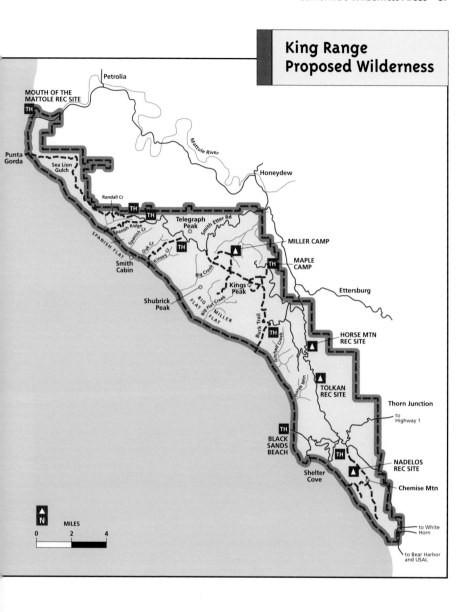

King Range
Proposed Wilderness

Petrolia

MOUTH OF THE
MATTOLE REC SITE
TH

Punta
Gorda

Sea Lion
Gulch

Mattole River

Honeydew

Randall Cr

TH

TH

SPANISH FLAT

Spanish Ridge

Spanish Cr

Oak Cr

Kinsey C

Telegraph
Peak

Smith Etter Rd

Smith
Cabin

TH

Big Creek

Kings
Peak

BIG
FLAT
FLAT Creek
Big Flat Creek
MILLER
FLAT

MILLER CAMP

MAPLE
CAMP

TH

Ettersburg

Shubrick
Peak

Buck Trail

TH

Gitchell Creek

HORSE MTN
REC SITE

TOLKAN
REC SITE

Horse Mtn

Thorn Junction

to
Highway 1

TH

BLACK
SANDS
BEACH

TH

Shelter
Cove

NADELOS
REC SITE

Chemise Mtn

N
MILES
0   2   4

to White
Horn

to Bear Harbor
and USAL

13

Marble Mountain Wilderness

The Marble Mountain Wilderness is a wondrous quarter-million acres of craggy peaks, meadows, and beautiful forests, all surrounded by rushing rivers.

The lush Elk Valley viewed from Marble Rim in Marble Mountain Wilderness.

LOCATION: 35 miles west of Yreka

SIZE: 242,500 acres

ELEVATION RANGE: 640 to 8,300 feet

MILES OF TRAILS: 600+

ECOSYSTEMS: chaparral, old-growth Douglas fir, mixed conifer forest

ADMINISTRATION: Klamath National Forest

MAPS: Klamath National Forest Map, Marble Mountain Wilderness Area Map

Floating like a green forested island and dotted with more than 100 subalpine, glacially carved lakes, the Marble Mountain Wilderness rises dramatically above the surrounding lowlands. South of the Klamath River and west of the Scott River, the wilderness protects 242,500 acres, one of the larger designated wildlands in California. Elevations vary from 640 feet along Wooley Creek to 8,300 feet on Boulder Peak.

Meadows are common at higher elevations while dense old-growth forest, mixed with chaparral, dominates lower elevations. Tree species include Pacific madrone, tan oak, canyon live oak, bigleaf maple, Douglas fir, sugar pine, red fir, white fir, Pacific yew, giant chinquapin, lodgepole pine, white pine, incense cedar, mountain hemlock, ponderosa pine, and Jeffrey pine. Many endemic and rare plant species abound.

Named for Marble Mountain, a mass of white metamorphosed limestone or marble, this wilderness contains a complex assortment of rock types, including metamorphic rocks such as marble, slate, quartzite, and metachert. Outcrops of serpentine and granitic rocks also occur, particularly along Wooley Creek and in the Upper North Fork Salmon River valley. The Marble and Black Marble Mountains are made of marble that was originally the coral reef of the tropical seas. The higher peaks were glaciated; U-shaped glacial valleys and cirque basins abound. The headwaters of nearly every major river or creek displays evidence of past glaciation.

Black bear are particularly common in the Marbles as are black-tailed deer. Elk have been recently re-established. Mountain lion, bobcat, wolverine, and fisher are known to occur here. Runs of salmon and steelhead are found in some of the streams draining the wilderness, including the North Fork of the Salmon, Wooley Creek, Elk Creek, Grider Creek, and Ukonom Creek. All of these streams are proposed additions to the Wild and Scenic Rivers system.

Several research natural areas are within the Marbles, including Haypress Meadows, where 12 conifer species and 200 vascular plants have been observed. Much of the forest cover is old-growth red fir. Bridge Creek contains large old-growth Douglas fir, plus some of the tallest giant chinquapin known.

The Marble Mountains region is surrounded by nearly 80,000 acres that could significantly enlarge the wilderness and increase its biological value. Among the more critical areas are those that link the Marbles and other wildlands. For example, a corridor between the Marble Mountain Wilderness and Trinity Alps Wilderness lies in the Portuguese Peak and Orleans Mountain Roadless Area, which is located on the southwest corner of the Marble Mountains. Grider Creek in the north is another important link between the Marbles and the Red Buttes Wilderness. Unfortunately, logging continues to isolate and shrink these roadless areas, each year stripping away the biological foundation of the region. In addition to the losses of roadless lands, livestock grazing continues to take its toll on riparian areas, meadows, and wildlife.

DAY HIKE: WRIGHT LAKES
One-way length: 4 miles
Low and high elevations: 3,800 to 7,400 feet
Difficulty: strenuous

This is a short but steep hike to one of the most spectacular glacial basins in the Marble Mountains. Boulder Peak, the highest in the range, towers above the lakes. Find the trailhead south of Fort Jones off the Scott River Road, cross the river on Indian Scotty Bridge, then follow signs along Canyon Creek Road to the trailhead.

Upper Wright Lake sits at 7,400 feet, making it the highest of the many lakes in the Marble Mountain Wilderness. The first part of the hike leads you through Douglas fir and black oak forests, but eventually the trail breaks out into flowery meadows with waterfalls and dramatic vistas of peaks. Both whitebark pine and the rare foxtail pine surround the lake basin. Foxtail pine is only common in the southern Sierra Nevada and a few places in northern California. From the lakes, it's possible to climb Boulder Peak.

> ## OVERNIGHT HIKE: LITTLE NORTH FORK TRAIL
> One-way length: 8 miles
> Low and high elevations: 2,000 to 6,800 feet
> Difficulty: strenuous

This trail accesses a host of lakes in the Chimney Peak and English Peak areas, with miles of trails that can be combined to make a multi-day loop. The trailhead is at the Little North Fork Campground along the North Fork of the Salmon River 3.5 miles west of Sawyers Bar on the southern edge of the wilderness. It's a long climb up to the first lakes, but from there, the possibilities are endless.

> ## OVERNIGHT HIKE: WOOLEY CREEK TRAIL
> One-way length: 25 miles to Anthony Mine Camp
> Low and high elevations: 600 to 2,600 feet
> Difficulty: moderate

The Wooley Creek Trail is at low elevation and is one of the few trails in the Marble Mountain Wilderness that can be hiked year round, offering numerous options for multi-day exploration. The trailhead is located along the Salmon River, 4.0 miles upstream from its confluence with the Klamath River and Highway 96.

Despite some minor ups and downs, the trail makes an overall gradual ascent along the forested canyon of Wooley Creek, a major salmon and steelhead spawning stream, and passes through stands of old-growth Douglas fir along the way. The trail begins by climbing a ridge before traversing a hillside above the creek. The first actual contact with the creek is two miles up the trail. It continues to swing back and forth between the creek and the hillside as the path negotiates cliffs and other obstacles adjacent to the stream.

There are a number of major campsites along the stream, as well as several connecting side trails that lead to other higher elevation lake basins. The Folwer Cabin, 9.0 miles upstream at the junction of Bridge and Wooley Creeks, is available for public use. Trails connecting to the Haypress Trail lake country take off from this point. Beyond Folwer Cabin, trail use falls off considerably. At 19.0 miles upstream, a junction with the Big Meadows Trail is reached. This trail accesses the English Peak lake country and eventually leads to the North Fork of the Salmon. It is possible to continue up Wooley Creek's major tributary, Big Elk Fork, and on to the Marble Rim; from there, numerous other trailheads are accessible that will complete a traverse of the entire wilderness.

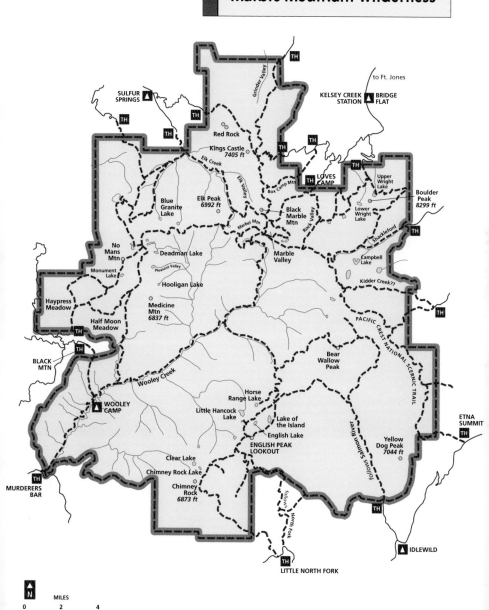

Marble Mountain Wilderness

to Ft. Jones

SULFUR
SPRINGS

KELSEY CREEK
STATION

BRIDGE
FLAT

Grinder Valley

Red Rock

Kings Castle
7405 ft

Elk Creek

Blue
Granite
Lake

Elk Peak
6992 ft

Elk Valley

Box Camp Mtn

LOVES
CAMP

Upper
Wright
Lake

Boulder
Peak
8299 ft

Black
Marble
Mtn

Lower
Wright
Lake

No
Mans
Mtn

Deadman Lake

Marbel Mtn

Marble
Valley

Rock Valley

Campbell
Lake

Shackleford

Monument
Lake

Pleasant Valley

Hooligan Lake

Kidder Creek??

Haypress
Meadow

Medicine
Mtn
6837 ft

Half Moon
Meadow

PACIFIC CREST NATIONAL SCENIC TRAIL

BLACK
MTN

Wooley Creek

Bear
Wallow
Peak

WOOLEY
CAMP

Horse
Range Lake

Little Hancock
Lake

Lake of
the Island

English Lake

ENGLISH PEAK
LOOKOUT

follows Salmon River

ETNA
SUMMIT

Yellow
Dog Peak
7044 ft

Clear Lake

Chimney Rock Lake

Chimney
Rock
6873 ft

MURDERERS
BAR

IDLEWILD

follows North Fork

LITTLE NORTH FORK

N

MILES

0   2   4

North Fork Wilderness

14

This heavily timbered, trailless area lies along the North Fork of the Eel River.

Alders leafing out in spring along a tributary of the North Fork of the Eel River in the trailless North Fork Wilderness.

LOCATION: 40 miles southeast of Eureka

SIZE: 8,100 acres

ELEVATION RANGE: 2,100 to 3,600 feet

MILES OF TRAILS: none

ECOSYSTEMS: Douglas fir, oak woodland

ADMINISTRATION: Six Rivers National Forest

MAP: Six Rivers National Forest Map

The North Fork Wilderness protects just over 8,100 acres of the North Fork of the Eel River within the Six Rivers National Forest. Like much of the North Coast Ranges, it is steep, rugged country covered largely with chaparral on its southern slopes while giant Douglas fir, ponderosa pine, incense cedar, and other equally large conifers cloak the northern slopes. The North Fork of the Eel is a Wild and Scenic River and contains a steelhead run. The area is an important deer winter range.

The area has no trail access, and even getting to its edge by road is not easy. Solitude is extreme. I've never met anyone who has hiked here; even the Forest Service people I contacted had never been in the North Fork. The most direct route is from Covelo to County Road 520 to Kettenpom Valley. You can then make your way on game trails to the river, the most obvious destination.

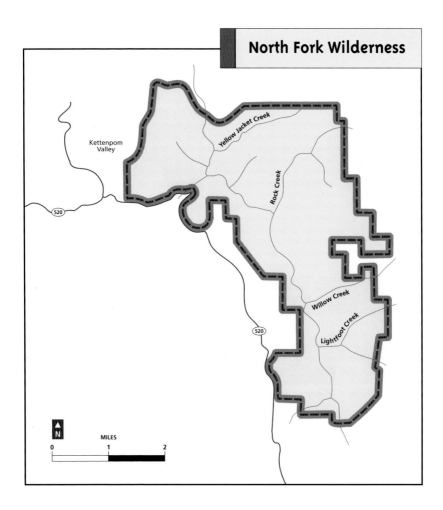

North Fork Wilderness

Point Reyes National Seashore— Phillip Burton Wilderness

15

Surrounded on all sides by the sea, the influence of the ocean is felt as well as seen here.

Lupine frames North Beach, Phillip Burton Wilderness.

LOCATION: 30 miles north of San Francisco

SIZE: 25,370 acres

ELEVATION RANGE: sea level to 1,400 feet

MILES OF TRAILS: 70

ECOSYSTEMS: grasslands, tidal estuary, oak woodlands, pine forest

ADMINISTRATION: Point Reyes National Seashore

MAP: Point Reyes National Seashore Map

Just north of San Francisco lies a sliver of land—the Point Reyes Peninsula. Some 71,000 acres of the peninsula are now part of the Point Reyes National Seashore, managed by the National Park Service. About a third of this landscape, or 25,370 acres, is permanently withdrawn from development as part of the Phillip Burton Wilderness. The land was set aside to honor Congressman Phillip Burton, who died in 1983. Burton was a long-time champion of parks and wilderness while he was chair of the House Subcommittee on National Parks and Insular Affairs. This wilderness is one of the best places to hike and camp adjacent to the Pacific Ocean outside of the far northern California coast.

The highest point is 1,407-foot Mount Wittenberg. Much of the peninsula consists of rolling hills covered with flowering meadows and dotted with pockets of timber, including the bishop pine. Long stretches of undeveloped beaches, many with seaside cliffs, offer numerous opportunities for solitary beachcombing. The national seashore is traversed by a number of roads and has some private inholdings, including active ranches and farms.

In 1579, English sea captain Sir Francis Drake sailed his ship, the Golden Hind, on a round-the-world voyage and landed at what is now Drake's Estero for boat repairs. He named the land "New Albion," meaning New England, and noted the resemblance of the Point Reyes coastal cliffs to the chalk cliffs of Dover back in England. Several other European sailing expeditions passed by the area, but it was Don Sebastian Vizcaino who cruised by the point in a storm on the Feast of the Kings Day in 1603 and bestowed the name "La Punta de Los Reyes," or the point of kings, in honor of the day. Ironically, though San Francisco Bay is one of the greatest harbors in the world, the narrow entrance at Golden Gate prevented its discovery by Europeans until 1769, when an overland expedition looking for mission sites stumbled upon the bay.

In 1821, Mexico gained its independence from Spain. California, as the northernmost extension of Mexico, was part of the frontier. To encourage settlement, the Mexican government granted huge land grants to Mexican as well as other settlers, many of them Americans. During this period, Point Reyes was divided into three large estates controlled by James Berry, Rafael Garcia, and Antonia Osio. After California passed under American control in 1848, these large land grants were divided up into dozens of small dairy farms and ranches.

After the gold rush of 1849, the booming city of San Francisco became a ready market for peninsula farm products. As early as 1935, there were calls to protect the Point Reyes area as a park, but local opposition stemmed serious consideration until the growing concern over San Francisco's growth post-World War II fostered a fear that the lands would be developed into housing tracts. Point Reyes National Seashore was authorized on September 13, 1962, and private holdings on the peninsula have gradually come under federal ownership.

The San Andreas Fault separates the Point Reyes Peninsula from the mainland. The nearly linear embayments of Tomales and Bolinas Lagoon mark the fault line. Rocks making up the Point Reyes Peninsula are similar to those found in the Santa Lucia Range and Tehachapi Mountains more than 300 miles south. They differ substantially from those immediately adjacent within the Golden Gate National Recreation Area. The peninsula's rocks have been transported northward as part of the Pacific Plate moving along the San Andreas Fault. When the 1906 San Francisco earthquake jostled the bay area, the Point Reyes Peninsula was thrust 20 feet further north and west. The Olema Valley marks the meeting of the North American and Pacific Plates.

Surrounded on all sides by the sea, the influence of the ocean is felt. Fog is common in summer; rain is the norm in winter. A cooling sea breeze is nearly constant. The maritime climate ensures fairly consistent year-round temperatures, with the winter mean of 50 degrees rising slightly to 55 in mid-summer.

There are essentially two seasons here—the rainy winter that begins in November and runs through March, and the nearly rainless summer. Interestingly, rainfall increases from the coast inland. Point Reyes itself receives only 18 inches of precipitation a year, while Bear Valley Visitor Center—15 miles away—records 36 inches annually.

Marine wildlife sightings are common at coast-side campsites, including observations of migrating gray whales. The whales feed and summer in Alaska and spend their winters in Baja, passing by Point Reyes twice during the year. The bulk of southward migrating whales pass Point Reyes in December, with the greatest peak in January. The whales only spend a few months in Baja before heading northward, passing Point Reyes again in March and early April.

It may be difficult to believe this since the area is so close to San Francisco, but relic spawning runs of salmon and steelhead still persist in Olema Creek and other streams entering Tomales Bay. It is also possible to see harbor seals, and in recent years the numbers of the much larger elephant seals have increased. They are particularly common in January when they haul out on remote beaches. The elephant seal has only recently recolonized the Point Reyes Peninsula, and the current small breeding population is the northernmost in California. Two other marine mammals likely to be seen along the coast are the California sea lion and the northern sea lion.

Winter is also the season for shorebird sightings. Many migrants, including black-bellied plover, dunlin, sanderling, western sandpiper, and willet, are concentrated along the beaches and estuaries of the peninsula. Other wintering species include white pelicans.

On land the wildlife is more typical for this part of California, with black-tailed deer the most common larger animal. Although the entire region was once home to large herds of Tule elk, these animals were extirpated from most of their native California habitat. In 1979, a small group of Tule elk were reintroduced to the Tomales Point area, and after a slow start, the herd has begun to grow.

In addition to these native species, a number of exotic deer also live on the peninsula, including fallow deer and axis deer. The fallow deer has a number of color phases, including white. Attempts to cull these exotics from the park have thus far been unsuccessful. Another alien species that roams the national seashore are domestic cattle. Of all exotics in the seashore, cattle probably cause the greatest damage to native plant communities and wildlife.

If these exotic species were eliminated, and the native elk and deer populations expanded, there is no reason why the peninsula couldn't support a larger population of native predators such as the mountain lion. We know lion are present, because there are many reports of sightings of the elusive animals. At one time the peninsula was also home to the grizzly bear, with several early records of bear sightings and killings. A brown color phase of black bear was also reported in the area, but neither these nor the grizzly are found here today.

Geologically isolated as it is, the Point Reyes Peninsula hosts a number of rare plant species, with at least 61 types found within the national seashore that are not known in the rest of Marin County. Thirty-four of these species reach their southern limit here, while 11 plants in the national seashore are at their northern limit.

There are a number of major forested communities, and the most unusual is the Bishop pine forests. Bishop pine are scattered along the California coast from Humboldt County south to Santa Barbara, with a few other stands in Baja. Until the Vision Fire in 1995, the groves in Point Reyes were among the largest stands in the state. The pine grows best on the granitic soils along Inverness Ridge. Bishop pine are one of several "closed cone" pines found in California that require periodic fire to regenerate. Within the national seashore, research has shown that the normal fire return interval is approximately every 80 years.

Douglas fir, the other major forest community type found on the peninsula, is more common on shale soils and on shadier north-facing slopes. Well established in the Sky Camp and Divide Meadow areas, these trees thrive under a regime of periodic fire.

Other trees common in the park unit include coastal live oak, California bay, bigleaf maple, madrone, California buckeye, and other non-coniferous species.

Although forest is common in some parts of the national seashore, it is open meadow that gives the area its charm. Once supporting herds of elk and antelope, much of this landscape was converted for use by domestic livestock. The introduction of exotic grass and other plant species often favored by heavy livestock grazing has dramatically altered this plant community. A number of native flowers continue to be threatened by the presence of domestic livestock grazing within the national seashore.

Nevertheless, there are still pockets of native prairie, and a wide variety of native flower species still cloak the slopes with color each spring. The early blooming species pop out in January; other flowering species reach their peak in April, when meadows are often covered with blooming fields of multi-colored hues. Common species include Douglas iris, blue-eyed grass, California poppy, owl's clover, meadow foam, and bush lupine.

A portion of the national seashore plant communities were rejuvenated by the Vision Fire, which burned a total of 12,354 acres of land. The fire also charred 45 homes in the community of Inverness. Like most larger fires in the West, the Vision Fire was fanned by high winds of up to 45 mph. Despite the ecological desirability of maintaining the influence of wildfire within the national seashore landscape, federal agencies were forced to aggressively fight the blaze almost from its inception due to the potential loss of private property. This resulted in the construction of 25 miles of bulldozer lines, as well as other major disturbances. Indeed, one of the longest-lasting impacts of fires are the scars resulting from the fire-fighting effort, including fire lines, which are a perfect seedbed for the invasion of exotic weedy plant species.

Although the loss of people's houses is an unfortunate consequence of some wildfires, in general periodic burns are beneficial to vegetative communities of the region. Nearly all of the plant communities on the Point Reyes Peninsula are invigorated by periodic fire. The Bishop pine forest, for instance, is dependent on fire to open its cones and provide the bare mineral soil its seedlings required for successful germination. Other species dependent on fire include madrone, Douglas fir, and many of the chaparral species. Even some animals benefit, such as the rare Myrtle's silverspot butterfly, whose favorite flowers grow in greater profusion after a burn. And new snags will provide greater opportunities for homes for cavity nesting birds.

There are 70 miles of hiking trails in the national seashore, but only four backcountry camping areas—Coast, Wildcat, Glen, and Sky. Each backcountry camp has up to a dozen tent sites, along with privies and water. Camping is restricted to designated sites. Since all are accessible by an interconnected trail system, it's possible to do longer trips of several days' length.

The Coast Camp lies on a grassy bluff high above the beach, and it is reached after an 8.9-mile hike from the Bear Valley Trailhead. Wildcat Camp lies in a meadow beside a small creek, 6.3 miles from the Bear Valley Trailhead. It provides good access to Wildcat Beach. Sky Camp is only 2.5 miles from the Bear Valley Trailhead, but it requires a stiff climb. Glen Camp lies in a small wooded valley just 5.0 miles from the Bear Valley Trailhead over nearly level terrain.

Most of the best wilderness hikes start from the Bear Valley Trailhead, where there is a visitor center and huge parking lot. Don't let a lot of cars discourage you! It's surprising how dispersed people are on the network of trails that radiate from this one location.

DAY HIKE: BEAR VALLEY–SKY CAMP
One-way length: 2.5 miles
Low and high elevations: 105 to 1,400 feet
Difficulty: moderate

Sky Camp lies at 1,024 feet on the slope of Mount Wittenberg. Though a designated overnight camp, it makes a great destination for day hikers as well. One can obtain commanding views of Drake's Bay and the surrounding meadows just above the camp. Though the higher parts of Sky Trail provide fantastic views, it gets the least use of the side trails branching off the Bear Valley trail system. The hike is a steady uphill walk practically to the top of Mount Wittenberg before it makes a short, steep descent to the campground. Nevertheless, when my daughter was only 18-months old, she hiked the entire distance without assistance, albeit slowly, and with frequent stops to examine pine cones, flowers, and other trailside prizes.

Sky Trail leaves the Bear Valley Trail just beyond the trailhead at the parking lot by the Bear Valley Visitor Center, and it climbs from 105 feet to 1,400 feet in 1.7 miles. Most of the walk is through lovely forests of Douglas fir, California bay, and bigleaf maple. Several small meadows provide some flowery interludes, but once you reach the top of the trail, you are treated to a spectacular view of Point Reyes and Drake's Lagoon. A short climb from the pass takes you up to the top of 1,407-foot Mount Wittenberg, which permits views to the southeast along the Olema Creek valley.

DAY HIKE: BEAR VALLEY–ARCH ROCK TRAIL
One-way length: 4.2 miles
Low and high elevations: 100 to 300 feet
Difficulty: moderate

The main hiking highway accessing the Philip Burton Wilderness is the Bear Valley Trail. The trailhead parking lot is across from the Bear Valley Visitor Center. A portion of the trail, formerly a wagon road, is actually outside the boundaries of the wilderness, thus open to mountain bikes. It is also wheelchair accessible, climbing 215 feet to Divide Meadow.

The Bear Valley Trail offers a relatively gentle grade to the ocean, but it has numerous side trails looping off of it that provide opportunities for multi-day backcountry treks or a variety of extended day trips. One of the more popular excursions is the 8.5-mile round-trip hike from the Bear Valley Visitor Center to Arch Rock. The first part of the trail winds through a meadow lined by coastal live oak, then it follows Bear Creek through a forest of Bishop pine and Douglas fir. At 1.5 miles out, the trail crosses Divide Meadow, a minor watershed divide, then follows Coast Creek to a bluff overlooking the Pacific Ocean at Arch Rock.

DAY HIKE: INVERNESS RIDGE TRAIL
One-way length: 3.1 miles
Low and high elevations: 900 to 1,300 feet
Difficulty: moderate

If you're looking for views, one of the best hikes to take is the Inverness Ridge Trail. There are two possible trailheads: One is located at 1,240 feet at the end of the Mount Vision Road, while the other is found along the Limantour Road at Bayview. The 3.1-mile trail generally follows the top of Inverness Ridge, with gentle rises and descents. The open meadows along the ridgeline offer great views of the Pacific Ocean.

For a longer loop with great views of Drake's Lagoon and the Pacific Ocean, start at the Mount Vision Trailhead and take the Inverness Trail for 0.5 mile to its junction with the Bucklin Trail. Descend the Bucklin Trail for 2.4 miles to the Muddy Hollow Trail. At this intersection, turn left (east) and hike for about 0.3 mile to the Drake's View Trail. Turn left here and ascend the slope 2.0 miles back to the Inverness Trail, then make another left and follow the trail along the ridge northwest back to the trailhead parking lot.

DAY HIKE: TOMALES POINT TRAIL
One-way length: 4.1 miles
Low and high elevations: 400 feet (more or less level)
Difficulty: moderate

One of the more popular hikes in the national seashore is the Tomales Point Trail. Beginning at the historic Pierce Point Ranch, a former dairy operation located at the end of the Pierce Point Road, this hike follows a ridge through flowery meadows that afford exceptional views of the Pacific Ocean, Bodega Bay, and the sea cliffs. It ends at Tomales Point, a wind-swept bluff overlooking the ocean. This is the heart of the Tule elk reintroduction area, so opportunities to see these animals are excellent. This is an exceptionally beautiful hike in the spring when the wildflowers are in bloom.

Point Reyes National Seashore—
Phillip Burton Wilderness

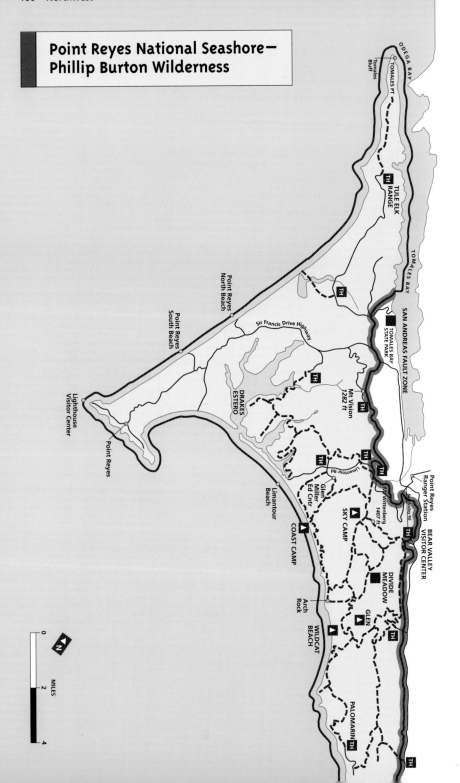

DAY HIKE: SOUTH BEACH TRAIL

One-way length: up to 10 miles
Low and high elevations: sea level
Difficulty: easy

The South Beach Trail is really a 0.1-mile walk from the parking lot off the Sir Francis Drake Highway to South Beach. Here, hikers have up to 10 miles of open sand beach to walk. Sand dunes, surf, and wind are the major features. Watch the tides!

OVERNIGHT HIKE: PALOMARIN–WILDCAT CAMP

One-way length: 5.5 miles
Low and high elevations: sea level to 563 feet
Difficulty: moderate

A great day hike or overnight trip is this 5.5-mile section of the Coast Trail from Palomarin by the Point Reyes Bird Observatory to Wildcat Camp. The trail has a few ups and downs and ins and outs as it climbs hills, drops into canyons, passes out to the coast, and comes back inland again. Few trails pack so much scenery in so few miles, with great coast vistas and opportunities to see seals, coastal wildlife, hawks, and other birds of prey, plus a waterfall, five lakes, and vistas of sea stacks. Along the way you'll pass through stands of coastal shrub, including black sage, coyote bush, and coffee berry. A short side trail takes you to view Alamere Falls as it cascades over a cliff onto the beach below. Wildcat Camp, which provides access to Wildcat Beach, sits on a meadowy bluff with a creek beside it. Camp here and hear the surf roll.

OVERNIGHT HIKE: COAST TRAIL

One-way length: 15 miles
Low and high elevations: sea level to 563 feet
Difficulty: moderate

The longest, most scenic direct hike in the national seashore is the 15-mile Coast Trail. If you want to do a trailhead-to-trailhead hike, it's best to have two cars, or better yet, hike the trail with friends who start out at the opposite trailhead and exchange car keys enroute. Although it's possible to do this hike in one long day, it makes a good multi-day hike if you obtain permits for overnight camping at Coast Camp and Wildcat Camp.

Most hikers begin at the trailhead next to the Point Reyes Youth Hotel off the Limantour Road. In 2.8 miles, you'll reach the first designated backcountry camp, the oceanside Coast Camp. The next leg of the trip is 6.6 miles long. The trail leaves Coast Camp and follows the beach for several miles before turning inland and winding down a canyon to Wildcat Camp. From here, you will pass by a series of lakes, climb a low ridge, and end at the Palomarin Trailhead 5.6 miles away.

OTHER RECREATIONAL ACTIVITIES: BOATING

With lagoons and bays, the area in and around Point Reyes offers a number of sea kayaking and canoeing options. Abbotts Lagoon is a good place for canoeing and is accessible by a portage from the Pierce Point Road. Other water bodies are best left to sea kayaks or covered canoes, since their larger size makes them more vulnerable to wind-generated waves. Nevertheless, on calm mornings or evenings, canoes that hug the shore can still find plenty of opportunities for exploration in Drake's Estero, Marin County's largest lagoon. With its multiple bays, Drake's Estero and the adjacent Limantour Estero offer miles of protected shoreline for canoeing or sea kayaking. There's an abundance of wildlife in the lagoon, including numerous shorebirds, herons, pelicans, and various ducks. Occasionally seals and sea lions enter the lagoon as well. Both Bolinas Lagoon and Tomales Bay are also potential sea kayaking areas. Both are wonderful bird-watching locations.

Sunset by Drakes Estero, Point Reyes.

Red Buttes Wilderness

16

This is a lightly-used wilderness of forested slopes with subalpine cirque lakes strung like beads along a granite crest.

Granite outcrop near Sucker Gap in Red Buttes Wilderness.

The Red Buttes Wilderness contains 25,900 acres on the Oregon–California border north of the Klamath River. Although most of the wilderness is in California, it is more easily accessed from Oregon's Applegate River headwaters. As late as the 1970s, there was more than 100,000 acres of roadless land in the Red Buttes area, but this number has shrunk dramatically as logging businesses have stripped the trees practically to timberline. Although not high, the elevational relief from the Klamath River to the highest peaks is more than one mile.

Red fir, white fir, noble fir, knobcone pine, sugar pine, Brewer's spruce, ponderosa pine, Jeffrey pine, mountain hemlock, and other species abound. Chaparral is common, even at higher elevations. There are small mountain meadows, some of them suffering serious erosion as a result of livestock grazing.

LOCATION: on the California–Oregon border

SIZE: 25,900 acres

ELEVATION RANGE: 1,600 to 7,000 feet

MILES OF TRAILS: 60

ECOSYSTEMS: mix of conifers including Douglas fir, knobcone pine, Brewer's spruce, and incense cedar

ADMINISTRATION: Rogue River National Forest, Siskiyou National Forest, Klamath National Forest

MAP: Klamath National Forest Map

The Red Buttes consists of a melange of rock types, including schists, greenstone, quartzite, chert, marble, and amphibolite, with intrusions of granite. Some serpentine rocks occur as well; the Red Buttes are red peridotite. This small wilderness contains glaciated cirques and tarns, plus a ridgeline of peaks that average around 6,000 feet in elevation.

Although the Red Buttes Wilderness is relatively small, it feels bigger because of the roadless areas that border it. The largest of these is known as the Kangaroo Roadless Area (RA). Lying south of the Red Buttes and north of the Klamath River, the 40,000-acre Kangaroo RA contains a portion of the Pacific Crest Trail. Over half of it is rock fields, brush fields, and meadows. The area contains the rare Baker's cypress, found only in a few areas of northern California and southern Oregon. However, much of Kangaroo burned in 1987 and "salvage" logging has destroyed some its natural integrity.

DAY HIKE: AZALEA LAKE TRAIL
One-way length: 6 miles
Low and high elevations: 4,500 to 5,900 feet
Difficulty: moderate

The hike to Azalea is one of the best in the wilderness, offering relatively level hiking (with two minor passes to cross) and traveling through meadows and forested glades. Enroute you will go through stands of the rare Brewer's spruce, knobcone pine, and sugar pine. Azalea Lake lies in a glacial cirque, with its namesake growing in profusion around the shores. One botanical oddity is the presence of lodgepole pine, a tree rather common in the Cascades but rare in the Siskiyous.

To reach the trailhead, drive south from Medford, Oregon, to Applegate Lake, then take Forest Road 1040 to Cook and Green Campground and continue another 8.0 miles to the trailhead.

OVERNIGHT HIKE: COOK AND GREEN LOOP
One-way length: 33 miles
Low and high elevations: 2,400 to 6,000 feet
Difficulty: strenuous

With Cook and Green Campground as your starting and ending point, this hike covers a good portion of the wilderness, traverses some of the roadless lands in the Kangaroo RA, and offers spectacular views of the Applegate and Klamath drainages from the crest of the Siskiyou Range.

Follow the previous directions to Cook and Green Campground south of Applegate Lake, located 30-plus miles south of Medford, Oregon. From the campground, hike 5.0 steep miles up the Horse Camp Trail to the Applegate–Klamath watershed divide, passing by tiny Elk Lake. Connect with the Pacific Crest Trail and head southwest along the top of the range to Kangaroo Mountain, Rattlesnake

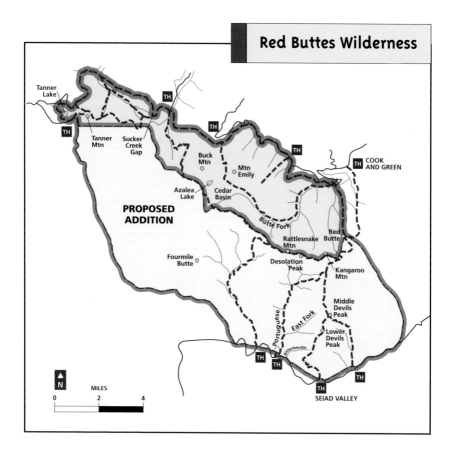

Red Buttes Wilderness

Mountain, and Cedar Basin by Azalea Lake. Head 9.0 miles down the Butte Fork of the Applegate River Trail to Cook and Green Campground. The Butte Fork is the only completely wild drainage in the wilderness, passing through forests of oak, sugar pine, ponderosa pine, bigleaf maple, Douglas fir, and dogwood. The blossoms of dogwood and azalea along its lower course are lovely in the spring.

OVERNIGHT HIKE: DEVIL'S PEAK–PORTUGUESE CREEK LOOP
Loop length: 14 miles
Low and high elevations: 1,380 to 5,900 feet
Difficulty: strenuous

This hike lies in California and is entirely outside of the Red Buttes Wilderness, but it is within the proposed Kangaroo RA addition to the wilderness. You can, however, use it to access trails from the south within the currently designated boundaries of wilderness. There are few campsites on the route, and most people will likely just make the day hike to the former lookout site on Lower Devil's Peak. Nevertheless, due to their low elevation and south-facing aspect, these trails are open to hiking earlier in the spring than most of those originating in Oregon. The Devil's Peak Trail and Portuguese Creek Trails both begin along the Klamath River just west of Seiad Valley on Highway 96. The Devil's Peak Trail is also the route of the Pacific Crest Trail.

From the trailhead, you will climb steadily via switchback through forests of ponderosa pine, madrone, oak, and sugar pine. There is only one spring, which is located in the first mile of the 5.0-mile climb to Lower Devil's Peak, so carry water. The bare, knobby summit of Lower Devil's Peak is the site of an old lookout tower, so it affords good views of Mount Shasta, Siskiyou Wilderness, and the Marble Mountains. For those wishing to make this a day hike, the peak is a good turn-around point.

If you've made it to Lower Devil's Peak, most of the elevational gain has been completed and the rest of the hike is less strenuous. The trail continues on approximately 2.0 miles, climbing another 1,000 feet as it skirts Middle Devil's Peak and Upper Devil's Peak. Just beyond Upper Devil's Peak, you will intersect the Portuguese Creek Trail coming in from the west. Just a short way down this trail is a level campsite beside a meadow known as Wildwood Camp, where water is nearby. One can continue on the Devil's Peak Trail to the Siskiyou Crest Trail, with numerous options for potential hikes along the way. But for those completing the loop, follow Portuguese Creek 7.5 miles down to the trailhead. The first mile after Wildwood Camp is very steep, with the trail dropping 2,400 feet in this short distance! After that, it's a relatively easy jaunt along the creek back to Highway 96 and the trailhead. Walk or hitchhike 2.5 miles to your starting point at the Devil's Peak Trailhead.

Russian Wilderness

17

The Russian Wilderness is a small area with 22 lakes set among glaciated granite peaks and one of the most diverse forests in California.

Looking down a glaciated valley of Russian Creek in Russian Wilderness.

The granite ribbed peaks of the Russian Wilderness lie between the Trinity Alps and the Marble Mountain Wilderness, with the Pacific Crest Trail running through it south to north. Much of it has been heavily glaciated: Twenty-two cirque lakes are nestled among the peaks, with the South Fork of Russian Creek, in particular, a classic example of a U-shaped glacial valley.

Though this wilderness is only 12,000 acres in size, it has one of the richest and most diverse coniferous forests in North America. This small wildlands has 17 species of conifers, including incense cedar, dwarf juniper, white fir, subalpine fir, red fir, Brewer's spruce, Engelmann spruce, whitebark pine, knobcone pine, foxtail pine, lodgepole pine,

LOCATION: 25 miles southwest of Etna

SIZE: 12,000 acres

ELEVATION RANGE: 4,800 to 8,200 feet

MILES OF TRAILS: 16

ECOSYSTEMS: diverse conifer forest

ADMINISTRATION: Klamath National Forest

MAPS: Klamath National Forest Map, Marble Mountains/ Russian Wilderness Areas Map

sugar pine, ponderosa pine, western white pine, Douglas fir, western hemlock, and Pacific yew.

The Duck Creek region may be a glacial refugium: It contains the only known stand of subalpine fir in California and one of two known stands of Engelmann spruce, both common species in the Rockies. Duck Creek also has Brewer's spruce, whitebark pine, and foxtail pine. The areas with the greatest tree diversity are the South Fork Russian Creek and the Duck Creek drainage.

DAY HIKE: PAYNES LAKE TRAIL
One-way length: 3 miles
Low and high elevations: 4,400 to 6,400 feet
Difficulty: moderate

This is a short but steep hike to the 17-acre Paynes Lake, which is set in a sparsely timbered glacial cirque with sparkling white granite domes rising above it and a meadow just beyond its shores. Need I say more? The trailhead is located on Forest Service Road 41N14. From Highway 3 by Etna, take French Creek Road west to its junction with Sugar Creek Road, then follow signs to the trailhead. Most of the elevation gain comes via switchback in the first 1.5 miles. An alternative route is the 5.0-mile hike via the Pacific Crest Trail from Etna Summit. The fishing is good and there are campsites for those interested in staying the night.

DAY HIKE: DUCK LAKES TRAIL
One-way length: 4 miles
Low and high elevations: 4,800 to 6,700 feet
Difficulty: moderate

The Duck Lakes Basin resembles the Sierra Nevada in miniature—granite domes, deep, glacially carved lakes, lovely woods, and the most diverse conifer forest in the West. The area contains, among other oddities, Pacific silver fir, not normally found south of Crater Lake in Oregon, and subalpine fir, foxtail pine, and Engelmann spruce. Big Duck Lake is 26 acres in size and 27 feet deep, and the slightly higher and smaller Little Duck Lake is only 18 feet deep. The trailhead is located off the French Creek–Sugar Creek Road west of Etna and Highway 3. It is a moderately steep hike to the lakes.

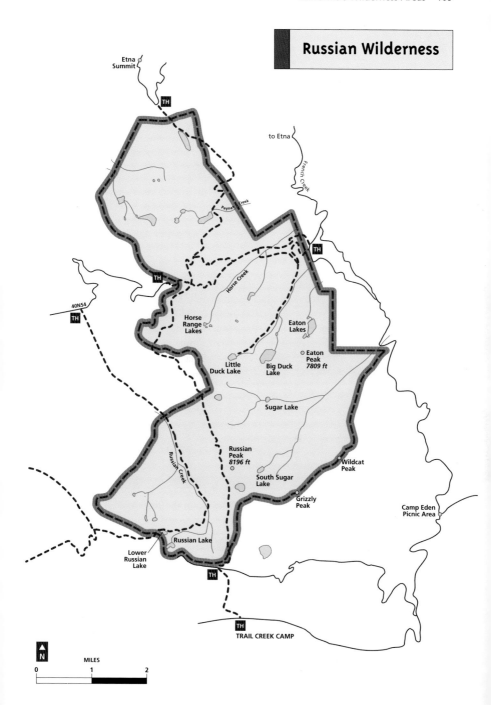

Russian Wilderness

Etna
Summit

TH

to Etna

French Creek

Paynes Creek

TH

40N54

TH

Horse Creek

Horse
Range
Lakes

Eaton
Lakes

Eaton
Peak
7809 ft

Little
Duck Lake

Big Duck
Lake

Sugar Lake

Russian Creek

Russian
Peak
8196 ft

South Sugar
Lake

Wildcat
Peak

Grizzly
Peak

Camp Eden
Picnic Area

Russian Lake

Lower
Russian
Lake

TH

TH

TRAIL CREEK CAMP

N

MILES

0   1   2

18 Siskiyou Wilderness

Glaciated ridgelines, clear streams, and diverse forest vegetation about in the Siskiyou Wilderness.

A look at Preston Peak across Clear Creek Valley from the Bear Lake Trail, Siskiyou Wilderness.

LOCATION: 40 miles east of Crescent City

SIZE: 153,000 acres

ELEVATION RANGE: 1,000 to 7,300 feet

MILES OF TRAILS: 70

ECOSYSTEMS: old-growth Douglas fir

ADMINISTRATION: Six Rivers National Forest, Klamath National Forest

MAPS: Six Rivers National Forest Map, Klamath National Forest Map

If you were to pick one area to view for lavish forest stands combined with sheer ruggedness of slope, the Siskiyou Wilderness would be hard to beat. Much of it is trailless, hence lightly used. Here is where the sense of the great Northwest exhibits its best charm.

The Siskiyou Mountains are another sub-range of the Klamath Mountain province, usually considered the area north of the Klamath River up to/into southern Oregon. The 153,000-acre Siskiyou Wilderness lies primarily in the Klamath and Six Rivers National Forests. The South Fork of the Smith River, a Wild and Scenic River, makes up much of the western border, while Clear Creek, a proposed Wild and Scenic River and tributary of the Klamath River, drains much of the eastern slope of the wilderness. Elevations range from 1,000 to 7,300 feet. Preston Peak is the highest summit and is a proposed Geologic Area due to its abundance of glacial features, including moraines, cirques, and tarns.

Clear Creek is the centerpiece of the present wilderness. Starting in subalpine meadows near Young Valley, the stream flows parallel to the main divide, then turns east. Deep pools, waterfalls, and slow, glassy glides all describe this stream. Magnificent stands of Port Orford cedar line its banks. Wilderness Falls, about six miles up the trail, presents a powerful sight as the entire creek pours through a narrow chute.

Geologically, the area consists of fragments of ocean basin crustal material that has been thrust up against the western edge of the North American Plate with intrusions of granitic rock—part of the Bear Mountain Batholith. The highest elevations have been glaciated; U-shaped valleys and cirque basins are common in the headwaters of Bear, Dillon, Clear, and other streams draining the wilderness. A 17-mile-long glacier with sources near Bear Mountain once occupied upper Clear Creek Valley. The Devil's Punchbowl is a glacial cirque with a 1,500-foot headwall.

Vegetation is very diverse. The upper headwaters of the major valleys typically have subalpine meadows and bogs, while lower creek courses are shaded by immense examples of trees typical of the region, including white fir, Douglas fir, Jeffrey pine, red fir, sugar pine, Pacific dogwood, canyon live oak, bigleaf maple, and tan oak. Rare species include the Brewer's spruce, sadler oak, Alaskan yellow cedar, and Port Orford cedar, with knobcone pine occurring here and there. The California pitcher plant along with coral root, twayblade, and lady's slipper orchids are common in bogs and seeps. The large blossoms of western azalea add color in early summer. The world's largest concentration of lily species is found here, including tiger lily and rare bolander's lily. The Elk Hole Botanical Area contains the southernmost known stand of Alaska yellow cedar.

Wildlife of the region includes the wolverine and fisher, both relatively rare. Black bear are common, as are black-tailed deer. Elk have recently reestablished themselves in the area and are increasing slowly. Dillon Creek and Clear Creek both support steelhead, as does the South Fork of the Smith River. Chinook and coho salmon are also found in Dillon Creek and the South Fork of the Smith River.

The Dillon Creek area is also an important biological corridor that could serve to link the Siskiyou and Marble Mountain Wilderness. Nearly 100,000 acres of additional roadless lands could be added to the wilderness, including large parcels of old-growth forest in Dillon Creek and the unroaded Five Mile Creek drainage. However, spreading logging roads and clearcuts are reducing this roadless heritage rapidly.

A small portion of the wilderness containing the lovely forested Blue Creek drainage is separated from the remainder of the wilderness by a narrow corridor. During the mid-1980s, the corridor was the center of a major controversy as the Forest Service attempted to complete construction of the Gasquet–Orleans Road (GO). Local Native Americans, along with conservationists, opposed the road, claiming construction would destroy both the wildlands and Native American religious sites. The issue was taken all the way to the Supreme Court, which ultimately stopped the road.

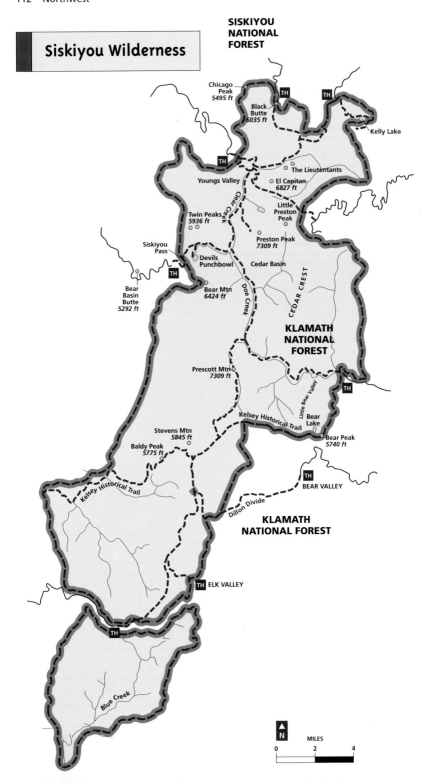

Siskiyou Wilderness

SISKIYOU
NATIONAL
FOREST

Chicago
Peak
5495 ft

TH

TH

Black
Butte
6035 ft

Kelly Lake

TH

The Lieutentants

Youngs Valley

El Capitan
6827 ft

Little
Preston
Peak

Twin Peaks
5936 ft

Preston Peak
7309 ft

Siskiyou
Pass

Devils
Punchbowl

Cedar Basin

Clear Creek

CEDAR CREST

TH

Bear
Basin
Butte
5292 ft

Bear Mtn
6424 ft

Doe Creek

KLAMATH
NATIONAL
FOREST

Prescott Mtn
7309 ft

Little Bear Valley

TH

Kelsey Historical Trail

Bear
Lake

Stevens Mtn
5845 ft

Baldy Peak
5775 ft

Bear Peak
5740 ft

TH

BEAR VALLEY

Kelsey Historical Trail

Dillon Divide

KLAMATH
NATIONAL
FOREST

TH   ELK VALLEY

TH

Blue Creek

N

MILES

0   2   4

DAY HIKE: BEAR LAKE
One-way length: 3 miles
Low and high elevations: 4,600 to 5,500 feet
Difficulty: moderate

Bear Lake is a lovely cirque set in an alpine bowl below Bear Peak in the heavily timbered Siskiyou Mountains. The Bear Lake hike is short, but it requires a steep descent to reach the lake. The trailhead is accessible off Highway 96, 10.0 miles southwest of Happy Camp. The trailhead is 11.5 miles off the highway.

The hike follows the historic South Kelsey Trail, a National Recreation Trail. The original 200-mile South Kelsey Trail was constructed in 1851 to bring supplies from Crescent City on the coast to Fort Jones near Yreka. Today, 16.5 miles of the trail remain between the South Fork of the Smith River and the Bear Lake Trailhead.

From the trailhead, the Bear Lake hike follows a ridge for 2.3 miles to 5,740-foot Bear Peak, passing through forests of white pine, white fir, red fir, Brewer's spruce, Jeffrey pine, and incense cedar. Just after you pass the Siskiyou Wilderness boundary sign, there should be a steep trail that descends to the lake. I couldn't find the trail, but one can bushwack to the lake. However, if you're not up for the 750-foot descent, you can continue on the South Kelsey Trail toward the main Siskiyou Crest, passing Red Hill, an outcrop of serpentine soil. If you aren't interested in a longer hike, Bear Peak makes a good turn-around point, offering great views of the Siskiyou Mountains that includes Preston Peak, the highest in the wilderness. A view to the south from this point will give you a look at the 100,000-acre Dillon Creek drainage, a proposed addition to the wilderness.

DAY HIKE: DEVIL'S PUNCHBOWL
One-way length: 5.5 miles
Low and high elevations: 3,278 to 4,750 feet
Difficulty: moderate

The Devil's Punchbowl occupies one of the more spectacular glacial cirques in the wilderness, and you will pay in sweat to reach it. Numerous switchbacks make the trail seem longer than its short mileage, and some may prefer to make this an overnight hike rather than a day hike. To find the trailhead, head up Highway 199 from Crescent City to the turnoff for Little Jones Creek Road, which you follow to another cutoff by Bear Basin Butte that leads to the trailhead at Siskiyou Pass. The area by Bear Basin has a unique blend of 16 conifers all in one small parcel.

The trail starts out at 4,124 feet and descends on an old mining road along Doe Creek to a trail junction at 3,278 feet. If you continue straight ahead on Doe Creek, you will soon reach Clear Creek, the major drainage in the wilderness. However, to reach the Punchbowl, you turn south and climb back up to the lake, which lies at 4,750 feet in a granite bowl with 1,000-foot cliffs.

OVERNIGHT HIKE: CLEAR CREEK NATIONAL RECREATIONAL TRAIL
One-way length: 21 miles
Low and high elevations: 1,500 to 4,400 feet
Difficulty: moderate

Clear Creek is the main waterway draining the Siskiyou Wilderness, and the 21-mile-long trail that follows its banks offers numerous side trips that can be linked to make up a 3 to 5 day trip into the heart of this mountain wildlands. Proposed for protection as a Wild and Scenic River, the creek is one of the best summer steelhead streams left in northwest California. The lower valley is lined by Port Orford Cedar, a tree endangered elsewhere by a root rot that is spread by the mud caked on logging truck tires.

Access is off Highway 96, 7.0 miles southwest of Happy Creek. Look for Clear Creek Road and follow signs to the trailhead. The trail follows the creek most of the way, offering occasional campsites. One destination is Wilderness Falls, 13 miles from the trailhead, where there is a nice campsite and a good swimming hole. One can continue up this green forested, azalea-covered corridor to Trout Camp and a trail junction. Head west up Doe Creek if you want to visit the Devil's Punchbowl and Buck Lake, or continue north to the Youngs Valley Trailhead.

Snow Mountain Wilderness | 19

*The Snow Mountain Wilderness protects one of the highest
portions of the North Coast Range.*

Ceonothus, Snow Mountain, Snow Mountain Wilderness.

Most of the North Coast Ranges have been developed and
roaded, but the Snow Mountain Wilderness is one of the
exceptions. Located at the south end of the North Coast
Range province on the Mendocino National Forest, Snow
Mountain is readily accessible from San Francisco. Most of
the 37,000-acre wilderness consists of the rolling summit of
Snow Mountain. Outstanding views of the entire North Coast
Ranges as well as the Central Valley to the Sierra Nevada are
possible on clear days. Although only slightly more than
7,000 feet in elevation, Snow Mountain's close proximity to
the ocean ensures abundant snowfall and a low timberline.

The geological base of the Snow Mountain Wilderness
consists of sedimentary rock, including sandstone, shale, and
chert. These all formed on the ocean floor and were accreted

LOCATION: 25 miles
northeast of Clear Lake

SIZE: 37,000 acres

ELEVATION RANGE:
1,800 to 7,056 feet

MILES OF TRAILS: 52

ECOSYSTEMS: black
oak-pine, mixed conifer,
and true fir forest

ADMINISTRATION:
Mendocino National
Forest

MAPS: Mendocino
National Forest Map,
Snow Mountain
Wilderness Area Map

to the edge of the North American Plate. Faults raised the mountain uplands, creating steep sides but leaving a gentle, rolling summit. Cirques created by past glaciation rim Snow Mountain's highest basins.

The area experiences the typical California Mediterranean climate of cool, wet winters, and dry, hot summers. It is actually quite cold on the crest zone in winter, with an average January temperature of 18 degrees. Precipitation at higher elevations is up to 60 inches, much of it as snow.

Typical vegetation consists of chaparral at lower elevations with mixed coniferous forests higher up, including ponderosa pine, Jeffrey pine, white fir, red fir, incense cedar, and oaks. Meadows, particularly in the high cirque basins, offer occasional fields of flowers.

Wildlife includes black bear, black-tailed deer, marten, and one of the highest populations of mountain lion in the state. Recently, Tule elk have been reintroduced in the forest and their numbers are expected to grow. Cattle, however, are the most likely animal to be encountered. I found the water in several campsites to be polluted by cattle excrement—yet another example of how we must tolerate private profit generated on public lands at the expense of the public's water, wildlife, and plant communities.

The South Fork of Stony Creek sustains a small trout populations, and the Middle Fork, a proposed Wild and Scenic River, contains the best native rainbow trout fishery in the area. Middle Fork, whose headwaters are in the glaciated basins below Snow Mountain, has carved a gorge exposing pillow basalt flows.

There are eight trailheads and, as with most wilderness areas, most of the use is focused on a few places—in this case, Snow Mountain's summit. Although this wilderness is not well known, hence relatively uncrowded, you might try Bearwallow, Upper Nye, or Trout Creek Trails if you want to avoid people, or get off the trail and explore the nearly impenetrable Middle Fork of Stony Creek.

DAY HIKE: WEST CROCKETT–SNOW MOUNTAIN LOOP
Loop length: 11 miles
Low and high elevations: 5,200 to 7,056 feet
Difficulty: moderate

This could be either a long day hike or an overnighter. The loop provides a good sample of the Snow Mountain Wilderness high country. The route begins at the West Crockett Trailhead by the primitive West Crockett Campground located along the northern boundary of the wilderness. The easiest way to reach the trailhead is to take Highway 162 from I–5 at Willows to Elk Creek, then drive west on Ivory Mill Road to its intersection with Forest Service Road M3, which leads to the trailhead.

The trail initially follows the North Fork of Stony Creek, which contains small trout, then climbs up a ridge to the eastern peak of Snow Mountain. Beware once you leave Stony Creek, because there is little water. There are occasional vistas once you climb up on the ridge, but the best views are from the treeless summit of Snow Mountain. After ascending the East Peak of Snow Mountain, take the Milk Ranch Trail, which loops back north along the headwaters of the Middle Fork Stony Creek, until you rejoin the North Ridge and continue back to the trailhead. This hike offers few camping sites with water, except near Snow Mountain and the Milk Ranch area.

Snow Mountain Wilderness

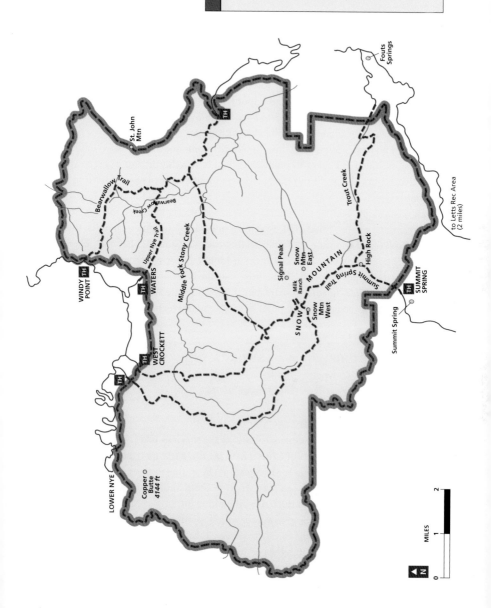

Fouts Springs

to Letts Rec Area
(2 miles)

TH

St. John
Mtn

Bearwallow Trail

Bearwallow Creek

Trout Creek

Upper Nye Trail

Middle Fork Stony Creek

Signal Peak

Snow
Mtn
East

High Rock

Summit Spring Trail

M O U N T A I N

S N O W

Milk
Ranch

Snow
Mtn
West

SUMMIT
SPRING

TH

WINDY
POINT

TH

WATERS

TH

Summit Spring

WEST
CROCKETT

TH

LOWER NYE

Copper
Butte
4144 ft

MILES

N

0   1   2

> **DAY HIKE: BEAR WALLOW TRAIL**
> One-way length: 6 miles
> Low and high elevations: 4,000 to 5,000 feet
> Difficulty: moderate

The main attraction of this trail is that not many other people hike it. So if you just want to wander through the lovely forests of the northern Coast Range by yourself, this is a good bet. A short connecting spur trail takes you to Bear Wallow Creek, where you can rest, obtain water, and have a picnic lunch. It's also often accessible in spring when the crest area is still laden with snow.

The Bear Wallow Trail links the Windy Point and Bear Wallow Trailheads and can be hiked as a point-to-point trip if you have a shuttle, but it isn't so arduous that it can't be hiked from trailhead to trailhead and back to your starting point in one long day. There is almost no water here in summer, and it can be hot, so plan accordingly. The hike begins at the Bear Wallow Trailhead. To reach it from Stonyford, take Forest Road M10, 10.0 miles to road 18N03. After 2.0 miles, turn on road 18N06 and continue 10.0 miles to the road's end and the trailhead. The trail contours north along the slopes of St. John Mountain for several miles, where it intersects the Upper Nye Trail. If you want, hike the Nye down to Bear Wallow Creek; otherwise, continue north approximately 3.0 miles to the Windy Point Trailhead, which will be your turn-around point or trail's end, if you have arranged a shuttle.

> **OVERNIGHT HIKE: SUMMIT SPRINGS–SNOW MOUNTAIN TRAIL**
> One-way length: 4 miles
> Low and high elevations: 5,000 to 7,056 feet
> Difficulty: moderate

This hike offers a lot of the same attributes as the previous hike, except perhaps more vistas due to the effects of a fire. There are also a few more obvious camping areas, making this a good trek for backpackers. First, find your way to Summit Springs Trailhead. From I–5 you need to get to Stonyford, then take Forest Service Road M10 about 25 miles to the trailhead parking lot.

The hike begins at a steady grade uphill, passing through the snags from a 1987 fire that rejuvenated the forest ecosystem. Like most fires, note how this blaze left an abundance of snags and downed logs, which are critical habitat for many wildlife species as well as providing nutrient storage and erosion control. Indeed, many ecologists believe dead trees are more important to the forest ecosystem— ecologically speaking—than live trees. Logging, on the other hand, leaves few if any snags or dead trees, removes nutrients, and increases erosion rates. The real lesson of the recent blaze is that a healthy forest ecosystem has an abundance of dead trees. Incidentally, the fire has also cleared away the timber, making for great views, but it means a hot climb if it's done on a warm summer afternoon.

You eventually switchback up the hill, pass High Rock, which offers great views southward, and then enter a forest of white fir, red fir, and Jeffrey pine until you reach Cedar Camp. This is a good camping spot, but be aware that cattle may have fouled the water. Ascend through a forest to a cirque basin between the twin summits of Snow Mountain, where there is usually water and another potential camping spot. The top of Snow Mountain is flat and broad enough for camping if you carry water up from the creeks on its flanks. The 360-degree views make an overnighter on the summit something to consider. On a clear day, you should be able to look up and down the Coast Range and out across the Sacramento Valley to Sutter Buttes and Sierra Nevada.

Snow Mountain's broad summit ridge.

20 Trinity Alps Wilderness

The is the largest and most spectacular mountain wilderness in northern California, offering deep canyons and glaciated peaks.

Canyon Creek by the outlet of Canyon Lake, Trinity Alps Wilderness.

LOCATION: 50 miles northwest of Redding

SIZE: 517,000 acres

ELEVATION RANGE: 1,360 to 9,000 feet

MILES OF TRAILS: 833

ECOSYSTEMS: diverse conifer forest to limited alpine terrain

ADMINISTRATION: Klamath National Forest, Six Rivers National Forest, Shasta–Trinity National Forest

MAPS: Shasta–Trinity National Forest Map, Klamath National Forest Map, Trinity Alps WIlderness Area Map

The 517,000-acre Trinity Alps Wilderness is the second largest designated wilderness in California and spans three national forest boundaries. Laced with trails, rivers, forests, and peaks, this is one wilderness where you can travel for weeks and never exhaust all the possible treks. A climb on the higher peaks with a sprawling sea of forested ridges and valleys gives this wildlands a sense of vastness not possible anywhere else in northwest California, except perhaps in the Marbles. Elevations range from 1,360 feet along the Trinity River to just over 9,000 feet at Thompson Peak. The trails up Canyon and Coffee Creeks lead into the heart of the Trinity Alps, the highest and most spectacular peaks. Because of their beauty, the Trinity Alps are heavily trafficked by hikers and are best avoided by those seeking fewer encounters with other people. Most of the trails leading off Highway 3 on the eastern edge of the wilderness are more heavily used, while trailheads accessing the western part of the wilderness offer tremendous opportunities for solitude.

Some divide the wilderness into the Green, Red, and White Trinities. The differently colored strata represent different geological rock layers that were welded on to each other to form the diverse geology of the Klamath Mountains region. The Green Trinities make up the western margin, a heavily timbered, low elevation area. This is the least visited region, and one where you're sure to find solitude on most trails. The Red Trinities consist of iron-rich meta-sedimentary rocks with rather unproductive soils, but numerous lakes. Finally, there are the White Trinities, the best known part of the wilderness, with granite peaks, meadows, and dozens of lakes. The Whites are often compared to the Sierra Nevada, with rugged peaks such as Sawtooth Ridge, and glaciated valleys such as Canyon Creek. Small glaciers still cling to the higher peaks around the headwaters of Grizzly and Canyon Creeks. As might be expected, with spectacular scenery and lots of lakes, this region receives the most visitation—avoid it if you prefer to have fewer encounters with other travelers.

An interesting phenomenon in the Trinities is the capture of the headwaters of Coffee Creek by the South Fork of the Salmon River. Moraines in Coffee Creek blocked the stream, while headwater erosion of the South Fork breached the gap separating the two drainages.

The area was first set aside as part of the 196,420-acre Salmon–Trinity Alps Primitive Area in 1932, with another 83,840 acres added in 1933. Even though the Trinities were one of the most spectacular areas in California, passage of the 1964 Wilderness Act did not see them become a designated wilderness as might be expected, partly due to their perceived timber values. Not until 1984, with the passage of the California Wilderness Act, did the Trinities finally gain the status and protection they deserved. There are also two designated Wild and Scenic Rivers within the wilderness: New River and North Fork Trinity River. Three other rivers are recommended for Wild and Scenic River status, including Canyon and Virgin Creeks and the upper 11.7 miles of the North Fork Trinity.

Due to the great elevation and soil types, it's not surprising that the Trinities support a diverse flora as well. Typical species of the region include Douglas fir, ponderosa pine, red fir, white fir, black oak, canyon live oak, California madrone, bigleaf maple, California buckeye, incense cedar, and Jeffrey pine. California's northernmost stand of digger pine is found here along the South Fork of the Salmon River.

Salmon and steelhead runs occur in a number of rivers whose headwaters lie in the wilderness, including the Stuart Fork River, South Fork of the Salmon River, North Fork Trinity River, and New River. Other wildlife includes black bear, black-tailed deer, wolverine, fisher, marten, pileated woodpecker, northern flying squirrel, spotted owl, band-tailed pigeon, and goshawk. The Trinity Alps are currently being considered for restoration of Roosevelt elk, a native species, and would be one of the better areas in northern California for the re-establishment of wolves.

Despite its superlative biological value, the Trinity Alps suffer from the scourge of livestock production, with nearly 100,000 acres—mostly occurring in the northeast corner of the wilderness—available to domestic cattle grazing. These animals trample meadows and spring areas and are a major source of water pollution. At the same time, the Forest Service demands that campers avoid trampling lakeshores and meadows, restricting numbers to minimize damage, while livestock grazing continues with almost no monitoring, much less any restrictions.

Trinity Alps Wilderness: West

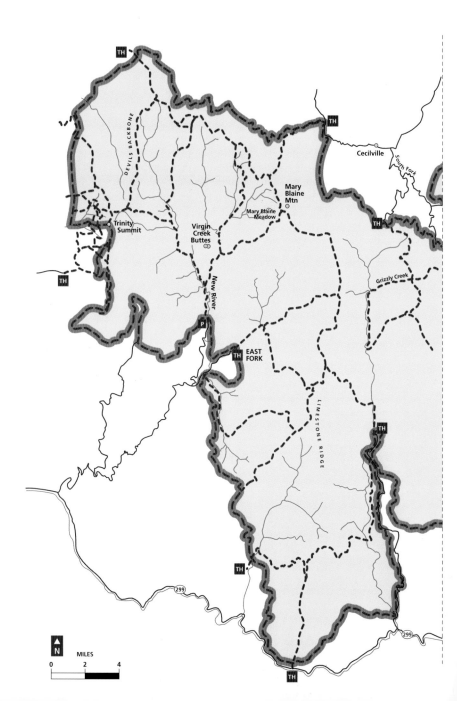

DEVILS BACKBONE

TH

TH

Cecilville

South Fork

Mary
Blaine
Mtn

Mary Blaine
Meadow

Trinity
Summit

Virgin
Creek
Buttes

TH

TH

New River

Grizzly Creek

TH

P

EAST
FORK

TH

LIMESTONE RIDGE

TH

TH

299

N
MILES
0   2   4

299

TH

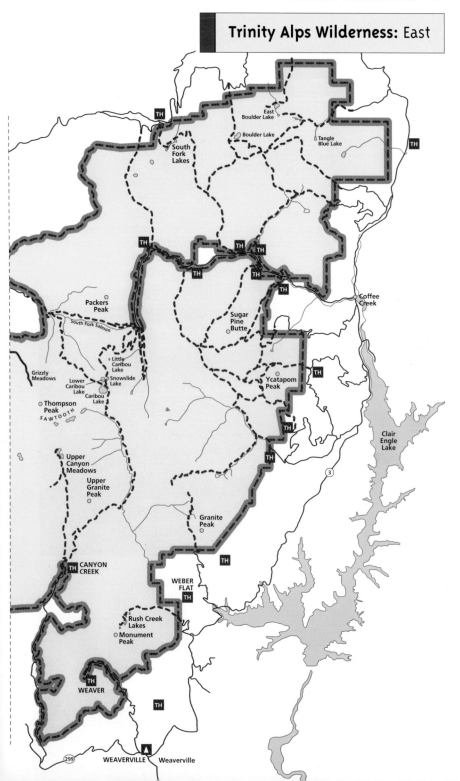

Trinity Alps Wilderness: East

East Boulder Lake

Boulder Lake

Tangle Blue Lake

South Fork Lakes

TH

TH

Coffee Creek

Packers Peak

South Fork Salmon

Sugar Pine Butte

TH

TH

TH

TH

Grizzly Meadows

Little Caribou Lake

Snowslide Lake

Lower Caribou Lake

Caribou Lake

Thompson Peak

SAWTOOTH

Ycatapom Peak

TH

TH

TH

Clair Engle Lake

Upper Canyon Meadows

Upper Granite Peak

3

Granite Peak

CANYON CREEK

TH

TH

WEBER FLAT

TH

Rush Creek Lakes

Monument Peak

TH

WEAVER

TH

WEAVERVILLE

299

Weaverville

DAY HIKE: EAST BOULDER LAKE
One-way length: 2 miles
Low and high elevations: 5,850 to 6,700 feet
Difficulty: moderate

Don't expect a lake less than two miles from a trailhead to be lightly used. The scenic, open basin of East Boulder Lake isn't a place to seek out solitude, but it does make for an easy, pleasant day hike that is particularly good for children. It is, unfortunately, often overrun with cows. To find the trailhead, drive on Forest Road 40N17 from Callahan. Following signs for McKeen Divide and East Boulder Lake, it is 6.0 miles to the trailhead located on the northern slope of the wilderness.

The trail follows Boulder Creek to the lake, passing a lovely waterfall enroute, then climbs steeply for the last 0.25 mile to the 32-acre lake, the largest in the northern Trinity Alps. The lake basin, open with scattered trees, is covered with sagebrush and rabbitbrush—plants one doesn't expect to see at this elevation in the "lush" Trinity Alps. The underlying serpentine soils may have something to do with limiting the vegetation in the area.

*A view of Caribou Mountain and Sawtooth Ridge
from above Steveale Creek, Trinity Alps.*

DAY HIKE: TANGLE BLUE LAKE TRAIL
One-way length: 3 miles
Low and high elevations: 4,500 to 5,700 feet
Difficulty: moderate

This short hike climbs 1,200 feet and provides access to one of the prettier lakes in the Trinity Alps Wilderness. The first part of the trail is an old mining road, which eventually passes beyond the wilderness boundary and becomes a real trail. There are some huge incense cedars about a mile up the trail from the wilderness boundary. The shallow Tangle Blue Lake lies in a large meadow.

DAY HIKE: GRANITE PEAK
One-way length: 4 miles
Low and high elevations: 4,100 to 8,091 feet
Difficulty: strenuous

This hike is short—just four miles—with a climb of nearly 4,000 feet on count-less switchbacks, but the views are worth it! There is a false summit 1,500 feet below the true peak, but the vistas of the surrounding mountains will keep your mind off the climb. The trail splits just before the final push for the top, with the left-hand fork leading to Red Mountain and Stonewall Pass and a traverse of high alpine country studded with lakes.

The trailhead is located 3.0 miles west of Highway 3 on a logging road that begins opposite the entrance for Bushy Trail Campground on Clair Eagle Lake.

OVERNIGHT HIKE: EAST FORK NEW RIVER LOOP
One-way length: 20 miles
Low and high elevations: 2,400 to 5,600 feet
Difficulty: strenuous

This hike along forested streams and over limestone ridges is located in the remote western part of the Trinity Alps Wilderness and is best done over a 3-to 4-day period. The trailhead is accessed by driving 32 miles west of Weaverville on Highway 299, then north on the Denny Road (County Road 402) to the Pony Buttes parking area.

The first part of the trip follows the East Fork New River and then Cabin Creek before climbing up Blue Ridge and continuing on to Limestone Ridge by Rattlesnake Lake. There's a few campsites here, but you will have to get your water from a signed spring nearby. From Rattlesnake Lake, the route turns south along the New River Divide Trail. There are great views—but little water—all along the ridge as you traverse the high country, passing 6,870-foot Cabin Peak enroute. This summit used to have a lookout, and an old trail leads to the top for excellent views.

Continue on southwest to tiny half-acre White Creek Lake by Pony Mountain, where there is a small campsite in western white pine at the fishless lake. From here, the trail heads northwest and mostly downhill, passing Upper Jakes Camp and Lower Jakes Camp and eventually linking up with the East Fork New River Trail just a few miles upstream from the trailhead.

OVERNIGHT HIKE: NEW RIVER TRAIL
One-way length: 9 miles
Low and high elevations: 2,400 to 6,000 feet
Difficulty: moderate

This trail follows the designated Wild and Scenic New River, located in the western, lower, and less frequently used portion of the wilderness. New River Trail passes such landmarks as Megram Cabin, Robbers Roost Mine, and Emmons Cabin, ending at Mary Blane Meadows, the final destination of the hike. It's possible to climb Mary Blane Mountain from this campsite. Longer, more extended trips are possible by linking with connecting trails that converge on the meadow.

> **OVERNIGHT HIKE: RED CAP LAKE TRAIL**
> One-way length: 4.1 miles
> Low and high elevations: 4,000 to 5,700 feet
> Difficulty: moderate

This relatively easy hike along the forested Salmon Summit National Recreation Trail to Red Cap Lake in the northwestern corner of the Trinity Alps Wilderness could easily be a day trip, but the seldom visited lake also makes a good overnight destination. The trail is accessed 18.5 miles from Orleans on Highway 96 by following Forest Road 10N01 to the trailhead.

The trail route is mostly in forests, providing shade from the summer sun, but as you approach the lake, the views open up. Initially, the trail climbs slightly to the Salmon Divide, then begins a descent just beyond Indian Rocks. About 2.75 miles from the trailhead, the Red Cap Lake Trail leaves the Salmon Summit Trail to descend to the lake. Red Cap Lake is reported to be fishless, but flowery scattered meadows and numerous campsites surround it, making it an attractive place to spend the night. You'll probably have the place to yourself.

> **OVERNIGHT HIKE: GRANITE LAKE AND SEVEN UP PEAK**
> One-way length: 5 miles
> Low and high elevations: 3,200 to 8,100 feet
> Difficulty: moderate

Granite Lake, as the name suggests, rests in a dramatic granite-lined bowl on the eastern edge of the wilderness. This trip takes you to the 18-acre lake at an elevation of 6,000 feet. For those with a bit more energy, a climb of Seven Up Peak offers spectacular views of the highest summits in the Trinity Alps. It's also possible to extend the trip into a multi-day loop by linking with several trail options that radiate from below Seven Up Gap. The trailhead is accessed from Highway 3 by Trinity Center. Take the Swift Creek Road 7.0 miles to the trail's start.

The first part of the trail follows the aptly named Swift Creek as it dashes its way down a canyon lined with azalea, Douglas fir, sugar pine, incense cedar, and Jeffrey pine. At 1.3 miles you will reach a trail junction: The trail along Swift Creek continues to Ward and Horseshoe Lakes—worth a trip in themselves—but the path to Granite Lake crosses Swift Creek and climbs up fern-lined Granite Creek, passing several waterfalls and a few flowery meadows, eventually arriving at Granite Lake. From the lake it's possible to climb by trail to Seven Up Gap, where there are scattered stands of mountain hemlock and the rare foxtail pine. From the gap, it's just a short scramble to the top of 8,134-foot Seven Up Peak.

If you're interested in making the trip more than an in-and-out from Granite Lake, consider hiking to the Bear Basin Trail or the Mumford Basin Trail, which course north from Seven Up Gap. Both trails eventually lead back to Swift Creek and the trailhead.

Yolla Bolly–Middle Eel Wilderness

This wilderness is one of the largest, but least-known wild areas in northern California. It offers many miles of lower elevation trails, making it a good hiking area in spring and fall.

Sunset on the slopes of the 8,092-foot Mount Linn, the highest peak in Yolla Bolly–Middle Eel Wilderness.

The Yolla Bolly–Middle Eel Wilderness lies at the northern end of the North Coast Ranges, approximately 50 miles west of Red Bluff. It's a wilderness area that has always seemed somewhat forgotten. Not quite as spectacular as the Trinity Alps to the north and too far from urban areas to attract crowds, hiking in the Yolla Bolly–Middle Eel feels accessible in a friendly sort of way, but remote. Since the area is lightly visited, long trips into its interior almost guarantee solitude. Managed by the Shasta–Trinity, Mendocino, and Six Rivers National Forests, along with nearly 9,000 acres of BLM lands proposed for transfer to the Forest Service, the wilderness consists of 156,000 acres of rugged, heavily-timbered slopes and valleys, a few peaks that rise to timberline, and the head-waters of the Middle Fork of the Eel River. Mount Linn, at

LOCATION: 50 miles west of Red Bluff

SIZE: 156,000 acres

ELEVATION RANGE: 2,000 to 8,083 feet

MILES OF TRAILS: 156

ECOSYSTEMS: mixed conifer, oak woodlands

ADMINISTRATION: Mendocino, Six Rivers, and Shasta–Trinity National Forests

MAPS: Mendocino N.F. Map, Six Rivers N.F. Map, Shasta–Trinity N.F. Map, Yolla Bolly–Middle Eel Wilderness Area Map

8,092 feet, is the area's highest summit. The name "Yolla Bolly" is reportedly a Native American word for "snow-covered peak."

Consisting of metamorphosed sedimentary rocks, most of the area has been eroded into narrow ridges and deep canyons by rivers. However, during the last Ice Age, the highest summits held glaciers that carved small cirques and tarns. Both North and South Yolla Bolly Mountains have evidence of glaciation. Geologically speaking, the northern part of the wilderness is the southernmost section of the Klamath Mountains region of northern California and southern Oregon. The rocks in North Yolla Bolly Mountain are composed of gray greenstone, an old metamorphosed lava. The South Yolla Bolly belong to the Franciscan formation, a sandstone that makes up much of the North Coast Range.

Originally set aside as a primitive area in 1931, the Yolla Bolly was one of the original designated wildernesses that came about with the passage of the 1964 Wilderness Act. Later in 1984, the area was expanded to include an additional 42,000 acres.

Perhaps one of Yolla Bolly–Middle Eel's greatest attractions is its forests. Beautiful, dense forests of red fir, Douglas fir, sugar pine, white fir, Jeffrey pine, ponderosa pine, and a variety of oaks cloak the slopes. A small grove of foxtail pine grows on South Yolla Bolly Mountain, and chaparral is common at lower elevations. Living among these forests are goshawk, spotted owl, black bear, northern flying squirrel, black-tailed deer, bobcat, mountain lion, ring tail, fisher, and marten. The Middle Fork of the Eel River courses through a narrow canyon with many deep, tree-shaded pools as it hosts spring-run chinook salmon and summer- and winter-run steelhead. A 24-mile stretch of the Middle Fork that lies outside of the wilderness is a designated Wild and Scenic River, and another 14 miles inside the wilderness are proposed for such status.

Due to the great variation in elevation, it's possible to hike here year round. Driving to trailheads in the winter can be problematic, due to snow or muddy conditions. Summers can be very warm except for the highest ridges, and as a consequence spring and fall are probably the best times to visit the area. The wilderness has a huge trail network, allowing for day hikes as well as loop trips of a week or more in duration.

DAY HIKE: PETTYJOHN TRAIL
One-way length: 4 miles
Low and high elevations: 5,600 to 7,135 feet
Difficulty: moderate

The Pettyjohn Trail is one of the major access points into the area of North Yolla Bolly Mountain (7,863) with a number of spur trails off of it, including short hikes to Black Rock Lake, North Yolla Bolly Lake, and Black Rock Mountain. Driving to the trailhead at Stuarts Gap, which is 78 miles west of Red Bluff and 19 miles from the Harrison Gulch Ranger Station, is all on paved roads except for the last two miles.

The trail follows a gentle ridge to the wilderness boundary and then heads to the Pettyjohn Basin, where there are paths leading to Black Rock Lake and North Yolla Bolly Lake. Good views of Black Rock Mountain and its glacial cirque are visible. Beyond the trail junctions, the Pettyjohn Trail switchbacks up to a ridge with a few wind-swept whitebark pine at about 7,000 feet. There is yet another trail junction with good views of the wilderness to the west and Mount Shasta to the north. The trail drops down through Cedar Basin and ends at the Humboldt Trail.

DAY HIKE: SOLOMON PEAK TRAIL
One-way length: 4 miles
Low and high elevations: 6,050 to 7,581 feet
Difficulty: moderate

This is one of the most remote trailheads in the Yolla Bolly–Middle Eel Wilderness, with some of the best views. You will hike up Solomon Peak, which is the headwaters of the Middle Eel River.

First drive to Covelo and the Round Valley Indian Reservation. Just east of Covelo, cross the Eel River and take Forest Service Road M1 (Indian Dick Road) for 28 miles to Indian Dick Guard Station. Just past the station, turn onto Soldier Ridge Road and follow it 3.0 miles to the trailhead.

The first 2.5 miles of the trail climbs gently up a moderate grade, passing grassy balds and windswept pine. You will come to a spring at Johnson Headquarters, and another 0.25 mile further, the trail divides. The left fork goes to Minnie Lake, and the right fork goes to Solomon Peak, which boasts a number of glacial cirques on its north face. The trail climbs the semi-open ridge nearly to the summit, with the last 0.25 mile and 300 feet up just a scramble. From here, you can backtrack to the trailhead or make it an overnight trek by continuing to Summit Trail, which winds northward along the Middle Eel Divide toward Devil's Hole Ridge and eventually reaches the North Yolla Bolly area.

DAY HIKE: IDES COVE NATIONAL RECREATION LOOP TRAIL
Loop length: 10 miles
Low and high elevations: 6,800 to 7,500 feet
Difficulty: moderate

This is an easy loop trail with great camping spots, lots of water, and wonderful views. Ides Cove provides access to the South Yolla Bolly Mountains area, which includes Mount Linn, the highest peak in the wilderness. The access is a long drive and rough in a few places, but it's normally passable for two-wheel-drive vehicles. From I–5 go west to Paskenta, bearing in mind that it's still another 34 miles to the trailhead. At Paskenta, get on Forest Service Road M2 to Cold Springs Guard Station, then take road M22, following the signs for 9.0 miles to the trailhead.

The first 3.0 miles of the trail are largely level with slight ups and downs, passing through forests of Jeffrey pine, ponderosa pine, and red fir. Throughout this section of trail, you will be treated to views of the North Yolla Bolly, Mount Shasta, Trinity Alps, and other mountains and ranges to the north. You will soon pass Square Lake, which is small but set in a lovely, meadowy glacial cirque below Mount Linn. Approximately 1.0 mile further is Long Lake, also set in a cirque.

Between Square and Long Lakes lies the Burnt Camp Trail, which provides a short-cut back to the Ides Cove Loop, effectively halving the mileage from 10 to 5. Four miles from the trailhead, you will intersect the Thomas Trail. A half mile further brings you to the return loop of the Ides Cove Trail, just below Harvey Peak, which is another side trip. You can access this summit easily from the high point of D Camp Trail by scrambling up the mountain. The return segment of the Ides Cove Loop has more trees and fewer views, but it does pass through nice meadows and by small creeks.

Yolla Bolly–Middle Eel Wilderness

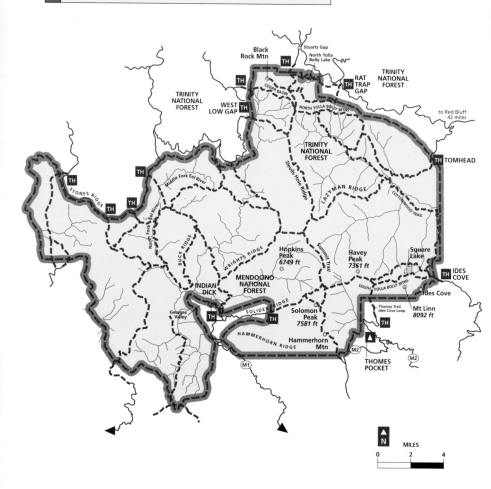

Yuki Proposed Wilderness 22

*The Yuki Proposed Wilderness, which contains portions of
Elk Creek and the Middle Fork of the Eel River, is the largest
unprotected wildlands in the northern California Coast Range.*

*Oak woodlands above Thatcher Creek
in the proposed Yuki Wilderness.*

You probably haven't heard of the Yuki Proposed Wilderness.
The area lies southeast of Round Valley in one of the most
forgotten parts of California—the northern Coast Range.
The region takes its name from the Yuki Indians, the tribe that
most recently occupied the area. This proposed wilderness is
made up of four separate wilderness study (WSA) and roadless areas (RA)—the Eden Valley WSA and Thatcher WSA,
and the Thatcher Ridge RA and Elk Creek RA. They are
administered by the BLM and the Forest Service, which
includes the Mendocino National Forest. Up until recently,
both agencies refused to consider the area as a unified whole
and therefore discounted its wildlands values. Another problem has been the private inholdings that lie along the upper
portion of the Middle Fork of the Eel. Nevertheless, there

LOCATION: 10 miles
southeast of Covelo

SIZE: 70,000 acres

ELEVATION RANGE:
1,200 to 3,500 feet

MILES OF TRAILS:
no maintained trails,
but a few old 4WD roads

ECOSYSTEMS:
riparian, oak woodlands,
chaparral, Douglas fir
forest

ADMINISTRATION:
BLM Ukiah District,
Mendocino National
Forest

MAP: Mendocino
National Forest Map

is growing support for a Yuki Wilderness, and the Forest Service has decided to manage its lands within the proposed wilderness so as to retain wildland values.

The area lacks the high glaciated peaks and spectacular scenery we often associate with protected wilderness, but that doesn't mean the Yuki doesn't have its charms. There are oak woodlands, shady old-growth Douglas fir groves, chaparral, and grasslands. The oaks are particularly special; 10 different species are recorded for the area, with the oak woodlands on Mendenhall Creek especially attractive. An additional feature of the area are the groves of Sargent cypress found in Deep Hole Creek.

Wildlife diversity is significant and includes Tule elk, black bear, mountain lion, bobcat, river otter, gray fox, goshawks, and golden eagles. The Middle Fork of the Eel, a Wild and Scenic River, bisects the proposed wilderness and supports summer steelhead and salmon runs. Both Elk and Thatcher Creeks have been recommended for Wild and Scenic designation, which will protect them for our enjoyment.

There are no official trails in the area, although the best access is off Forest Road M1 near Skunk Rock and Grizzly Flat. The road is accessible from Covelo after crossing the Eel River near Eel River Campground.

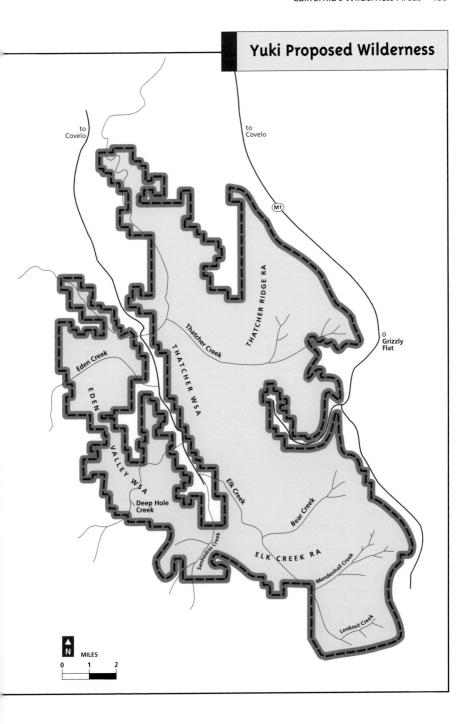

Yuki Proposed Wilderness

Sierra Nevada: The Northern, Central, and Southern Sierras

Naturalist John Muir wrote that the Sierra "…seemed not clothed with light, but wholly composed of it, like the wall of some celestial city… It seemed to me that the Sierra should be called, not the Nevada or Snowy Range, but the Range of Light." Muir's poetic description accurately describes the Sierra Nevada, which is the quintessence of mountain wildlands for most Californians—the standard against which all others are measured. Other parts of the state are more remote and have more wildlife, but almost everyone agrees that the Sierra Nevada is special—a landscape that commands awe and admiration.

Straddling the California–Nevada border for more than 400 miles, the Sierra Nevada is the longest, highest, and one of the most spectacular mountain ranges in the state with more than half of the designated wilderness acreage. Countless lakes, domes, peaks, waterfalls, oak-studded foothills, alpine meadows, and great, haunting forests add to the Sierra's appeal. The mountains form a barrier to everything from weather to highway construction. For example, there is a 150-mile stretch of the Sierra from Tioga Pass in the north to the Sherman Pass Road in the south, where not a single road traverses the range.

The litany of superlatives continues: Lake Tahoe is the tenth-deepest lake in the world; Kings Canyon, at 8,240 feet, is the deepest in the United States. The 2,425-foot drop of Yosemite Falls is the third highest in the world. Mono Lake, just east of the range, is the oldest continually existing body of water in the nation. And the trees *Sequoia gigantea*, scattered in 75 groves along the western slope of the range, are the largest living things on earth.

If this isn't enough, the southern Sierra Nevada, with nearly 2.8-million acres of roadless country, lays claim to having the second-largest roadless area left in the coterminous 48 states! Only the unroaded wildlands complex that surrounds and includes Idaho's Frank Church–River of No Return Wilderness is larger.

The obstacle the Sierra poses cannot be understated: It is an enormous block of upthrusted granite, volcanic, sedimentary, and metamorphic rock that, in area, almost equals the state of Maine. Rising from nearly sea level in the Central Valley, the Sierra climbs more than two miles into the sky, culminating in the 14,495-foot Mount Whitney, the highest peak

Mount Russell from the summit of Mount Whitney, Sequoia National Park.

in the contiguous United States. In the 150-mile stretch of rockbound lakes and jagged summits, familiarly called the "High Sierra" and located between Yosemite Park and Cottonwood Pass on the south, more than 500 peaks 12,000 feet or higher rake the sky. Hundreds of small glaciers, including the most southerly in the United States, sculpt these crags.

The Kern River divides the southern Sierra into two major arms, with Mount Whitney and other high peaks forming the eastern section. The western branch is made up of the Great Western Divide, with peaks exceeding 13,000 feet.

The western and eastern flanks of the range are dramatically different. The eastern side of the Sierra soars as much as 11,000 feet above the floor of the Owens Valley near Lone Pine, while the western side is a gentle, long steady incline. Uplift of the range is still occurring. The 1872 Owens Valley Earthquake raised the range 23 feet near Lone Pine!

The highest and most dramatic portion of the range is typically south of Yosemite. Here are the lakes, granite basins, and soaring peaks for which the Sierra is justly known. Further north, beyond Yosemite, the range is increasingly dominated by volcanic rock that produces a more subdued landscape with fewer lakes, similar to the Carson–Iceberg Wilderness. Nevertheless, in this portion of the range there are granitic outcrops such as those found in the Desolation Wilderness and Granite Chief Wilderness. North of I–80, the Sierra becomes rolling and heavily timbered, and heavily logged, as well. The Bucks Lake Wilderness is the only designated wild-lands, but several other roadless parcels, including the Sierra Buttes area, may eventually gain wilderness protection in the future.

When most people think of the Sierra, they think granite. Granites are formed deep in the earth, where molten rock cools slowly forming dense, hard rock resistant to erosion. Dozens of granite bodies were intruded into the roots of the Sierras between 87 and 115 million years ago. Granites only occur at the surface where erosion has stripped away the overlying rock layers. Volcanic rock can be made from the same basic material, but are exploded or oozed out on the surface, resulting in different texture and chemical composition. They tend to be darker in color and softer, thus more easily eroded.

It is the light-colored granite that prompted John Muir to call these mountains the "Range of Light." Perhaps this is because the most famous vistas from Half Dome to Mount Whitney are dominated by granitic out-crops. Nevertheless, much of the range, particularly north of Yosemite, is made up of volcanics and metamorphic rocks rather than granites. The Carson–Iceberg and Mokelumne Wilderness Areas primarily consist of bedrock of volcanic origin. But even in Yosemite and further south, non-granitic rocks crop out here and there. Mount Dana along the eastern edge of Yosemite as well as Mount Banner and Mount Ritter further south in the Ansel Adams Wilderness are composed primarily of metavolcanic rock. And the dark rocks of the Kaweah Ridge area in Sequoia National Park also consist of metavolcanics. Similarly, most of the foothill "Mother Lode" country consists of metamorphic sedimentary rock, not granitic bodies.

Much of the volcanic rock dominating the surface north of Yosemite is the result of volcanic activity that began about 20 million years ago. Sonora Peak, Mount Rose, the Dardanelles, and Castle Peak are all remnants of this period. But the volcanic activity isn't over: Mammoth Mountain is an active volcano that could explode any time, and eruptions as recent as the 1800s have occurred in the Mono Lake area.

The finishing touches to the Sierra occurred during the past two million years as successive waves of glaciation washed over the range. Most of the higher elevations were enveloped in ice sheets. Valley glaciers carved deep, U-shaped gorges such as those found in the Kern Canyon and Tuolumne River. Cirque glaciers carved the peaks into jagged spires. Water carved deep river canyons, in part hastened by the uplift that occurred during this time. Uplift is on-going, and the Sierra is rising at a rate of more than an inch a year.

The wall of peaks wrings moisture from every passing winter storm system, giving the Sierra the distinction of being one of the snowiest places in the lower 48 states, outside of the Pacific Northwest. In 1911, 32.6 feet of snow buried the town of Tamarack near Lake Tahoe, and more than 86 feet smothered Donner Pass during the winter of 1982–1983. Yet, due to its Mediterranean climate, only three percent of the annual precipitation falls in summer. The dominance of clear summer skies allows the Sierra to enjoy more sunshine than any other temperate region mountain range in the world, and it is one reason for its appellation as a "Gentle Wilderness."

Precipitation follows a north–south gradient. At 5,000 feet near Mount Lassen, annual precipitation may be 90 inches. At the same elevation at Yosemite in the central Sierra, it drops to 55 inches, while in the south end of the range, no more than 30 inches may be recorded. A west–east gradient also exists, with the western slope receiving the bulk of annual precipitation. At 5,500 feet in the central Sierra by Yosemite, annual precipitation of 75 inches has been measured, while at the exact same elevation on the eastern flank, the measurable precipitation drops to 20 inches.

The temperature and moisture gradients affect tree distribution. At the lowest elevations in the Sierra foothills, between 3,000 feet in the south to 1,000 feet in the north, grow annual grasses such as wild oat mixed with scattered stands of digger pine and blue oak. At slightly higher elevations, between 5,000 and 3,000 feet, grow ponderosa pine and black oak, mixed in with Douglas fir in the north. Douglas fir is not found south of the San Joaquin in the Sierra. Gradually, between 5,000 feet or higher in the south and approximately 4,000 feet in the north, white fir, incense cedar, and Jeffrey pine replace the ponderosa and black oak. The giant sequoia grow in a band at about 6,000 to 8,000 feet along the western slope. The big tree is most abundant in the southern Sierra and reaches its northern limits near I–80.

As you climb higher still, one encounters the "snow forest" or red fir zone. This occurs at the elevation of maximum snowfall, typically between 8,000 or even 9,000 feet in the south to 6,000 feet or less in the north. Red fir is often mixed with lodgepole pine, but lodgepole typically spans a greater elevational range, often growing to timberline. Species at this altitude include foxtail pine in the southern Sierra, as well as western white pine, whitebark pine, western juniper, and mountain hemlock in the north. Alpine tundra dominates above 11,000 feet in the south to less than 8,000 feet in the north.

On the drier, eastern flanks, many of the same species dominate, but they tend to be found at higher elevations than typically found on the western flanks. Furthermore, many species fall out and are not found on the eastern slope at all, or only in small specialized habitats. For example, black oak, a common west slope species, is restricted to a few southern Sierra east side canyons. Other species, such as Douglas fir and sequoia, never cross the Sierra divide to the eastern flank. Aspen, along with pinyon pine, are more abundant on the eastern side of the range.

Many wildlife species such as mule deer, mountain lion, black bear, and the yellow-bellied marmot are found throughout the range, while others such as the Mount Lyell salamander, found only in a narrow alpine strip in and near Yosemite National Park, have a very restricted range. Bighorn sheep, once abundant, are restricted to five small herds, all on the eastern flank.

The Sierran red fox and wolverine are two animals of the subalpine zone that are extremely rare. Very few sightings have been documented during the past twenty years, and these animals may be facing extirpation in the Sierra. Pine marten and fisher, both members of the weasel family, are associated with old-growth forests and are fewer in areas of heavy logging or in the more open forests of the arid eastern flank.

More than two thirds of the Sierra Nevada is administered by public lands agencies—52 percent in nine national forests, 10 percent in national parks, and seven percent among scattered BLM holdings. Nineteen wilderness areas totaling more than 3.3 million acres are scattered from one end of the range to the other. Most of this protected landscape lies in the southern and central Sierra, south of Donner Pass and I–80.

The popularity of these federal lands for recreation is undisputed. More than 30 million people live within a half-day's drive of the Sierra. Mammoth Mountain Ski Resort has more skier days than any other ski area in the United States. Yosemite is the third most visited national park in the country. The John Muir Wilderness is the most heavily used designated wilderness in the nation. Out of 166 national forests in the country, the Inyo, on the eastern flank of the Sierra, is fifth in recreational use. And the national forests of the Sierra account for an eighth of all national forest recreation in the entire country.

Yet, despite all the hoopla about "loving our wildernesses and parks to death," it is not recreation, for the most part, that poses the greatest threat to the Sierra's overall ecological function and health. One factor is the lack of complete ecosystem representation—from the foothills to the alpine—in our protected areas. Only one sixth of the Sierra Nevada has any protective status as designated wilderness, and most of it lies at higher elevation. As Jim Eaton of the California Wilderness Coalition put it, "We've done a good job of protecting a lot of rocks and ice, and that's not necessarily bad…. Nevertheless, by focusing all our efforts on the dramatic landscapes, we've wound up doing a poor job of protecting the biological diversity of the Sierra."

Most of the lower elevation areas with good timber-producing potential lie outside of designated wilderness. Eric Beckwith of the Sierra Biodiversity Project has mapped the remaining old-growth forests of the entire range and reports that only 10 to 15 percent of the Sierran forests are covered with closed canopy old-growth forest stands. Says Beckwith somewhat cynically, "They took efforts to keep heavy volume timber stands out of designated wilderness."

Heavy logging and the accompanying roads fragment forests and reduce wildlife habitat available for old-growth-dependent species. Increasingly, it's clear that to save wildlands ecosystems, we need to include the lower elevation areas that are perhaps less spectacular, but possibly more important biologically than the spartan alpine zones that dominate so much of the protected Sierra Nevada wildlands. Some environmentalists are talking about wildlands restoration—allowing previously logged areas to return to their natural condition—as well as the establishment of buffers and corridors linking protected lands.

But designation of new wildlands or even wildland restoration will not solve all problems. Smog from the Central Valley envelopes the Sierra each summer in a brown poisonous cloud. Researchers at Sequoia National Park have recorded the highest 24-hour ozone level of any unit in the National Park System, including urban parks such as Gateway in New York. And a 1988 study in Yosemite National Park found that 58 percent of the Jeffrey pine had ozone-damaged needles. Smog is literally killing the Sierran forest.

Finally, fire suppression has altered natural forests to such an extent that they are far more vulnerable to drought, insects, and other periodic permutations than in the past. Despite years of Smoky the Bear propaganda on the dangers of forest fires, many forest ecologists now recognize that wildfire is an essential and natural element of Sierran forests and, in fact, of most California ecosystems. Recognizing this, some land managers are attempting to reintroduce fire into ecosystem functioning. However, as more and more people move into the Sierran landscapes, it becomes increasingly difficult to allow fires to burn unrestrained.

Periodic fires kill some trees, reducing competition for water and nutrients and helping to maintain the health of the forest ecosystem. Fires are to forests what wolves are to a deer herd—they thin it out, keeping it healthy. Fires recycle nutrients, create snags that benefit cavity-nesters, and produce woody debris that provides habitat for small mammals and fish, if the logs should tumble into a stream. Logging does not emulate most fire functions and without fire, our wilderness areas will not be truly representative of pristine landscapes.

Despite these problems, the Sierra Nevada is probably the best place in the state to implement ecosystem-wide planning and protection. Recent conferences and discussions have focused on management of the entire Sierra Nevada range as one unit, much as the Tahoe Basin is managed in miniature. This would require looking at the cumulative impacts of all human activities upon the ecological health of the range, linking corridors between wildlands units and increasing the size of buffer zones.

The most heavily used wildernesses in the Sierra include the John Muir, Ansel Adams, Hoover, Golden Trout, and the backcountry portions of Yosemite, Sequoia, and Kings Canyon National Parks. Lightly used wildlands include Bucks Lake, Domeland, Granite Chief, Monarch, Kaiser, and South Sierra.

There are a number of important roadless areas that should be designated as wilderness in the future. These lands are scattered throughout the Sierra and are too numerous to describe in detail. Readers are encouraged to discover these areas on their own and help to garner protection for them. To find out more about them, contact the appropriate National Forest offices.

Beginning in the north and working south, the more important roadless lands in the Sierra Nevada include: Chips Creek along the Feather River, Sierra Buttes near Sierra City, Upper Little Truckee River near Webber Lake, Castle Peak along I–80, Duncan Creek on the American River, Echo–Carson and the Caples Creek area, both north of Carson Pass, Freel Peak near South Lake Tahoe, Pacific Valley near Ebbetts Pass, Bald Peak by Sonora Pass, West Walker River west of Bridgeport, Log Cabin–Saddlebag west of Lee Vining, San Joaquin Ridge by Mammoth Lakes, Wheeler Ridge and Coyote Southeast by Bishop, Sherman Peak and Cannell Peak just north of Lake Isabella, and the Piute Mountains to the south of Lake Isabella.

23 Ansel Adams Wilderness

Lakes, high peaks, and meadows characterize this wilderness that lies at the headwaters of the San Joaquin River.

A view of Garnet Lake below Banner Peak from the John Muir Trail within the Ansel Adams Wilderness.

LOCATION: 80 miles west of Merced, south of Yosemite

SIZE: 228,669 acres

ELEVATION RANGE: 7,600 to 13,157 feet

MILES OF TRAILS: 125

ECOSYSTEMS: alpine tundra, red fir, mixed conifer forest

ADMINISTRATION: Inyo National Forest, Sierra National Forest

MAPS: Sierra National Forest Map, Inyo National Forest Map, Ansel Adams Wilderness Area Map

The Ansel Adams Wilderness was originally known as the Minarets Wilderness. The 228,669-acre area was renamed for famed landscape photographer Ansel Adams, best known for his stunning black and white photographs of Yosemite National Park. The wilderness encompasses the headwaters of the Middle and North Fork of the San Joaquin River just south of Yosemite National Park and west of Mammoth Mountain. The San Joaquin, a candidate for Wild and Scenic River status, is one of few rivers that starts east of the main Sierra crest and ends up flowing west. The wilderness is managed by the Inyo and Sierra National Forests.

For a long time, conservationists worried about development of a proposed trans-Sierra highway that would have followed the San Joaquin drainage up and over the

range to Mammoth Mountain. When the Ansel Adams Wilderness was designated in 1984, it closed the gap between the John Muir Wilderness and Yosemite National Park and killed the highway plans.

Dozens of glacial lakes dot the uplands, and spectacular peaks—including 13,157-foot Mount Ritter and 12,945-foot Mount Banner—create a distinctive skyline recognizable from miles around. The jagged profile of the Minarets, needle-like peaks in the Ritter Range seen from Minaret Summit, is one of the most spectacular views in the entire Sierra.

Like other parts of the Central Sierra, the mountains in this stretch of the range are composed of both granitic rock and metamorphic and volcanic rock. The Ritter Range is largely metamorphosed volcanic rock, but you will see granite outcroppings by Thousand Island Lake and Marie Lake. Metamorphic sedimentary rock also forms a band along San Joaquin Mountain between Agnew Meadow and Gem Lake.

Evidence of past and recent glaciation abounds. A number of small glaciers still cling to the higher peaks, plus some of the best examples of lateral moraines found anywhere on the east side of the mountains are located at the mouths of canyons that empty from the wilderness, including Parker, Walker, and Gibbs Canyons.

Several major Native American trails pass through the wilderness, including Bloody Canyon, which crosses the Sierra via Mono Pass in Yosemite National Park. Another major trail that crosses the Sierra by way of the Middle Fork of the San Joaquin was used for Native American trade, particularly of obsidian from Casa Diablo to the tribes living in the Central Valley.

Modern trails where most recreation use is concentrated include the John Muir and Pacific Crest Trails. In summer, spectacular floral displays occur along the Middle Fork of the San Joaquin River Canyon. Equally dramatic, but less visited, are the string of peaks and lakes that are located between Madera Peak and Rodger Peak along a 14-mile stretch of the Ansel Adams Wilderness adjacent to Yosemite National Park. Because the area receives more precipitation than areas further east, timberline is lower and the entire reach has a very alpine character.

Some of the eastside canyons have sizable aspen patches, which are visually spectacular in the autumn. They are important fawning areas and summer habitat for mule deer, and the Casa Diablo herd, numbering in the thousands, summers in the area between Parker and Walker Lakes.

One of the largest proposed additions to the Ansel Adams Wilderness includes Glass Creek Roadless Area, which lies south of June Lake and north of Mammoth. It includes San Joaquin Ridge and encompasses some of the finest Jeffrey pine forest in California. The Inyo National Forest has recommended non-wilderness designation, perhaps in part to accommodate a proposed expansion of ski lift facilities at Mammoth Mountain.

Ansel Adams Wilderness: East

Ansel Adams Wilderness: West

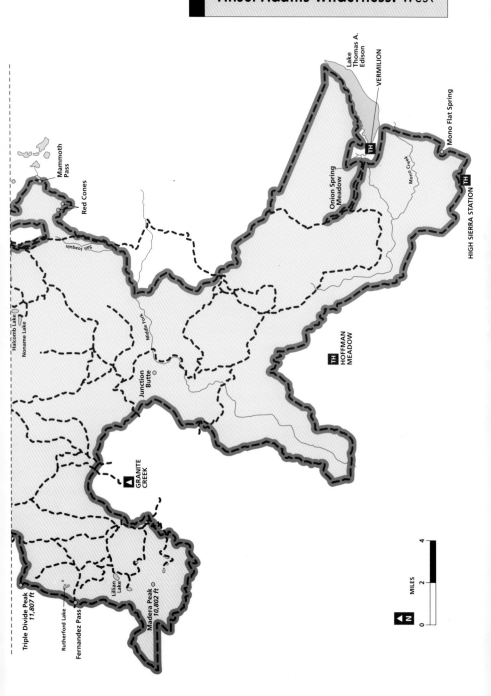

Lake Thomas A. Edison

VERMILION

Mono Flat Spring

Mammoth Pass

Red Cones

Onion Spring Meadow

Mono Creek

HIGH SIERRA STATION

San Joaquin

Halcomb Lake

Noname Lake

Middle Fork

HOFFMAN MEADOW

Junction Butte

GRANITE CREEK

Triple Divide Peak 11,807 ft

Rutherford Lake

Fernandez Pass

Lillian Lake

Madera Peak 10,802 ft

MILES

N

0   2   4

DAY HIKE: SARDINE LAKE
One-way length: 3.5 miles
Low and high elevations: 8,400 to 9,890 feet
Difficulty: moderate to strenuous

This is a spectacular hike up a glaciated canyon on the steep eastern face of the Sierra. Trailhead access is off the paved June Lake Loop Road by Grant Lake— follow the dirt road to the trailhead.

The first part of the trail climbs a glacial moraine, then descends to Walker Lake. When you get to the shoreline trail, head up the canyon toward Sardine Lake some 3.0 miles away. You will cross the boundary for the Ansel Adams Wilderness in 1.2 miles as the trail continues to climb via switchback through aspen groves, open sage-flower hillsides, and patches of timber, but with great views throughout. You will pass a waterfall and arrive at the lakeshore, where you will have superb views of Mono Lake. Should you feel inclined, you can continue another 2.5 miles up to Mono Pass on the Yosemite National Park border.

DAY HIKE: SHADOW LAKE
One-way length: 3.6 miles
Low and high elevations: 8,330 to 8,750 feet
Difficulty: moderate

Shadow Lake lies in a rocky glacial cirque just below the 13,157-foot Mount Ritter, the highest peak in the Ansel Adams Wilderness. The trail to the lake is heavily used because it accesses such spectacular country and is the major route into the Ansel Adams Wilderness. If you're hoping to find solitude, you'd best look elsewhere! However, if you want stunning flowery meadows and striking alpine scenery, this is a good bet.

From Highway 395, take Highway 209 to Mammoth Lakes and continue to the Devil's Postpile National Monument. (*Note:* If you're not camping in the monument area, you may be required to leave your car at Mammoth Lakes and take an Intravalley shuttle bus. Be sure to check locally.) After you pass the entrance station, go a few miles further, then turn on the road for Agnew Meadows Campground. The trailhead is just beyond the campground.

From here, the path gradually drops through open sage-covered flowery slopes and scattered timber to the Middle Fork of the San Joaquin River. At 2.0 miles, you will reach Olaine Lake, and another 0.3 mile beyond this brings you to the Shadow Lake Trail junction. The river trail continues straight ahead, but the route to Shadow Lake turns west and crosses the river. The trail now switchbacks uphill until you reach Shadow Lake's rocky shore. Take time to enjoy the vista of Mount Ritter, Banner Peak, and the Minaret Crest. For those wishing a more extended hike or a longer backpack trip, connect with the John Muir Trail at Shadow Lake's western shore to access other lakes both north and south.

OVERNIGHT HIKE: RUTHERFORD LAKE
One-way length: 10 miles
Low and high elevations: 7,500 to 9,780 feet
Difficulty: moderate

This alpine lake is situated at timberline surrounded by barren granite peaks of the Clark Range just south of the Yosemite National Park border. Although there are several ways to get to the trailhead, the one with the least turns is the Minarets Road, which leaves the community of South Fork just south of Bass Lake. Follow the paved road beyond Minarets Work Station to the trailhead at the Clover Meadow Campground. If you have a good backroad vehicle, there are several other trailheads at the end of dirt roads to the west that shave some of the distance off the hike.

About 1.0 mile of slightly uphill hiking from the Clover Meadow Trailhead will bring you to another parking area and trailhead where the route to Rutherford Lake heads north (right). This hike, which travels 2.5 miles through forested terrain to the wilderness boundary, crosses Madera Creek and heads northwest toward Lillian Lake, passing several other trail junctions in rapid succession. Two miles along the trail, you will reach the junction for Lillian Lake, which continues west. The trail heading to Rutherford Lake is to the north (right). Continue through sparse woodlands for 1.4 miles to where the junction for Rainbow Lake heads west. Maintain your northerly hike for another 1.0 mile to Fernandez Creek, which you need to cross. The trail now climbs rather steeply for another 1.0 mile to another trail junction. Straight ahead is Fernandez Pass and Yosemite National Park; to the right and uphill 0.5 mile or so lies Rutherford Lake.

OVERNIGHT HIKE: MINARET LAKE
One-way length: 7.4 miles
Low and high elevations: 7,000 to 9,793 feet
Difficulty: moderate

Minaret Lake sits in a spectacular granite glacial bowl below the ragged peaks of the Minarets. The trailhead is located at the Devil's Postpile National Monument Campground, accessible from Highway 395 via Mammoth Lakes. A mandatory shuttle bus operates between 7:30 a.m. and 5:30 p.m. during the summer months; camping quotas exist, so check with the Mammoth Ranger Station for the latest information.

From the trailhead, hike 1.5 miles north along the John Muir Trail by Johnson Lake to the junction with the Minaret Lake Trail, which heads west along Minaret Creek, climbing steadily to timberline and the lake. The trail circles the lake to the north, offering potential campsites. It's possible to continue a mile or so more to the north to camp at Ceilia and Iceberg Lakes.

24 Bucks Lake Wilderness

Bucks Lake Wilderness, which contains a portion of the Pacific Crest Trail, is best described as a small area of gentle terrain with glaciated granite basins holding a few lakes.

Near Silver Lake in Bucks Lake Wilderness.

LOCATION: 15 miles west of Quincy in northern Sierra

SIZE: 21,000 acres

ELEVATION RANGE: 2,000 to 7,017 feet

MILES OF TRAILS: 25

ECOSYSTEMS: chaparral, red fir, and mixed conifer-oak forest

ADMINISTRATION: Plumas National Forest

MAPS: Plumas National Forest Map, Bucks Lake Wilderness Area Map

The 21,000-acre Bucks Lake Wilderness lies 15 miles west of Quincy in the Plumas National Forest. It is currently the only designated wilderness in the Sierra Nevada north of I–80 and was given protection as part of the 1984 California Wilderness Act. The wilderness takes its name from Bucks Lake, a hydroelectric reservoir built in 1925. The area is generally rolling in topographic relief, except for where it plunges into the North Fork of the Feather River Canyon. The lowest elevations, located along the North Fork, are at 2,000 feet, while the highest point is 7,017-foot Spanish Peak. The Pacific Crest Trail runs through the wilderness from south to north, with secondary trails providing access to lake basins off the main divide.

The wilderness is dominated by granitic outcrops, although some bands of serpentine rock are found in the area. All of the higher elevations have been heavily glaciated, providing a number of small lakes and basins. Silver Lake, found on the eastern border of the wilderness, lies in a glacially carved valley.

Most of the higher elevations are forested with red fir interspersed with mountain hemlock. The lower elevations are mixed conifer forests that include ponderosa pine, black oak, Douglas fir, and other species. The 1,300-acre Mount Pleasant–Spanish Peak proposed Research Natural Area lies within the wilderness and protects a representative sample of red fir forest–mesic meadow complex.

A portion of the Bucks Mountain deer herd winters in the lower elevations along the North Fork of the Feather River Canyon. One bald eagle is known to nest in the wilderness, as well as the rare California spotted owl. Domestic livestock grazing still occurs in this wildlands.

If roadless lands along the North Fork Canyon were added and a few dirt roads closed in the Bucks Creek drainage, it would be possible to expand this wilderness by at least another 20,000 acres. Partially adjacent to and immediately north of the North Fork of the Feather River lies the 12,700-acre Chips Creek Roadless Area, one of the largest undesignated wildlands in the Plumas National Forest. Its designation would significantly increase the biological value of the Bucks Lakes Wilderness and allow for a larger wildlands block, albeit divided by the highway and railroad corridor along the North Fork Feather River. Chips Creek is also known for its huge old-growth Douglas fir, white fir, ponderosa pine, and Jeffrey pine.

DAY HIKE: SILVER LAKE TO PACIFIC CREST TRAIL
One-way length: 2.2 miles
Low and high elevations: 5,000 to 6,700 feet
Difficulty: moderate

This hike begins at beautiful Silver Lake, where there is a Forest Service campground on the shore that makes for a good weekend base. From the campground, the trail climbs through open scattered timber past a number of small lakes, including Gold and Rock Lakes, then reaches the Pacific Crest Trail, which runs north-south along the top of a major ridge that marks the center of the wilderness. From this perspective, you are rewarded with great views of the glacially carved Silver Lake and the rolling northern Sierra Nevada. If you are inclined to hike more, the Pacific Crest Trail offers miles of exploration both north and south.

Bucks Lake Wilderness

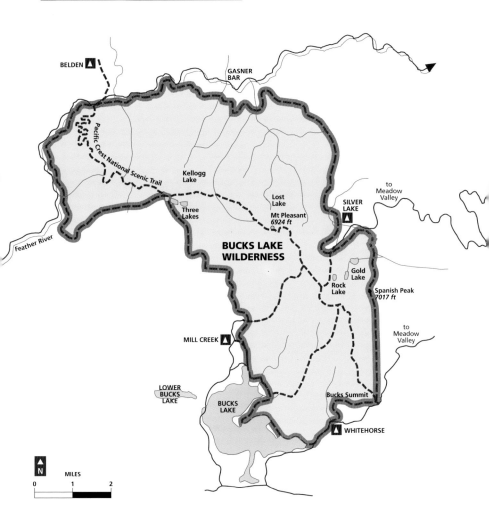

BELDEN

GASNER BAR

Pacific Crest National Scenic Trail

Kellogg Lake

Lost Lake

to Meadow Valley

SILVER LAKE

Three Lakes

Mt Pleasant 6924 ft

Feather River

BUCKS LAKE WILDERNESS

Gold Lake

Rock Lake

Spanish Peak 7017 ft

to Meadow Valley

MILL CREEK

LOWER BUCKS LAKE

BUCKS LAKE

Bucks Summit

WHITEHORSE

N

MILES

0   1   2

OVERNIGHT HIKE: PACIFIC CREST TRAIL / BUCKS SUMMIT
TO NORTH FORK FEATHER RIVER
One-way length: 20 miles
Low and high elevations: 2,300 to 6,900 feet
Difficulty: moderate

As a good introduction to the Bucks Lake Wilderness, with a sampling of different vegetation from red fir forest to oak woodlands, this hike has much to offer. As described, it is basically a point-to-point shuttle trip, but one can hike part way and return along the same track from either trailhead. To avoid having to haul a heavy pack up out of the Feather River Canyon, the recommended starting point is Bucks Summit west of Quincy. You reach the trailhead by driving 11.0 miles west on the Bucks Lake Road to Bucks Summit.

The first part of the trail climbs through chaparral and scattered trees until you reach the rolling ridgeline that makes up the bulk of the Bucks Lake Wilderness. The Pacific Crest Trail turns north, passing through open, red fir forest. About 5.0 miles into the hike, there is a side trail that descends to Rock, Gold, and Silver Lakes, where water is available if needed. About 15.0 miles out, you will pass Three Lakes, where it's possible to camp for the night. The final 5.0 miles descends rather steeply into the North Fork of the Feather River Canyon, passing through a lovely mixture of canyon oak, bigleaf maple, and Douglas fir forests. The Feather Canyon section of the Pacific Crest Trail is hikeable most of the winter, when the higher elevation trails are closed.

Carson–Iceberg Wilderness

The Carson–Iceberg Wilderness features twelve peaks exceeding 10,000 feet, long valleys with meadows, and the headwaters of Carson, Stanislaus, and Mokelumne Rivers.

A view from Sonora Peak toward White Mountain, showing the glaciated volcanic rock that makes up the Carson–Iceberg Wilderness.

LOCATION: 40 miles east of Sonora

SIZE: 160,000 acres

ELEVATION RANGE: 5,000 to 11,459 feet

MILES OF TRAILS: 190

ECOSYSTEMS: riparian meadows, red fir, western white pine, alpine tundra

ADMINISTRATION: Stanislaus National Forest, Toiyabe N.F.

MAPS: Toiyabe N.F. / Bridgeport Ranger District Map, Stanislaus N.F. Map, Carson–Iceberg Wilderness Area Map

The 160,000-acre Carson–Iceberg Wilderness straddles the Sierra crest, with the Pacific Crest Trail crossing the wilderness south to north. Though it exhibits heavily glaciated peaks, this wilderness is dominated by volcanic rock that harbors fewer lakes than tends to dominate granitic-based portions of the Sierra. The Dardanelles, highly prominent battlement-like peaks in the southwest corner of the wilderness near the Clark Fork River, are one of the sites of andesite volcanic flows that poured out across the region 20 million years ago. The Dardanelles Cone is a hard plug of andesite lava that was eroded from other softer surrounding volcanic rock. Most of the lava erupted from a volcano near Bridgeport some nine million years ago. One tongue of lava flowed down the Stanislaus River as far as Knights Ferry; another tongue went down the Tuolumne

River and can be seen at Rancheria Mountain within Yosemite National Park. Other volcanic centers within the wilderness include Silver Peak, Markleeville Peak, and Highland Peak.

The lowest point of the wilderness barely exceeds 5,000 feet near Donnell Lake, while more than a dozen peaks along the crest exceed 10,000 feet. Sonora Peak, at 11,459 feet, is the highest point.

The eastern flank is arid and dominated by open meadows that have spectacular floral displays in summer, as well as sagebrush, aspen, and pockets of timber. The western side has a greater timber component. Major tree species include aspen, red fir, white fir, lodgepole pine, sugar pine, and Jeffrey pine. One giant western juniper has a measured girth of 36 feet! The tree, located along the Corral Valley Trail, is thought to be the largest juniper in the Sierra Nevada.

The Carson–Iceberg is home to the threatened Paiute cutthroat trout. The fish is native only to Silver King Creek, a tributary of the East Fork of the Carson River that lies within the wilderness. With one of the smallest native ranges of any trout in the West, a series of waterfalls has isolated it long enough for it to develop into a separate species, similar to the Lahontan cutthroat to which it is most closely related. Paiute trout is also found in Coyote Valley and Corral Valley Creeks.

The name "Carson–Iceberg" honors Kit Carson, a frontier fur trapper who crossed the Sierra Nevada with John Fremont in 1844 just north of the present-day wilderness. Later, in 1861, the town of Silver Mountain City was founded after Norwegian miners discovered the mineral along the aptly named Silver Creek, which forms the northern boundary of the wilderness area. Silver Mountain City was the county seat until that honor was bestowed on Markleeville in 1875. Silver Mountain City soon slipped into ruin and was replaced by Silver King, located on Silver King Creek. Silver King was both a mining and lumbering center. The Nevada mining boom required massive amounts of timber for mine shaft supports, firewood, house construction, and railroad ties, and nearly all of it came from the eastern side of the Sierra, including the upper Carson River drainage.

The next boom involved livestock. Like most of the Sierra, the free grazing on the public domain attracted sheep and cattle herders; as a result, the entire region was severely overgrazed. With the establishment of national forests, grazing came under some regulation, but not nearly enough to eliminate ecological damage to the landscape. Today, ten livestock allotments are allowed in this wilderness. According to the Stanislaus Forest Plan, the vast majority of rangelands on the forest are in unsatisfactory condition due to overgrazing, with more of them declining rather than improving.

According to the California Department of Fish and Game, cattle-damaged riparian areas are one of the major reasons for the decline of the threatened Paiute cutthroat trout. A portion of the Silver Fork was fenced (at taxpayer expense), but according to state fishery biologists, livestock still trample the surrounding landscape and destroy springs and seeps that feed the main stretch of stream, increasing sedimentation and decreasing habitat effectiveness.

The Carson–Iceberg Wilderness was designated as part of the 1984 California Wilderness Act and includes portions of the Stanislaus, Eldorado, and Toiyabe National Forests. Unlike many newly designated areas, visitor use decreased after Carson–Iceberg was declared wilderness, but now visitation is on the rise.

Nearly 100,000 roadless acres adjoin this wilderness. The largest parcels include the 10,000-acre Pacific Valley RA, located just west of Ebbetts Pass. At one time, a ski resort was planned here, but the Forest Service has recommended against development of the area and plans to maintain its naturalness. The Pacific Valley RA is a critical link between the Carson–Iceberg and Mokelumne Wilderness Areas. Between 7,000 and 9,600 feet in elevation, Pacific Valley contains glaciated valleys, meadows, and dramatic summits such as Lookout Peak.

To the south between the Clark Fork Valley Road and the Sonora Pass Road lies the 20,500-acre Bald Peak RA, which is comprised of considerable granitic outcrops, scattered timber, and summits of up to 11,462 feet. In its Forest Plan, the Stanislaus National Forest has recommended that the Bald Mountain area be added to the Carson–Iceberg Wilderness.

DAY HIKE: DARDANELLES LOOP
Loop length: 7 miles
Low and high elevations: 7,200 to 8,100 feet
Difficulty: moderate

This is a good day hike or short overnighter, providing numerous views of the spectacular Dardanelles, a volcanic castle-like landmark visible from throughout much of the southwest corner of the Carson–Iceberg Wilderness. Be forewarned that the trail can sometimes be difficult to follow in places where cattle have made numerous trails of their own, so bring a map and compass and keep your eyes open.

To find the trailhead, look for a paved road to the north signed for the Clark Fork of the Stanislaus, located on Highway 108 approximately 17.0 miles west of Sonora Pass. Just about 1.0 mile from the highway, turn left on Forest Road 6N06 and head west approximately 7.0 miles to the County Line Trailhead.

From the trailhead, hike northeast (right) toward McCormick Creek, passing through forests of Jeffrey pine and white fir. Just after passing a meadow, a trail junction is reached. Take the left-hand trail, which is marked with red blazes on trees, and begin ascending switchbacks through a red fir forest to a saddle at 8,100 feet. To the east lies the 9,500-foot Dardanelles Cone, while to the southwest lies another 8,834-foot peak, part of the Dardanelles system. From the saddle, the trail—often faint and sometimes difficult to distinguish from all the cattle trails— heads in a generally north and westerly direction for perhaps 0.3 mile before it turns to the southwest. If you lose the trail in the confusion of cow pies, just hug the northwest-facing slope of the 8,834-foot peak and head southwest. Eventually, you will enter a small drainage that you can continue to follow downslope through miles of red fir, white fir, and western white pine until you intercept the well-worn trail from Sword and Lost Lakes, about 2.25 miles from the saddle. Turn southeast (left) on this trail and proceed back to the trailhead.

Carson–Iceberg Wilderness

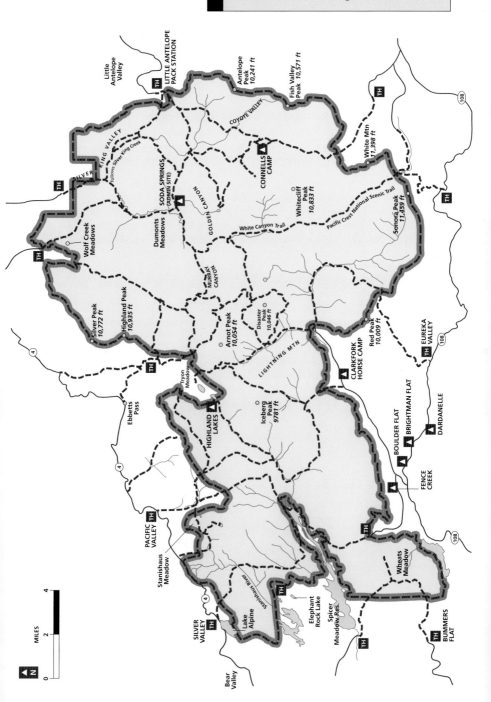

DAY HIKE: SONORA PEAK
One-way length: 5 miles
Low and high elevations: 9,400 to 11,459 feet
Difficulty: moderate

This is a hike to the highest peak in the Carson–Iceberg Wilderness, which offers spectacular views of the surrounding landscape. The trailhead is located at Sonora Pass on Highway 108.

From Sonora Pass, follow the Pacific Crest Trail for approximately 1.5 miles. You'll be crossing open slopes with scattered timber in a generally north-northwest direction. This area is testimony to the abuse domestic livestock impose upon our lands. Along the entire route, there is evidence of highly degraded plant communities and severely eroding slopes as a consequence of livestock grazing. Where the Pacific Crest Trail turns sharply to the east, begin to hike up the slope in a north-northwesterly direction. You'll continue to climb until you reach a broad sloping shoulder of Sonora Peak. Follow the slope to the summit.

OVERNIGHT HIKE: EAST CARSON RIVER TRAIL
One-way length: 23 miles
Low and high elevations: 6,240 to 10,300 feet
Difficulty: moderate

This trail, a good way to get into the heart of the Carson–Iceberg Wilderness, has more privacy and plenty of campsites, if you don't mind sharing them with cows. The trailhead is located south of Markleeville. Drive Highway 4 and 89 to Wolf Creek Road, turn east and go to Wolf Creek Meadows, then turn left at a sign for the trailhead.

The trail first heads southeast to Gray's Cross in Silver King Valley along East Carson River, where you pass out of the wilderness. It crosses the river, which can be difficult in the spring, then follows an old jeep trail up through Vasquero Cow Camp. The road brings you back to the river, which must be crossed again, as you re-enter the wilderness. Here you continue up the East Carson Valley in a southwest direction until the jeep trail ends and the hiking trail begins. You will cross several large clearings, including Dumonts Meadow and Fall Meadows, and pass Carson Falls. From the falls, the trail continues 4.5 miles along the river, passing White Canyon enroute until you intercept the Pacific Crest Trail. You will continue on the Pacific Crest Trail 6.0 miles to Wolf Lake, which lies just below 11,459-foot Sonora Peak.

Desolation Wilderness **26**

With granite basins, rolling alpine country, and more than 130 lakes, Desolation Wilderness, located just west of South Lake Tahoe, makes for heavy use, but lovely hiking terrain.

Lake Tahoe from Mount Talac, Desolation Wilderness.

Averaging 12.5 miles long by 8 miles wide, the compact 63,475-acre Desolation Wilderness lies directly southwest of Lake Tahoe in the Eldorado National Forest, taking in much of the high country in a sub-range of the Sierra known as the Crystal Range. The highest peak, Pyramid, is 9,983 feet in elevation. Several other summits, including Mount Tallac, Mount Price, Dicks Peak, Jacks Peak, and Ralston Peak, all exceed 9,000 feet, but the average elevation lies between 7,500 and 8,300 feet. Originally set aside as the Desolation Primitive Area, the status was upgraded to wilderness in 1969.

There are over 100 lakes and numerous streams dotting this wilderness. Combined with dramatic cliffs, bald granitic peaks, and meadows, Desolation Wilderness is one of the more scenic areas in California's wilderness system.

LOCATION: west of South Lake Tahoe

SIZE: 63,475 acres

ELEVATION RANGE: 6,500 to 10,000 feet

MILES OF TRAILS: 75

ECOSYSTEMS: alpine, red fir, mixed conifer forest

ADMINISTRATION: Eldorado National Forest

MAPS: Eldorado N.F. Map, Tahoe Basin N.F. Map, Desolation Wilderness Area Map

The largest water body, Lake Aloha, was formed by damming its outlet, flooding several small lakes that sat in the valley. The view of Lake Tahoe from Mount Tallac is perhaps one of the finer vistas in the entire Sierra.

The wilderness takes its name for the barren, rocky basins that characterize its heights. The area is not particularly high by Sierra standards, but the heavily glaciated landscape—still largely devoid of soil, hence vegetation—and the heavy snowfall that limits tree growth make for a spectacular, if not stark country.

Like much of this section of the Sierra, the rocks of the Desolation are a mixture of granitic basement rock interspersed with metasedimentary rock. Jacks Peak and Dicks Peaks both have a combination of the two basic rock types, while the area that includes Susy Lake and Mount Tallac consists of metavolcanic rock.

The granitic rock that makes up the Desolation area were intruded between 80 to 100 million years ago. Molten rock cooled deep in the earth, later to be uplifted and eroded to expose the present granitic basins of the wilderness.

Beginning approximately 33 million years ago, periodic volcanic eruptions occurred, bringing molten rock to the surface where it was thrown out with explosive force. This continued on and off for millions of years, until about seven million years ago, when eruptions nearly ceased. Meanwhile, uplift of the range began and has quickened in just the last two million years, with the main Sierra and Carson Ranges continuing to rise while the intervening valley subsided to create the Tahoe Basin. New eruptions dammed the Truckee River, flooding the basin and creating Lake Tahoe.

The finishing touches to the landscape occurred during the past two million years when several major glacial periods buried the high country of the wilderness in glacial ice. Most recently, ice sheets over 1,000 feet thick smothered all but the highest peaks, grinding out the granitic basins, creating the lakes, and removing most of the soil, leaving behind the barren landscape. Tongues of this glacial ice flowed down toward Lake Tahoe, creating Emerald Bay, Fallen Leaf, Cascade Lake, and Echo Lake.

In essence, the region's geological history determined its subsequent human use. Areas where the volcanic rocks have not been stripped away tend to have deeper soils and fewer lakes, as found in the Carson–Iceberg area further south. Had it not been for glaciation, the preponderance of granitic bedrock, and the lack of suitable soil, much of what is now Desolation Wilderness would be treed and have likely been logged and never set aside in any kind of protective status. Such is the fate granted by differing geology.

The heavy precipitation favors forests of red fir, white fir, Jeffrey pine, western white pine, mountain hemlock, western juniper, and whitebark pine. Red fir is probably the most abundant species.

Given its proximity to Lake Tahoe and I–80, it's not surprising that Desolation Wilderness receives some of the heaviest recreational use in the Sierra. The most popular trailheads include Fallen Leaf Lake, Echo, Eagle Falls, and Glen Alpine. Those seeking solitude should consider other trails! The Forest Service, arguing that human use was degrading the wilderness, now restricts access through a daily quota system. Ironically, while this agency restricts backpackers and hikers, who for the most part, have little real impact on the land, it does permit livestock grazing, a far more damaging activity, to occur in the wilderness. (See page 303 for more information about grazing's impact on wildlands.)

Other significant roadless areas proposed for wilderness near Desolation include the Echo–Carson RA south of Highway 50. Here, the Carson Range and main crest of the Sierra merge at the headwaters of the Truckee River, forming meadows that are a popular destination for hikers.

Just east of the Echo–Carson RA is the Freel Peak RA, located in the Carson Range southeast of South Lake Tahoe. A portion of the Tahoe Rim Trail passes through this roadless area. Freel meadows and the alpine cushion plant communities on Freel Peak are major attractions of this proposed wilderness.

The best hiking period is after July 1, prior to that time, snow cover is still more or less continuous. September and early October can be great times to visit, since there are fewer people and no bugs. There's almost no place in the Desolation Wilderness you can't reach in a long day hike, although it would be easy to put together loops and trips that could be overnighters.

DAY HIKE: GROUSE LAKE TRAIL
One-way length: 2.2 miles
Low and high elevations: 7,000 to 8,200 feet
Difficulty: easy

The trail to Grouse Lake is an easy hike to a forested glacial basin, with several other lakes located less than a mile away in the southwest corner of the wilderness. To find the trailhead, travel Highway 50 to Wrights Lake Road, which is 13.0 miles west of Echo Summit. The trailhead is located at the eastern shore of Wrights Lake, approximately 9.0 miles from Highway 50. It is about 1.25 miles from the trailhead at Wrights Lake Inlet to the wilderness boundary, where the trail splits: The left fork goes to Twin Lakes and Island Lakes—both worthy destinations themselves—and the right fork heads into Grouse Lake Basin. At first, the trail continues upward at a gentle grade, then becomes steep over open granite mixed with scattered trees to the rockbound lakeshore. Smith Lake, about 0.25 mile further, lies at 8,700 feet— nearly at timberline—and offers great views of the basin.

DAY HIKE: RALSTON PEAK
One-way length: 4.5 miles
Low and high elevations: 6,600 to 9,235 feet
Difficulty: strenuous

Ralston Peak offers a great day hike destination for those willing to climb for a view. The trailhead is located right on Highway 50 at Camp Sacramento about 5.5 miles west of Echo Summit. The trail climbs continuously upward on a giant glacial moraine in a general northerly direction. As you ascend the slope, you are treated to views of Lake of the Woods and Lake Aloha—the largest water body in the wilderness. Eventually, the trail turns to the southwest and heads toward the summit of Ralston Peak. Directly below Ralston Peak lies three cirque lakes: Cagwin, Ralston, and Tamarack. Great views of Desolation Wilderness spread out to the north, and in the distance one can see Lake Tahoe and Mount Tallac.

Desolation Wilderness

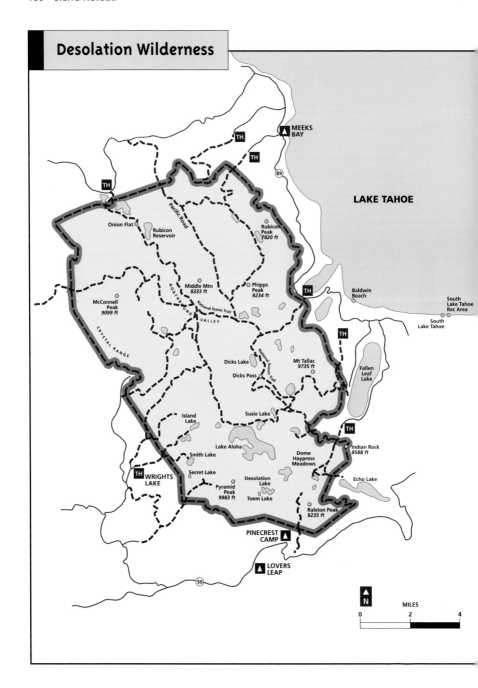

DAY HIKE: MOUNT TALLAC
One-way length: 4.6 miles
Low and high elevations: 6,500 to 9,736 feet
Difficulty: moderate

Mount Tallac offers one of the more spectacular views in the entire Sierra and certainly one of the best vistas for effort expended. From the top, Lake Tahoe spreads out below with views of Desolation Wilderness visible behind you. Do not climb this without a camera and time to spend enjoying the view. You can reach the trailhead by driving Highway 89 north from South Lake Tahoe. In about 3.2 miles, you will pass the Forest Service Lake Tahoe Visitor Center; go approximately 1.0 mile and watch for a signed road for Baldwin Beach on the right (north). Directly opposite, on the left or south, is the turn you want for the trailhead. In about 1.0 mile, you will come to the parking area.

The hike climbs a thinly forested moraine, offering great views of the glacially carved Fallen Leaf Lake. You will enter Desolation Wilderness about 1.5 miles up the trail, just as you encounter Floating Island Lake. The route continues past Cathedral Lake up a glacial headwall and on to the final open slope that climbs toward Mount Tallac's summit.

OVERNIGHT HIKE: MEEKS CREEK DRAINAGE
One-way length: 8.1 miles to Rubicon Lake
Low and high elevations: 6,250 to 8,400 feet
Difficulty: moderate

This hike provides access to a lesser-used part of Desolation Wilderness along Meeks Creek, with eight lakes strung along the length of the drainage. Geologists call this string of glacially carved water bodies "paternoster lakes," so named for their resemblance to rosary beads.

To find the trailhead, drive Highway 50 north approximately 16.5 miles from South Lake Tahoe to Meeks Bay Campground, where the trailhead is a couple hundred yards north from the entrance. The first part of the trail follows an old road that climbs gently and turns into a path at the Desolation Wilderness boundary. Continue to ascend southwest through forests of red fir, lodgepole pine, Jeffrey pine, and western white pine, passing several potential campsites along Meeks Creek. Eventually, the trail climbs to Lake Genevieve, which is 4.5 miles from the trailhead. About 0.3 mile further, you will reach Crag Lake with Crag Peak rising above it. There are good campsites here. The trail to Stoney Ridge Lake continues along tumbling Meeks Creek, passing enroute shallow Shadow Lake. Stoney Ridge Lake is the largest of the lakes in this basin and has numerous places to camp along its shore. The final 1.5 miles to Rubicon Lake is steep, and most people just doing an overnighter will probably wish to stop here at one of the many campsites around the lake. However, those with more time might consider going further. Another 1.0 mile takes you to Phipps Pass, where it's possible to continue to Phipps Lake or down to Middle Velma Lake 13.0 miles from the trailhead. It's possible to take the Pacific Crest Trail north to a junction with a trail to Lake Genevieve, then back to Meeks Bay, thus making a loop of the trip.

27 Dinkey Lakes Wilderness

This wilderness, comprised of timbered, rolling terrain with a few lakes, is separated from the larger John Muir Wilderness by just a single road.

Sunset at Mystery Lake, Dinkey Lakes Wilderness.

LOCATION: 70 miles east of Fresno

SIZE: 30,000 acres

ELEVATION RANGE: 8,000 to 10,619 feet

MILES OF TRAILS: 44

ECOSYSTEMS: red fir and mixed conifer forest

ADMINISTRATION: Sierra National Forest

MAPS: Sierra National Forest Map, Dinkey Lakes Wilderness Area Map

South and east of Huntington Lake lies the 30,000-acre Dinkey Lakes Wilderness. Managed by the Sierra National Forest, Dinkey Lakes was designated in 1984. The John Muir Wilderness lies to its east and is separated from it by a single off-highway vehicle route.

According to popular lore, Dinkey Lakes was named in the 1860s for a hunter's dog, Dinkey, who was injured in a fight with a bear. Lying between 8,000 and 10,619 feet, most of the Dinkey Lakes Wilderness is a rolling, timbered plateau that was formerly glaciated. Two prominent peaks—Dogtooth and Three Sisters—provide good views of the surrounding high country. The glaciers carved 16 small lakes that are popular with fishers. A few meadows dot the area, and nearly all of them suffer from the ill effects of livestock grazing.

DAY HIKE: MYSTERY LAKE
One-way length: 1.6 miles
Low and high elevations: 8,590 to 9,000 feet
Difficulty: easy

Mystery Lake is little more than a stroll through the woods, but the setting is quite nice. A rugged granite dome rises over the lake, which has a nice forested shoreline. To find the trailhead, first drive Highway 168 to Shaver Lake, then take Dinkey Creek Road 9.0 miles until you come to a sign for an unpaved road on your left, leading to the trailhead. Continue on this dirt road, following signs at all road junctions for approximately 7.0 miles to the trailhead.

The hike begins gently through forests to the wilderness boundary sign 0.5 mile from the trailhead. Follow Dinkey Creek for 1.3 miles to a trail junction, where you turn right (south) and switchback up a slope to the lake. It's possible to continue on this trail, passing Swede Lake, South Lake, and First Dinkey Lake, and return to the trailhead along Dinkey Creek to make a loop of about 7.0 miles.

DAY HIKE: DINKEY LAKES
One-way length: 7.5 miles
Low and high elevations: 8,400 to 9,930 feet
Difficulty: moderate

The Dinkey Lakes Trail provides access to the cluster of lakes in the southwest corner of the wilderness. The trailhead is located adjacent to Courtright Reservoir, 36 miles from Shaver Lake. To get to the trailhead, take Highway 168 to Shaver Lake and drive Dinkey Creek Road toward Wishon Reservoir, then follow signs to Trapper Springs Campground on Courtright Reservoir, where the trailhead is located.

From the trailhead, you will hike generally northwest on a gradual incline through forest, passing an arm of Courtright Reservoir at the border of the wilderness. At 3.0 miles, you will pass a junction for a trail to Helms Meadow; continue straight ahead toward Cliff Lake, which is 5.0 miles from the trailhead and the first water body on this hike. Just above Cliff Lake is another trail heading northeast to Helms Meadow: Keep left, climb to a small pass, and descend to Rock Lake. Just beyond Rock Lake is Second Dinkey Lake. Another 1.0 mile brings you to meadow-rimmed Dinkey Lake.

Dinkey Lakes Wilderness

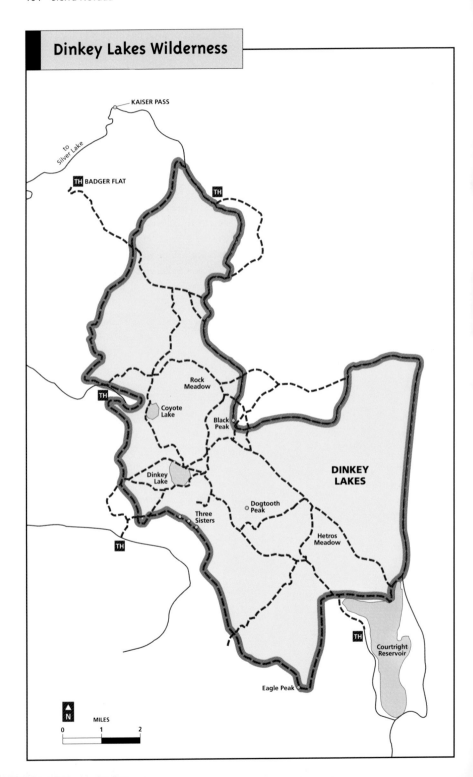

KAISER PASS

to Silver Lake

TH BADGER FLAT

TH

TH

Rock Meadow

Coyote Lake

Black Peak

DINKEY LAKES

Dinkey Lake

Dogtooth Peak

Three Sisters

Hetros Meadow

TH

TH

Courtright Reservoir

Eagle Peak

N

MILES

0   1   2

Domeland Wilderness 28

Containing the South Fork Kern River, Domeland Wilderness is a forested plateau known for its "church" domes of white granite.

Granite outcrops frame Pilot Peak on the southern fringe of the Domeland Wilderness.

Taking in the southern end of the Kern Plateau, the 130,986-acre Domeland is the southernmost wilderness in the Sierra Nevada. Elevations range from 3,000 to 9,730 feet. The South Fork of the Kern runs the length of the wilderness and is a designated Wild and Scenic River. Below Rockhouse Meadow, the South Fork enters a steep, granitic gorge that has no trail access for 15 miles. Although granitic bedrock dominates the region, volcanic outcrops occur between Taylor and Manter Creeks and a basalt flow is evident in Dark Canyon near the northwest border.

As a consequence of its general aridity as well as lower elevation, the Domeland offers year-round access. The rounded domes of Yosemite come to mind when visiting this wilderness. Not nearly as crowded as Yosemite, solitude is a

LOCATION: 70 miles northeast of Bakersfield

SIZE: 130,986 acres

ELEVATION RANGE: 3,000 to 9,730 feet

MILES OF TRAILS: 45

ECOSYSTEMS: pinyon pine, Jeffrey pine, mixed conifer

ADMINISTRATION: Sequoia National Forest, BLM Bakersfield

MAPS: Sequoia National Forest Map, Domeland Wilderness Area Map

hallmark of the region, especially if you venture off the major access routes, including the Pacific Crest Trail that runs through the northwest corner of the area. Manter Meadow on the western fringe is another popular destination. As with other southern Sierra wildernesses, the Domeland often seems more like a cow pasture than a wildlands. According to the California Department of Fish and Game, severe degradation of riparian areas and meadows continues to threaten fisheries and other wildlife here.

Pinyon pine woodlands dominate the eastern side of the wilderness, while Jeffrey pine covers much of the higher elevations to the west. Black oak is found along the western margins and adds a bit of color, especially in the fall. Lodgepole pine and red fir are scattered here and there.

Along the western border of the Domeland Wilderness lies the Sirretta Peak Wilderness Study Area. The top of Sirretta Peak is part of the Twisselmann Botanical Area. The 859-acre area encompasses the summit and slopes of 9,978-foot Sirretta Peak, which is the southernmost known range for foxtail pine in the Sierra. In addition, limber pine as well as nine other plant species also reach their southernmost known distribution in this same area.

The California Wilderness Act of 1984 added 32,000 acres to the original Domeland Wilderness, including the Woodpecker Meadow drainage in the northwest corner. Bald Mountain Botanical Area lies just north of here along the wilderness boundary. Composed of metasedimentary rocks, the soils produced from them hold moisture better than the surrounding granitic material, hence the mountain is home to more kinds of plants, including limber pine and the endemic Bald Mountain potentilla, than many surrounding areas. A lookout was built atop the mountain in 1951.

The 1994 California Desert Bill greatly expanded the Domelands Wilderness by adding roadless BLM lands, mostly along the eastern border to the existing Forest Service wilderness. Arid and covered with pinyon pine, the Chimney Creek drainage contains massive granitic outcrops and contains the largest concentration of *Nolina parryi,* a large flowering yucca that reaches heights of 15 feet.

DAY HIKE: LONG VALLEY TRAIL
One-way length: 3 miles
Low and high elevations: 4,800 to 5,270 feet
Difficulty: moderate

This hike takes one into the Domeland Wilderness to the South Fork of the Kern, a Wild and Scenic River in the heart of the wilderness. The trail begins at the BLM's Long Valley Campground, reachable from Highway 178 by the BLM's Chimney Peak Backcountry Biway. The hike begins at the far end of the campground, which is set in a grove of large Jeffrey pine. If possible, tank up on water in the campground, as the scourge of southern California wilderness areas—cows—usually have trampled and polluted the water downstream. The trail basically follows Long Valley Creek to the river, occasionally switching from side to side as the creek pinches off the path. There are a few narrow gorges where you may have to negotiate your way around an occasional slab of granite.

Domeland Wilderness

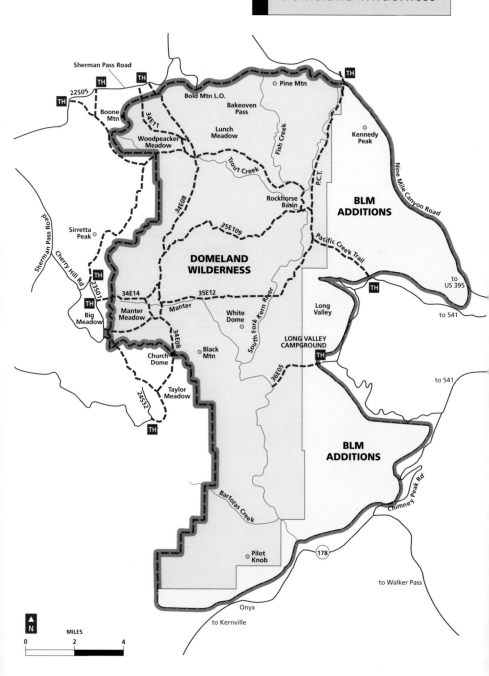

Sherman Pass Road

22S05

TH

Boone
Mtn

34E11

Woodpeacker
Meadow

Bold Mtn L.O.

Pine Mtn

Bakeoven
Pass

Lunch
Meadow

Fish Creek

Kennedy
Peak

Nine Mile Canyon Road

Trout Creek

Rockhorse
Basin

P.C.T.

BLM
ADDITIONS

Sherman Pass Road

Cherry Hill Rd

Sirretta
Peak

34E08

35E109

DOMELAND
WILDERNESS

Pacific Creek Trail

to
US 395

to 541

23S01

TH

TH

Big
Meadow

34E14

35E12

Manter
Meadow

Manter

White
Dome

South Fork Kern River

Long
Valley

TH

34E08

Church
Dome

Black
Mtn

LONG VALLEY
CAMPGROUND

TH

to 541

24S32

Taylor
Meadow

36E05

TH

BLM
ADDITIONS

Bartolas Creek

Chimney Peak Rd

Pilot
Knob

178

to Walker Pass

Onyx

to Kernville

N

MILES

0   2   4

OVERNIGHT HIKE: MANTER/WOODPECKER LOOP TRAIL
Loop length: 24 miles
Low and high elevations: 6,600 to 8,250 feet
Difficulty: strenuous

This is a good 2 to 3 day backpacking trip that gets you into the heart of the Domeland Wilderness. When other trails further north are still under snow, this trek is usually negotiable as soon as late May or early June.

The trailhead is on the western side of the wilderness. From Kernville drive toward Sherman Pass on Forest Service Road 22S05. At Burton Camp, turn south (right) on the Poison Meadow Road (22S12) and follow signs for Horse Meadow/ Big Meadow. Approximately 2.0 miles beyond Horse Meadow Campground, there is a left-hand fork to Forest Service Road 23S07, which will take you the rest of the way to the parking area.

From the parking area where your trip will end, walk the road along Big Meadows south about 1.0 mile to Manter Trailhead on the left (east). Take Manter Trail approximately 3.0 miles to Manter Meadow, follow the Woodpecker Trail (34E08) north to its junction with the Rockhouse Basin Trail (35E16), then turn west to Woodpecker Meadow and Trout Creek, which is reputed to be good fishing. From Woodpecker Meadow, hike west and then south to Sirretta Peak, which is a scramble, and Sirretta Pass. From the pass, continue southwest down to Cannell Trail (33E32), where you bear right and south about 1.0 mile to the parking area.

Emigrant Wilderness 29

Emigrant Wilderness, located west of the Sierra crest just north of Yosemite, abounds with granite landscapes, lakes, and rolling forested terrain.

A view of the 50,000-acre proposed West Walker River addition to the eastern border of the Emigrant Wilderness.

The 112,191-acre Emigrant Wilderness lies on the western slope of the Sierra crest, immediately north of Yosemite National Park and south of Sonora Pass. It is a 25- by 15-mile complex of volcanic peaks, rounded granitic domes, barren basins, and more than 100 lakes, all managed by the Stanislaus National Forest. Most of the wilderness, except for the steep canyon of the Stanislaus, is an undulating granitic plateau.

The area south of Sonora Pass, however, is dominated by volcanic rock. One of the best places in the entire Sierra to see andesite mudflow is Blue Canyon, located on the northeast border along Deadman Creek. Here, volcanic rock 2,000 feet thick has been exposed by erosion. The contact with underlying quartz-monzonite (granitic rock) that makes up much of the remainder of the wilderness is obvious as well.

LOCATION: 35 miles northwest of Bridgeport

SIZE: 113,000 acres

ELEVATION RANGE: 5,000 to 11,570 feet

MILES OF TRAILS: 185

ECOSYSTEMS: alpine tundra, red fir, western white pine-lodgepole forest, mixed conifer forest

ADMINISTRATION: Stanislaus National Forest

MAPS: Stanislaus National Forest Map, Emigrant Wilderness Area Map

Elevation ranges from 5,000 feet by Cherry Lake to 11,570-foot Leavitt Peak on the Sierra crest, the highest summit in the wilderness.

Prior to the gold rush of 1849, few whites ventured into this part of the Sierra, but once minerals were discovered both in California as well as Nevada, travel across the Sierra increased. The pathway over Sonora Pass became a standard route for travelers going to and from the gold and silver fields of Nevada and the Central Valley. A formal road was constructed for wagons by 1864.

The road also became a livestock driveway. As early as 1861, domestic cattle and sheep were being grazed in the Emigrant Wilderness area. Cattle were grazed along the South Fork of the Stanislaus by an early settler named W. F. Cooper, and Cooper Meadow and Cooper Pocket within the wilderness are named for him. Cattle grazing still occurs in the wilderness today, with many documented impacts to the landscape.

Emigrant Wilderness was established as a Forest Service Primitive Area in 1931 and designated a wilderness in 1975. Today, an estimated 20,000 people visit the wilderness annually—a small number when compared to nearby Yosemite. The heaviest use occurs at Kennedy Meadows and Deer, Wood, and Buck Lakes. With about 185 miles of trails and open terrain conducive to cross-country travel, there is no reason why anyone should feel crowded or at a loss for solitude in this wilderness.

Since much of the Emigrant includes high country with its rocks and ice, it's not the best wildlife habitat. Nevertheless, 85 species of birds, 46 mammals, six reptiles, three amphibians, and six fish species are known to occur within the wilderness. Wildlife typical of the Sierra Nevada in general occurs here.

Just west of the Emigrant Wilderness lies the 50,000-acre West Walker–Leavitts Meadow RA, one of the largest undesignated potential wildernesses left in the Sierra. The area, highly scenic and offering outstanding recreational opportunities, will no doubt be added to the wilderness system in the future.

DAY HIKE: BLUE CANYON LAKE
One-way length: 1.7 miles
Low and high elevations: 8,820 to 10,100 feet
Difficulty: moderate

This trail starts high and goes higher, entering a wonderful cirque basin occupied by Blue Canyon Lake. The trailhead is located off of Highway 108, 4.0 miles west of Sonora Pass.

The trail immediately descends and crosses Deadman Creek, then begins to ascend the glaciated Blue Canyon. The meeting of two geological features is obvious: The older granites (circa 100 million years) that underlay most of Emigrant Wilderness are covered by younger (20 million years old) volcanics. The trail switchbacks to a crossing of Blue Canyon Creek and eventually leads to a small meadow that frames the moraine-dammed 3.5-acre Blue Canyon Lake.

Emigrant Wilderness

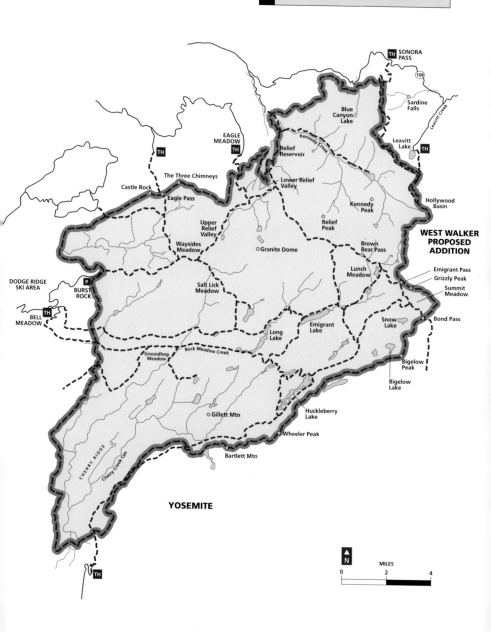

SONORA PASS

TH

108

Sardine Falls

Leavitt Creek

Blue Canyon Lake

EAGLE MEADOW

TH   TH

Kennedy Creek

Relief Reservoir

Leavitt Lake

TH

The Three Chimneys

Castle Rock

Lower Relief Valley

Hollywood Basin

Eagle Pass

Kennedy Peak

Upper Relief Valley

Relief Peak

WEST WALKER PROPOSED ADDITION

Waysides Meadow

Granite Dome

Brown Bear Pass

DODGE RIDGE SKI AREA

P

BURST ROCK

Salt Lick Meadow

Lunch Meadow

Emigrant Pass
Grizzly Peak
Summit Meadow

BELL MEADOW

TH

Emigrant Lake

Snow Lake

Bond Pass

Long Lake

Groundhog Meadow

Buck Meadow Creek

Bigelow Peak

Bigelow Lake

Gillett Mtn

Huckleberry Lake

CHERRY RIDGE

Cherry Creek Can

Wheeler Peak

Bartlett Mtn

YOSEMITE

TH

N

MILES

0   2   4

DAY HIKE: LEAVITT LAKE PASS
One-way length: 1.7 miles
Low and high elevations: 9,600 to 10,640 feet
Difficulty: strenuous

This shortcut into the Emigrant Wilderness travels from a spectacular alpine lake to the crest of the entire range. Drive to the trailhead from Highway 108 to the signed road for Leavitt Lake, about 3.8 miles east of Sonora Pass. The road to the lake is rough, and you may want to consider walking the 2.9 miles to the lakeshore parking area; check with the Forest Service prior to your drive to determine current conditions. Once you arrive at beautiful Leavitt Lake, this easily visible trail takes off to the southeast and climbs a ridge. The trail, an old jeep road, was bulldozed in 1943 to access a tungsten mine; the mine floundered, and the road has since been closed. Part way up the ridge, you pass a sidetrack (another old road) leading to Ski Lake, a good day hike destination or an overnight campsite. Meanwhile, the goal, Leavitt Lake Pass, is several switchbacks ahead. Upon attaining the summit, the views are tremendous, including many of the higher peaks in the northern part of Yosemite, such as Matterhorn, Conness, and Dana.

The Pacific Crest Trail is just below the pass, offering trails both north and south that can be used for longer day hikes or overnighters. A good longer loop is to head north 6.0 miles along the Pacific Crest Trail to Sonora Pass, where one can either hike back to their vehicle at Leavitt Lake or have prearranged a pickup.

OVERNIGHT HIKE: EMIGRANT MEADOWS TRAIL
One-way length: 12.5 miles
Low and high elevations: 6,500 to 9,680 feet
Difficulty: moderate

This is one of the major pathways into the Emigrant Wilderness, leading to the namesake meadows and lake. The views of Emigrant Meadows from Brown Bear Pass is one of the most spectacular in the entire Sierra. The trailhead is located off Highway 108 at Kennedy Meadows. After passing the privately owned Kennedy Meadows Lodge, the trail follows the Middle Fork of the Stanislaus River through Kennedy Meadows and crosses the wilderness boundary shortly beyond. Continue past Relief Reservoir to Saucer Meadow on Summit Creek, about 6.0 miles from the trailhead. In another 1.5 miles of ascent through forests, you come to Lunch Meadows. The trail steepens somewhat as you approach 9,786-foot Brown Bear Pass. Upon reaching the top, Emigrant Meadows spreads below you. Another 1.0 mile of descent brings you to Emigrant Lake, a wonderful place to camp and spend some time in the Sierra backcountry.

OTHER RECREATIONAL OPPORTUNITIES

Winter camping and cross-country skiing in the Emigrant Wilderness is possible, although access takes time. The best entryway is via Dodge Ridge east of Pinecrest. Here, the Forest Service has laid out marked ski trails that generally follow old logging roads, with a few connecting to trails that enter the wilderness.

Golden Trout Wilderness 30

A forested plateau with large meadows, Golden Trout Wilderness is one of the largest in the Sierra.

Looking west from Cottonwood Pass to Big Whitney Meadows in Golden Trout Wilderness.

In some ways, the Golden Trout Wilderness is one of the most delightful wildlands in California. It's a large roadless area with a good trail system and open, rolling terrain that is easily traversed, making it a hiker's paradise. The wilderness is punctuated by a multitude of meadows—Big Whitney, Horseshoe, Mulkey, Templeton, and Little Whitney—and isolated, high peaks affording outstanding views. Some consider the unrestricted panoramic vista from Kern Peak one of the best in the entire Sierra. Overall, this is a more arid wildlands than the High Sierra areas, and water is not nearly as abundant as it is further north.

The 308,287-acre wilderness was designated in 1978 and is the second largest national forest wilderness in the Sierra Nevada (several national park areas are larger). Taking in the

LOCATION: 100 miles east of Bakersfield

SIZE: 308,287 acres

ELEVATION RANGE: 4,800 to 12,900 feet

MILES OF TRAILS: 147

ECOSYSTEMS: oaks, chaparral, pinyon pine, mixed conifer, red fir

ADMINISTRATION: Sequoia National Forest, Inyo National Forest

MAPS: Sequoia N.F. Map, Golden Trout/ South Sierra Wilderness Areas Map

southern end of the Sierra drained by the Kern and Little Kern Rivers, its elevations range from 3,700 feet along the Kern River to 12,432-foot Mount Florence along the border of Sequoia National Park, to 12,900-foot Cirque Peak on the border with the John Muir Wilderness. Olancha Peak (12,123) on the southern edge of the wilderness is the most southerly high summit in the Sierra. Overall, the highest peaks generally follow the Great Western Divide, which runs south from Mineral King in Sequoia National Park, forming a bowl of high peaks that surround the Little Kern drainage in the western portion of the wilderness. Some 20 miles of the South Fork of the Kern and 11 miles of the North Fork of the Kern are designated Wild and Scenic Rivers.

Except for the highest peaks, most of the wilderness was not glaciated, hence there are few lakes. Granitic rock dominates most surface features, but there are outcrops of metamorphic and volcanic rocks denoted by such names as Malpais Lava, Volcano Creek, and Volcano Meadow. Templeton Mountain is a cinder cone.

Vegetation is dominated by ponderosa pine and Jeffrey pine at lower elevations, with white fir, sugar pine, and incense cedar at mid-elevations, grading to red fir and lodgepole pine at higher elevations. Limber pine and western white pine occur sporadically, with juniper and pinyon pine found mostly east of the Sierra crest. Foxtail pine, unique to California, is found from the Kern Plateau northward to Onion Valley near Kearsarge Pass in the John Muir Wilderness. The Last Chance Meadow Research Natural Area was established in 1982 to provide research opportunities on foxtail pine.

The name of the wilderness refers to the fact that the Kern drainage is the original ancestral home of the golden trout, an endemic colorful distant cousin of the rainbow trout and California's state fish. The golden trout lives only at high elevations and was originally restricted to the southern Sierra, although it has been successfully stocked in many other parts of the Sierra, as well as the rest of the West. The world's record golden trout came from Wyoming's Wind River Range, not California.

The Kern once flowed into the San Joaquin River drainage. The early form of golden trout swam up into the Kern and was subsequently isolated long enough to develop into a genetically distinct species. There are two forms recognized, the Volcano golden trout, sometimes called the "South Fork of the Kern golden trout," and the Little Kern golden trout. Both are found in the Golden Trout Wilderness.

The fish have reddish to orange bellies, greenish backs, and bright golden sides, with a reddish lateral band similar to a rainbow trout. The Little Kern golden trout was listed as a federally threatened species in 1977. Two factors are responsible for this listing: (1) Degradation of habitat due to livestock grazing has damaged much of the fish's native environment, and (2) strong competition and hybridization from non-native fish introduced into golden trout waters has led to a decline in the species. At one time the fish were reduced to 10 percent of their former range.

Since 1975, the Forest Service, along with the California Fish and Game Department, has undertaken a golden trout recovery program. Competing fish are eradicated from a stream or lake using rotenone, a selective poison that kills only fish. After a few days, a detoxicant is mixed into the waterway, then the stream is restocked with golden trout.

The rolling terrain and aridity of the area has favored the formation of many large meadows, which have been severely degraded by domestic livestock grazing. Nearly the entire wilderness is covered by existing grazing allotments. In its brochure on the

Golden Trout Wilderness, the Inyo National Forest tries spin control to evoke a feeling that cattle grazing is just an "old time" use of the land where cattlemen "drive their cattle over historic trails, use pack stock to supply cow camps built of native materials, and cook over woodstoves by lantern light." Unfortunately, the effects of livestock grazing are all too evident in the Golden Trout Wilderness, where many wet meadows have been turned into sagebrush flats with incised stream channels and excessive erosion. The Forest Service continues to expend a great deal of taxpayer money trying to mitigate these effects, including construction of erosion control devices, fencing, and water developments, but the agency never considers removing the source of the problem in the first place. And, contrary to popular belief, corporations, not small family ranchers, control many of the largest public lands' grazing allotments. For instance, Anheuser–Busch beer corporation is holder of the Templeton and Mount Whitney allotments, located in the Golden Trout and nearby South Sierra Wildernesses.

In addition, much of the area outside of the wilderness has been subject to heavy logging. Finding your way to a trailhead is often complicated by the maze of logging roads. Be sure you have a current map.

DAY HIKE: COTTONWOOD PASS
One-way length: 4 miles
Low and high elevations: 9,950 to 11,250 feet
Difficulty: moderate

This is a hike that will get your lungs in shape as you climb to the top of Cottonwood Pass on the northeastern edge of the Golden Trout Wilderness. To find the trailhead, take the Whitney Portal Road off of Highway 395 in Lone Pine, go 3.2 miles and veer left for Horseshoe Meadows, then drive nearly 20 miles on this paved road to the trailhead.

The hike skirts cattle-damaged Horseshoe Meadows and climbs west up a slope with scattered foxtail pine. About 2.0 miles from the trailhead, the path begins to switchback up the slope (18 of them!), with good views of Owens Valley to the east. At mile 2.9, you will cross a small meadow full of flowers then climb a few more switchbacks to the 11,150-foot pass. Although the views east are exceptional, climb the rocky ridges west of the pass to get a better view.

OVERNIGHT HIKE: BLACKROCK GAP TO KERN PEAK
One-way length: 13.3 miles
Low and high elevations: 8,940 to 11,510 feet
Difficulty: strenuous

This hike takes you into the heart of the Golden Trout Wilderness to a peak that many believe affords one of the best views in the southern Sierra Nevada. Be prepared to meet cows along the way. The trailhead is 60 miles from Kernville. Find the trailhead by driving Kern River Road from Kernville to the Sherman Pass

Road, which is Forest Service Road 22S05. Go over Sherman Pass and continue 17.2 miles to a four-way junction, where you will continue north on road 21S03 to Blackrock Ranger Station. From here, drive another 8.0 miles to the parking area.

There are several stream crossings along this route, so it's best to wait until mid-summer or later to attempt the hike. The first part of the trail heads north to Cas Vieja Meadows, where a trail to Jordan Hot Springs heads to the northwest. For this hike, however, continue due north, crossing Lost Trout Creek on the way to Beer Keg Meadow. You will pass River Spring, which features good drinking water uncontaminated by cattle, so drink heartily—it may be the only pure source you will encounter. Continue north to Redrock Meadow, which makes a good campsite with its small streams and abundant wood. For those interested in climbing Kern Peak, continue northeast, ascending steeply in a red fir forest to a 10,250-foot pass in the Toowa Range. From the pass, the remainder of the distance is cross-country. Hike west along the Toowa Range Divide; after 1.0 mile, you must make a short scramble up a steep slope with foxtail pine to the summit, where there are the remains of an old fire lookout tower.

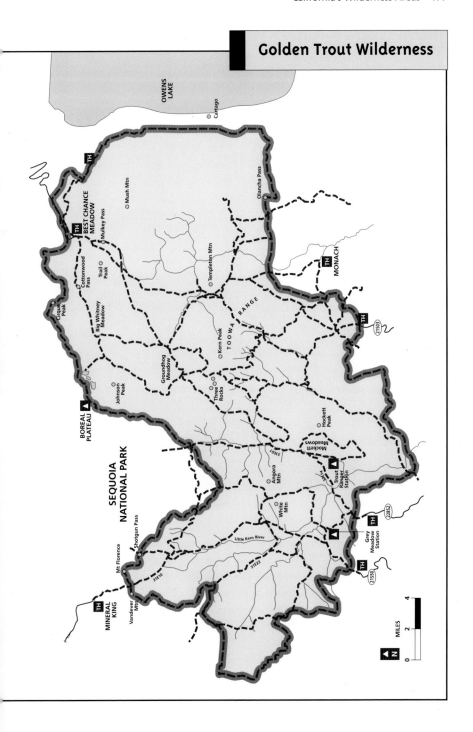

Golden Trout Wilderness

OWENS LAKE

Cartago

Olancha Pass

Mush Mtn

TH

BEST CHANCE MEADOW

Mulkey Pass

Templeton Mtn

MONACH

Cottonwood Pass

Trail Peak

TH

Cirque Peak

Big Whitney Meadow

Kern Peak

T O O W A   R A N G E

21S50

Groundhog Meadow

Johnson Peak

Three Rocks

Hockett Peak

BOREAL PLATEAU

Modett Meadows

33E01

SEQUOIA NATIONAL PARK

Angora Mtn

35E14

Trout Ranger Station

22E52

White Mtn

TH

Grey Meadow Station

Little Kern River

21S50

Shotgun Pass

Mt Florence

35E10

31E23

TH

MINERAL KING

Vandever Mtn

MILES

N

0   2   4

31 Granite Chief Wilderness

This wilderness encompasses the headwaters of the American River and has a landscape dominated by rolling granite slabs with small meadows and lovely forested ridges.

Aspen in Five Lakes Basin, Granite Chief Wilderness.

LOCATION: by Squaw Valley Ski Area, south of Truckee

SIZE: 25,784 acres

ELEVATION RANGE: 4,600 to 9,886 feet

MILES OF TRAILS: 36

ECOSYSTEMS: red fir, lodgepole pine, western white pine

ADMINISTRATION: Tahoe National Forest

MAPS: Tahoe Basin N.F. Map, Granite Chief and Wentworth Springs 7.5' USGS Topo Maps

If you walk up the lifts at Squaw Valley to the ridgeline and look west, you will be viewing the 25,784-acre Granite Chief Wilderness on the Tahoe National Forest. The wilderness includes the headwaters of the North Fork and Middle Fork of the American River, as well as the scenic Five Lakes Basin. A portion of a state game refuge overlaps the western part of the wilderness. The Pacific Crest Trail winds through the area, with several linking trails that begin at Squaw Valley and Alpine Meadows Ski Areas. The highest peak, Granite Chief, is 9,886 feet in elevation. The wilderness was designated as part of the 1984 California Wilderness Act.

The entire area was scoured by glaciation, creating cirque basins and U-shaped valleys. Snowfall is heavy, with

Golden Trout Wilderness

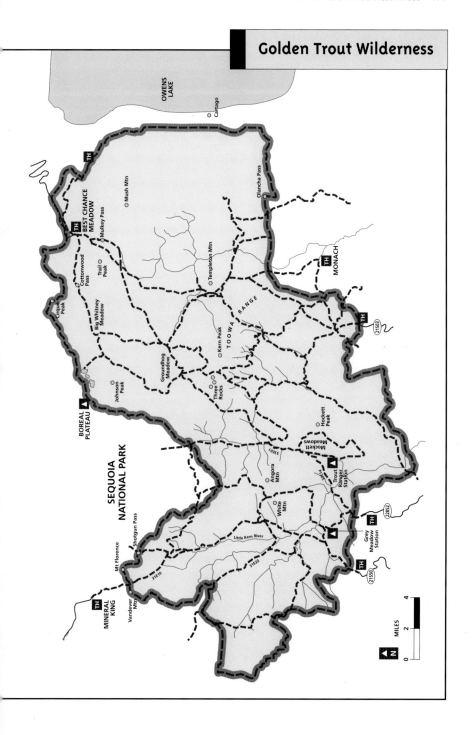

31 Granite Chief Wilderness

This wilderness encompasses the headwaters of the American River and has a landscape dominated by rolling granite slabs with small meadows and lovely forested ridges.

Aspen in Five Lakes Basin, Granite Chief Wilderness.

LOCATION: by Squaw Valley Ski Area, south of Truckee

SIZE: 25,784 acres

ELEVATION RANGE: 4,600 to 9,886 feet

MILES OF TRAILS: 36

ECOSYSTEMS: red fir, lodgepole pine, western white pine

ADMINISTRATION: Tahoe National Forest

MAPS: Tahoe Basin N.F. Map, Granite Chief and Wentworth Springs 7.5' USGS Topo Maps

If you walk up the lifts at Squaw Valley to the ridgeline and look west, you will be viewing the 25,784-acre Granite Chief Wilderness on the Tahoe National Forest. The wilderness includes the headwaters of the North Fork and Middle Fork of the American River, as well as the scenic Five Lakes Basin. A portion of a state game refuge overlaps the western part of the wilderness. The Pacific Crest Trail winds through the area, with several linking trails that begin at Squaw Valley and Alpine Meadows Ski Areas. The highest peak, Granite Chief, is 9,886 feet in elevation. The wilderness was designated as part of the 1984 California Wilderness Act.

The entire area was scoured by glaciation, creating cirque basins and U-shaped valleys. Snowfall is heavy, with

Golden Trout Wilderness

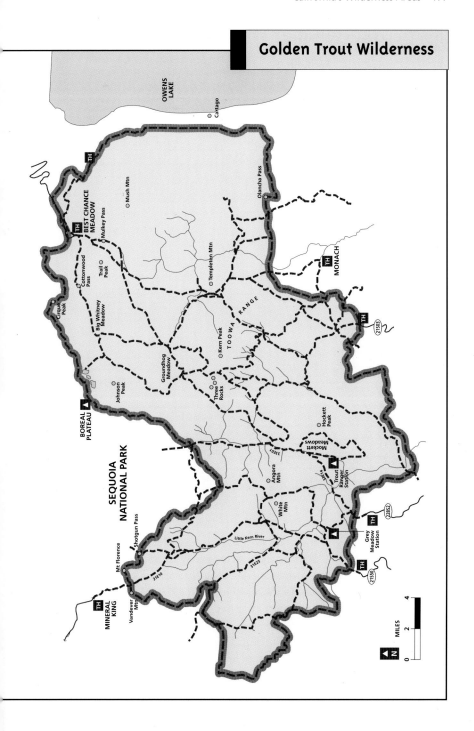

OWENS LAKE

Cartago

TH

Mush Mtn

BEST CHANCE MEADOW

Mulkey Pass

Olancha Pass

Cottonwood Pass

Trail Peak

Templeton Mtn

MONACH

TH

Cirque Peak

Big Whitney Meadow

Kern Peak

TOOWA RANGE

TH
21503

Groundhog Meadow

Johnson Peak

Three Rocks

BOREAL PLATEAU

Hockett Peak

Mockett Meadows

31E01

SEQUOIA NATIONAL PARK

Angora Mtn

31E14

Trout Ranger Station

White Mtn

22E52

TH

Shotgun Pass

Little Kern River

Grey Meadow Station

Mt Florence

31E10

31E23

TH
21E50

MINERAL KING

Vandever Mtn

N

MILES

0   2   4

31 Granite Chief Wilderness

This wilderness encompasses the headwaters of the American River and has a landscape dominated by rolling granite slabs with small meadows and lovely forested ridges.

Aspen in Five Lakes Basin, Granite Chief Wilderness.

LOCATION: by Squaw Valley Ski Area, south of Truckee

SIZE: 25,784 acres

ELEVATION RANGE: 4,600 to 9,886 feet

MILES OF TRAILS: 36

ECOSYSTEMS: red fir, lodgepole pine, western white pine

ADMINISTRATION: Tahoe National Forest

MAPS: Tahoe Basin N.F. Map, Granite Chief and Wentworth Springs 7.5' USGS Topo Maps

If you walk up the lifts at Squaw Valley to the ridgeline and look west, you will be viewing the 25,784-acre Granite Chief Wilderness on the Tahoe National Forest. The wilderness includes the headwaters of the North Fork and Middle Fork of the American River, as well as the scenic Five Lakes Basin. A portion of a state game refuge overlaps the western part of the wilderness. The Pacific Crest Trail winds through the area, with several linking trails that begin at Squaw Valley and Alpine Meadows Ski Areas. The highest peak, Granite Chief, is 9,886 feet in elevation. The wilderness was designated as part of the 1984 California Wilderness Act.

The entire area was scoured by glaciation, creating cirque basins and U-shaped valleys. Snowfall is heavy, with

Golden Trout Wilderness

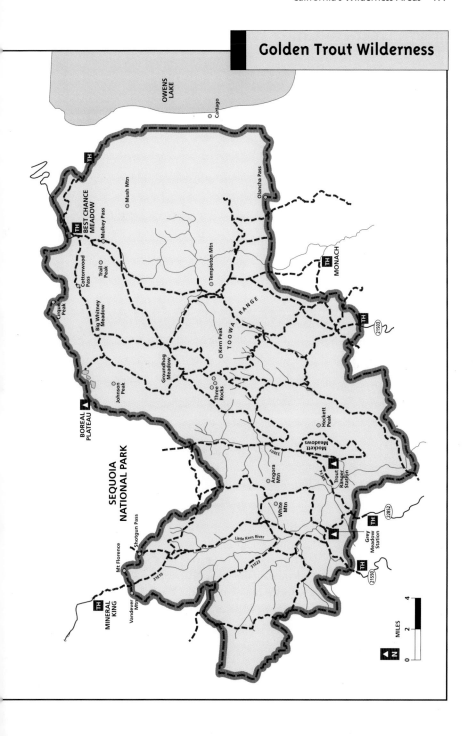

OWENS LAKE

Cartago

Olancha Pass

Mush Mtn

MONACH

BEST CHANCE MEADOW

Mulkey Pass

Templeton Mtn

Cottonwood Pass

Trail Peak

21503

TOOWA RANGE

Cirque Peak

Big Whitney Meadow

Kern Peak

BOREAL PLATEAU

Groundhog Meadow

Johnson Peak

Three Rocks

Hockett Peak

Mockett Meadows

33E01

SEQUOIA NATIONAL PARK

Angora Mtn

35E14

Trout Meadow Ranger Station

White Mtn

22E52

Grey Meadow Station

Shotgun Pass

Little Kern River

31E10

31E23

21E50

Mt Florence

Vandever Mtn

MINERAL KING

MILES

0   2   4

N

31 Granite Chief Wilderness

This wilderness encompasses the headwaters of the American River and has a landscape dominated by rolling granite slabs with small meadows and lovely forested ridges.

Aspen in Five Lakes Basin, Granite Chief Wilderness.

LOCATION: by Squaw Valley Ski Area, south of Truckee

SIZE: 25,784 acres

ELEVATION RANGE: 4,600 to 9,886 feet

MILES OF TRAILS: 36

ECOSYSTEMS: red fir, lodgepole pine, western white pine

ADMINISTRATION: Tahoe National Forest

MAPS: Tahoe Basin N.F. Map, Granite Chief and Wentworth Springs 7.5' USGS Topo Maps

If you walk up the lifts at Squaw Valley to the ridgeline and look west, you will be viewing the 25,784-acre Granite Chief Wilderness on the Tahoe National Forest. The wilderness includes the headwaters of the North Fork and Middle Fork of the American River, as well as the scenic Five Lakes Basin. A portion of a state game refuge overlaps the western part of the wilderness. The Pacific Crest Trail winds through the area, with several linking trails that begin at Squaw Valley and Alpine Meadows Ski Areas. The highest peak, Granite Chief, is 9,886 feet in elevation. The wilderness was designated as part of the 1984 California Wilderness Act.

The entire area was scoured by glaciation, creating cirque basins and U-shaped valleys. Snowfall is heavy, with

an average of almost 70 inches of precipitation a year. The abundant winter moisture supports forests dominated by large, old-growth western white pine, lodgepole pine, red fir, and mountain hemlock, while aspen and other shrubs provide color in the fall. Wetlands make up approximately eight percent of the area.

The forest supervisor of the Tahoe National Forest recently decided not to require permits for day use in this area, in part because of the agency's conclusion that most damage comes from stock use rather than hikers and backpackers. Recreational stock will not be permitted within 600 feet of any lake, and a limit of animals per party is being implemented. The Forest Service plan also calls for the phasing out of domestic livestock grazing in the Picayune Valley.

Ten-thousand acres of roadless land surrounds the Granite Chief Wilderness, and another 50,000 acres of roadless areas are in the North Fork of the American River, a designated Wild and Scenic River located immediately west of the existing wilderness. The closure of just two dirt roads could unite these areas into one cohesive unit of more than 85,000 acres, providing significantly more biological value and protecting the water quality of the river.

DAY HIKE: FIVE LAKES BASIN
One-way length: 2.3 miles
Low and high elevations: 8,000 to 9,400 feet
Difficulty: moderate

The Five Lakes Basin is one of the easiest accesses into the Granite Chief Wilderness, hence one of the most used. It is, however, a delightful walk, despite the crowds you will no doubt encounter. To find the trailhead, drive south from Truckee on Highway 89 and turn up the road for Deer Park and Alpine Meadows Ski Area. The trailhead is on the north side of the road about 3.0 miles from Highway 89. The first part of the trail switchbacks up to a ridge, then it levels out for about 1.9 miles as it passes into the Granite Chief Wilderness. This stretch of trail has some very large red fir and western white pine along it before it descends to the first lake in the Five Lakes Basin. Just beyond the lakes, it's possible to hook up with the Pacific Crest Trail and travel north or south in the wilderness.

DAY HIKE: POWDERHORN–HELLHOLE TRAIL
One-way length: 4 miles
Low and high elevations: 5,500 to 6,400 feet
Difficulty: moderate

Here's one with fewer crowds. It's mostly a walk in a forested canyon, but it follows rushing mountain streams most of the way. The first test of your mettle is to find the trailhead. From Highway 89 near the Kaspain Picnic Area on Lake Tahoe's

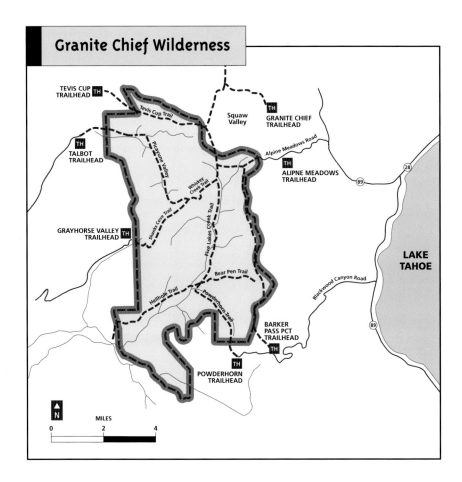

Granite Chief Wilderness

TEVIS CUP
TRAILHEAD TH

Tevis Cup Trail

Squaw
Valley

GRANITE CHIEF
TRAILHEAD TH

TH
TALBOT
TRAILHEAD

Picayune Valley

Alpine Meadows Road

ALIPNE MEADOWS
TRAILHEAD TH

28

89

Whiskey
Creek Trail

GRAYHORSE VALLEY
TRAILHEAD TH

Shanks Cove Trail

Five Lakes Creek Trail

LAKE
TAHOE

Bear Pen Trail

Blackwood Canyon Road

Hellhole Trail

Powderhorn Trail

BARKER
PASS PCT
TRAILHEAD TH

89

TH
POWDERHORN
TRAILHEAD

N

MILES

0   2   4

POWDERHORN–HELLHOLE TRAIL: CONTINUED

west shore, turn west on Blackwood Canyon Road. Go 7.0 miles to Barker Pass, where the pavement ends, and go another 2.3 miles to the Powderhorn Trailhead.

The 4.0-mile-long Powderhorn Trail leads downhill (remember you have to walk back up again) to Diamond Crossing. Most people turn around at this point, but if you want to continue, ford Powderhorn Creek and intersect the Hellhole Trail. At this point, you will almost immediately have to cross Five Lakes Creek. It is 6.5 miles to Hellhole Reservoir, elevation 4,580 feet, with two more creek crossings. You can continue around the reservoir to roads and campgrounds if you've prearranged a shuttle or pickup; otherwise, it's back up to the trailhead.

Hoover Wilderness

Hoover Wilderness offers alpine lakes, jagged peaks, and small glaciers—all adjacent to Yosemite National Park.

North Peak from the Steelhead Lake area in Hoover Wilderness.

The Hoover Wilderness encompasses 48,601 acres in a long, thin sliver no more than four miles wide. It borders Yosemite National Park east and north of Tioga Pass and is managed jointly by the Toiyabe and Inyo National Forests.

There are a number of small glaciers in this wilderness, nestled among peaks that exceed 12,000 feet, including Conness, Matterhorn, Excelsior, and Dunderberg. Major glaciated valleys include Green, Virginia, Robinson, and Buckeye Creeks. Dozens of lakes and tarns dot the area. Most of the wilderness is alpine in nature, with forests covering only 10 percent of the area. White fir, aspen, and Jeffrey pine dominate the lower valleys, while lodgepole pine, limber pine, western juniper, red fir, western white pine, and mountain hemlock are scattered about at higher elevations.

LOCATION: 10 miles west of Bridgeport

SIZE: 48,601 acres

ELEVATION RANGE: 8,000 to 12,590 feet

MILES OF TRAILS: 30

ECOSYSTEMS: mostly alpine tundra

ADMINISTRATION: Toiyabe National Forest, Inyo National Forest

MAPS: Toiyabe N.F./ Bridgeport Ranger District Map, Inyo N.F. Map, Hoover WIlderness Area Map

The geology dictates the appearance of the individual peaks. Some of the Hoover takes in a belt of metamorphic rock of volcanic origin, which crowns the granitic rock that lies beneath. This belt of rocks lies along the eastern border of Yosemite, as well as north and south of the park. Volcanic peaks tend to be more easily eroded, so they take on a rounded appearance. Dunderberg Peak is an example of a mountain of volcanic origins. Mineralization lead to early development for mining, and traces of this mining past are evident in the numerous miner's cabins and other relics of that age, including an old road from Saddlebag Lake to the Hess Tungston Mine, which operated until the 1950s. Granitic peaks, on the other hand, are very resistant to erosion and tend to take on a more jagged, craggy look. Sawtooth Ridge, visible from Bridgeport, is an example of a granitic summit eroded by glaciation into a knifelike crest.

One of the attractions of the wilderness is bighorn sheep. They were reintroduced into Lee Vining Canyon in 1985, and the herd has grown and expanded its range. Besides sheep, one is likely to see pika, yellow-bellied marmot, Belding ground squirrels, and mule deer.

A special feature of the Hoover Wilderness is the 3,883-acre Hall Creek Natural Area, which was set aside for protection in 1933 for scientific study of the representative alpine tundra plant communities. It is one of the few habitats between 10,000 and 12,000 feet within the Sierra that is readily accessible by road.

Although there are plenty of lakes and basins for camping within the wilderness, longer treks usually involve a swing into Yosemite National Park. Some 72,000 acres of additional roadless areas are proposed for wilderness designation to expand the Hoover Wilderness, including Crater Crest, Eagle Peak, Log Cabin–Saddlebag, and Flatiron Ridge. Combined, these areas would nearly double the size of the existing wilderness.

Among the least-used trails in Hoover Wilderness are Tamarack Lake, Buckeye, Burt Canyon, and Molybernite Canyon. If you want to avoid crowds, consider hiking these trails, which you will find on your map.

DAY HIKE: STEELHEAD LAKE
One-way length: 4 miles
Low and high elevations: 10,087 to 11,200 feet
Difficulty: moderate

The scenery at Saddlebag Lake, the starting point for this hike, is enough to take your breath away, never mind the thin air of the 10,000-foot elevation. But it only gets better from here. To find the trailhead, take the Tioga Pass Road, Highway 120 from Lee Vining, west 10.0 miles toward Yosemite National Park's eastern entrance. Just a few miles before the park, you'll see a sign for the Saddlebag Lake Road. It's 2.0 miles to the lake and trailhead.

The trail is an old mining road, so it's generally easy to follow. First walk north around the shore of Saddlebag Lake to Greenstone Lake. Continue in a general northwesterly direction (the old road is obvious) past Wasco Lake and you'll soon reach Steelhead Lake by the old Hess Tungsten Mine. The lake is nestled in alpine country, surrounded by 12,000-foot peaks, and it offers a good place to picnic and enjoy the high country terrain. It is possible to hike cross-country to the northwest and climb up to the top of Shepherd Crest, where great views of the Yosemite back-country, including McCabe Lake, are visible. Otherwise, wander the upper basin and retrace your steps back to Saddlebag Lake.

DAY HIKE: EAST LAKE TRAIL
One-way length: 3.5 miles
Low and high elevations: 8,200 to 9,480 feet
Difficulty: moderate

This short hike takes you into superb alpine country to a small glacially carved cirque lake. To find the trailhead, drive south from Bridgeport on Highway 395 4.5 miles to a signed road heading southwest for Green Lakes Campground, which is about 6.0 miles further on. The trail begins just beyond the campground. The first part of the route passes through open slopes with scattered patches of aspen, which are lovely in the fall, then you quickly pass beyond the Hoover Wilderness sign. In 2.0 miles of hiking through open terrain, often covered with flowers during the summer, you come to a trail junction. Green Lake lies straight ahead, but to reach West Lake, a worthwhile goal in itself, take the north (right-hand) fork of the trail. Ascend 1,000 feet by switchback to the rocky basin that contains West Lake. East Lake is 1.5 miles further on the south (left-hand) fork of the trail.

OVERNIGHT HIKE: SUMMIT LAKE
One-way length: 5 miles
Low and high elevations: 9,000 to 11,008 feet
Difficulty: moderate

This is an easy backpack to a beautiful alpine lake lying right on the border with Yosemite National Park. To find the trailhead, take Highway 395 south from Bridgeport for 13.0 miles to Conway Summit, where there is a sign for a turn west to Virginia Lakes. The trailhead is located at the end of the Virginia Lakes Road. The hike is mostly upward at first, going by Blue Lake in less than 1.0 mile from the trailhead and eventually passing Conney and Frog Lakes as well. Switchbacks finally take you to an 11,008-foot pass, where you will get the first glimpse of Summit Lake and numerous 12,000-foot peaks walling in the alpine landscape. From the pass it is another 1.5 miles—mostly downhill—to the lake, which has numerous potential campsites in the vicinity.

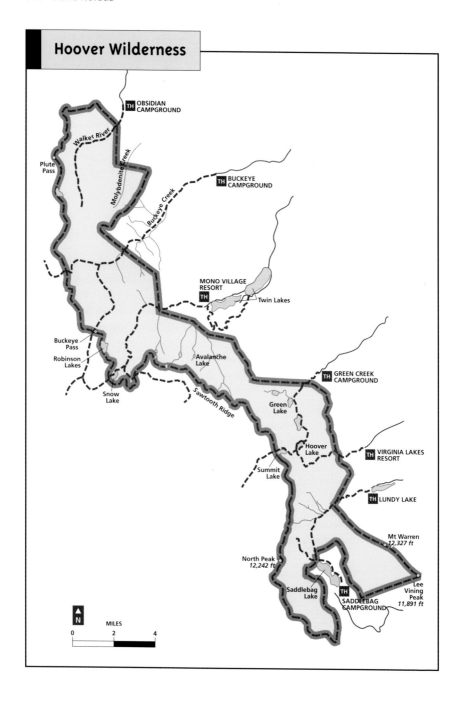

Hoover Wilderness

OBSIDIAN
CAMPGROUND

Walker River

Plute
Pass

Molybdenite Creek

Buckeye Creek

BUCKEYE
CAMPGROUND

MONO VILLAGE
RESORT

Twin Lakes

Buckeye
Pass

Robinson
Lakes

Avalanche
Lake

GREEN CREEK
CAMPGROUND

Snow
Lake

Sawtooth Ridge

Green
Lake

Hoover
Lake

VIRGINIA LAKES
RESORT

Summit
Lake

LUNDY LAKE

Mt Warren
12,327 ft

North Peak
12,242 ft

Saddlebag
Lake

SADDLEBAG
CAMPGROUND

Lee
Vining
Peak
11,891 ft

N

MILES

0   2   4

Jennie Lakes Wilderness 33

A small plateau of rolling timber with two lakes, the Jennie Lakes Wilderness lies adjacent to Sequoia National Park.

Weaver Lake as seen from Shell Mountain, Jennie Lakes Wilderness.

Tucked in the northeast corner of Sequoia National Park in the Kings River drainage lies the 10,500-acre Jennie Lakes Wilderness. Designated in 1984 as part of the California Wilderness Act, the heavily forested wilderness contains just two water bodies: Weaver Lake and the namesake Jennie Lake. The high point is 10,365-foot Mitchell Peak, located in the northwest corner of the wilderness. Besides a loop trail that connects the two lakes, much of the traffic through this wilderness is to access trail systems in the adjacent Sequoia National Park.

LOCATION: 60 miles east of Fresno

SIZE: 10,500 acres

ELEVATION RANGE: 8,400 to 10,365 feet

MILES OF TRAILS: 20

ECOSYSTEMS: mixed conifer forest

ADMINISTRATION: Sequoia National Forest

MAPS: Sequoia National Forest Map, Monarch/Jennie Lakes Wilderness Areas Map

Jennie Lakes Wilderness

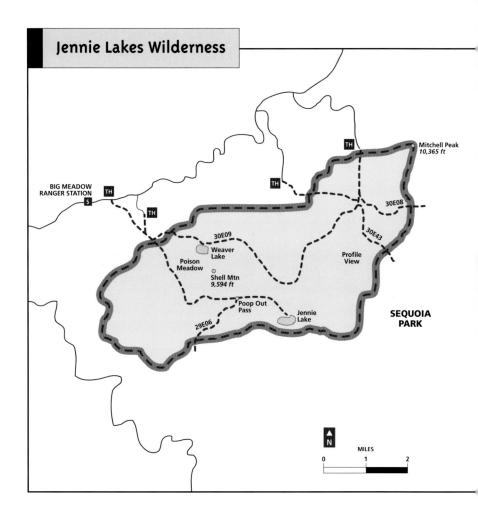

BIG MEADOW
RANGER STATION

TH

S

TH

TH

TH

TH

Mitchell Peak
10,365 ft

30E08

30E43

30E09

Weaver
Lake

Poison
Meadow

Shell Mtn
9,594 ft

Profile
View

Poop Out
Pass

Jennie
Lake

29E06

SEQUOIA
PARK

N

MILES

0   1   2

DAY HIKE: WEAVER LAKE
One-way length: 2.1 miles
Low and high elevations: 7,900 to 8,700 feet
Difficulty: moderate

This is a good hike for a family with young children passing through gorgeous red fir forests enroute. Finding the trailhead can be confusing due to new logging roads, but the following directions will get you in the right vicinity. Take Highway 180 from Fresno, enter Kings Canyon National Park, and turn right toward Sequoia National Park. Go 7.0 miles, watching for the signed left turn for Big Meadows Road. Follow the signs at all junctions, heading for Big Meadows Campground and passing Big Meadows enroute. The campground sprawls along Big Meadows Creek. Just after you cross a bridge over the creek, there is a right turn (south) onto a logging road, which is rough, but passable. At all junctions, take the more traveled road, generally staying parallel to Fox Creek. The trailhead is approximately 1.4 miles south.

The directions to the lake are easier than finding the trailhead. From the parking lot, which is a log landing, cross Fox Creek and hike up through a red fir forest about 0.25 mile to a junction with a trail that comes from the Big Meadows Campground. You need to turn left onto this trail, but be sure to note the junction, and don't daydream as you hike back or you'll miss the turnoff and wind up back at the campground instead of your vehicle. I'm speaking from experience! At about 0.7 mile you'll come to another trail junction for the Jennie Lake Trail. You need to bear left here and climb an open flowery hill, and you will soon pass a sign marking the border of the Jennie Lakes Wilderness. Continue to climb through lovely forests of lodgepole pine, red fir, and flowery understory to another trail junction some 1.9 miles from the trailhead. Stay to your left to reach Weaver Lake, less than 0.25 mile beyond.

OVERNIGHT HIKE: JENNIE LAKE
One-way length: 5.2 miles
Low and high elevations: 7,900 to 9,180 feet
Difficulty: moderate

This hike takes you to Jennie Lake, set in a bowl of granite at 9,000 feet right on the border with Sequoia National Park. The trailhead is the same as the previous hike for Weaver Lake. After leaving the trailhead, go 0.7 miles to a trail junction, where you bear right and head south. The trail climbs to Poison Meadow and levels for a while before rounding the southwest shoulder of Shell Mountain. Here, it begins climbing to timbered Poop-out Pass, some 3.7 miles from the trailhead. Just after the pass, the trail descends steeply for about 1.0 mile before it climbs again for the final pitch to the lovely Jennie Lake at 5.2 miles. From Jennie Lake, it's possible to continue south to Lodgepole Campground in Sequoia National Park, as well as combine this trail with others to make a very long loop trip.

34 John Muir Wilderness

Easily the granddaddy of Sierra Nevada wilderness areas, the John Muir Wilderness has the highest peaks, the greatest amount of area above timberline, and numerous alpine lakes and waterfalls.

Duck Lake from Duck Pass in John Muir Wilderness.

LOCATION: 60 miles east of Fresno and 25 miles west of Bishop

SIZE: 580,675 acres

ELEVATION RANGE: 4,000 to 14,500 feet

MILES OF TRAILS: 450

ECOSYSTEMS: ponderosa pine, mixed conifer, red fir, alpine tundra

ADMINISTRATION: Sierra National Forest, Inyo National Forest

MAPS: Sierra N. F. Map, Inyo N. F. Map, John Muir/Sequoia/ Kings Canyon Wilderness Areas Map

The 580,675-acre John Muir Wilderness, managed by the Sierra and Inyo National Forests, is the largest designated wilderness in California. It encompasses most of the eastern slope of the Sierra Nevada, from Mammoth Mountain south to Cottonwood Lakes by Lone Pine, as well as wrapping around the northern portion of Kings Canyon National Park, to take in a major chunk of the western slope of the Sierra. The John Muir Wilderness contains the headwaters of the South and Middle Forks of the San Joaquin River, the North Fork of the Kings River, and many smaller streams that drain into Owens Valley. Elevations range from 4,000 to 14,495 feet at the apex of Mount Whitney.

It is appropriate that the state's most dramatic and largest wildlands is named after one of the Sierra's most eloquent and ardent supporters, for nowhere else is there such an abundance of stark, glaciated peaks, waterfalls, and lake-studded alpine basins as here. Nor does any other part of the Sierra more appropriately reflect the appellation given to it by John Muir—the "Range of Light."

John Muir was born in Scotland, came to America as a child, and was raised on a stump farm in Wisconsin. After attending college in Madison and then incurring a number of mishaps—including an eye injury that nearly blinded him and malaria he contracted during a thousand-mile walk from the Midwest to Florida—Muir wound up in California. He was immediately drawn to the Sierra, where he lived for several years. He spent his time mapping glaciation and sequoia distribution and climbing peaks, including one of the earliest ascents of Mount Whitney. He eventually became one of the prime advocates for protection of the range. His writings evoked an almost religious tone that graphically described the wonders of the mountain range to an eager national audience. His books and articles helped to create the necessary political support for the establishment of Yosemite National Park, as well as other parks, including Sequoia National Park, Grand Canyon National Park, and Glacier Bay National Park and Preserve. Muir went on to found the Sierra Club and became its first president, a post he held until his death in 1914.

Most of the John Muir Wilderness consists of granite. Indeed, as one travels southward from Yosemite, more and more of the exposed rock in the Sierra consists of granites, but there are still some extensive areas of metamorphic rock. The oldest exposed rock in the Sierra, at 500 million years, is seen at the base of Mount Morrison near Convict Lake. Roof pendants, or relics of the overlying dark metamorphic sedimentary rocks that used to cover all of the Sierra, crown a number of peaks, including Red Slate Mountain, Mount Humphreys, Mount Emerson, Red and White Mountain, and elsewhere. Metamorphic volcanic rocks make up the darker, nearly black rock seen at Black Divide, Black Kaweah, and Blackcap Mountain.

The John Muir Wilderness is the most popular wilderness area in California, and for good reason. Combine the abundance of glaciated lakes, waterfalls, soaring jagged peaks, alpine meadows, magnificent forests, a wealth of excellent trails with the nearly perfect summer weather that characterizes the Sierra Nevada as a whole, and you have the necessary ingredients for heavy use. Although a significant number of people enter the wilderness, the vast size, rugged nature of the landscape, and the numerous hidden basins and valleys still provide plenty of opportunity for solitude—if one makes the effort to avoid the major access points and popular destinations.

The eastern side of the wilderness provides the most ready access to the high country, but trails are steep and climb quickly to high passes. Western slope trailheads offer a gentler, but longer, entry. Take your choice of misery.

Both the John Muir and Pacific Crest Trails traverse the wilderness. The John Muir is the earliest major hiking trail constructed in California. It was proposed by Theodore Solomons of the Sierra Club and was supported by other Sierra Club members, such as Joseph LeConte, a professor at the University of California, Berkeley. LeConte had explored the Sierras for decades, and in 1908 he set off from Yosemite, hiking south to explore the general route of the proposed trail. LeConte and other supporters managed to persuade the state legislature to appropriate funds for the trail, and construction began the following summer. The John Muir Trail was completed in 1916, linking Happy Isles in Yosemite with Whitney Portal some 225 miles south.

One of the attractions of the John Muir is the large number of high peaks. One cluster, the Palisades, embraces six summits that exceed 14,000 feet, including 14,242-foot North Palisade Peak, which cradles the Sierra's southernmost and largest glacier—the Palisade Glacier. This region of spectacular peaks and glaciers is readily accessible via a nine-mile trail from the Big Pine Canyon Trailhead.

The other major cluster of high peaks surrounds and includes 14,495-foot Mount Whitney, the highest peak in the lower 48 states. The peak lies on the border between the John Muir Wilderness and Sequoia National Park. Named in 1864 for the director of the California Geological Survey, Josiah Dwight Whitney, the peak rises more than 10,000 feet above Lone Pine in the Owens Valley. With its multiple granite pinnacles on its eastern face, Mount Whitney presents a forbidding aspect; the western slope, however, is relatively gentle, with a trail all the way to the top. The first known ascent of Mount Whitney was in 1873 by three fishermen. That same summer, John Muir also climbed the peak, but he chose the sheer eastern face for his ascent, still known today as the Mountaineer's Route. A stone hut was built on the mountain's summit in 1909, and it still stands today. About 5,000 people a year make the pilgrimage to the top of Whitney. It's not a place for a wilderness experience, but it's a fine point from which to experience the sheer majesty of the Sierra.

Large mammals are relatively rare in the Sierra, but one of the species that commands interest is the bighorn sheep, an animal John Muir observed on numerous occasions near the headwaters of the Kings and San Joaquin Rivers. About the size of a deer but chunkier, both sexes of the bighorn sheep possess horns, but those of the rams tend to grow in large spirals that sweep back and curl around to nearly form a circle in mature males. Sheep tend to group in herds, with ewes and lambs separate from the males most of the year, except during breeding season in the late fall. Disease introduced from domestic livestock, along with market hunting, decimated sheep herds up and down the Sierra. Today, native bighorns are concentrated in several areas of the John Muir Wilderness; around Mount Williamson south of Independence, and from Kearsarge Pass to Taboose Pass. I once found an old, weathered ram's horn above Duck Pass near Mammoth Lakes—an area where, sadly, wild sheep no longer roam.

Another feature of the John Muir and adjacent areas of the Kings Canyon and Sequoia National Park Wildernesses is foxtail pine, a California endemic, found only in the southern Sierra and the Klamath Mountains in the northern portion of the state. This tree has a distinctive dense coverage of needles that gives a bushy appearance— like a fox's tail—hence the name. With its reddish-brown bark and open crown, the tree is readily identified. The foxtail pine, closely related to the bristlecone pine that is seen in the Great Basin, is found in similar subalpine timberline habitat, growing equally as gnarled and picturesque.

A number of roadless areas adjoin the John Muir Wilderness and should be added to its expanse. They include the 16,229-acre Wheeler Ridge RA, near Rock Creek, where bighorn sheep have been reintroduced. The 55,588-acre Coyote Southeast RA, located southwest of Bishop, is the largest proposed addition to the John Muir Wilderness. Major peaks include the Hunchback, Round Mountain, and Sugarloaf Mountain.

DAY HIKE: DUCK PASS
One-way length: 5 miles
Low and high elevations: 9,050 to 10,477 feet
Difficulty: moderate

This is one of the more popular day hikes in the entire wilderness, for several reasons. The trailhead is already quite high; the pass is "low," as Sierra Nevada passes go; Mammoth Lakes, a popular resort community, lies just down the road; and the scenery coming and going is outstanding. To locate the trailhead, find your way from Mammoth Lakes to Coldwater Campground, just beyond Lake Mary. The trailhead parking area lies just beyond the campground. The trail switchbacks past a host of glacially carved lakes, including Arrowhead, Skeleton, Woods, Red, and Barney, before climbing to the pass, which offers tremendous views across Duck Lake to the Silver Divide.

DAY HIKE: HILTON LAKES BASIN
One-way length: 5 miles
Low and high elevations: 9,840 to 10,400 feet
Difficulty: moderate

The Hilton Lakes Basin, with more than 10 lakes of the same name, is accessed from the Rock Creek Road. To locate the trailhead, turn off of Highway 395 at Tom's Place onto Rock Creek Road. About 0.5 mile past the Rock Creek Resort, look for a trailhead on the right (north). From the trailhead, the path climbs a mere 500 feet to cross the Hilton Creek–Rock Creek Divide then drops to meet the main trail running up and down Hilton Creek. Most of the Hilton Lakes are located up the drainage basin, but the largest, Hilton Lake #2, is downstream to the right.

DAY HIKE: BISHOP PASS
One-way length: 5 miles
Low and high elevations: 9,800 to 11,980 feet
Difficulty: moderate

This hike provides access to numerous glacial lakes and the backcountry of Kings Canyon National Park. From Highway 395 in Bishop, turn west on Line Street (Highway 168 West) and drive 23 miles to South Lake. The Bishop Pass Trail stays to the east side of South Lake, passing through a forest of lodgepole pine and aspen. Great views of Mount Thompson and Mount Goode are visible from the trail. In rapid succession, the trail passes Long Lake, Spearhead Lake, Saddlerock Lake, and the upper Bishop Lakes, making the final steep switchback ascent to Bishop Pass. The lake-studded Dusy Basin, in Kings Canyon National Park, lies just over the pass.

John Muir Wilderness: West

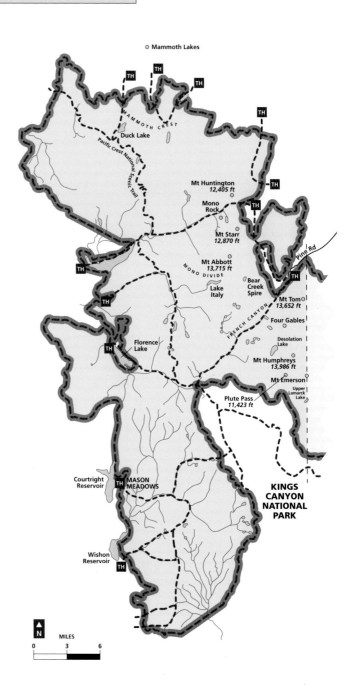

Mammoth Lakes

MAMMOTH CREST

Duck Lake

Pacific Crest National Scenic Trail

Mt Huntington
12,405 ft

Mono
Rock

Mt Starr
12,870 ft

Mt Abbott
13,715 ft

MONO DIVIDE

Lake
Italy

Bear
Creek
Spire

Pine Rd

Mt Tom
13,652 ft

Four Gables

FRENCH CANYON

Desolation
Lake

Florence
Lake

Mt Humphreys
13,986 ft

Mt Emerson

Upper
Lamarck
Lake

Plute Pass
11,423 ft

Courtright
Reservoir

MASON
MEADOWS

KINGS
CANYON
NATIONAL
PARK

Wishon
Reservoir

N

MILES

0   3   6

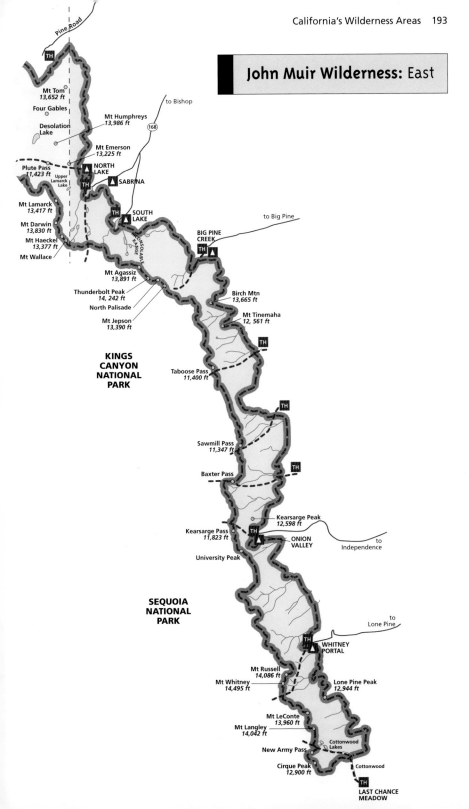

John Muir Wilderness: East

DAY HIKE: MOUNT WHITNEY TRAIL
One-way length: 10.7 miles
Low and high elevations: 8,365 to 14,496 feet
Difficulty: strenuous

Climbing Mount Whitney, the highest peak in the lower 48 states, is more like visiting a shrine than doing a wilderness trek. It is the hiking analogy of a sojourn to Mecca, and I believe it should be treated as such and not as a wilderness hike where solitude is of prime importance. Unfortunately, the Forest Service believes it must manage the Whitney hike as if the primary goal of most hikers is solitude, implementing strict quotes on numbers of people hiking the trail instead of recognizing its other values. Though the heavy use does create some minor impacts, they pale by comparison to the effects of livestock, pack stock use, and other influences typically found in wilderness areas that ecologically are far worse. One way to reduce the heavy trail traffic would be to remove the trailhead and roadhead from Whitney Portal to a lower site in the Alabama Hills. The longer hike would significantly reduce use of the trail without having to implement offensive direct control methods, such as permits and quotas.

The hike up Whitney wouldn't ordinarily be considered a day hike, except that restrictions on overnight camping placed by the Forest Service makes it difficult for most people to get a permit to climb the mountain over a period of days. Doing the climb in one day is long and strenuous. Consider not only the length of the trail (22 miles round trip), but the net elevation gain and loss. Also, remember that there is no water past Trail Camp at the 6.0-mile mark. Nevertheless, hiking Whitney in one day is possible.

First, find your way to Whitney Portal by driving 13.0 miles west of Lone Pine on the Whitney Portal Road. From the trailhead, the trail switchbacks up through red fir and foxtail pine, passing Outpost Camp at 3.5 miles, Mirror Lake at 4.0 miles, and Trail Camp at 6.0 miles, the last location for overnight campers to comfortably set up a tent. Its location directly below the granite Whitney spires is awesome. The scenery along this entire stretch is just stunning, but as good as it is, it gets better. Now the hardest part begins. There are more and more switchbacks as one climbs to Trail Crest, over 13,800 feet in elevation and 8.2 miles from the trailhead. The views are spectacular from here, but those feeling the altitude should turn around. If you're not gasping for air, proceed to the top: The remaining stretch of trail is less steep, but it's still another 2.5 miles to the broad, rocky summit of Mount Whitney.

The last part of the trail is actually in Sequoia National Park. The views from the top of Whitney are incomparable, with the entire Sierra Nevada spread out before you—an ocean of peaks as far as one can see north and south. The nearly as high White–Inyo Mountains to the east also contribute to the visual feast. To see a sunset or sunrise from this location is an unforgettable experience. It is possible to camp on top of the mountain, if there is snow that can be melted for water or if you had the foresight and energy to haul it from Trail Camp. I once spent two nights in a row on top of Mount Whitney—the stars seem closer, because they are!

OVERNIGHT HIKE: TABOOSE CREEK–BENCH LAKE
One-way length: 13 miles
Low and high elevations: 5,500 to 11,400 feet
Difficulty: strenuous

Taboose Pass is one of the least used and most difficult access points into the High Sierra. The trail starts out low and climbs high: It's steep and long—9.0 miles from the trailhead to the pass. It goes almost the entire way in open sagebrush, offering little in the way of shade on a hot summer day. But for those who cherish solitude, Taboose is the pass to consider. From Highway 395 north of Independence, watch for a sign on the west for the Taboose Creek Campground. Take that road 5.0 miles to the trailhead parking area.

From the trailhead to the top of the pass is pretty straightforward—just follow the creek and the switchbacks. Once you cross the pass, you enter Kings Canyon National Park. From the pass, another 2.5 miles brings you to the junction with the Pacific Crest Trail, should you wish to head north toward Mather Pass. However, to reach Bench Lake, watch for cairns about 1.0 mile below the pass that mark a trail heading southwest, and follow it until you reach the confluence with the Pacific Crest Trail. After the Pacific Crest Trail, you will soon come to another junction. If you head south here, you will come to Lake Marjorie; if you head west, in 1.5 miles you will reach Bench Lake, which sits directly below Arrow Peak.

If you're really adventurous and want to do some exploring, much of the area accessed by Taboose Pass is trailless backcountry, including the lower gorge of the South Fork of the Kings, plus several basins north and west of the river that are sprinkled with dozens of alpine lakes. The entire area is perfect for those who want to get off the beaten path, and in much of this country, you won't find a path!

OVERNIGHT HIKE: NORTH FORK–PALISADES TRAIL
One-way length: 9 miles
Low and high elevations: 7,750 to 12,400 feet
Difficulty: strenuous

The hike up the North Fork Big Pine Canyon to Palisades Glacier holds a special place in my heart, since it was the first place I ever backpacked in the Sierra. It was an unforgettable trip. The trail up North Fork Big Pine accesses some of the highest summits in the Sierra Nevada, with several peaks exceeding 14,000 feet in elevation. The Palisades Glacier is also the largest in the range. The trailhead is located west of Highway 395 in Big Pine. Take Crocker Street out of town and follow it approximately 10.0 miles up Big Pine Canyon to the end of the road. The North Fork Trail begins in sagebrush, but switchbacks up through lodgepole pine forest, passing a stone cabin built by actor Lon Chaney. As you ascend past First, Second, and Third Lakes, glacial flour—finely ground pieces of glacier—begins to color the water. Campsites with trees are found along this stretch of trail. About 0.5 mile beyond Third Lake, turn south (left) and ascend the switchbacks to Sam Mack Meadows, then hike on the boulders to the glacier. Crampons and an ice ax are necessary to safely travel on the glacier.

OVERNIGHT HIKE: HUMPHREYS BASIN
One-way length: 6 miles
Low and high elevations: 9,400 to 11,400 feet
Difficulty: moderate

The hike into lake-studded Humphreys Basin is like a trip to Greenland—stark, barren, bleak, and rocky. These are the adjectives that describe this truly alpine area. The trailhead is located west of Bishop off Highway 168 toward Lake Sabrina. Just before the lake, there is a right-hand turn (north) to North Lake, located about 2.0 miles up a narrow dirt road, where trailhead parking is available.

From the parking lot at North Lake, the trail climbs through woodlands of aspen and conifer, reaching Loch Leven Lake at 10,740 feet at about 2.0 miles from the trailhead. Continue on to Piute Lake at the 4.0-mile mark, then hike another 1.0 mile to Piute Pass at 11,423 feet, where the barren Humphreys Basin opens up before you. Summit Lake is less than 1.0 mile down the gentle pass, but that isn't your only option. The open terrain makes cross-country travel easy, and with several dozen tarns and lakes to choose from, it isn't difficult to locate a quiet place to camp. The spectacular lakes and glacier in Goethe Cirque lie just to the south. Desolation Lake, looking like a pool from the Barrenlands of the Northwest Territory, lies to the north. Or one can continue down Piute Creek to the John Muir and Pacific Crest Trails. Days, or even weeks, could be spent exploring and sampling all that this one basin has to offer.

OTHER RECREATIONAL OPPORTUNITIES

There is probably no better cross-country skiing in the Sierra Nevada than that found in the John Muir Wilderness. Most of the skiers follow summertime trails up side canyons. The most accessible skiing lies on the eastern side of the Sierra, fronting Highway 395. In years past, a few of the access roads have been kept plowed while others were snowed under, offering a good broad ski surface. Among the more accessible ski areas are the Mammoth Lakes region and Bishop Canyon. Ski up the unplowed portions of Cottonwood Creek, Whitney Portal, and Rock Creek Roads for excellent access to the high country beyond.

Kaiser Wilderness 35

*Made up of a rugged granite ridge, the Kaiser Wilderness
provides spectacular views of the main Sierra crest with
several cirque lakes.*

Kaiser Ridge above Idaho Lake in Kaiser Wilderness.

Established in 1976, the island-like heights of the 22,700-acre
Kaiser Wilderness lie just north of Huntington Lake. It is named
for Kaiser Ridge, a long, high, east-west divide, capped by
10,320-foot Kaiser Peak. From this summit, you will see an
arresting panorama of the Sierra that stretches from the Clark
Range by Yosemite to Mount Whitney.

The southern half of the wilderness slopes up from
Huntington Lake through forests of Jeffrey pine and red fir,
with four trailheads accessing the southern boundary. The
northern portion of the Kaiser Wilderness has been glaciated,
with 18 small glacially carved lakes resting below Kaiser Ridge.
There are also four trailheads accessing the northern part,
although most people actually hike over the ridge from
the south. Trail access to the entire area is good. Like most

LOCATION: 70 miles
east of Fresno

SIZE: 22,700 acres

ELEVATION RANGE:
7,200 to 10,320 feet

MILES OF TRAILS: 40

ECOSYSTEMS:
alpine-rock, Jeffrey
pine, chaparral, red fir

ADMINISTRATION:
Sierra National Forest

MAPS: Sierra National
Forest Map, Kaiser
Wilderness Area Map

wilderness areas in the Sierra, the Forest Service requires quotas to limit the presumed "impacts" of backpackers and hikers, while domestic cattle are free to trample and trash the landscape.

DAY HIKE: IDAHO LAKE TRAIL
One-way length: 3 miles
Low and high elevations: 8,800 to 9,200 feet
Difficulty: moderate

The trail to Idaho Lake and beyond to Potter Pass is relatively even with little climbing, but it offers a pleasant walk to a glacial cirque lake. The trailhead is located at Kaiser Pass east of Huntington Lake. From the trailhead, the route winds through open forests of red fir, lodgepole pine, and Jeffrey fir to pretty Idaho Lake at about 2.0 miles. Continue to traverse to 9,149-foot Potter Pass for good views to the south.

DAY HIKE: KAISER PEAK
One-way length: 5.3 miles
Low and high elevations: 7,150 to 10,320 feet
Difficulty: moderate to strenuous

Kaiser Peak is the highest point in the Kaiser Wilderness, and it offers a tremendous 360-degree view of the central Sierra Nevada. The trailhead is located near the Kinnikinnick Campground north of Huntington Lake off Highway 168. As you start the climb, you will pass the wilderness boundary sign. At 3.0 miles, you will pass College Rock, then arrive at a saddle at 4.3 miles. From here, the trail really gets steep for the final approach to the summit. On a clear day you should be able to see Mount Ritter to the north and Mount Goddard to the south.

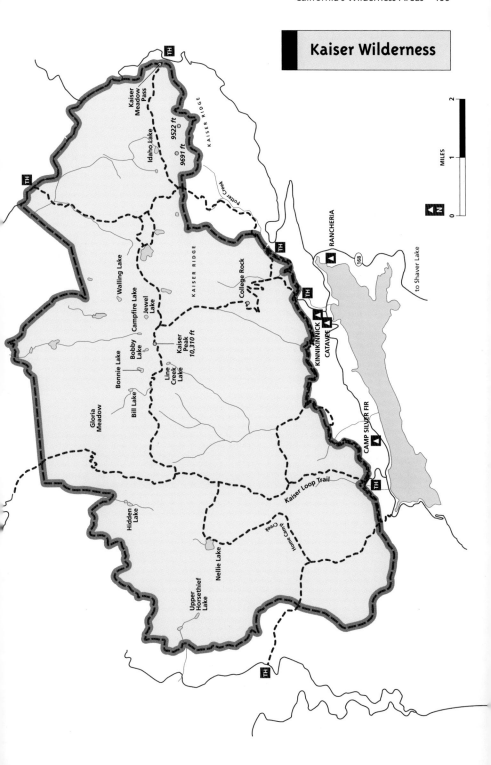

Kaiser Wilderness

N

0   1   2
MILES

TH

Kaiser Meadow Pass

KAISER RIDGE

Idaho Lake

9522 ft

9691 ft

TH

Potter Creek

Walling Lake

KAISER RIDGE

College Rock

RANCHERIA

168

to Shaver Lake

TH

TH

Campfire Lake

Jewel Lake

Bobby Lake

Kaiser Peak
10,310 ft

Line Creek Lake

KINNIKINNICK

CATAVEE

Bonnie Lake

Bill Lake

Gloria Meadow

CAMP SILVER FIR

Hidden Lake

Kaiser Loop Trail

TH

Home Camp Creek

Nellie Lake

Upper Horsethief Lake

TH

36 Mokelumne Wilderness

The Mokelumne Wilderness is distinguished by rugged canyons, rolling uplands, numerous lakes, and sections of the Pacific Crest Trail.

Roundtop Peak near Winnemucca Lake, Mokelumne Wilderness.

LOCATION: 15 miles west of Markleeville

SIZE: 105,165 acres

ELEVATION RANGE: 3,960 to 10,380 feet

MILES OF TRAILS: 89

ECOSYSTEMS: alpine tundra, red fir, ponderosa pine, white fir forest

ADMINISTRATION: Eldorado N.F., Stanislaus N.F., Toiyabe N.F.

MAPS: Eldorado N.F. Map, Stanislaus N.F. Map, Toiyabe N.F. Map/ Carson Ranger District, Mokelumne Wilderness Area Map

Situated on the Sierra crest between Ebbetts and Carson Passes at the headwaters of the West Fork of the Carson and Mokelumne Rivers, the 105,165-acre Mokelumne spans portions of three national forests: Toiyabe, Eldorado, and Stanislaus. Elevations range from 3,960 feet near Salt Springs Reservoir rising to 10,380 feet on the summit of Round Top Peak, the highest point in the wilderness. Much of the terrain is rolling uplands at or near timberline, but the canyon of the Mokelumne River is quite rugged.

The Mokelumne Wilderness was part of the territory used by both the Washo and Miwok tribes. The first whites to enter the area were in the trapping party of Jedidiah Smith, for whom the Smith River in northern California is named. Smith, along with two others, journeyed over the Sierra in

1826 somewhere in this vicinity, thus becoming the first Euro-Americans to success-fully cross the Sierra. But their journey had only begun: They next trekked across Nevada and northern Utah, becoming the first group to successfully cross the Great Basin Desert as well.

John Fremont and guide Kit Carson crossed the Sierra near here in 1844, by Carson's namesake, Carson Pass. Fremont's party is credited with discovering Lake Tahoe. Carson's name is not only attached to the pass, but to a river, mountain range, and wilderness area (Carson–Iceberg), as well.

Gold and silver mining flourished briefly in the 1860s near Blue Lake, but interest subsided after the deposits played out. Most human use after that time consisted of sheep grazing, which came under moderate control once the area became part of the 1897 Stanislaus Forest Reserve, later to become the Stanislaus and Eldorado National Forests. Livestock grazing still occurs here, with the obvious results, generally destroy-ing many of the values associated with wilderness preservation. The Mokelumne, one of the original wilderness areas designated with passage of the 1964 Wilderness Act, was expanded to its present size in the 1984 California Wilderness Act.

The oldest exposed rocks in the wilderness consist of dark metamorphosed sedimentary and volcanic rocks, deposited in ancient seas some 100 to 230 million years ago. Most of these old rock layers have been stripped away by erosion, but their remnants still cap Mokelumne Peak.

Approximately 80 to 95 million years ago, magma was intruded into over-lying rock layers, where it cooled slowly to form granite. Uplift and subsequent erosion has exposed much of this granitic bedrock throughout the wilderness. Some four to 20 million years ago, new volcanic eruptions buried the region in ash, lava flows, and mud. Round Top Peak is a relict volcanic vent, created from this event. Lastly, glaciation scraped and sculpted the surface of the wilderness into cirques and U-shaped valleys, such as Summit Creek and Thornburg Canyon.

Common trees include ponderosa pine at lower elevations graduating into Jeffrey pine, white fir, red fir, lodgepole pine, and whitebark pine at higher altitude. Hikers will notice mountain hemlock as they approach timberline.

As with many wildernesses, the majority of the use is concentrated in a few areas. The loop trails to Winnemucca Lake and Round Top Peak receive the bulk of recreational visitation, while other portions of the wilderness are virtually ignored. Lesser-used areas include the Thornburg Canyon and Pleasant Valley Trails leading in from Markleeville, as well as trails originating by Salt Springs Reservoir. The Forest Service has recently changed regulations regarding use of these areas, so one should check to obtain the latest information. The Pacific Crest Trail runs through a portion of the wilderness.

Expansion of Mokelumne could be accomplished by a few minor road closures. For instance, a major intrusion is the Blue Lakes Road that splits the wilderness into two units. Expansion to the west into the Bear River–Thimble Peak area could be accomplished by closure of one low standard dirt road. All total, there are approximately 60,000 acres of additional roadless areas that could be added to this wilderness.

Mokelumne Wilderness

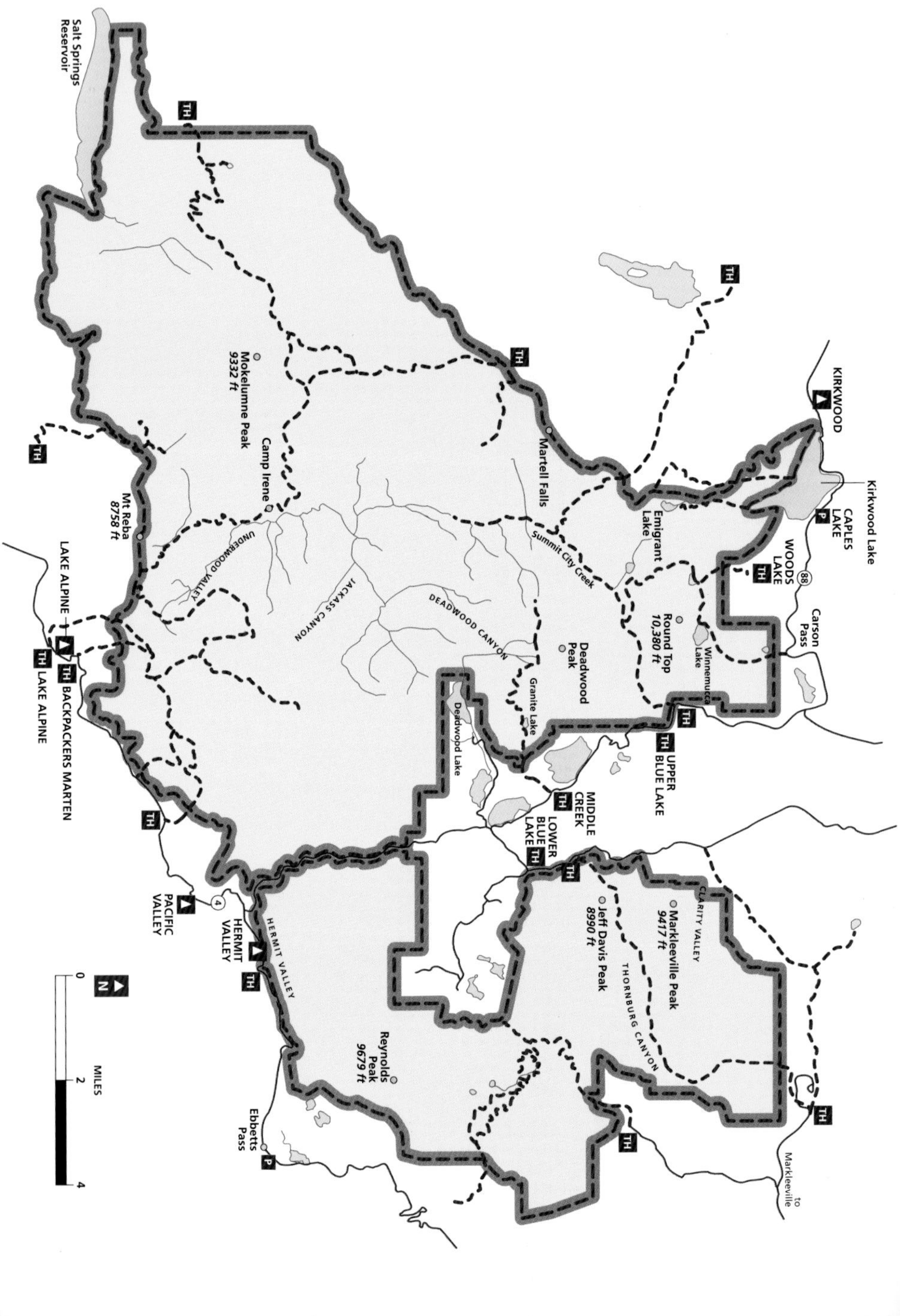

Salt Springs
Reservoir

TH

TH

TH

KIRKWOOD

Kirkwood Lake

CAPLES
LAKE

P

Mokelumne Peak
9332 ft

Camp Irene

WOODS
LAKE

Martell Falls

88

Carson
Pass

Mt Reba
8758 ft

UNDERWOOD VALLEY

JACKASS CANYON

Summit City Creek

Emigrant
Lake

LAKE ALPINE

DEADWOOD CANYON

Deadwood
Peak

Round Top
10,380 ft

Winnemucca
Lake

TH

LAKE ALPINE

BACKPACKERS MARTEN

Granite Lake

Deadwood Lake

TH

UPPER
BLUE LAKE

TH

MIDDLE
CREEK

TH

LOWER
BLUE
LAKE

TH

TH

CLARITY VALLEY

TH

PACIFIC
VALLEY

4

Jeff Davis Peak
8990 ft

Markleeville Peak
9417 ft

HERMIT
VALLEY

THORNBURG CANYON

TH

HERMIT VALLEY

N

0

2

MILES

4

Reynolds
Peak
9679 ft

Ebbetts
Pass

P

TH

Markleeville
to

DAY HIKE: GRANITE LAKE
One-way length: 2.2 miles
Low and high elevations: 8,100 to 8,700 feet
Difficulty: moderate

The scenic hike to Granite Lake is relatively short and easy, with great views of the surrounding wilderness both on the way in and on nearby ridges that surround the lake itself. The trailhead is located near Middle Creek Campground on the Blue Lakes Road, which is off of Highway 88 just 6.3 miles east of Carson Pass. It is 13.0 miles to the campground. The trail ascends gently at first, then climbs steeply after passing the wilderness boundary. The good views here make the ascent easier to ignore. The final stretch is less steep as you arrive at the aptly named lake, situated in a granite basin with whitebark pine, mountain hemlock, and lodgepole pine scattered around.

DAY HIKE: WINNEMUCCA AND ROUND TOP LAKE LOOP
Loop length: 4.8 miles
Low and high elevations: 8,400 to 9,400 feet
Difficulty: moderate

This is one of the more popular loops in the Mokelumne Wilderness, so be prepared to meet other hikers. However, for the amount of effort involved, the rewards are great with fantastic views, flowery meadows, and dashing streams. The trailhead is located at the Woods Lake Campground just 1.8 miles west of Carson Pass off Highway 88. The trail for Winnemucca Lake takes off from the east side of Woods Lake, climbing gently 1.5 miles through scattered woodlands to the beautiful lake located below Round Top Peak. After pausing at the lake to admire the scenery, head west through a small saddle before dropping to Round Top Lake. From here, it's an easy traverse downhill back to Woods Lake. For those with more time and energy, the views from the summit of 10,381-foot Round Top Peak are worth the climb. From Round Top Lake, head south along the eastern shore and follow a faint trail toward the saddle west of the peak, then scramble among boulders to the summit.

DAY HIKE: EMIGRANT LAKE
One-way length: 4.6 miles
Low and high elevations: 7,798 to 8,600 feet
Difficulty: moderate

Emigrant Lake sits in a glacial cirque near timberline and makes for a pleasant day hike or easy overnight trek. The trailhead is located near the outlet of Caples Lake, 5.0 miles west of Carson Pass on Highway 88. The first 2.0 miles of the trail is nearly level and follows the shoreline of Caples Lake. Once you pass the end of the reservoir, the trail begins to climb more steeply, then becomes very steep with switchbacks for the last 0.5 mile before the lake.

37 Monarch Wilderness

Taking in the steep gorges of the Middle and South Forks of the Kings River, the Monarch Wilderness is one of the more inaccessible wildlands of the western Sierra.

Looking across Monarch Wilderness toward the Middle Fork of the Kings River Canyon.

LOCATION: 60 miles east of Fresno

SIZE: 45,000 acres

ELEVATION RANGE: 2,400 to 11,000 feet

MILES OF TRAILS: 16

ECOSYSTEMS: chaparral, mixed conifer forest

ADMINISTRATION: Sierra National Forest, Sequoia National Forest

MAPS: Sierra N.F. Map, Sequoia N.F. Map, Monarch Wilderness/ Jennie Lakes Wilderness Areas Map

As one drives along Highway 180 to Cedar Grove in Kings Canyon National Park and the South Fork of the Kings River, you round a curve by Horseshoe Bend and are treated to an immense thousand-foot wall of limestone that makes up Junction Ridge. Most people don't realize it, but they are looking at the heart of the 45,000-acre Monarch Wilderness, formerly called the High Sierra Primitive Area.

The wilderness, managed by both the Sequoia and Sierra National Forests, takes in both sides of the highway and includes much of the dramatic, deep canyon of the Middle Fork of the Kings River. Both the South Fork and the Middle Fork are designated Wild and Scenic Rivers. The main drainage in the wilderness is Grizzly Creek, whose headwaters contain the two small Grizzly Lakes.

Lower elevations are cloaked with chaparral, ponderosa pine, and Jeffrey pine. At high elevations you will see whitebark pine, the southernmost occurrence of this species in the Sequoia National Forest.

The wilderness is bordered on the north and east by Kings Canyon National Park and on the north by the John Muir Wilderness. Elevations range from 2,400 feet along the river to summits of more than 11,000 feet, including Spanish Mountain (10,051), Obelisk Peak (9,700), Mount Harrington (11,005), and Wren Peak (9,450). The views from Spanish Mountain across the Kings River Canyon are exceptional, with terrain so steep that U.S. Geological Survey field crews studying the area in the early 1970s had to move their camps by helicopters. As a consequence of its nearly vertical aspect, there are almost no trails within the wilderness. Cross-country travel would be extremely difficult, if not impossible.

DAY HIKE: DEER COVE TRAIL
One-way length: 4 miles
Low and high elevations: 4,400 to 7,800 feet
Difficulty: moderate

This south-facing trail can be hot in summer, climbing steeply to a lovely creek and Wildman Meadow, a good spot to camp or turn around, in the Monarch Wilderness. The trailhead is located north of the highway just before Cedar Grove in Kings Canyon National Park.

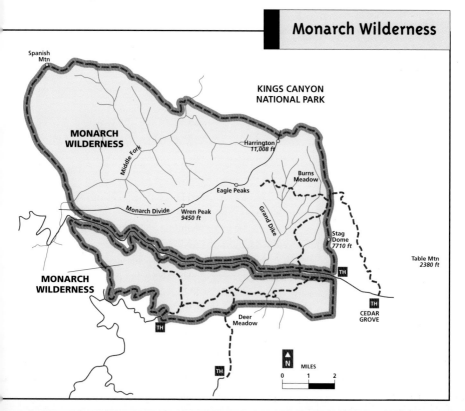

Monarch Wilderness

Sequoia–Kings Canyon National Park Wilderness

This wilderness contains the most elevated country of the High Sierra, with hundreds of alpine lakes and jagged peaks full of miles of trails.

Alpen glow on Mount Darwin in Sequoia–Kings Canyon National Park Wilderness.

LOCATION: 80 miles southeast of Fresno

SIZE: 736,980 acres

ELEVATION RANGE: 1,300 to 14,500 feet

MILES OF TRAILS: 800

ECOSYSTEMS: oak woodlands, mixed conifer, sequoia, alpine tundra

ADMINISTRATION: National Park Service

MAPS: Sequoia–Kings Canyon National Park Map, John Muir/Sequoia/Kings Canyon Wilderness Areas Map

Though the names are different, both Sequoia and Kings Canyon National Parks are managed as one unit. Ninety percent of their backcountry, some 736,980 acres, were designated wilderness by the California Wilderness Act of 1984, making it the largest single wilderness in the state under one management agency. Two other parts of the park are also under study for wilderness protection — 56,000 acres of the Hockett Plateau and 35,000 acres on Redwood Mountain/North Fork Kaweah.

The area that would later become the largest Sierran parks complex was first explored by whites when William and John Bubbs prospected Kings Canyon in 1860. Bubbs Creek is named for them. In 1864, William Brewer, after which Mount Brewer is named, and four others with the California Geological Survey explored the area at the head of the Kern and Kings Rivers. The men sighted Mount Whitney and named it after their director, Josiah Whitney. Another early visitor was Frank Dusy, who explored Tehipite Valley. Dusy Basin, located just west of the Palisades, is named for him. In 1873, John Muir explored the Kings River country, which was already being ravaged by domestic livestock. This prompted him to work for its protection. He was back again in 1877 to further his survey of the southern Sierra. Mount Muir and Muir Pass are two park landmarks named for this intrepid mountaineer.

In 1881, the first bill to establish a national park in the southern Sierra was introduced into Congress by John Miller of California. It would have established a park approximately the size of today's combined parkland but it failed because it was considered too bold for the time. Park supporters did not give up, however, and by 1890 they successfully established a smaller Sequoia National Park, making it the second national park created in the nation. The park's purpose was to protect some of the largest sequoia groves in the southern Sierra.

Almost as soon as it was established, John Muir was lobbying to expand it. In an 1891 article he published in *Century Magazine,* Muir argued that everything from the headwaters of the Kings and Kern Rivers as far east as Mount Whitney should be incorporated in the new area. The park has been enlarged several times, most recently in 1978, when the Mineral King area was added, ending a long heated battle against ski resort development in that valley.

The 450,000-acre Kings Canyon National Park was established in 1940. It is unique among national parks in the lower 48 states because, from the start, it was managed primarily as a wilderness park. Except for a road that ends at Cedar Grove, nearly the entire park has remained undeveloped. Its namesake, Kings Canyon, is more than 8,200 feet in depth—the deepest canyon in North America, exceeding the Grand Canyon by 2,000 feet. The 3,000-foot cliff face on Tehipite Dome along the Middle Fork of the Kings Canyon is often compared to Half Dome in the Yosemite Valley. During the last Ice Age, a glacier 23 miles long gouged out the Middle Fork Valley into a magnificent U-shaped canyon. The only reason it isn't better known is that its only access is by trail.

The Kings River is not the only major glaciated canyon. Deep in Sequoia National Park's backcountry lies the fault-controlled Kern River, the only Sierra waterway that flows south for any distance. The Kern is cutting into the granitic rocks as seismic activity uplifts the entire region. On either side of it are old erosional surfaces—the Chagoopa and Boreal Plateaus—and the mountains seem to split here as well. The main Sierra crest, including such 14,000-foot peaks as Mount Russell, Mount Muir, Mount Langley, and Mount Whitney, forms the higher eastern arm, while the Great Western Divide, a range of 13,000-foot peaks, forms the western branch. The highest water body in California, 12,802-foot Tulainyo Lake, lies just north of Mount Russell.

Major cross ridges and divides, such as Monarch, LeConte, Black, Goddard, and Glacier Divides, give depth to this part of the Sierra. Stand on any high summit, and the ragged array of peaks that puncture the sky in every direction give an overwhelming sense of vastness.

Elevations in these parks range from 1,500 feet to the 14,495-foot summit of Mount Whitney. Given this elevational difference, it's not surprising that the vegetation and wildlife are varied and diverse. At the lowest elevations, chaparral dominates, along with blue oak savanna and California buckeye. Higher up, typical Sierran forest species are found, such as red fir, white fir, sugar pine, Jeffrey pine, incense cedar, lodgepole pine, and the giant sequoia, for which the park was established. Aspen often fringe the meadows.

Wildlife of the lower elevations includes gray fox, ringtail, bobcat, striped and spotted skunks, raccoon, woodrat, pocket gopher, and a wide variety of lizards and snakes, including the whiptail lizard, gopher snake, and Pacific rattlesnake. In the forested mid-elevations, golden mantled ground squirrels, chickaree, mountain lion, mule deer, and black bear are common in summer. At the highest elevations, marmots, pika, wolverine (rarely seen), and white-tailed jackrabbit can be observed, along with rosy finch, Clark's nutcracker, golden eagle, and raven.

The black bear are mostly vegetarian, subsisting upon acorns, grass, berries, and insects. They are, however, adept at raiding camper's food supplies and are quite intelligent in their abilities to discern potential food sources. Black bear in Sequoia have learned to break into cars to steal food from coolers. Every effort should be made to keep food from bears—a human-food adapted bear usually winds up a dead bear, sooner or later.

Trails crisscross the backcountry, permitting numerous loop trails, cross-Sierra hikes, and through hikes on the Pacific Crest, John Muir, and High Sierra Trails. For sheer beauty of scenery, ease of access, opportunity for variety of routes, good weather, and abundance of water, there is probably no finer backpacking area in the United States.

DAY HIKE: HEATHER LAKE
One-way length: 4.2 miles
Low and high elevations: 7,280 to 9,500 feet
Difficulty: moderate

Heather Lake is more an excuse for hiking somewhere than a destination in itself. It is closed to camping, so most visitors have a picnic before turning around and heading back down the trail. The route follows the Marble Fork of the Kaweah River for part of the distance and offers a good introduction to the west slope of the Sierra forests. The trailhead is located off the Generals Highway. Take the Wolverton turnoff for Lodgepole Campground and drive 1.5 miles, watching for signs indicating trailhead parking. The first part of the trail climbs through red fir forest until you reach a trail junction at 1.8 miles, where you need to bear left for Heather Lake. At 2.1 miles, there is a trail junction, with both trails ultimately reaching Heather Lake. The left branch, which is Watchtower Trail, is longer but more scenic.

DAY HIKE: ALTA PEAK TRAIL
One-way length: 6.3 miles
Low and high elevations: 7,260 to 11,204 feet
Difficulty: moderate

This hike offers one of the better vistas accessible by trail in the Sequoia–Kings Canyon National Park. The trailhead is located at Wolverton 3.0 miles northeast of Giant Forest in Sequoia National Park.

You will reach a junction after a short distance on the trail; bear right for the path to Alta Peak, heading east then southeast along Wolverton Creek through a red fir forest. At 2.6 miles, you will reach the intersection of the Wolverton Creek and Alta Trails at Panther Gap. Views of the Great Western Divide can be discerned to the east. Continue east to Mehrten Meadow, where camping is permitted for those backpacking. In another 1.0 mile, you will reach another trail junction. If you want to backpack to Moose Lake and the Tablelands, continue straight ahead. For Alta Peak, turn left (north) onto the Alta Peak Trail, passing Tharps Rock enroute. The trail ascends through a forest of western white pine and scattered foxtail pine until the trail fades just below the summit. Scramble up granite blocks to the top of the peak for an expanded view of the entire southern Sierra. Just south, across the Middle Fork of the Kaweah River, lies the jagged Castle Rocks and on a clear day, Mount Whitney can easily be seen to the east.

DAY HIKE: EAGLE LAKE
One-way length: 3.4 miles
Low and high elevations: 7,800 to 10,000 feet
Difficulty: moderate

Eagle Lakes lies in a pretty glacial pond set in a bare granite bowl. First, find your way to Mineral King area at the end of a twisty, rough, 25-mile dirt road that will take you three hours to drive. The first part of the trail climbs a flower-scented and sagebrush-lined trail along the East Fork of the Kaweah River. Gradually, the trail enters a red fir forest and the grade steepens. At 1.1 miles, you will reach a trail junction; keep right and climb the switchbacks. At 2.0 miles, there is another trail junction. This time, bear left for Eagle Lake and climb more switchbacks until you reach the lake at 3.4 miles. It is possible to camp here, and a few backpackers do so.

DAY HIKE: REDWOOD CREEK LOOP
Loop length: 6.2 miles
Low and high elevations: 6,200 to 6,950 feet
Difficulty: moderate

There are 75 major sequoia groves on the western slope of the Sierra Nevada. (*Note:* Sequoias were sometimes called "redwoods" by early settlers, but the true California redwood is found only along the coast.) A few, such as Grant Grove and Giant Forest, are accessible by car and are thronged by visitors. This hike to Redwood Mountain, currently a wilderness study area, offers a fine day trip through a magnificent giant sequoia forest. The trailhead is located south of the Generals Highway in Sequoia National Park. From the junction of Highway 180 and the Generals Highway, drive 3.5 miles to a Forest Service road signed for Hume Lake. Just opposite, to the south off the Generals Highway, is a dirt road signed for Kings Canyon National Park. Drive 1.9 miles to Redwood Saddle, with another 0.1 mile to the trailhead.

Take the Sugarbowl Trail, which heads south just east of Redwood Mountain's crest through a forest of white fir, sugar pine, and sequoia. Eventually, you will descend off the mountain into Redwood Creek's canyon, observing the granite face of Big Baldy Mountain along the way. At Redwood Creek, a trail junction is reached. Turn left and pass many fine sequoias as you follow Redwood Creek upstream approximately 2.0 miles to the trailhead.

OVERNIGHT HIKE: FARWELL GAP AND BULLFROG LAKES
One-way length: 7 miles
Low and high elevations: 7,000 to 10,700 feet
Difficulty: moderate

The trek to Farwell Gap, the gateway to hikes into the Golden Trout Wilderness to the south, makes a good day hike. The trailhead is located on the western slope of the Sierra at Mineral King Valley in Sequoia National Park. You can reach it via Highway 198 to Three Rivers, then drive 25.0 miles on the windy Mineral King Road.

The hike to Farwell Gap is relatively easy. It follows a road, then climbs through open slopes and scattered timber to treeline. From the gap you have two options: You can drop down to the headwaters of the Little Kern River, reaching the official trail junction for Bullfrog Lakes in about 1.0 mile. The Bullfrog Trail climbs northeast for about 0.75 mile to the lower of the two lakes; or you can traverse the open slopes for 1.0 mile to the lakes, saving yourself the descent and extra mile of hiking.

For those who wish to make a longer loop, it's possible to continue down the Little Kern River to a trail junction that leads to Shotgun Creek and Silver Lake. Cross Shotgun Pass back into Sequoia National Park and continue north to a trail junction leading to Franklin Lakes. From here, it's a quick 5.0-mile downhill run back to the trailhead.

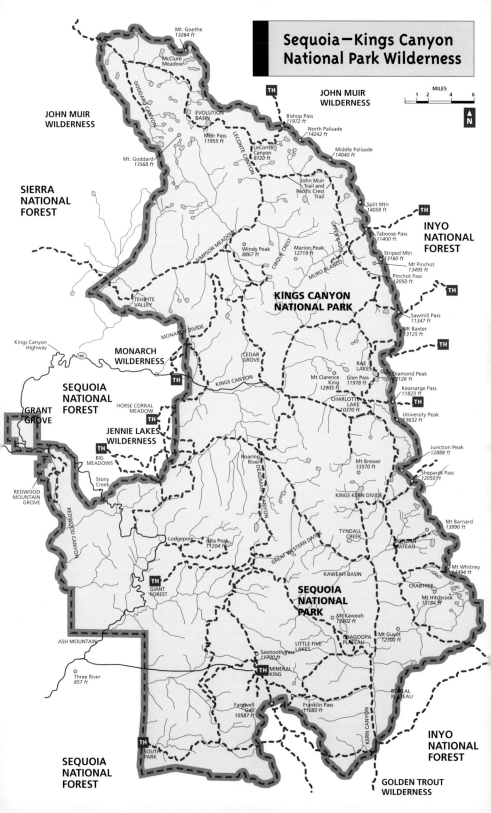

OVERNIGHT HIKE: ONION VALLEY TO CEDAR GROVE
One-way length: 23.5 miles
Low and high elevations: 4,800 to 11,813 feet
Difficulty: strenuous

This is one of the classic trans-Sierra hikes that is also one of the shortest. Of course, if you plan to go only one way, there is a very long shuttle that must be prearranged. At 9,200 feet, Onion Valley Trailhead, one of the highest in the Sierra, is the main approach to Kearsarge Pass and is one of the shortest access points crossing the main Sierra crest, which means it is also one of the most popular. Those seeking solitude need not travel this route. From Highway 395, the trailhead is located west of Independence.

But if solitude isn't your goal, then by all means consider this hike. The first part of the trail switchbacks up from the trailhead to 11,813-foot Kearsarge Pass, a great day hike. It is just four—albeit steep—miles, passing some lovely lakes enroute. From the pass, you will see the spectacular Kearsarge Pinnacles just below. Beyond lie the Kearsarge Lakes, which make a good stopping point for those not trying to set a record getting to Cedar Grove. Bear in mind that the next lake, Bullfrog, is closed to camping. From Bullfrog Lake, the trail drops more than 1,000 feet into the glaciated gorge of Bubbs Creek Canyon, where there are good camping opportunities. From Vidette Meadows, it's a 14-mile trek to Cedar Grove. For those who aren't willing to do a long shuttle and need to go back to the Onion Valley Trailhead, a return trail via Paradise Valley and Rae Lakes over Glen Pass makes for a nice loop of 50 miles.

OTHER RECREATIONAL OPPORTUNITIES

There are almost unlimited cross-country skiing opportunities in Sequoia–Kings Canyon National Park. Skiing the trails that link the sequoia groves makes for good winter fun. The Giant Forest–Lodgepole area is a good ski base with numerous trails in the vicinity. One of the most popular ski treks is the Big Meadows ski tour, which borders the Jennie Lakes Wilderness on Sequoia's northwest edge. Other popular backcountry trips are the 6.0-mile ski to Pear Lake Hut, which takes off from the Wolverton Trailhead, and the tour up the Mineral King Road, which is unplowed in the winter.

South Sierra Wilderness 39

*This wilderness is accented by gently rolling,
forested terrain with a steep eastern face.*

South Fork of the Kern River in South Sierra Wilderness.

Established in 1984, the 63,000-acre South Sierra Wilderness
lies along the southern Sierra crest, just south of the Golden
Trout Wilderness which it adjoins. Rising steeply from 4,240 feet
in the Owens Valley on the eastern side of the Sierra escarpment, the highest point lies at 12,123 feet on the summit of
Olancha Peak, the most southerly 12,000-foot peak in the
Sierra. Encompassing the South Fork of the Kern, a designated
Wild and Scenic River, the terrain is mostly rolling with no
lakes. The main access is from Kennedy Meadows, where there
is a trailhead for the Pacific Crest Trail, the major north-south
trail in the wilderness. Only 30 miles of trails are found in
the entire area, but the open forests and gentle terrain make
cross-country travel easy.

The western portion of the wilderness has stands of
old-growth Jeffrey pine and ponderosa pine, while lodgepole

LOCATION: 10 miles
west of Olancha

SIZE: 63,000 acres

ELEVATION RANGE:
6,100 to 12,123 feet

MILES OF TRAILS: 30

ECOSYSTEMS:
pinyon pine, mixed
conifer, Jeffrey pine

ADMINISTRATION:
Inyo National Forest

MAPS: Inyo National
Forest Map, Golden
Trout/ South Sierra
Wilderness Areas Map

pine is abundant in the colder basins. Red fir grows on Kingfisher Ridge. In the most easterly portion of the wilderness, pinyon pine is found, along with greasewood and sagebrush.

The South Fork of the Kern contains the South Fork of the Kern golden trout, sometimes known as the Volcano golden trout. According to Eric Gerstrung, Endangered Fishery Biologist with the California Department of Fish and Game, much of the South Fork is severely degraded as fish habitat because of livestock grazing.

Two large Roadless Area Review Evaluation (RARE) II roadless areas abut the wilderness, both recommended for non-wilderness. The Monache Mountain RA, sandwiched between the Golden Trout Wilderness and South Sierra, contains the largest meadow complex in the southern Sierra. It has been compromised by unregulated off-road vehicle use, as well as livestock grazing. This area is so severely degraded that the Forest Service is considering using bulldozers to totally restructure the stream channel. The Haiwee Creek RA, located on the eastern escarpment, takes in a sliver of one to four miles all along the eastern border of the South Sierra.

DAY HIKE: KENNEDY MEADOWS TO CLOVER MEADOWS
One-way length: 5.5 miles
Low and high elevations: 6,000 to 7,100 feet
Difficulty: moderate

This hike is a modest walk along the South Fork of the Kern River to Clover Meadows, passing through forests of pinyon pine, Jeffrey pine, and lodgepole pine. There are few views and limited access to the river, so it's mostly just an opportunity to hike through the forest. The Kennedy Meadows Trailhead can be reached by driving Nine Mile Canyon Road from Highway 395 to Kennedy Meadows Road and following it to the trailhead. This route uses the Pacific Crest Trail, taking hikers north to Clover Meadow. It occasionally fords the adjacent stream, and there is one crossing that may be difficult early in the season. Clover Meadows makes for a nice picnic spot and turnaround point, although the Pacific Crest Trail continues north to skirt Monache Meadows.

OVERNIGHT HIKE: HAIWEE CREEK–DUTCH JOHN FLAT
One-way length: 6.3 miles
Low and high elevations: 5,000 to 7,965 feet
Difficulty: moderate

This hike provides access into the heart of the South Sierra Wilderness, with opportunities to connect with the Pacific Crest Trail and South Fork of the Kern River. To find the trailhead on Highway 395, drive approximately 9.0 miles south of Olancha and look for a dirt road heading off to the west. It is approximately 3.0 miles up this road to the trailhead. Follow Haiwee Trail 37E01 west along Haiwee Creek 2.7 miles, with a final steep ascent to Haiwee Pass at 7,965 feet. This route was once proposed for a trans-Sierra highway, but the designation of the South Sierra Wilderness precluded any chance for future construction. From the pass, it is basically downhill to the South Fork of the Kern. Once on the South Fork, turn upstream to find nice campsites among oaks at Dutch John Flat.

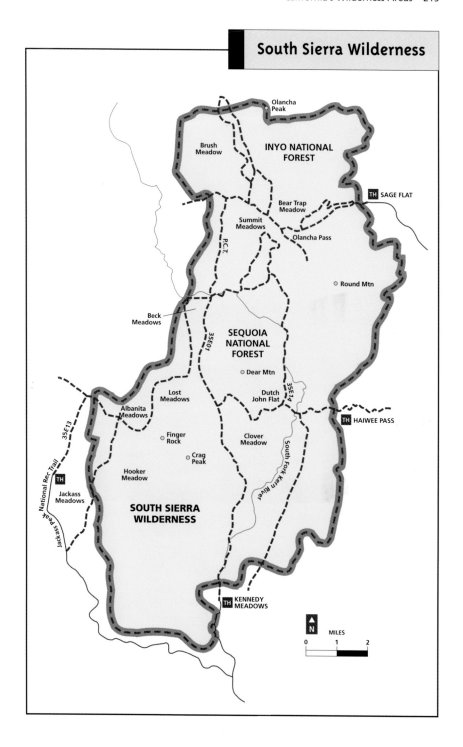

South Sierra Wilderness

Olancha
Peak

Brush
Meadow

INYO NATIONAL
FOREST

TH SAGE FLAT

Bear Trap
Meadow

Summit
Meadows

Olancha Pass

P.C.T.

Round Mtn

Beck
Meadows

SEQUOIA
NATIONAL
FOREST

35E01

Dear Mtn

Lost
Meadows

Dutch
John Flat

35E14

Albanita
Meadows

TH HAIWEE PASS

Finger
Rock

Clover
Meadow

Crag
Peak

South Fork Kern River

Hooker
Meadow

35E13

National Rec Trail

Jackass
Meadows

SOUTH SIERRA
WILDERNESS

Jackass Peak

TH KENNEDY
MEADOWS

N

MILES

0   1   2

40 Yosemite National Park Wilderness

Yosemite National Park is one of the largest wilderness areas in California. Despite the crowds that may jam its valley, Yosemite's backcountry offers everything from solitude to alpine lakes and beautiful forested valleys.

The view northeast from Mount Hoffman, Yosemite Wilderness.

LOCATION: 70 miles east of Merced

SIZE: 681,150 acres

ELEVATION RANGE: 2,100 to 13,000 feet

MILES OF TRAILS: 800

ECOSYSTEMS: chaparral, oak woodlands, mixed conifer, alpine

ADMINISTRATION: Yosemite National Park

MAPS: Yosemite National Park Map, Yosemite National Park Topo Map

Some 681,150 acres of Yosemite National Park were granted wilderness status as part of the 1984 California Wilderness Act. Even though it is divided into two halves by the Tioga Pass–Tuolumne Meadow Road, the overall wildlands complex is much larger because the park is surrounded by designated wilderness on three sides. Although the park is better known for its crowds than its isolation and wilderness, solitude is easily attainable for those willing to make the effort. I've spent days at a time in the Yosemite backcountry, even during the height of the summer tourist season, without encountering another soul.

With granite domes, hundreds of waterfalls, jagged peaks, deep canyons, lovely virgin forests, miles of beautiful granitic basins, and more than 300 lakes, Yosemite is a visual feast for the eye. The elevations range from around 2,000 feet along the Merced River to over 13,000 feet along the Sierra crest. There are two named mountain sub-ranges in the park: Cathedral Range and Clark Range.

Yosemite lays claim to a host of superlatives. El Capitan is the largest cliff face in the world. Tuolumne Meadows, located in the center of the park, is the largest meadow in the entire Sierra Nevada. Yosemite Falls is the third highest in the world. It is no wonder that Yosemite was declared a World Heritage Site.

Most of the bedrock exposed in Yosemite consists of granitic materials. This rock was implanted as molten magma deep in the earth, where it cooled and hardened. Only later was it uplifted and the overriding rocks scraped away by erosion to expose the granite beneath. Although superficially similar, the granitic rocks in Yosemite are made up of numerous plutons or granitic intrusions of varying age and chemical composition. Why the rock faces of Yosemite vary from cliff to rubble, such as what is seen by El Capitan in the Yosemite Valley, depends on the different chemical properties of these unique magma intrusions.

After uplift, the entire wilderness area was heavily glaciated during the last Ice Age. Relict glaciers that are hidden among the higher peaks such as Dana, Lyell, and others, formed during the last mini-Ice Age that occurred only 300 to 400 years ago.

Yosemite displays more effects of glaciation than the areas both north and south of it for two reasons. Lying almost due east of the Golden Gate and San Francisco Bay, Yosemite is perfectly aligned to receive the westward sweeping air masses off the ocean, which proceed inland almost uninterrupted. For the same reason, a lot of snow falls in the high country each winter. A lot of snow falls in the Lake Tahoe area as well, but it is not as glaciated. The important difference is height. With peaks of 13,000 feet in elevation, Yosemite is high enough to capture a great deal of snow and is positioned close to the pathway of moisture-bearing air masses.

During the last Ice Age, a gigantic glacial ice sheet covered much of the high country along the Sierra crest. Huge valley glaciers flowed down existing river canyons, sculpting and deepening them. The rugged Grand Canyon of the Tuolumne was carved by the Tuolumne Glacier, which, at 60 miles in length, is the longest valley glacier in the Sierra. Most of the higher lakes fill glacially carved rock basins.

Yosemite was the first parklands set aside merely to protect its scenic splendor. In 1864, the Yosemite Valley was ceded from the federal government to the state of California to be retained as a public park. Livestock grazing continued to degrade the uplands. John Muir, wilderness prophet of the Sierra Nevada, lobbied to have the head-waters of the Tuolumne and Merced Rivers surrounding the Yosemite Valley State Park protected as a national park in order to preclude further livestock grazing. In 1890, Muir, along with the help of many others, succeeded in persuading Congress to desig-nate Yosemite as our third national park. Later the state park in the valley was ceded back to the federal government.

Although declared a protected area, not all wildlife survived. The last grizzly bear was killed in 1895 near Wawona, and bighorn sheep were extinct by 1914. Sierran red fox and wolverine may have disappeared as well. Fortunately, recent reintroduction of bighorn in Lee Vining Canyon have spread into the park, returning these animals to the high country along the Sierran crest. Originally, fish were not found in Yosemite above the 4,000-foot elevation. Native fish such as salmon and steelhead, which once ran up the Merced into the park, are extinct due to dams on the lower San Joaquin River. However, as a result of stocking, fish are now found in more than 100 of the 318 lakes in the park. While this may bring a smile to the fisherman's face, fish stocking has serious ecological impacts. It is thought to be one factor responsible for the decline in the park's frog population and throughout the Sierra Nevada. (See page 309 for more information about fish stocking.)

Though the Yosemite high country is dramatic, the mid-elevation forests are among the most overlooked aspects of Yosemite's attractions. The park was established early enough to protect representatives of forests that were left out of other wildlands in the Sierra. For example, some of the best examples of old-growth sugar pine found in the entire state are located in Yosemite's backcountry. Besides sugar pine, the park is home to beautiful stands of ponderosa pine, incense cedar, Jeffrey pine, western white pine, white fir, red fir, lodgepole pine, mountain hemlock, and whitebark pine. Hardwoods include Pacific dogwood, azalea, bigleaf maple, aspen, black oak, and canyon live oak.

Like many parts of the Sierra Nevada, permits are required to spend the night in the Yosemite National Park backcountry. Part of the justification for this is to reduce the impacts associated with human use. Ironically, on some of the heavily used trails, the majority of the impact is from horse use, mostly from commercial outfitters either supplying the High Sierra camps or bringing people to them. The camps were grandfathered in after the park's backcountry obtained legal wilderness status. They provide family-style meals, hot showers, and overnight accommodations—if you can afford the cost. The presence of the camps is controversial, since they concentrate use and bring their own impacts, such as the need for proper sewage deposal. It has been proven that each horse is equal to 25 to 50 backpackers, in terms of impact to trails and campsites. Some argue that elimination of horse use would substantially reduce backcountry impacts, but horse users counter with the suggestion that horses allow travel into the wildlands by those who would otherwise find it inaccessible. The controversy is not likely to be settled anytime soon. (See page 307 for more information about the environmental effects of pack stock use.)

DAY HIKE: NORTH DOME TRAIL
One-way length: 3.7 miles
Low and high elevations: 7,542 to 8,150 feet
Difficulty: moderate

North Dome, which lies along the lip of the glaciated Yosemite Valley, provides great views of the entire Yosemite Valley region. The trailhead is located by the Porcupine Creek Campground off the Tioga Pass Road (Highway 120) west of Tuolumne Meadows. The trail travels southwest primarily through forest and passes several intersections, including a side trail about 2.0 miles out that leads up Indian Rock. The route to North Dome continues in a southwest direction. Some of the trail is across granite slabs, so watch for cairns indicating the proper direction.

Yosemite National Park Wilderness

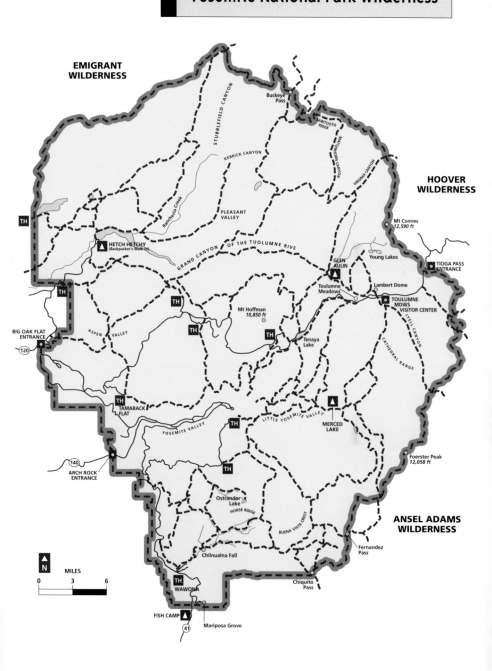

EMIGRANT WILDERNESS

HOOVER WILDERNESS

ANSEL ADAMS WILDERNESS

STUBBLEFIELD CANYON

Buckeye Pass

SAWTOOTH RIDGE

KERRICK CANYON

MATTHORN CANYON

VIRGINIA CANYON

Rancheria Creek

PLEASANT VALLEY

TH

Mt Connes 12,590 ft

HETCH HETCHY
(Backpacker's Walk-in)

GRAND CANYON OF THE TUOLUMNE RIVE

GLEN AULIN

Young Lakes

TIOGA PASS ENTRANCE

TH

Toulumne Meadows

Lambert Dome

TOULUMNE MDWS VISITOR CENTER

BIG OAK FLAT ENTRANCE

ASPEN VALLEY

TH

Mt Hoffman 10,850 ft

TH

LYELL CANYON

120

TH

Tenaya Lake

CATHEDRAL RANGE

TH
TAMARACK FLAT

YOSEMITE VALLEY

TH

LITTLE YOSEMITE VALLEY

MERCED LAKE

140

TH

Foerster Peak 12,058 ft

ARCH ROCK ENTRANCE

TH

Ostrander Lake

HORSE RIDGE

BUENA VISTA CREST

N

MILES

0   3   6

Chilnualna Fall

Fernandez Pass

TH
WAWONA

Chiquito Pass

FISH CAMP

41

Mariposa Grove

> **DAY HIKE: CATHEDRAL LAKES**
> One-way length: 3.5 miles
> Low and high elevations: 8,500 to 9,600 feet
> Difficulty: moderate

Cathedral Lakes lie in a rocky, glaciated basin below the horned spire of Cathedral Peak, a major landmark of the central Yosemite backcountry. The trailhead is located on the Tioga Pass Road (Highway 120) 1.0 mile west of the Tuolumne Meadows Visitor Center. The route heads in a generally southwest direction and climbs somewhat steeply, but it also has stretches that are more or less level. It passes through forests of lodgepole pine mixed with red fir and other species. If you want to get some good views, travel 0.25 mile past Cathedral Lake to Cathedral Pass, which opens up beautiful vistas to the south.

> **DAY HIKE: MOUNT HOFFMAN**
> One-way length: 3.5 miles
> Low and high elevations: 8,847 to 10,850 feet
> Difficulty: moderate

Mount Hoffman offers one of the best views from the center of Yosemite National Park. From the summit, you have a 360-degree panorama. The trailhead is located along the Tioga Pass Road 26 miles from the Crane Flat Junction, where there is a sign for May Lake on the north side of the highway. Take that road for 2.0 miles to the parking lot.

The hike up Mount Hoffman first travels on a mostly level trail to May Lake, about 1.0 mile from the trailhead. Then it begins to climb, first west, then northwest to the peak summit, passing through mountain hemlock forest enroute, one of the southernmost stands of the tree in the Sierra. The effects of glaciers are abundantly evident. Good views of Half Dome, Cathedral Peak, and the Matterhorn, among other high peaks, are evident from Hoffman's summit.

> **OVERNIGHT HIKE: EVELYN LAKE**
> One-way length: 10 miles
> Low and high elevations: 8,600 to 10,328 feet
> Difficulty: moderate

Evelyn Lake occupies an alpine cirque in the Cathedral Range and makes a good destination for overnight trips. Almost half the route is along meadows. The hike begins at the Tuolumne Meadows Campground just off the Tioga Pass Road. The first part of the hike follows the John Muir Trail up the Lyell Fork of the Tuolumne River through Lyell Canyon, passing several spur trails. Expect to meet lots of other hikers on this section. After 5.5 miles, you leave the John Muir Trail, keeping right at the trail junction fork. At 8.0 miles, the side trail to Ireland Lake heads to the southwest. This tarn is worth a visit, but be prepared to climb 700 feet and walk an extra 1.5 miles one way. The main destination for now is Evelyn Lake, which lies 2.0 miles ahead along the right fork. The lake sits in a grassy basin, offering many campsite possibilities.

OVERNIGHT HIKE: WAWONA LOOP
Loop length: 30 miles
Low and high elevations: 4,000 to 9,080 feet
Difficulty: strenuous

This loop makes for a good 3 to 4 day outing, passing Chilnualna Falls and several high alpine lakes. Because the first part of the route is fairly low in elevation, it is a good trail to hike in the spring. The trailhead is located behind Wawona Ranger Station.

There are a number of trail junctions on this loop, making it seem complicated, but, in fact, the route is fairly easy to follow. The first part of the trail gently ascends through beautiful forests of ponderosa pine, incense cedar, black oak, canyon oak, and Douglas fir. At about 3.5 miles, the trail dips close to Chilnualna Creek, then climbs by way of switchback up above the creek to Chilnualna Falls—a good place for day hikers to turn around.

Those on an overnight trip should continue past several small meadows, now and then adjacent to the stream, to the Buck Lake Trail. Bearing right at the junction and heading more or less east, the path climbs through lodgepole pine forest past Grouse and Crescent Lakes before descending slightly to Johnson Lake at 8,310 feet. The trail continues another 1.0 mile to the trail junction. The route to Buck Camp continues east. Bear left (north) and take the trail to Royal Arch Lake (8,700) or continue on to Buena Vista Lake (9,080). There are good campsites all along this route.

One half mile beyond Buena Vista Creek, you will reach another trail junction; hikers should bear left for Chilnualna Lakes, where there are more good camping spots. Continue west and down the trail until you reach the junction with the Buck Camp Trail. Follow this about 0.8 mile northwest toward Turner Meadows, where you will reach another junction with a 2.9-mile trail descending to Chilnualna Falls. It is 5.3 miles back to the Wawona Ranger Station.

OVERNIGHT HIKE: GRAND CANYON OF THE TUOLUMNE
One-way length: 50 miles
Low and high elevations: 3,720 to 8,000 feet
Difficulty: strenuous

The northern part of Yosemite has far less use than the higher country south of Tuolumne Meadows, and the hike down the Tuolumne River offers a great long-distance backcountry trip that passes some of the most spectacular backcountry waterfalls and glaciated gorges in Yosemite National Park. To do the hike properly, one needs a shuttle or to be dropped off at the trailhead in Tuolumne Meadows. The best time of year to do the hike is early summer, when the waterfalls are roaring and flowers are abundant.

From Tuolumne Meadows Trailhead, proceed on the Pacific Crest Trail to Glen Aulin, following the Tuolumne River most of the way. At Glen Aulin, there is a nice aspen flat. Here the Pacific Crest Trail turns north, while the Tuolumne River Trail continues west. The next stretch of trail has some of the best scenery on the entire route, as the river drops from 7,800 feet at Glen Aulin to 5,000 feet in Muir Gorge. Along the way, the trail passes California, LeConte, and Waterwheel Falls. The Muir Gorge, gouged by giant glaciers 15,000 years ago, is one of the more inaccessible areas of the park, and yet one of the most dramatic. The trail through here literally hangs on the cliff walls. After Muir Gorge, the route reaches Pate Valley, with trail junctions heading north and south. Pate Valley has numerous oaks and Native American pictographs. To complete this route, hike up Rancheria Mountain Trail and follow it northeast; bear left at a trail junction and continue to Pleasant Valley, where the trail again descends to Rancheria Falls and Hetch Hetchy Reservoir, the terminus of the trip.

OTHER RECREATIONAL OPPORTUNITIES

Yosemite offers outstanding cross-country skiing in the winter months. Although there is seldom any snow in the Yosemite Valley, the high country offers plenty of the white stuff long into spring. Both day skis and longer cross-Sierra treks are possible. Some ski the snow-covered Tuolumne–Tioga Pass Road, which is closed to vehicle traffic in winter. The road provides access to numerous other backcountry sites. Another favorite location is where a number of nordic ski trails begin at Badger Pass Ski Area, an operating downhill ski facility. Again, skiing the road or venturing onto the backcountry trail system is possible. One popular overnight ski is the nine-mile trail to Ostrander Lake Ski Hut, a stone shelter located at Ostrander Lake. For really dedicated skiers, the 42-mile trans-Sierra route from Mammoth to the Yosemite Valley is always popular. The basic route goes up the John Muir Trail to Banner Lake over Donahue Pass, down the Lyell Fork to Tuolumne Meadows, then down Snow Creek into the Yosemite Valley.

Glacial erratics on bedrock near the headwaters of Lewis Creek, looking toward Clark Range, Yosemite National Park.

South Coast Ranges: The Santa Lucia, Diablo, and Sierra Madre Mountains

The South Coast Ranges contain some of the most unique parts of California. Here one finds wildlands that border the Pacific Ocean— steep, rugged, and nearly inaccessible. These coastal ranges, immortalized in John Steinbeck novels and Robinson Jeffers poetry, capture the essential element of early California as I imagine it to have been: huge forests of oaks and redwoods, rivers full of salmon and steelhead, and the whale and grizzly not an unusual sight. Some of these are now gone—the grizzly no longer roams the beaches of Monterey Bay, feeding on whale carcasses, and salmon and steelhead runs are nearly extinct. Yet this region, perhaps more than any other, holds a special attraction for me. To hike the open ridges of the Ventana Wilderness in spring when the hills are green, cloaked with poppies and lupine that frame the blue Pacific, is an experience unique to California.

The South Coast Ranges are separated from the North Coast Ranges by San Francisco Bay. They stretch south to Santa Barbara, where they merge in a confused jumble with the Transverse Ranges that circle the northern edge of the Los Angeles Basin. The famous San Andreas Fault runs the entire length of the region. North-south trending valleys such as the Santa Clara, Salinas, and Santa Ynez divide these mountains into distinctive sub-ranges, including the Santa Cruz Mountains, Diablo Range, La Panza Range, Gabilan Range, Santa Lucia Range, San Raphael Mountains, Tremblor Range, Sierra Madre Mountains, and others.

North of Monterey Bay, most of the ranges are privately owned or part of the state park system. Some of the most extensive state wildlands holdings, 80,000 acres in the oak-spangled Diablo Range, are found in Henry Coe State Park, while the Santa Cruz Mountains' Big Basin State Park, the oldest in California, is the setting for another state wilderness area. However, most of the federal wilderness areas, with the exception of Pinnacles National Monument Wilderness, are south of Monterey within the 1.7-million-acre Los Padres National Forest—the third largest in California. First established as the Santa Barbara Forest Reserve, its name was changed in 1936 to the Los Padres National Forest, in recognition of the fact that nine missions bordered the area during the Spanish colonial period.

In general, the western portions of the South Coast Ranges drop abruptly into the sea, which is best seen along the Big Sur Coast. Cone

Looking down Church Creek, Ventana Wilderness.

Peak rises to 5,155 feet within three-and-one-half miles of the ocean, providing tremendous vertical relief. Big Pine Mountain, at 6,828 feet in the San Raphael Range, is the highest peak within the agreed-upon boundaries of the South Coast Ranges, though some geographers consider Mount Pinos part of the South Coast Ranges as well, and it reaches 8,826 feet in elevation.

One of the major rivers in the South Coast Ranges is the Salinas, which runs north before emptying into Monterey Bay. Other rivers include the Big Sur, Little Sur, Ventana, Sespe, Nacimiento, Sisquoc, and Arroya Seco.

The rocks that now make up the South Coast Ranges were originally formed elsewhere and accreted to the western edge of California. The South Coast Ranges mark the border between two major crustal plates—the Pacific and the North American. The Pacific Plate is sliding past the North American at a rate of 2.2 inches a year. A large part of the South Coast Ranges are made up of the Salinian Block, a 300-mile long by 30-mile wide sliver of the earth's crust, composed primarily of granites and metamorphic rocks. These rocks had their origins further south; they were torn from their original anchorage and rafted north-ward over the past 25 million years along the San Andreas Fault to their present location. Most of the granitic rocks are similar to those found in the Sierra Nevada, and some geologists believe they were once part of the southern portion of that range. Active earthquakes, such as those that rattled Santa Cruz and San Francisco in 1990, are a reminder that this movement is by no means over.

West of the Salinian granites and metamorphic rocks and marked by the Nacimiento Fault are "young," ten-million-year old sedimentary rocks dominated by sandstones and shales that were formed in shallow seas. The coast has only been uplifted above the sea for one to two million years, a short time by geological standards. Old beach terraces are easily seen along the coast north of Santa Cruz and elsewhere. The sedimentary layers have trapped oil, which was once so abundant that it actually flowed from seeps on the surface. In 1884, the first wells were drilled in the Sespe oil fields—the only working oil wells on national forest lands in California.

Steep slopes, nearly impenetrable chaparral, and dense forests make much of the Los Padres National Forest inaccessible. In part because of its rugged terrain, over 823,366 acres, or roughly 46 percent, of the forest is designated wilderness in 10 wilderness areas—Dick Smith, Sespe, Chumash, Matilija, Garcia, Silver Peak, Santa Lucia, Machesna

Mountain, San Rafael, and Ventana. Three rivers are designated Wild and Scenic—Sespe Creek, Big Sur River, and Sisquoc Creek. The Ventana and Silver Peak Wilderness Areas lie along the Big Sur Coast in the north. The Santa Lucia, Garcia, and Machesna Mountains are clustered near San Luis Obispo, while east of Santa Barbara there are nearly a million acres of roadless country, the majority protected in the San Rafael, Dick Smith, Matilija, Chumash, and Sespe Wilderness Areas. In addition, the Pinnacles Wilderness, a national park service unit, lies within Pinnacles National Monument in the Gabilan Range east of Salinas.

Overall precipitation varies tremendously. Heavy winter rainfall may exceed 120 inches in the Santa Cruz Mountains and Santa Lucia Range, encouraging the growth of the southernmost coast redwood forests. Drier conditions prevail inland and further south, where stands of ponderosa pine, sugar pine, Coulter pine, Douglas fir, Jeffrey pine, lodgepole pine, and limber pine may be found. Sycamore, cottonwood, and bigleaf maple are common riparian deciduous trees. Oaks, including coast live oak, valley oak, black oak, and blue oak, are found in various parts of the range. However, chaparral dominates most south-facing slopes and recently burned areas. Some 77 percent of the 162 vascular plant families found in California have been noted in the Los Padres National Forest as well. This variety of plants is only exceeded by the Klamath Mountains in northern California.

Wildlife varies from sea otter and gray whales seen along the Big Sur Coast to California condor, which was recently reintroduced into the wild country of the Sespe and San Rafael Wildernesses. Grizzlies once ranged throughout the entire South Coast Ranges, but are now extinct. Deer, black bear, mountain lion, and non-native wild boar are the largest land mammals found here today.

Chumash Wilderness

41

The Chumash Wilderness includes the high forested slopes of Mount Pinos, one of the loftier mountains along the South Coast of California.

Limber pine snag on Mount Pinos, Chumash Wilderness.

LOCATION: 7 miles west of Frazier Park

SIZE: 38,000 acres

ELEVATION RANGE: 4,200 to 8,831 feet

MILES OF TRAILS: 20

ECOSYSTEMS: chaparral, mixed conifer

ADMINISTRATION: Los Padres National Forest

MAP: Los Padres National Forest Map/Ojai Ranger District

The 38,150-acre Chumash Wilderness is part of the larger 85,000-acre Mount Pinos/Cuyama Badlands Roadless Area. The name honors the Chumash Indians, who roamed the area prior to Spanish colonization.

Set off by the San Andreas Fault, 8,831-foot Mount Pinos is the highest point in the Santa Barbara region. The mountain summit is broad and rolling and is high enough to have a wind-influenced timberline. Groves of limber pine, relatively rare in southern California, have been sculpted by the wind as they sit high on the rocky ridges of the summit. Just below the limber pine grow lodgepole pine, a species common in the Sierra and in the higher mountains surrounding the Los Angeles Basin, but not found elsewhere in the Santa Barbara region. Dense forests of Jeffrey pine and white fir cover the lower slopes. This is one of the few areas in the region where snowfall is regular enough to provide good cross-country skiing. Most of the rugged Cuyama badlands were left out of the Chumash Wilderness. This area of colorful eroded volcanic ash has the look and feel of southern Utah. If all the roadless lands in this area were designated wilderness—from the Chumash borders to the Lockwood Road on the west and to Highway 33 on the north—it would nearly join the Dick Smith–San Rafael, Sespe, and Chumash Wildernesses, making them into an 800,000-acre roadless wildlands complex. Hopefully, future wilderness designations can achieve this worthy goal.

> **DAY HIKE: MOUNT PINOS RIDGE**
> One-way length: 3.4 miles
> Low and high elevations: 8,000 to 8,831 feet
> Difficulty: moderate

Mount Pinos, the highest peak in Kern and Ventura Counties and in the Los Padres National Forest, marks the border of the Chumash Wilderness. To find the trailhead, take I–5 to Gorman and exit at Frazier Park, then follow the signs for Mount Pinos Campground; from there, go another 2.0 miles to Chula Vista Campground and the trailhead. Take the road with a locked gate; hike it to the top of Mount Pinos for exceptional views. From the peak, head west on a trail that runs up and down through pine forest past Sawmill Mountain to Grouse Mountain. There aren't a lot of good views here, but the hiking through the pine forest is enjoyable. Return the way you came.

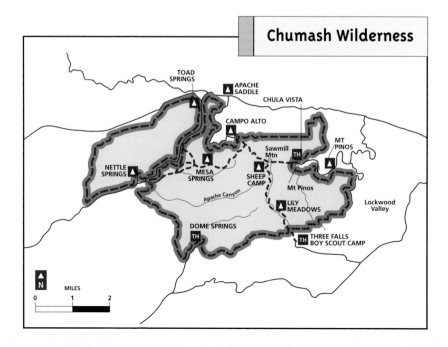

42 Dick Smith Wilderness

*This wilderness consists of many rugged mountains
with small drainages and few trails.*

Hikers in Rancho Nuevo Canyon, Dick Smith Wilderness.

LOCATION: 12 miles
east of Santa Barbara

SIZE: 64,700 acres

ELEVATION RANGE:
3,750 to 6,541 feet

MILES OF TRAILS: 49

ECOSYSTEMS:
chaparral, pine

ADMINISTRATION:
Los Padres National
Forest

MAPS: Los Padres
National Forest/Barbara
Ranger District Map,
Dick Smith Wilderness
Map

The 64,700-acre Dick Smith Wilderness lies immediately
south of the San Rafael Wilderness. The two wildernesses
are separated by the Sierra Ridge Road, which is closed to
motorized use but open to mountain bikes.

The wilderness area is named for Dick Smith, who
was born in Detroit Lakes, Minnesota, in 1929 and moved
to Santa Barbara in 1948 to work as a newspaper reporter
for the *News–Press*. During the 1950s, he became acquainted
with the Santa Barbara backcountry, beginning a life-long
career dedicated to its exploration and preservation. Among
other things, Smith wrote one of the first trail guides to this
area, which was published in 1962, as well as his classic book,
Condor Journal, which documented the natural history and
the plight of the condor. Smith died in 1977 and the new
wilderness was named to honor his efforts.

The Dick Smith is similar to the San Rafael in both terrain and vegetation. The highest summit is 6,541-foot Madulce Peak, which means "strawberry" in Spanish. The old Mono–Alamar Trail, used for centuries by the Chumash Native Americans to travel between the coast and the San Joaquin Valley, crosses through the wilderness. After the Chumash revolted against Spanish rule, they fled across the mountains to the San Joaquin, using this trail. Later, they were recaptured by Captain Pablo de la Portillo. During the return trek, Portillo and the Chumash are thought to have camped near today's Dutch Oven Camp on Alamar Creek. Still in use, the trail begins at Santa Barbara Canyon, continues past Madulce Peak, then travels down Mono Creek.

The high country around the peak supports ponderosa, incense cedar, big-cone Douglas fir, and a variety of oaks. It is a lovely setting. Near the peak is the Madulce Guard Station, built in the 1930s and now a historic site. Built in the 1880s, the cabin was originally the homestead of Old Marlowe and was taken over by the Forest Service when the area became part of the Forest Reserve in 1898. The original structure was torn down in 1929 and rebuilt. Today, the historic cabin has been restored and is on the National Register of Historic Places.

Steep canyons, sometimes resembling the canyon country of Utah, rise above small streams and creeks. There are only 49 miles of trail, compared to the 125 miles in the San Rafael, but the opportunity for solitude is greater. Some of the trails are not very passable nor easy to follow, but on the plus side, that also reduces use. Despite the proximity to Santa Barbara, and easy driving distance from Los Angeles, I did an overnight backpack here during the Fourth of July weekend and did not see another soul—not even another vehicle at the trailhead!

DAY HIKE: UPPER RANCHO NUEVO CAMP
One-way length: 4.8 miles
Low and high elevations: 3,500 to 4,000 feet
Difficulty: moderate

This hike makes a good day trip or an easy overnighter to a camp on the eastern edge of the Dick Smith Wilderness. Rumor has it that the Cuyama Valley was first settled by the Reyes family, who had traveled overland with their livestock from San Fernando Valley to the south. They named the area Nuevo Rancho, or "new ranch." Upper Rancho Nuevo is located on the creek of the same name. To reach the trailhead, drive Highway 33 from Ojai up the Sespe River and cross the mountains to the upper Cuyama River drainage. The trailhead is at the Rancho Nuevo Campground, which is located north of the highway at the end of Tinta Canyon Road. The trail to Upper Rancho Nuevo follows the creek upstream, making a few stream crossings and hiking through forests of big-cone Douglas fir, pinyon pine, and chaparral.

OVERNIGHT HIKE: MADULCE PEAK
Loop length: 23 miles
Low and high elevations: 3,540 to 6,000 feet
Difficulty: moderate

This hike traverses the western portion of the Dick Smith Wilderness and the eastern part of the San Rafael Wilderness, climbing over the Sierra Madre Mountains before looping back to the starting point.

Find the trailhead by taking Highway 33 from Ojai up the Sespe Valley and over to Cuyama Valley. Just 2.0 miles east of the Forest Service's Ventucopa

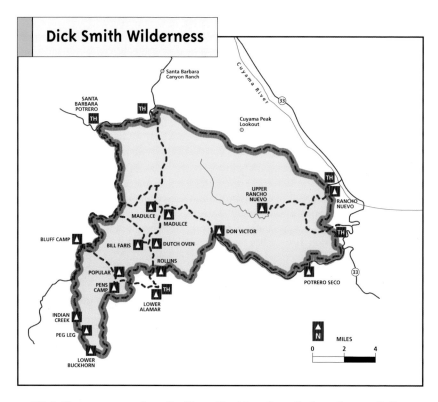

Work Center, turn north on Buckhorn Road into Santa Barbara Canyon. Follow this to the trailhead, which begins just after Cox Flat.

The first part of the loop takes you up Santa Barbara Canyon, following an old jeep trail with numerous stream crossings. At 4.5 miles, the trail heads up a side canyon, climbs to a ridge, and drops into Pine Creek, where the historic Madulce Cabin, an old Forest Service Guard Station built in the 1930s, is located. Nearby is Madulce Camp, set in a forest of ponderosa pine, Douglas fir, incense cedar, and oak, with a nearby spring as a water source. Madulce Camp, at 5,000 feet, makes a good first-night camp.

Follow the Madulce Trail 2.5 miles west through a conifer forest to Big Pine Road. Once on the road, head south 1.0 mile to Alamar Saddle. Here, turn west again and descend the upper Sisquoc River Trail, entering the San Raphael Wilderness. Follow this trail to Bear Camp at 5,283 feet. The Sisquoc River bubbles out of the ground nearby. Continue down through Lower Bear Camp, which makes a good overnight camp if you're ready to stop for the day; otherwise, continue past the Devil's Slide—an area of steep, loose shale—and Upper Sisquoc Falls Camp, where there is a magnificent waterfall. From here, it is another 3.0 miles to Heath Camp, an oak- and sycamore-shaded spot at 3,440 feet that makes a good campsite with plenty of water, swimming, and fishing. The Sisquoc River is a Wild and Scenic River.

The final day is a long haul up the Judell Canyon Trail, which climbs out of the Sisquoc River Canyon to the top of the Sierra Madre Mountains. In 4.7 miles, you will reach the Santa Barbara Potrero on the Sierra Madre Road. Follow the road less than 1.0 mile to its junction with the Big Pine Road, where you will turn left (east) and walk 3.0 miles back to your vehicle.

Garcia Wilderness 43

A small wilderness, the Garcia is comprised of steep slopes largely covered with chaparral.

Looking across Trout Creek to Garcia Mountain, Garcia Wilderness.

The Hi Mountain Road separates the 14,100-acre Garcia Wilderness from the Santa Lucia Wilderness. The Garcia represents the southernmost protected area in the Santa Lucia Range. As with other parts of the Santa Lucia Range, steep slopes, narrow V-shaped canyons, and knife-edge ridges characterize the Garcia Wilderness. Chaparral dominates the area, but pines occur on the aptly named Pine Ridge. Only a few trails lace this wilderness and its two designated campsites—the Buckeye, set within a dense oak forest, and Balm of Gilead, located in Garcia's northeast corner.

LOCATION: 15 miles southeast of San Luis Obispo

SIZE: 14,000 acres

ELEVATION RANGE: 1,500 to 3,000 feet

MILES OF TRAILS: 20

ECOSYSTEMS: chaparral, limited pine

ADMINISTRATION: Los Padres National Forest

MAP: Los Padres National Forest/Santa Lucia District Map

Garcia Wilderness

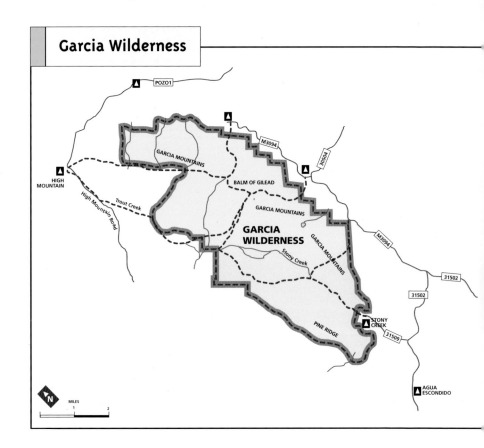

DAY HIKE: CALDWELL MESA–AVENALES TRAIL
One-way length: 4 miles
Low and high elevations: 1,200 to 2,000 feet
Difficulty: moderate

This trail is located in the southern part of the wilderness and begins at Stony
Creek Campground. To reach the campground, take Grand Avenue east from
Arroyo Grande to Huasna Road, then to Arroyo Seco Road. Follow this eastward
to a locked gate; park here and follow the road to Stony Creek Campground. From
the campground, cross into the wilderness and descend 2.0 miles on the Caldwell
Mesa Trail. At the trail junction, turn right (north) and follow the Avenales Trail
2.0 miles to historical Avenales Station. The private land lying beyond the station
requires that you backtrack here to Stony Creek Campground.

Henry Coe State Park— Orestimba Wilderness

*Located in the Diablo Range south of San Jose,
the Henry Coe offers beautiful oak-studded hills,
ponderosa pine, and grasslands.*

Digger pine and oaks at Poverty Flat, Henry Coe State Park.

This park encompasses one of the more beautiful California landscapes—the oak-grass savanna. To visit this area of rolling hills in the spring when the wildflowers are in their prime is a not-soon forgotten experience. One of the unique features of the park is the ponderosa pine growing on Pine Ridge. Except for a small number of pine in the Santa Cruz Mountains, the nearest ponderosa pine are found in the Sierra Nevada, and further south in the South Coast Ranges.

Coyote Creek is the major watershed in the park; it was named by Juan Bautista de Anza in 1776 on an expedi-

LOCATION: 14 miles east of Morgan Hill

SIZE: 79,500 acres

ELEVATION RANGE: 1,200 to 3,000 feet

MILES OF TRAILS: 40

ECOSYSTEMS: oak woodlands and grasslands

ADMINISTRATION: Henry Coe State Park

MAP: Henry Coe State Park Map

tion from Mexico to San Francisco. Henry Coe arrived in the area around 1883 and began to develop a large ranch. His daughter eventually donated the ranch holdings to the state for use as a park. The Henry Coe is large enough to permit loop hikes of 70 miles or more. There are few wildlands of this size so close to San Francisco.

OVERNIGHT OR DAY HIKE: CHINA HOLE LOOP
Loop length: 9.3 miles
Low and high elevations: 1,200 to 2,600 feet
Difficulty: moderate

This hike is a good introduction to the oaks and grasslands that dominate the Henry Coe State Park backcountry. To find the trailhead, drive to the park via Highway 101 to Morgan Hill and exit on Dunne Avenue East. Follow this to park headquarters, where the hike begins. There are numerous trail intersections that permit one to develop longer or shorter loops, making this hike almost any length desired. Take a good map!

To do this 9.3-mile loop, head east from park headquarters on the trailhead along an oak savanna-covered hill above Soda Springs Canyon. A little over 0.5 mile, there is a three-way trail junction. Take the right-hand fork to the Springs Trail, which passes through ponderosa pine and oaks as it descends gradually. At 2.0 miles, you will come to Coit Route, a ranch road; turn right here and hike for about 0.3 mile to Blue Oak Horse Camp and Bass Pond. Continue on Coit Route, passing Manzanita Point Camp. Some 2.7 miles from the trailhead, you will reach Madrone Soda Springs Trail. Turn right here and hike for 1.0 mile to Madrone Soda Springs, passing digger pine, California buckeye, and oaks enroute.

A little beyond the springs, the trail name changes to Mile Trail. Continue another 1.0 mile, passing through lovely bigleaf maple, oaks, and laurels to Coyote Creek. Here you will follow Coyote Creek upstream to China Hole and beyond.

At the 5.0-mile mark, you will come to a fork in the trail; take the lower one. About another 0.5 mile further, you will need to ford Coyote Creek and get on the Pacheco Road; once you reach the road, turn left and pass through Poverty Flat—a nice area with oaks. Continue for about 2.0 miles on Pacheco Road, passing the Cougar and Middle Ridge Trails and fording Coyote Creek once more.

At 7.5 miles from the trailhead, you will come to a junction with the Forest Trail. Turn right here and hike another 1.0 mile to the intersection with the Pacheco Route, which is opposite the Springs Trail, and turn right to finish the loop.

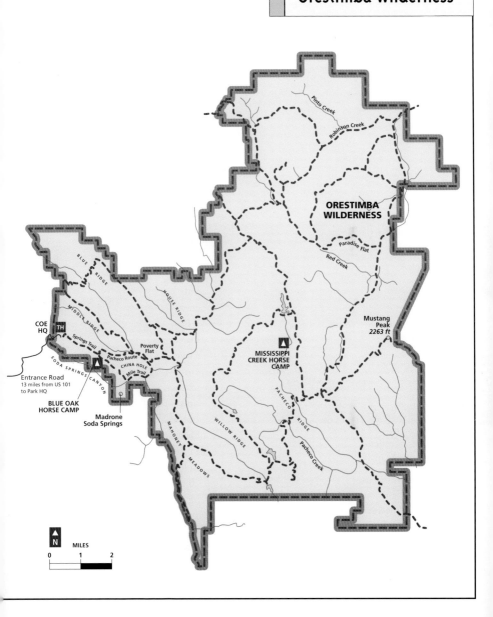

Henry Coe State Park— Orestimba Wilderness

ORESTIMBA
WILDERNESS

Pinto Creek

Robinson Creek

Paradise Flat

Red Creek

Mustang
Peak
2263 ft

BLUE RIDGE

HOUSE RIDGE

MIDDLE RIDGE

COE
HQ   TH

Springs Trail

Poverty
Flat

Pacheco Route

CHINA HOLE

Mile Trail

SODA SPRINGS CANYON

Entrance Road
13 miles from US 101
to Park HQ

BLUE OAK
HORSE CAMP

Madrone
Soda Springs

MISSISSIPPI
CREEK HORSE
CAMP

PACHECO RIDGE

Pacheco Creek

MAHONEY
MEADOWS

WILLOW RIDGE

N
MILES
0   1   2

45 Machesna Mountain Wilderness

*With intimidating terrain made up of rugged cliffs,
the Machesna Mountain Wilderness offers forests
of lovely Coulter pine and oak woodlands.*

*Sandstone outcrops at Castle Crags,
Machesna Mountain Wilderness.*

LOCATION: 25 miles
southeast of San Luis
Obispo

SIZE: 20,000 acres

ELEVATION RANGE:
1,500 to 4,063 feet

MILES OF TRAILS: 14

ECOSYSTEMS:
chaparral, Coulter pine

ADMINISTRATION:
Los Padres National
Forest

MAP: Los Padres
National Forest/Santa
Lucia District Map

East of the Santa Lucia Range lies the La Panza Range,
crowned by 4,063-foot Machesna Mountain, the highest point
in the 20,000-acre Machesna Mountain Wilderness. Most
of this area is drained by the American Creek via American
Canyon. The higher ridges are relatively gentle and rolling with
a steep eastern escarpment, but the Castle Crags, lying along
the northern border of the range, consists of rugged cliffs and
outcrops of sandstone. Scattered groves of Coulter pine and
digger pine, along with grassy meadows and oaks, break up the
chaparral that dominates the area. The larger wildlife encountered here are Tule elk. Because of the rugged terrain, trail
access is limited in these mountains. Off the beaten path and
far from any major population centers, this is one wilderness
where you won't meet many other people.

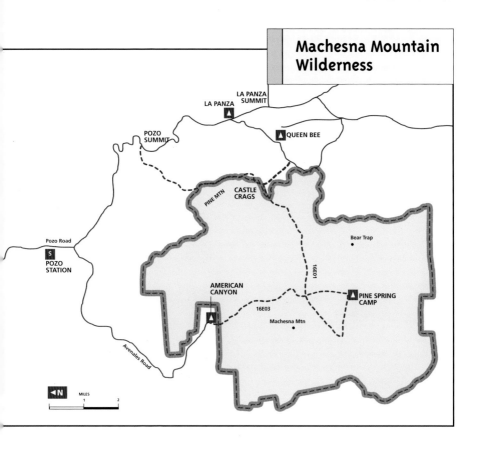

DAY HIKE: AMERICAN CANYON
One-way length: 5 miles
Low and high elevations: 1,700 to 3,500 feet
Difficulty: moderate

Access to this trail is restricted to August and September. The trail starts in oak woodlands at American Creek Campground and ends at the shady Pine Springs Recreation Site. To find the campground, take Highway 58 to Pozo Road and drive it to Avenales Road. Turn right and go 7.0 miles to a sign for the campground; make a left here and go 1.2 miles to the trailhead. Beginning at the campground, the trail ascends gradually through chaparral and pine to Pine Springs, where there is a water trough for horses, a toilet, and fire ring. There are good views of the surrounding La Panza Mountains along the trail.

46 Matilija Wilderness

These rugged chaparral-covered mountains offer a good-flowing perennial stream, all located just outside of Ojai in the Matilija Wilderness.

Matilija Creek, Matilija Wilderness.

LOCATION: 5 miles northwest of Ojai

SIZE: 29,600 acres

ELEVATION RANGE: 1,500 to 6,000 feet

MILES OF TRAILS: 8

ECOSYSTEMS: chaparral, riparian

ADMINISTRATION: Los Padres National Forest

MAP: Los Padres National Forest/Ojai Ranger District Map

The newly created 29,600-acre Matilija Wilderness lies near the headwaters of the Ventana River northeast of Ojai. The wilderness was established in 1992 as part of the Los Padres Condor Range and River Protection Act. The main attraction is Matilija Creek, 16 miles of which are being studied for Wild and Scenic River designation. Evidence of the Santa Ynez Fault can be seen in the tilted sedimentary layers visible in the North Fork of Matilija Creek Canyon. The canyon is steep-sided and largely covered with chaparral, but bigleaf maple and oaks are common along the stream course, with big-cone Douglas fir occurring along Ortega Hill. The main trail along the North Fork of Matilija Creek is 7.0 miles from end to end.

DAY HIKE: NORTH FORK MATILIJA CREEK
One-way length: 7 miles
Low and high elevations: 1,500 to 4,974 feet
Difficulty: moderate

The hike along the North Fork Matilija Creek is the main access to this rugged wilderness. If you plan to hike the entire distance, it is best to start at the upper trailhead by Cherry Creek Campground, which is located off of Highway 33. However, most people will choose to start from the bottom and hike only partway. To find the lower trailhead, drive north on Highway 33 about 5.0 miles from Ojai and turn left onto Matilija Canyon Road. Park here at the locked gate. Hike the road through private property to the trailhead at the mouth of the North Fork Matilija Canyon. The first 1.0 mile of the trail, which follows the creek to Matilija Camp, is relatively flat and easy to hike, even for children.

Beyond this point, the trail alternatively follows the creek or climbs above it and makes several crossings. Eventually you will reach oak-shaded Middle Matilija Creek Camp. The trail beyond here passes through more Douglas fir, California bay, and oak, as well as chaparral, then climbs out of the canyon, offering views of the Pacific. The upper canyon burned in the 1985 Wheeler Fire and is a good place to see how fires rejuvenate a landscape. The trees at Maple Camp at 3,800 feet are bigleaf maple, which persisted after the fire, along with chokecherry and Douglas fir. From Maple Camp it is a short, steep 1.0 mile to the other trailhead, located at Ortega Hill and Cherry Creek Campground.

Matilija Wilderness

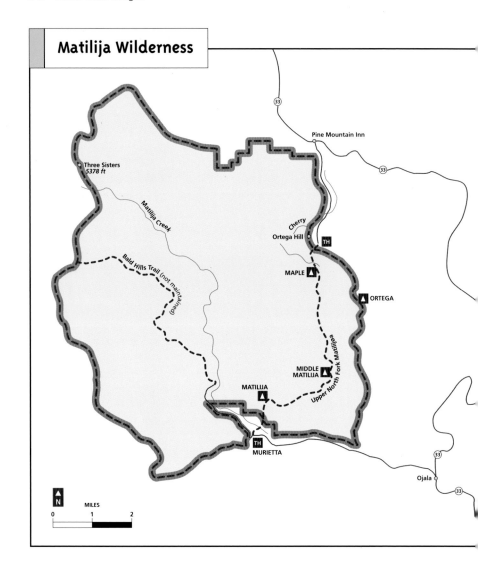

Pine Mountain Inn

33

33

Three Sisters
5378 ft

Matilija Creek

Cherry

Ortega Hill

TH

Bald Hills Trail (not maintained)

MAPLE

ORTEGA

MIDDLE
MATILIJA

Upper North Fork Matilija

MATILIJA

MURIETTA
TH

33

Ojala

33

N

MILES

0   1   2

Pinnacles Wilderness

The Pinnacles Wilderness, located south of Monterey, presents dramatic volcanic cliffs and lovely oak woodlands.

View of the Pinnacles on High Peaks Trail, Pinnacles National Monument.

LOCATION: 34 miles south of Hollister

SIZE: 12,952 acres

ELEVATION RANGE: 1,200 to 3,300 feet

MILES OF TRAILS: 28.5

ECOSYSTEMS: chaparral, pine, oak woodland

ADMINISTRATION: Pinnacles National Park

MAP: Pinnacles National Monument Map

The 12,952-acre Pinnacles Wilderness takes in most of the 16,222-acre Pinnacles National Monument, which was established in 1908. The monument lies east of Soledad in the arid Gabilan Mountains, one of John Steinbeck's favorite ranges. The name refers to the 600-foot-tall spires and crags of rust-colored rock that bisect the park's main ridge, remnants of an ancient volcano. The highest peaks barely exceed 3,000 feet, but the overall terrain is dissected by canyons and is relatively steep, rising more than 1,200 feet above the canyon floors.

The volcano that spewed forth the rock that now makes up the crags of the monument erupted more than 23 million years ago. At that time, the rocks that now comprise the monument were located further south; they were rafted northward on top of the earth's crust along the San Andreas Fault.

Although originally set aside because of its unusual geological formations, Pinnacles is the only national park unit that has a complete example of the Coast Range chaparral community. Composed of manzanita, buckbrush, hollyleaf cherry, toyon, and chamise, chaparral is specially adapted to withstand winter rains and summer droughts.

Common birds found in this wilderness are the acorn woodpecker, brown towhee, California quail, and scrub jay. Mammals infrequently seen include the gray fox, bobcat, and mule deer.

There are a number of trails that access much of the central core of this area's peaks, but the longest trail is only nine miles in length. Most recreational use consists of day hiking and bird watching. Springtime, when flowers are in bloom, is considered the best season to visit the Pinnacles Wilderness.

DAY HIKE: HIGH PEAKS TRAIL
One-way length: 5.4 miles
Low and high elevations: 1,200 to 2,600 feet
Difficulty: moderate

The High Peaks Trail offers good views of the entire park and surrounding country-side and is an introduction to the Pinnacles backcountry. Drive to the monument, which lies a few miles west of Highway 25. The trailhead starts at the Chalone Creek picnic area and ends at Bear Gulch parking lot. The first part of the trail climbs a ridge, following the ridgeline around the highest peaks before descending again to Bear Gulch. Altogether, there is a 1,650-foot elevation gain. Take water!

DAY HIKE: CHALONE PEAK TRAIL
One-way length: 5 miles
Low and high elevations: 1,200 to 3,300 feet
Difficulty: moderate

The hike to 3,198-foot South Chalone Peak takes you past 3,300-foot North Chalone Peak enroute—the highest point in the monument. Start at the Pinnacles Monument Visitor Center and hike on a level forested trail to Bear Gulch Reservoir, where the path sidehills up to the main ridgeline leading to North Chalone Peak. Follow this trail, much of it in chaparral, to the peak and take the short spur trail to a fire look-out for fine views. Continue on to South Chalone, dropping into a saddle before you climb to the top of the peak.

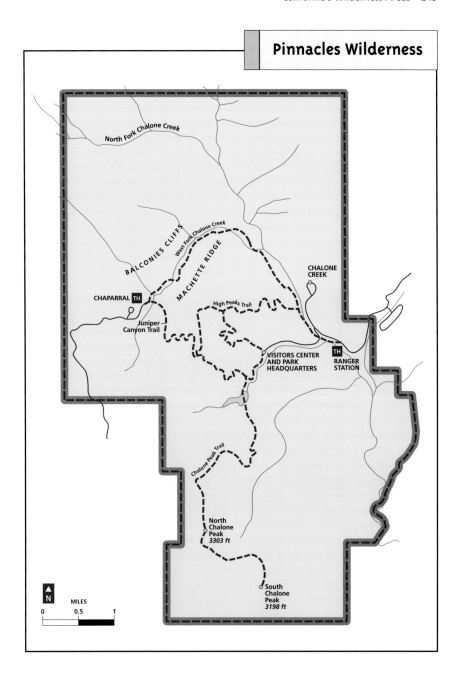

Pinnacles Wilderness

North Fork Chalone Creek

BALCONIES CLIFFS

West Fork Chalone Creek

MACHETTE RIDGE

CHALONE CREEK

CHAPARRAL TH

High Peaks Trail

Juniper Canyon Trail

VISITORS CENTER AND PARK HEADQUARTERS

TH RANGER STATION

Chalone Peak Trail

North Chalone Peak 3303 ft

South Chalone Peak 3198 ft

N MILES
0   0.5   1

48 San Rafael Wilderness

*Steep ridges, chaparral-covered slopes, pine forests,
and beautiful rivers accentuate the San Rafael Wilderness,
located just east of Santa Barbara.*

Waterfall on Mission Creek, San Rafael Wilderness.

LOCATION: 15 miles east of Santa Barbara

SIZE: 197,570 acres

ELEVATION RANGE: 1,700 to 6,828 feet

MILES OF TRAILS: 125

ECOSYSTEMS: chaparral, oak woodlands, pine forest

ADMINISTRATION: Los Padres National Forest

MAP: Los Padres National Forest/Santa Barbara Ranger District Map

The 197,570-acre San Rafael Wilderness is just one of the mountain ranges located east of Santa Barbara. It is drained by the Sisquoc, a recently designated Wild and Scenic River.

The area was first withdrawn from the public domain, as part of the Pine Mountain and Zaca Lake Forest Reserves, prior to the establishment of the national forest system in 1905. It was renamed the Santa Barbara National Forest in 1908 by President Theodore Roosevelt. In 1931, a portion of the forest was set aside as the San Rafael Primitive Area. In 1937, the Sisquoc Condor Sanctuary was established within the San Rafael Primitive Area to provide undisturbed nesting habitat for the large birds. In 1968, the San Rafael became the first primitive area to be designated a wilderness after passage of the 1964 Wilderness Act. Then in 1984,

2,000 additional acres, under the California Wilderness Act, were added to the San Rafael. Finally, in 1992, another 48,000 acres were added along the northern border of the wilderness.

Two mountain ranges, the San Rafael and Sierra Madre, form high forest and chaparral-covered ridges that are drained by the Sisquoc River and Manzana Creek. Composed of easily eroded sedimentary sandstones, conglomerates, siltstones, and shales, the terrain is steep with narrow canyons. Higher peaks include Big Pine Mountain (6,828) and San Rafael Mountain (6,593). Hurricane Deck is a large outcrop of sandstone that is devoid of vegetation.

Much of the wilderness is covered by chaparral and yucca, but you will see groves of Coulter pine, big-cone Douglas fir, Jeffrey pine, ponderosa pine, and digger pine, while oaks, Fremont cottonwood, sycamore, white alder, and an occasional bigleaf maple line the streams. California's southernmost stand of Sargent cypress is found here. Spring wildflowers are exceptional, particularly in the small meadows that dot some of the stream riparian areas and higher basins.

The Sisquoc River was one of the last known haunts of the endangered California condor. Present plans call for reintroducing condors into this area within the next year. Lizards are the most abundant wildlife you'll see, along with dozens of bird species. Trout are found in the major rivers and streams. Deer, raccoon, ring-tailed cat, gray fox, coyote, black bear, and mountain lion are also present.

Although the rugged terrain of the San Rafael Wilderness thwarted most development schemes, it was, for a time, settled by several families, most of whom eventually left the country for more favorable lands. Remains of one settlement can still be seen along the Sisquoc River near its confluence with Manzana Creek. Here, Hiram Preserved Wheat and a group of religious fundamentalists settled in the 1880s. A post office, schoolhouse, and small farms made up the community. They grew a few crops and raised livestock, living a largely self-subsistent lifestyle. However, faith could not overcome droughts and floods, and by 1902 only two families remained. Building foundations and other relics of this era can still be seen near Wheat Peak, located along the northern boundary of the wilderness.

More than 100,000 additional roadless acres surround this wilderness and the adjacent Dick Smith Wilderness. Designation of these remaining lands and permanent closure and restoration of the Sierra Ridge Road could create a 381,000-acre wildlands complex, which some believe would be large enough to support a grizzly bear population.

San Rafael Wilderness

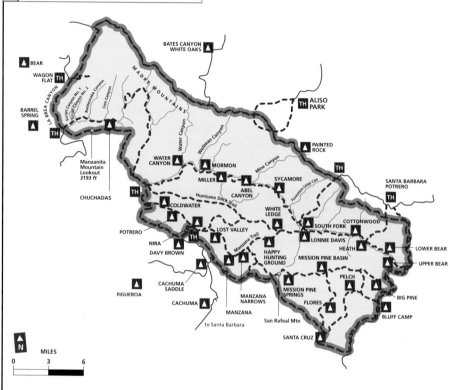

DAY HIKE: MANZANA CREEK TRAIL

One-way length: 3.25 miles to Manzana Camp

Low and high elevations: 2,000 to 3,100 feet

Difficulty: moderate

Manzana Creek is a major tributary of the Sisquoc River. With beautiful riparian vegetation and a gentle grade up the creek, this makes a good day hike, as well as a potential overnight backpack. This hike begins at NIRA Campground, a major auto camp. To reach the trailhead, travel from Santa Barbara on Highway 101 to Highway 154, follow it to Armour Ranch Road, then turn onto Happy Canyon Road and drive 17.0 miles to NIRA Campground, where you will find the trailhead.

The trail crosses Manzana Creek and follows the north bank upstream. In 1.0 mile, you will reach Lost Valley Camp—a potential overnight campsite and a trail junction, where you can head east to the Hurricane Deck. For this hike, continue following Manzana Creek upstream, where you will stay primarily on the north bank, occasionally crossing the stream as the canyon narrows. At 3.25 miles, you will come to Manzana Creek Camp, a lovely spot with lots of tent sites, big live oak and sycamores, and several swimming holes. This is a good place to turn around, but it is possible to continue upstream to several other camps and a trail that heads over to the Sisquoc River.

DAY HIKE: McPHERSON PEAK
One-way length: 4 miles
Low and high elevations: 3,000 to 5,740 feet
Difficulty: moderate

McPherson Peak lies on the dry eastern side of the San Rafael Wilderness. This trail leads to a lookout on the flat summit of the peak, which not only provides outstanding vistas of the San Rafael Wilderness and areas to the east in Cuyama Valley, but also a chance to see the endangered California condor. Most of the trail passes through roadless, but undesignated, wilderness. To find the trailhead, take Highway 166 to New Cuyama and proceed 2.5 miles further to Aliso Canyon Road, following it to Aliso Campground. From here, follow trail 27W02 uphill through scattered brush to a ridge, crossing the Sierra Madre Road; just beyond is McPherson Peak. An alternative route to the peak or a way to make a complete loop is to go up an old jeep road that follows the canyon from Aliso Campground 2.2 miles to Hog Pen Springs Camp. Here, a trail switchbacks steeply to the Sierra Madre Road, which you will hike north to the summit of McPherson Peak.

49 Santa Lucia Wilderness

*This long, narrow ridge is characterized by the
chaparral-covered slopes of the steep Santa Lucia Range
and occasional sweeping views of the ocean.*

*Looking toward Lopez Canyon from the Hi Mountain area,
Santa Lucia Wilderness.*

LOCATION: 10 miles
east of San Luis Obispo

SIZE: 21,704 acres

ELEVATION RANGE:
800 to 3,000 feet

MILES OF TRAILS: 13

ECOSYSTEMS:
chaparra

ADMINISTRATION:
Los Padres National
Forest

MAP: Los Padres
National Forest/Santa
Lucia Ranger District
Map

Lying east of San Luis Obispo, the 21,704-acre Santa Lucia
Wilderness was established in 1978 as one of the 17 areas
designated by passage of the Endangered Wilderness Act. This
long, thin wilderness takes in the narrow, southern ridgeline
of its namesake mountain range. The lowest elevations are
about 800 feet along Lopez Canyon, while the highest elevations barely exceed 3,000 feet. Steep terrain, mostly covered by
chaparral, dominates this area, however, riparian vegetation
along streams offers shade from hot summer sun. A few groves
of the rare Santa Lucia fir occur at higher elevations. The most
popular trails include Lopez and Big Falls Canyons. Good
views of the Pacific Ocean are possible on clear days. Spring
and fall are the best times to visit the area. Lopez Creek is a
candidate for Wild and Scenic River designation. Much of
the area burned in the 1985 Las Pilitas fire.

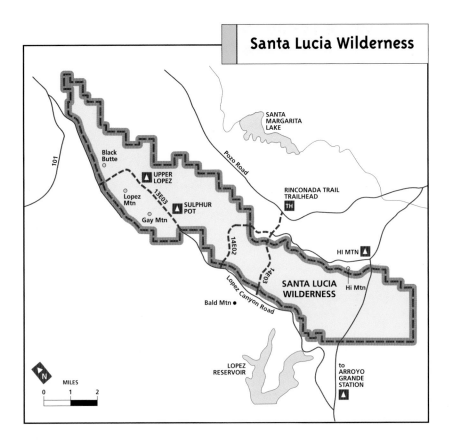

Santa Lucia Wilderness

DAY HIKE: BIG FALLS CANYON
One-way length: 1.5 miles
Low and high elevations: 800 to 1,080 feet
Difficulty: moderate

There are few trails in the Santa Lucia Wilderness, but one of the nicer hikes follows Big Falls Canyon. There are several ways to access the canyon, and the one given here is on the west side of the range. From San Luis Obispo, drive south on Highway 101 to Highway 227, then head east to Lopez Lake. Cross the dam and drive 1.0 mile to a left-hand turn onto Upper Lopez Canyon, which will take you up and around the reservoir. Follow this dirt road approximately 3.5 miles to an unmarked trailhead, located beside the Big Falls Canyon. The trail winds from side to side up the canyon, which is shaded by live oak, sycamore, and lots of poison oak. You pass numerous pools and a few waterfalls enroute.

50 Sespe Wilderness

The Sespe Wilderness offers pine-covered mountains, chaparral-studded hills, and clear streams, with a good chance to see the endangered California condor.

The view across Sespe River to Pine Mountain, Sespe Wilderness.

LOCATION:
5 miles east of Ojai

SIZE: 219,000 acres

ELEVATION RANGE:
3,000 to 7,510 feet

MILES OF TRAILS: 53

ECOSYSTEMS:
chaparral, mixed conifer forest, oak woodlands

ADMINISTRATION:
Los Padres National Forest

MAP: Los Padres National Forest/Ojai Ranger District Map

The 219,700-acre Sespe Wilderness protects a portion of the 320,000-acre Sespe RA, one of the largest Forest Service roadless areas left in California. The wilderness was created in 1992 with the passage of the Los Padres Condor Range and River Protection Act. The Sespe takes in much of the drainage of Sespe Creek, with 31.5 miles of designated Wild and Scenic River. A portion of Piru Creek, a candidate for Wild and Scenic River status, also lies in the wilderness, which includes much of the Sespe Condor Sanctuary. The new wilderness lies in the rugged country east of Ojai and reaches its highest peak on 7,510-foot Reyes Peak.

The most dramatic areas of the wilderness are the sandstone cliff faces that line Pine Mountain, from which you will have extraordinary views of the Sespe Creek drainage thousands of feet below. Forests of white fir, Jeffrey pine, sugar pine, and incense cedar cover the top of the mountain, while lower elevations are largely chaparral and yucca.

Another attraction is Sespe Hot Springs, reachable only on foot by hiking 17 miles of trail that require a half-dozen river crossings. Reportedly, the springs bubble out of the ground with a temperature in excess of 200 degrees. Despite the distance, the area is still a popular destination for hikers. The trail continues on toward Devil's Gate, passing pools, sandstone gorges, and groves of alder, sycamore, and oaks.

Nelson's bighorn sheep were once common in the area, but disease borne by domestic livestock led to their local extinction. They have been successfully re-established near Sespe Hot Springs.

Condors have been released into the Sespe and, with luck, may also re-establish themselves. Two other species that are rare and of concern are the steelhead, a sea-run form of rainbow trout that used to inhabit Sespe Creek, and the arroyo toad. It is not known if steelhead still run up Sespe Creek, but the toad is presently being considered for listing under the Endangered Species Act.

DAY HIKE: BEAR TRAP CAMP
One-way length: 5 miles
Low and high elevations: 3,960 to 5,060 feet
Difficulty: moderate

This hike takes one on a trail where the ghosts of grizzly bear that once roamed these mountains can be imagined. Bear Trap Camp is named for the grizzly trapping activities of the Reyes family, who ran cattle in the Cuyama Valley and successfully made these mountains safe for livestock by killing off the grizzlies.

To reach the trailhead, take Highway 33 from Ojai or from the Cuyama Valley, turn south for about 4.0 miles on the paved Lockwood Valley Road to the turn for Reyes Creek Campground, and go to the campground and trailhead. Follow the trail through chaparral past Upper Reyes Camp—located on perennial Reyes Creek—up and over a ridge to Bear Trap Camp, which is nestled along Bear Trap Creek among Douglas fir, sugar pine, incense cedar, and ponderosa pine.

DAY HIKE: PORTRERO JOHN TRAIL
One-way length: 1.6 miles
Low and high elevations: 3,700 to 4,400 feet
Difficulty: easy

The Portrero John Trail provides year-round access to the southwest corner of the Sespe Wilderness. The trailhead is located just off Highway 33 in the Sespe River Gorge. At first, the trail is steep, then moderates as you travel up canyon. Portrero John Camp is set on a flat in the shade of live oaks. The trail deadends just beyond the camp.

Sespe Wilderness

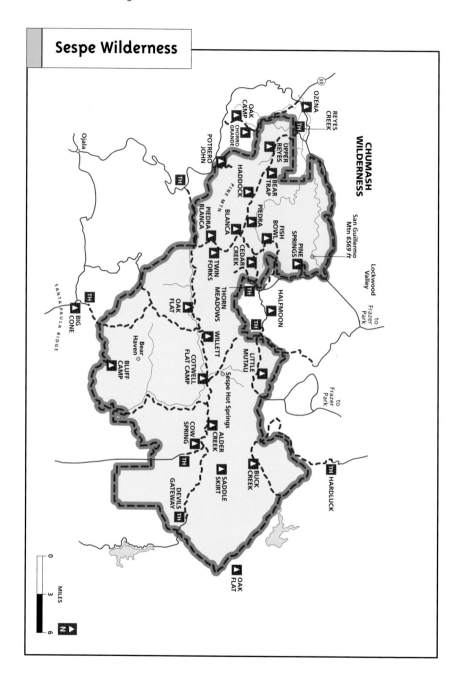

OVERNIGHT HIKE: PIRU CREEK LOOP
One-way length: 13 miles
Low and high elevations: 4,750 to 5,400 feet
Difficulty: moderate

The Piru Creek Loop makes for an easy overnight trip with several lovely potential campsites set among pine and oaks. To reach the trailhead, take the Frazier Park exit from I–5 near Gorman. Follow Frazier Mountain Road for 3.0 miles to Lake of the Woods and bear left for Lockwood Valley Road. Follow this to Thorn Meadows Road and drive to Cedar Creek Trailhead near Thorn Meadows Campground.

The first 3.0 miles or so of Trail 21W06 follows Cedar Creek then the South Fork of Piru Creek to Cedar Creek Camp, situated in a little basin with Douglas fir and incense cedar. From the camp, climb 1.2 miles to a ridge, where there is a trail junction. Bear right onto the Fishbowl Trail (22W05) and follow the ridge northwest up, then down, until you descend to Piru Creek and Fishbowl Camp. Just upstream, you will find some deep potholes worn into the soft sandstone of the creekbed. It is about 6.2 miles back down Piru Creek Trail (21W05) to Grade Valley Road, which you follow another 1.0 mile along the road to your vehicle at the parking area.

51 Silver Peak Wilderness

The dramatic Silver Peak Wilderness presents steep slopes that rise directly from the sea, as well as meadows and redwoods, making this a lovely hiking area throughout the year.

Hikers on the Buckeye Trail in the Silver Peak Wilderness are treated to a spectacular view of the Pacific Ocean.

LOCATION:
50 miles north of
San Luis Obispo

SIZE: 14,500 acres

ELEVATION RANGE:
300 to 3,590 feet

MILES OF TRAILS: 22

ECOSYSTEMS:
redwoods, chaparral,
grasslands

ADMINISTRATION:
Los Padres National
Forest

MAP: Los Padres
National Forest/Santa
Lucia Ranger District
Map

Just south of the Ventana Wilderness and rising almost directly from the sea is the 14,500-acre Silver Peak Wilderness, established in 1992. After passage of the 1984 California Wilderness Act, Silver Peak was the first roadless area originally released for development to subsequently be protected as a new unit in the wilderness system. Part of the Santa Lucia Range, this wilderness rises nearly 3,600 feet within two miles of the ocean. Despite its small size, the area is separated by a single dirt road from a huge roadless area found on the Fort Hunter Liggett Military Base, so the actual roadless value of Silver Peak is significantly greater than acreage would indicate.

Unlike many of the higher portions of the Ventana Wilderness, which is composed of granites of the Salinian Block, Silver Peak is made up of younger rocks from the Nacimiento Block. These rocks are primarily sandstones, shales, greenstones, and cherts.

Vegetation and wildlife are similar to that of the larger Ventana Wilderness: Open meadows with oaks dominate ridgelines, while conifers occur in the stream bottoms, including California's southernmost redwoods, found along Salmon Creek. Both steelhead and salmon runs are found in Salmon Creek. A number of trails lace this wilderness, but level camping areas are rare. The Forest Service has three designated botanical areas in the Silver Peak Wilderness.

OVERNIGHT HIKE: SALMON CREEK LOOP
Loop length: 14 miles
Low and high elevations: 300 to 3,000 feet
Difficulty: moderate

This route can be hiked partway to make a delightful day hike or lengthened into a 2-day overnight hike. The trail will take you through open grasslands, oak woodlands, and into redwood-lined ravines. Travel Coast Highway 1 to Salmon Creek Ranger Station, where parking is available. The trail is located on the south side of Salmon Creek.

The trail climbs immediately across flowery slopes, providing good views of Salmon Creek Falls. You will eventually cross the creek, passing into a Douglas fir forest; 2.0 miles from the highway, you will reach the junction for Spruce Creek Camp, a good site for overnighters not interested in going far. The main trail continues up Salmon Creek to Estrella Camp, located at 1,500 feet elevation on a grassy spot along Salmon Creek. This is a good turnaround point for day hikers. From here, there is no water or shade available for 2.5 miles as the trail climbs steeply to South Coast Range Road, which separates the Silver Peak Wilderness from Fort Hunter Liggett.

Once on the road, turn left (north) and walk less than 0.1 mile to the Cruickshank Trail. This will bring you to Lion's Den Camp, which has water. Continue descending from here into Villa Creek, where there are some flat campsites. Less than 1.0 mile beyond this point, you will hit the junction with the Buckeye Trail, which you will ascend up and over a wooded ridge and down again into Redwood Creek drainage. Eventually, your trail climbs up and passes Buckeye Camp, which has a spring, and traverses an open meadowy slope with great views of the Pacific Ocean. This brings you back to Highway 1 and the parking area.

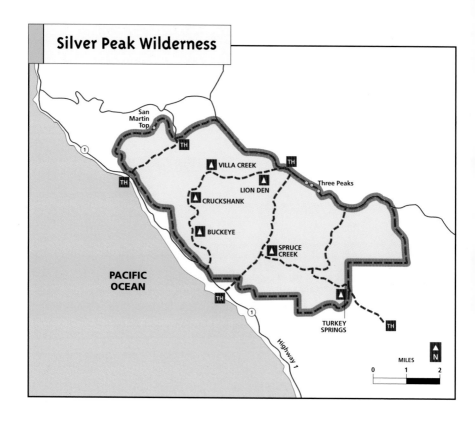

Silver Peak Wilderness

San Martin Top

TH

VILLA CREEK

TH

Three Peaks

LION DEN

CRUCKSHANK

BUCKEYE

TH

SPRUCE CREEK

PACIFIC OCEAN

TH

TURKEY SPRINGS

TH

Highway 1

MILES

0   1   2

N

Ventana Wilderness   52

Steep mountains that drop into the Pacific, redwoods, oak woodlands, and flowered meadows characterize the Ventana Wilderness, one of the most delightful wildlands in California.

The trailless granite gorge of the Little Sur River in the Ventana Wilderness.

LOCATION: 25 miles south of Monterey

SIZE: 216,500 acres

ELEVATION RANGE: 600 to 5,862 feet

MILES OF TRAILS: 260

ECOSYSTEMS: redwoods, oak woodland, mixed pine, chaparral

ADMINISTRATION: Los Padres National Forest

MAPS: Los Padres National Forest/ Monterey Ranger District Map, Ventana Wilderness Area Map

The Ventana Wilderness takes in the higher northern portion of the Santa Lucia Mountains in what is commonly known as the Big Sur Coast region. Most of the wilderness is part of the Salinian Block and consists of granitic as well as metamorphic rocks, such as marble, schists, and slates. Hot springs occur in a few locations, including the popular Styes Hot Springs, only accessible by foot.

In some places of the Ventana, the wilderness boundary comes to within a quarter mile of the ocean. This area's western boundary is almost always within sight of Coast Highway 1, the scenic road that was built by convict labor during the depression years.

Set aside as the Ventana Primitive Area in 1931 by the chief of the Forest Service, it originally contained 45,520 acres, but this was enlarged to 55,884 acres in 1937. In 1969, it became part of the National Wilderness system and was renamed Ventana Wilderness. It was subsequently enlarged in 1978 and 1984. In 1992, another 38,000 acres were added in the Horse Creek and Rocky Creek areas on the eastern edge of the wilderness, bringing its total up to the present 216,500 acres.

The Ventana is steep. Knife-edge ridges drop precipitously into narrow, V-shaped canyons. There are some 260-plus miles of trails, with longer loop trips and backpacking possible. Some 90 percent of Ventana's use occurs on just two trails—Pine Ridge/Carmel River Trail and the hike up the Big Sur River to Styles Hot Springs. If you want to find solitude, avoid these trails. However, don't *stray* from the trails: Unlike the Sierra Nevada and other areas, traveling off-trail can be extremely difficult, due to steep terrain and dense vegetation. One Thanksgiving break, I was backpacking here and tried to travel cross-country from Ventana Cones to Bottchers Gap. I soon discovered that crawling through a trailless country of chaparral with a backpack on and shimmying over huge, wet, downed redwood boles taller than two people required a bit more effort than I had bargained for. It took me two exhausting days in nearly continuous rain to cover eight miles! Oh, but what isolation.

The highest summit in the Santa Lucias is 5,862-foot Junipero Serra Peak. This may not seem high compared to the Sierra Nevada or other high ranges of the state, but keep in mind that nearly all this relief is from sea level. These mountains rise more than a mile out of the Pacific, and for those hiking the trails, it can sometimes seem as though you are climbing sheer cliffs, so vertical is the terrain. The lowest portion of the wilderness is 600 feet, lying along the Big Sur River.

Annual precipitation occurs mostly between November and April, with as much as 75 inches falling along the coast and as little as 25 inches just a few miles inland. In summer, fog bathes the coastal side of the mountains, but it seldom reaches more than a few miles inland.

The Ventana has one of the more diverse vegetative communities found anywhere. You may camp among redwoods and bigleaf maples or traverse up through an oak savanna to break out in open grassy meadows—all in the course of one mile. Ponderosa pine, Coulter pine, sugar pine, and knobcone pine dominate the areas with frequent fires. Douglas fir, along with Santa Lucia fir, dominate the moister, higher elevations. The aptly named Pine Valley with its large stately stands of ponderosa pines seems more like the Sierra Nevada than a coastal mountain valley. However, chaparral covers more than 60 percent of the area.

The Santa Lucia fir, found nowhere else on earth but in these mountains, is sometimes called bristlecone fir because of the bracts that stick out of its cones. The fir tends to grow at higher elevations on north-facing slopes where fires are infrequent. This tree was first discovered by botanists Thomas Coulter, for whom Coulter pine is named, and David Douglas, of Douglas fir fame. Most of this vegetative diversity is maintained by wildfire, and fortunately for the Ventana, the 1977 Marble Cone fire blazed across 175,000 acres—nearly 90 percent of the wilderness—creating new wildlife habitat and rejuvenating vegetative communities.

Black bear, mountain lion, mule deer, and bobcat are common forest mammals. Non-native wild boar escaped from the Hearst Estate to the south and are now common. Steelhead—sea-run rainbow trout—still ascend the Big Sur and Little Sur Rivers and Big Creek in small numbers.

Most of Ventana's use occurs in the spring, when flowers are blooming and temperatures are optimal, but hiking in the wilderness is possible year round. Even in summer, westside valleys are often cool due to morning fog and shady canyon environments, while in late fall and winter, the east side offers some respite from the heavy rain common at that time of year.

> **DAY HIKE: CONE PEAK**
> One-way length: 2.3 miles
> Low and high elevations: 3,720 to 5,155 feet
> Difficulty: moderate

This is a steep climb (1,400), but the magnificent views of the Pacific Ocean and the entire Santa Lucia Range make this a premier hike on a clear day. To reach the trailhead, turn off of Coast Highway 1 by the Mill Creek Picnic Area onto the Nacimiento–Fergusson Road. This highly scenic route winds 7.5 miles up the mountains to Redwood Springs Campground, where it intersects Forest Road 20S05, sometimes known as the Coast Ridge Road. From the trailhead parking area, the hike follows the closed road a short way, then it splits to form a separate trail that follows a ridge, passing through oak woodlands. Eventually, the trail switchbacks, passing through Coulter pine, sugar pine, and the rare Santa Lucia fir, on the final 0.25 mile of spur trail to the summit lookout.

> **DAY HIKE: VICENTE FLAT**
> One-way length: 4.3 miles
> Low and high elevations: 300 to 1,780 feet
> Difficulty: moderate

The Vicente Flat Trail takes you from near sea level at the coast up through the Santa Lucia Mountains and ends at a lovely redwood grove along a murmuring creek. The trailhead is located near Kirk Creek Campground just east of Coast Highway 1. With beautiful views of meadows and oak woodlands, the trail ascends by switchback through chaparral and grasslands, often studded with flowers in March and April. You will continue climbing to a ridge, then traverse along the side of the Hare Creek drainage to the redwood-lined banks of the creek at Vicente Flat, which makes a great overnight camp as well as a good picnic spot and goal for day hikers.

Ventana Wilderness

OVERNIGHT HIKE: PINE VALLEY LOOP
Loop length: 23.1 miles
Low and high elevations: 1,600 to 4,750 feet
Difficulty: moderate

The Pine Valley Loop takes one past waterfalls, pine forests, and beautiful meadows. As might be expected, this is a popular route, so it's best to avoid it during major holidays and during summer when it can be very hot. To reach the trailhead, turn west off Highway 101 by Greenfield on County Road G16. Take this county road 29.0 miles to Tassajara Road, then turn south to China Campground, where there is trailhead parking for the Pine Ridge Trail.

At first, the trail goes up and down as it makes its way to Church Creek Divide, with views of flowery meadows just above the trail. Continue north to Pine Valley, where there is an overnight campsite, a lovely place with large ponderosa pine somewhat reminiscent of the Sierra Nevada. From Pine Valley, it's an easy hike to view Pine Creek Falls, and the pool below makes a good swimming hole on a hot day. To continue the loop, head down the Carmel River Trail, which crosses the stream a number of times. This can be difficult if water levels are high—usually a concern only in winter. Good campsites are located at Hiding Camp and Buckskin Flat. The Carmel River Trail is joined by the Miller Canyon Trail at Carmel River Camp. If you have previously arranged a shuttle or want to hitchhike back to your vehicle—which is risky, given the limited traffic—you can continue 5.0 miles down the Carmel River to the Carmel River Ranger Station by the reservoir. To complete the loop by trail, take the Miller Trail 9.4 miles uphill to your vehicle at China Campground. Alternatively, it is possible to camp enroute at Miller Canyon Camp and have an easy jaunt out the next day.

Pine Creek Falls, Santa Lucia Range, Ventana Wilderness.

CONDORS

The entire Santa Barbara backcountry, including the San Rafael, Sespe, Dick Smith, and other wilderness areas, used to be the haunt of the endangered California condor. The condor once ranged over much of the West and was found as far north as southern British Columbia and east into Arizona, New Mexico, and Texas. The first record of a condor was made by the Lewis and Clark Expedition, who saw the birds feeding on dead salmon along the Columbia River in 1806.

Condors range widely, sometimes up to 100 miles from nesting sites to feeding areas. One of the last known nesting spots was not in the Santa Barbara region, but the southern Sierra.

The condor is the largest flying bird in North America, reaching a weight of 20 pounds with a wingspan of 10 feet. Overall, the bird is black with a naked head. In captivity, they have lived up to 45 years. They reach maturity at six years and produce a single egg every other year.

The condor flies over open country—pastureland and meadows—looking for dead animals that it locates both by sight as well as smell. At night it roosts in trees or cliffs, often communally.

Condors began a rapid slide toward extinction with the settlement of the West. They were shot by miners because their quill feathers were considered good for storing gold. Ranchers and hunters shot them because they were thought to prey on livestock and game animals. An estimate in the 1930s put the bird's numbers at only 60 to 70 over its entire range.

By 1937, concern for the bird's declining numbers lead to the establishment of the 1,200-acre Sisquoc Condor Sanctuary in what is now the San Rafael Wilderness. The goal of the refuge was to provide undisturbed nesting and roosting habitat for the condors. In 1947, the 53,000-acre Sespe Sanctuary in what is now the Sespe Wilderness was created and later expanded. Neither sanctuary proved sufficient to slow the condor's slide toward extinction.

Predator poisoning programs done at taxpayer expense to benefit live-stock producers took its toll, as did lead poisoning, when the big birds consumed wounded deer or other game animals hunters failed to find or retrieve. The birds use the bullet opening to access the carcass, often consuming the lead bullet in the process. By 1965, only 40 birds were thought to be alive, and by 1983, there were only 20 wild condors left.

To reverse this trend, the U.S. Fish and Wildlife Service launched a captive breeding program in 1981. By 1987, the last wild condor was captured and placed in captivity. Normally, a condor lays one egg every other year, however, if the egg is removed, the birds produce another. Using this method, the captive breeding program had increased the number of birds to 52 by 1992. Beginning that year, the first captive-bred condors were released back into the wild and are once again sailing above the sky of the Santa Barbara backcountry. It is still too early to gauge the final success of the program.

Southern California: The Transverse and Peninsula Ranges

Wilderness in Southern California? Well, maybe on the freeways. That's probably the reaction most people have to any suggestion that there could be anything natural or wild left south of the Sierra. Despite the millions who live here, Southern California has a remarkable amount of land that is undeveloped, with even a few pockets of relative solitude. This region contains 10 national forest wildernesses and several state wilderness areas, including San Jacinto State Wilderness and Cuyamaca Rancho State Park.

Southern California is usually defined as the area south of the Transverse Ranges—the Santa Ynez, Santa Monica, San Gabriel, and the San Bernardino Mountains, as well as the Peninsula Ranges. This includes the San Jacinto, Santa Rosa, Laguna, Santa Ana, and Palomar Mountains located east of San Diego.

Between the Los Angeles Basin and the area around San Diego live more than half of the state's population, and the reason they're there is climate. It is seldom excessively hot in the summer, especially near the coast, and it's pleasant all winter. Most precipitation comes in the winter months, but even then sunshine prevails much of the time. Another reason for the popularity of the region is the extreme natural beauty. From the coastal strand to the desert sands, mountains and hills dominate every horizon. Physically, the natural landscape of southern California is one of the most arresting in the state.

Part of the reason a few pockets of Southern California remain undeveloped is due to their rugged terrain. Some of the steepest mountains in California are found here, with the loftiest rising as much as 10,000 feet above the surrounding lowlands. Peaks such as the San Gabriel and San Bernardino, whose highest summit, Mount San Gorgonio, is 11,502 feet, occur in the Transverse Ranges. John Muir, not one to shy away from difficult hiking, noted the tough going these ranges represented when he observed"…the slopes are exceptionally steep and insecure to the foot and they are covered with thorny bushes from five to ten feet high."

The Transverse Ranges are aligned east–west, distinctively different from most of the mountains in the state that follow a more or less north–south orientation. This alignment is the result of rotation by the northward migration of the Pacific Plate along the San Andreas Fault, which has twisted these southern California mountains into their present position. Powerful earthquakes regularly rock the region.

Limber pine on Mount San Gorgonio, San Gorgonio Wilderness.

All these Southern California mountain ranges are fault-block induced, thus they tend to have at least one steep side, while those aligned between parallel faults tend to be precipitous along both sides of the axis. The majority of uplift has only occurred during the past two million years. As a consequence, these ranges are geologically young, with little time for erosion to strip away the overlying rock formations.

Granitic rocks underlie all southern California mountains, but in the Transverse Ranges, they are still overlain by older rocks, such as the 1.7-billion-year-old gneiss that can be seen along the Angeles Crest Highway. Sedimentary rocks, such as sandstones, limestones, shales, and schists, also occur primarily in the San Gabriel and San Bernardino Mountains.

Unlike the Sierra Nevada, there was little glacial activity in these southern California mountains that were, for the most part, too low and too far south to maintain glaciers. However, Mount San Gorgonio did support a few cirque glaciers, making it the southernmost edge of glaciation in California.

The area is dominated by chaparral, which covers some 12 million acres of California. The word "chaparral" is Spanish, and was originally used to describe thickets of evergreen shrub oaks. Now its meaning has broadened to include any dense shrub habitat. Although chaparral is found throughout various sub-regions of the state, it is most abundant in Southern California.

Much of the lower elevation chaparral is known as "coastal sage shrub." It is very drought resistant, but as a community, the majority of the plants are not frost-hardy. The species commonly found in this area differ between the north- and south-facing slopes. Those on the southern slopes include California sagebrush, California encelia or brittle-bush, California buck-wheat, black sage, purple sage, white sage, and bush monkeyflower. The north-facing slopes have greater shade, less evaporation, and cooler temperatures, which encourage the growth of shrubs such as toyon, lemonadeberry, and coyote brush.

There has been a tremendous loss of the coastal sage chaparral community. At first, much of this plant community was bulldozed to make way for agriculture, particularly cow pastures and orange groves. Now, in many parts of Southern California, the pastures and orange groves have been replaced by shopping malls and housing tracts. Because of this loss, many species associated with this distinctive community have been significantly reduced and threatened with extinction. This includes the California gnatcatcher, a small wren-like bird that nests exclusively in the coastal sage shrub community.

At slightly higher elevations, frost-tolerant chaparral plants dominate. This is southern California's most common plant community, which includes species such as chamise and a number of species of ceanothus, manzanita, and shrub oak. Plants at this elevation tend to be evergreen with small, drought-resistant leaves. They also have a two-layered root system: Shallow roots that absorb moisture as soon as it hits the ground, and a deeper set of roots to tap into long-term soil moisture supplies. To deal with heat, many of these plants have serrated leaves or roll their leaf margins—both adaptations to help dissipate heat or reduce surface area exposed to the sun.

Perhaps the most important adaptation of this community is its propensity to burn. Many chaparral species require periodic fires to remain healthy and vigorous and actually contain oils that make them extremely flammable. One of the common adaptations to fire is root sprouting. Even if the above-ground parts are completely burned off, new growth sprouts from the root crown. Some chaparral plants have hard seed coatings that only open after they are heated. They can remain dormant in the soil for decades, waiting for a fire to release them for growth.

Of conifer species, one of the most unusual is big-cone Douglas fir, locally called "big cone spruce," which explains why there are so many place-name references to spruce scattered about the southern California mountains. Found only in Southern California and the South Coast Ranges, big-cone Douglas fir is related to the Douglas fir that dominates the North Coast and the Pacific Northwest, except that it has cones twice as large. Adapted to fire, it has the ability to sprout after a burn—a useful trait in the fire-prone Southern California forests.

Another common conifer in the Southern California mountains is Coulter pine. It looks something like a ponderosa pine, but with enormous cones that may at times approach the size of a bowling ball! Growing in open stands, it occupies a similar ecological niche as digger pine—lower elevation forests. In the more desert ranges, such as the eastern slope of the Santa Rosa Range, stands of pinyon pine and juniper take over the same ecological niche.

Above the Coulter pine forest grow the more typical Sierran pine species, such as ponderosa and Jeffrey pine. However, both species are absent from the Santa Monica and Santa Ana Mountains. Also mixed in with these species are white fir and incense cedar. At very high elevations in the San Bernardino, San Jacinto, and San Gabriel Mountains, there are stands of lodgepole pine and, in a few places, limber pine. The southernmost limber pine are found on Toro Peak on the edge of the Santa Rosa Wilderness.

Oak trees, including black oak, golden cup oak, and coast live oak, are very abundant in some of these ranges. Coast live oak grows at the lowest elevations, particularly on north-facing slopes. Golden cup oak, or canyon live oak, as it is often called, is widely distributed. Found at slightly higher elevations than coast live oak, it is frequently associated with canyons and other shady, moist sites, hence its common name. Black oak, which is deciduous and has beautiful golden leaves in the fall, is often found growing among Coulter pine and ponderosa pine stands.

Riparian species include California sycamore, white alder, flowering ash, and Fremont cottonwood. Occasionally, one will also find Pacific madrone and California laurel, as well.

A wide variety of wildlife typical of Southern California can be found here, including coyote, ringtail, mule deer, gray fox, bobcat, and the mountain lion. The lion, in particular, is far more common than people might suspect, but their generally shy nature makes it an unusual occurrence to spot one. As more and more people have moved into mountain lion territories, conflicts have risen, with a few people suffering attacks on their pets annually. Again, the risk of lion attack is small, and just driving to a park or wilderness is far more risky than hiking in mountain lion country. We must show tolerance for the mountain lions: They have no place else to go, but people do.

Black bears, not native to the southern California mountains, were introduced and are now relatively common. The "Bear" canyons that adorn Southern California place-names refer to the grizzly, once very prevalent in the region. In 1845 a local rancher, along with Mexican troops, killed more than 22 grizzlies in two days in the Bear Valley area of the San Bernardino Mountains. Today, the grizzly is extinct throughout California, the last one killed in 1922.

The San Gabriel Mountains were among the first forested areas to receive protection within the country. In 1892, President Harrison set aside the San Gabriel Timberland Reserve, the second in the country after Yellowstone. One year later, the San Bernardino Forest Reserve was established, and today it ranks as the second largest national forest in California, with an area larger than the state of Rhode Island!

Around the turn of the century, these forested mountain areas became fashionable as a hiking region, with many lodges and camps springing up to serve the public. The Angeles Crest Highway was built between 1929 and 1956, providing more access. The Rim of the World Highway in the San Bernardino Mountains offered similar access.

Most of these wilderness areas, what some call "weekend wildernesses," are relatively uncrowded during the week. In fact, except for the San Jacinto Wilderness and a couple of weekends in the San Gorgonio Wilderness, I did not encounter another hiker in any of the Southern California wildernesses I visited once I got more than a few miles from a trailhead. People who suggest hikers are "loving wilderness to death" are focused on cosmetic aspects, such as campfire rings, compacted campsites, and the like. Ecologically speaking, in the big picture of wilderness, what is affecting the wildlands are creeping urbanization and agriculture that are now at the very fringes of some Southern California wildernesses. The fields, housing tracts, highways, and other developments fragment these landscapes, making it difficult for wildlife to travel between ranges.

Another problem with development, particularly in mountain canyons and on slopes, is that demand for wildfire control grows, despite the fact that nearly all native plant communities are dependent upon fire for their continued health and survival. Even more insidious is the smog that envelopes southern California every summer. An acid fog with a pH of 1.7 was recorded in one southern California location in 1982. (To compare, neutral pH is 7.0.) Smog, particularly high levels of ozone, has been shown to damage the needles on ponderosa and Jeffrey pine and has contributed to a significant death among those sensitive species.

It is doubtful that human population growth overrunning southern California will halt any time soon. The best that can be hoped for is that some pockets of the natural landscape will remain intact to function as ecological preserves and as reminders of what first attracted people to this land of sunshine and beauty.

53 Agua Tibia Wilderness

Its chaparral-covered hills and the many streams located in the northern end of the Palomar Mountains make this a good wildlands to explore in spring and fall.

Chaparral dominates the vegetation along the Dripping Springs Trail in Agua Tibia Wilderness.

LOCATION: 10 miles east of Temecula

SIZE: 15,933 acres

ELEVATION RANGE: 1,700 to 5,000 feet

MILES OF TRAILS: 17.4

ECOSYSTEMS: chaparral, oak-pine woodlands

ADMINISTRATION: Cleveland National Forest

MAP: Cleveland National Forest Map

Agua Tibia means "warm water" in Spanish, and this wilderness was supposedly named after the small sun-warmed pools that are commonly found along its streams during the summer. Since lower elevations are less than 2,000 feet and summer temperatures often exceed 100 degrees, it's easy to understand how this might be an appropriate name.

The Agua Tibia was first given protection as a primitive area in 1931 and was officially designated a wilderness area in 1975. Located 75 miles southeast of Los Angeles on the Cleveland National Forest in the Palomar Range, the 15,933-acre wilderness is only 3 miles wide by 5 miles across. The "palomar" of the Palomar Range is another name derived from Spanish and means "pigeon roost," an appellation given to these mountains for the large numbers of band-tailed pigeons known to live here.

Most of the wilderness encompasses steep, brushy mountain slopes with 69 percent of the area in chaparral and only seven percent in coniferous forest. Most of the chaparral consists of black sage, chamise, red shank, buckwheat, and various species of ceanothus. Due to the dense shrub cover and limited supplies of grass and water, the area has never had livestock grazing. Most of the conifers occur on or near 5,077-foot Eagle Crag Peak and 4,779-foot Agua Tibia Mountain. These stands consist of Coulter pine, big-cone Douglas fir, incense cedar, and white fir. Deciduous species include black oak, red alder, bigleaf maple, interior live oak, Fremont cottonwood, and California sycamore. One of the southernmost occurrences of Pacific madrone is located just outside of the wilderness on Mount Palomar.

Due to the dense chaparral, nearly all recreational use occurs on trails or old fire roads bulldozed up the ridges. The most popular route is Dripping Springs Trail, which goes from Dripping Springs to Agua Tibia Mountain.

DAY HIKE: DRIPPING SPRINGS–PALOMAR DIVIDE TRAIL
One-way length: 6.8 miles
Low and high elevations: 1,600 to 4,779 feet
Difficulty: moderate

The Dripping Springs Trail accesses Aqua Tibia Mountain (4,779), passing giant chaparral that hasn't burned in more than 100 years. To find the trailhead, take Highway 79, 10.0 miles east from I–15 to the Dripping Springs Campground. The trail immediately crosses Arroyo Seco Creek, the only source of water along this entire hike. Bear in mind that there is almost no shade, and the hike should be avoided on a hot sunny afternoon. The trail continues to climb as Vail Lake comes into view. At 3.5 miles, it passes through giant chaparral up to 20 feet in height. If you continue to the Palomar Divide Truck Trail—an old fire road—you will gradually enter scattered stands of oak and pine. In this open landscape, you will see fine views of the San Jacinto Mountains and perhaps even the Pacific Ocean, more than 40 miles away.

DAY HIKE: MAGEE–PALOMAR TRAIL
One-way length: 6 miles
Low and high elevations: 3,900 to 4,800 feet
Difficulty: moderate

This route is a continuation of the Dripping Springs Trail, traveling across the highest parts of the Aqua Tibia Wilderness. Access is via Dripping Springs Trail. From Aqua Tibia Mountain, the trail descends to the chaparral-covered Crosley Saddle at 3,900 feet. From here, the trail rises again, entering coniferous and oak woodlands on Eagle Crag.

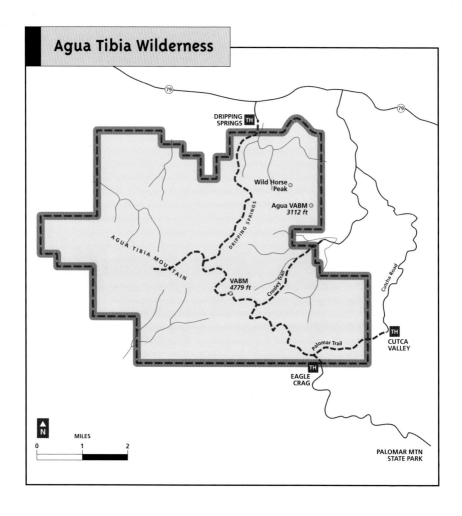

Agua Tibia Wilderness

DRIPPING
SPRINGS TH

Wild Horse
Peak

Agua VABM
3112 ft

AGUA TIBIA MOUNTAIN

DRIPPING SPRINGS

VABM
4779 ft

Crosley Trail

Cutcha Road

Palomar Trail

CUTCA
VALLEY

EAGLE
CRAG

N

MILES

0   1   2

PALOMAR MTN
STATE PARK

Cucamonga Wilderness 54

*This small forested wilderness has steep slopes
and a lovely, cool creek.*

Cascade on Icehouse Creek, Cucamonga Wilderness.

The easternmost of the three wildernesses in the San Gabriel
Mountains, the Cucamonga is perhaps the most heavily used.
This 12,981-acre wilderness was among the original wild-
lands designated by the passage of the 1964 Wilderness Act.
It was subsequently enlarged as part of the 1984 California
Wilderness Act.

Ranging from 5,000 feet in Icehouse Canyon to
nearly 9,000 feet at Telegraph Peak, the wilderness contains
its namesake, 8,859-foot Cucamonga Peak. As one of the most
remote mountains in the entire range, you must hike a minimum of six miles to ascend this peak, with unsurpassed views
of the Los Angeles Basin from its lodgepole pine-studded
summit as your reward.

Much of San Antonio Canyon, which borders the
wilderness on the western edge, burned in the 1980 Thunder

LOCATION: 5 miles
north of San Antonio
Heights

SIZE: 12,981 acres

ELEVATION RANGE:
5,000 to 9,000 feet

MILES OF TRAILS: 26

ECOSYSTEMS:
chaparral, mixed
conifer

ADMINISTRATION:
San Bernardino
National Forest

MAPS: Angeles N.F.
Map, San Bernardino
N.F. Map, Cucamonga
Wilderness Area Map

Mountain Fire. Strong Santa Anna winds powered the blaze, creating a patchwork of burned and unburned forest—a classic textbook example of a burn mosaic. Beautiful riparian vegetation is found along boulder-strewn Icehouse Canyon.

DAY HIKE: ICEHOUSE CANYON–CUCAMONGA PEAK
One-way distance: 6 miles
Low and high elevations: 5,000 to 8,859 feet
Difficulty: moderate

This trail follows Icehouse Creek to Icehouse Saddle and then to the top of 8,859-foot Cucamonga Peak, passing through marvelous incense cedar, sugar pine, and ponderosa pine forest enroute. To find the trailhead, drive Highway 83 from Upland to the Mount Baldy Village on the San Antonio Canyon Road, then continue 1.5 miles to Icehouse Canyon Resort; park there.

The first half of this trail is actually outside of the formally designated wilderness and passes many private inholdings. You will pass through a forest of oaks, big-cone Douglas fir, and incense cedar along the way and eventually reach a junction some 1.5 miles from the trailhead. The new trail to the left is the Chapman Trail. It is gentler but longer by almost 2 miles than the old trail that continues straight ahead; both eventually rejoin at Columbine Spring, the last water along the route. From the spring, it's another 0.6 mile through lovely pine and fir forest to Icehouse Saddle, where there are several options. One can continue down into the Middle Fork Lytle Creek or head north to Timber Mountain and Telegraph Peak. To reach Cucamonga Peak, the goal of this hike, turn right (south) and follow the trail 2.4 miles as it skirts the shoulder of Bighorn Peak. Then climb steeply up the north side of Cucamonga Peak to the summit.

DAY HIKE: MIDDLE FORK LYTLE CREEK
One-way distance: 2.3 miles
Low and high elevations: 4,000 to 5,200 feet
Difficulty: moderate

This hike follows the beautiful stream draining Cucamonga Peak, the highest in the wilderness. One of the least used entries into the wilderness, it's located just a few miles from millions of people. The Middle Fork of Lytle Creek, proposed for protection as a Wild and Scenic River, is also home to a small herd of bighorn sheep. To find the trailhead, take the Sierra Avenue exit off I–15, head north to Lytle Creek Road, then drive on Middle Fork Road to the trailhead parking area.

The hike begins with a short switchback over a ridge then drops into the Middle Fork Lytle Creek drainage, passing through live oak and big-cone Douglas fir as it descends to a stream with lush riparian vegetation of bigleaf maple and sycamore. Just 0.5 mile from the trailhead lies Stone House Camp—a good potential camping spot for someone who wants to make an overnight trip without a lot of hiking. From here, the trail climbs more steeply to Third Crossing Camp, 2.3 miles from the trailhead. This is a good place to turn around, but it is possible to continue another 1.5 miles to Commanche Camp, then another 2.0 steep miles to Icehouse Saddle.

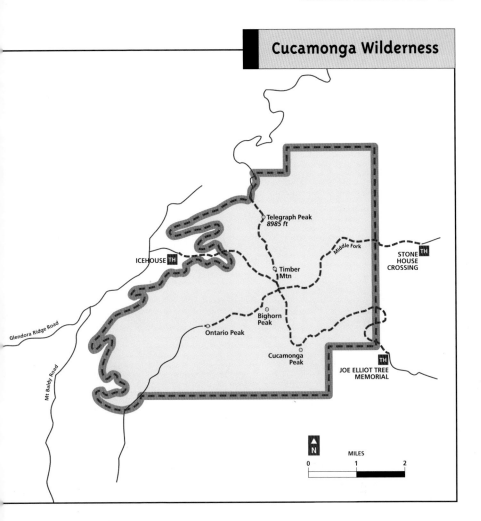

Cucamonga Wilderness

Telegraph Peak
8985 ft

Middle Fork

ICEHOUSE TH

STONE TH
HOUSE
CROSSING

Timber
Mtn

Glendora Ridge Road

Bighorn
Peak

Ontario Peak

Cucamonga
Peak

JOE ELLIOT TREE TH
MEMORIAL

Mt Baldy Road

N

MILES

0   1   2

55 Pine Creek and Hauser Wildernesses

Chaparral and perennial creeks dominate these granite-knobbed wildlands, all within sight of the Mexican border.

A chaparral-covered slope by Pine Valley Creek in Pine Creek Wilderness.

LOCATION: south of I–8 east of Alpine

SIZE: 13,100 acres (Pine Creek), 8,000 acres (Hauser)

ELEVATION RANGE: 2,000 to 4,000 feet Pine Creek; 2,000 to 3,681 feet Hauser

MILES OF TRAILS: 5

ECOSYSTEMS: chaparral, riparian

ADMINISTRATION: Cleveland National Forest

MAPS: Cleveland N.F. Map, Pine Creek/Hauser Wilderness Areas Map

In the Laguna Mountains of southern California, just off I–8 east of San Diego, lie two adjacent pocket wildernesses—the 13,100-acre Pine Creek Wilderness and the 8,000-acre Hauser Wilderness. Both are managed by the Cleveland National Forest.

Of the two, Pine Creek is likely to attract the most recreational use. This long, thin wildlands is sliced by deep canyons, and the largest is its namesake—Pine Creek Canyon. Elevations vary from 2,000 to 4,000 feet. Looking across the canyons and ridges at sunrise, one feels as though they may be lost in some remote part of Mexico, far from the hustle and noise of southern California.

Tranquil Pine Creek flows over smooth, granite slabs and boulders and holds lovely pools suitable for taking a dip in on hot summer days. Trout are found in the creek along this narrow, but lush, riparian zone, consisting of willows, Fremont cottonwood, California sycamore, and scattered stands of coast live oak. Chaparral covers most of the rest of the slopes. When I visited the area in July, the air was alive with the buzzing of dozens of hummingbirds.

The Espinoza Trail dissects the wilderness from east to west, while another trail parallels Horsethief Canyon on the west. Unfortunately, cattle have the run of the place, decreasing its desirability as a wildlands sanctuary.

Lying just south of Pine Creek Wilderness and separated from it by a single dirt road in Skye Valley lies the trailless Hauser Wilderness. Granite boulders and ridges covered with dense chaparral dominate this area, whose high point is just 3,681 feet. The only access is the old Hauser Creek Road, which follows the stream along the southern edge of the wilderness. Hauser Creek is lined by California sycamore, live oak, cottonwood, and willows. The Pacific Crest Trail passes just to the east of the wilderness, and cattle graze its few meadows. The 8,000-acre wilderness was designated in 1984.

DAY HIKE: PINE CANYON
One way length: 3 miles
Low and high elevations: 2,000 to 2,200 feet
Difficulty: moderate

The hike down to Pine Canyon is delightful as it follows a side canyon with large oaks and sycamores. The creek itself slides over granite boulders and into clear pools that invite one to spend time lingering there. To find the trailhead, exit I–8 at Highway 79 and head south to Japatul Fire Station. Turn onto Horsethief Canyon Road and head north to the trailhead, looking for trail 3E05. The path descends for 1.0 mile to Pine Creek, then turns south, passing through large flats with scattered trees. The trail only occasionally intersects the creek and eventually just peters out.

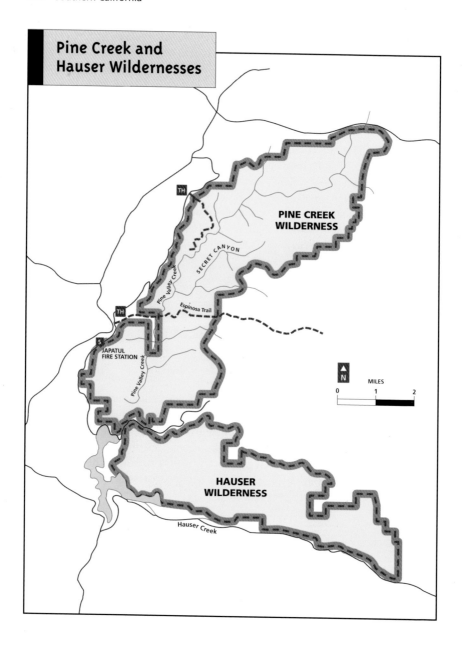

Pine Creek and Hauser Wildernesses

PINE CREEK WILDERNESS

SECRET CANYON

Pine Valley Creek

Espinosa Trail

TH

TH

5

JAPATUL FIRE STATION

Pine Valley Creek

HAUSER WILDERNESS

Hauser Creek

N

MILES

0   1   2

San Gabriel Wilderness 56

*Steep mountains, high peaks, and small streams
characterize this wilderness that lies just above millions
of people.*

*The view toward Twin Peaks from Waterman Mountain Trail,
San Gabriel Wilderness.*

The San Gabriel Mountains, which contain three wilderness
areas, provide a dramatic background for the cities of the Los
Angeles Basin. The 36,118-acre San Gabriel, managed by the
Angeles National Forest, is the westernmost of the wildernesses.
Dominated by very steep V-shaped canyons and narrow
ridgelines cut into granitic rock, a majority of the San Gabriel's
slopes exceed 50 degrees. As a consequence of the rugged
terrain, there are only 27 miles of trails in this pocket wildlands. The longest trails are the 14-mile Mount Waterman
and the 10.2-mile Bear Creek Trails. Accessible portions of
the wilderness receive heavy use since chaparral vegetation
makes cross-country travel almost impossible. Originally
part of the Devil Canyon–Bear Canyon Primitive Area
established by the Forest Service in 1932, the San Gabriel

LOCATION: just north
of Los Angeles

SIZE: 36,118 acres

ELEVATION RANGE:
1,600 to 8,200 feet

MILES OF TRAILS: 27

ECOSYSTEMS:
chaparral, mixed
conifer forests

ADMINISTRATION:
Angeles National Forest

MAP: Angeles National
Forest Map

Mountains were among the original wilderness areas designated by passage of the 1964 Wilderness Act.

The two year-round flowing streams, one each in Devil and Bear Canyons, are tributaries of the San Gabriel River. Both streams harbor trout.

Chaparral, a dominant plant community within the wilderness, consists of buckthorn, toyon, chamise, manzanita, ceanothus, and sugarbush. At higher elevations, one encounters forests of ponderosa pine, Jeffrey pine, Coulter pine, big-cone Douglas fir, and white fir, as well as black oak and bigleaf maple.

Wildlife includes the black bear, which were introduced from Yosemite decades ago, and bighorn sheep, seen frequently scampering among the crags.

The Angeles Crest Highway provides access from the north, while Highway 39 lies to the east, separating San Gabriel from Sheep Mountain Wilderness.

DAY HIKE: DEVIL'S CANYON
One-way distance: 3.5 miles
Low and high elevations: 3,500 to 5,000 feet
Difficulty: moderate

Though Los Angeles is less than 18 miles from the San Gabriel Wilderness, it's sights and sounds fade quickly once you descend along the Devil's Canyon Trail. This route wanders from the Chilao Visitor Center downhill to Devil's Canyon, alternately passing through pine forest and back into chaparral. This is steep country, and remember you have to hike back up to get to the trailhead. But once you get to the creek, you can enjoy soaking your feet in the water. Some people extend the hike by boulder-hopping down Devil's Creek, enjoying seldom visited waterfalls with beautiful plunge pools below.

DAY HIKE: TWIN PEAKS
One-way distance: 4.5 miles
Low and high elevations: 6,300 to 7,761 feet
Difficulty: moderate

This trail starts high with some occasional ups and downs as it passes through Jeffrey pine forests along the northern border of the San Gabriel Wilderness. To locate the trailhead, drive the Angeles Crest Highway beyond Horse Flats, continuing toward Buckhorn Campground. Watch for a blocked road to the south. The trail switchbacks up to a ridge where you will get great views south into the Bear Creek drainage. Hike the trail to Twin Peaks saddle, where you can follow an informal trail to the top of the peaks.

San Gabriel Wilderness

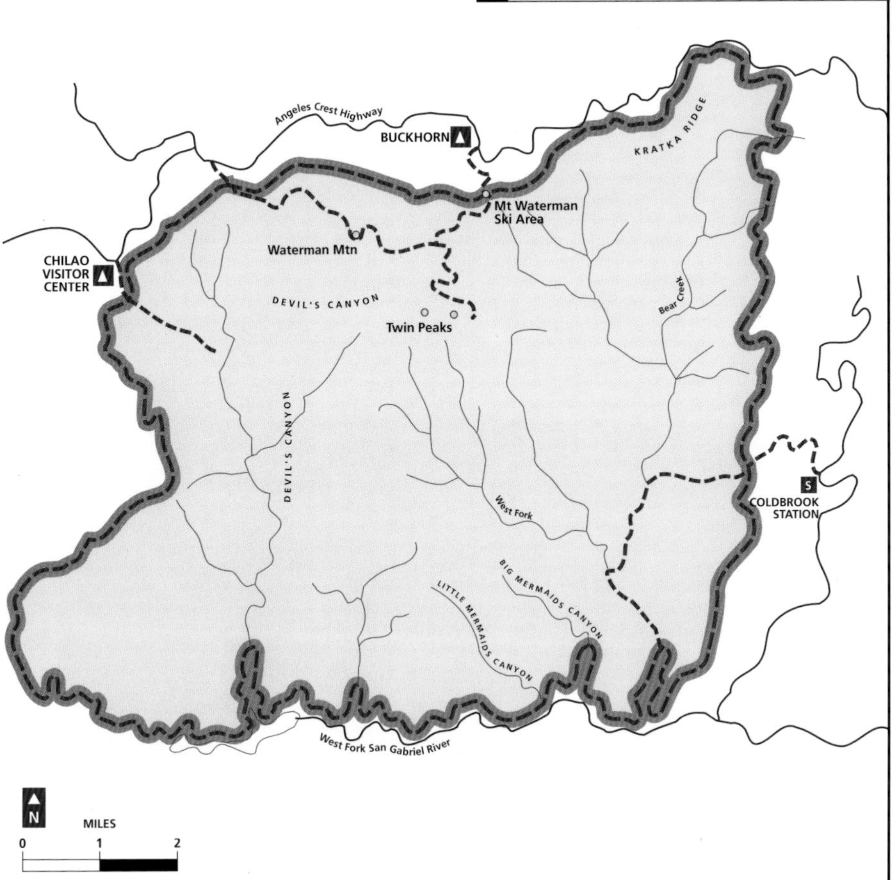

Angeles Crest Highway

BUCKHORN ▲

KRATKA RIDGE

Mt Waterman
Ski Area

Waterman Mtn

CHILAO
VISITOR ▲
CENTER

DEVIL'S CANYON

Bear Creek

Twin Peaks

DEVIL'S CANYON

West Fork

COLDBROOK
STATION

S

BIG MERMAIDS CANYON

LITTLE MERMAIDS CANYON

West Fork San Gabriel River

N

MILES

0   1   2

57 San Gorgonio Wilderness

Rising from desert to the alpine summit of San Gorgonio, this wilderness is very rugged and steep.

Lodgepole pine on Mount San Gorgonio frame Mount San Jacinto, San Gorgonio Wilderness.

LOCATION: 15 miles east of San Bernardino

SIZE: 94,702 acres

ELEVATION RANGE: 2,300 to 11,502 feet

MILES OF TRAILS: 106

ECOSYSTEMS: chaparral, mixed conifers, alpine

ADMINISTRATION: San Bernardino N.F., BLM Palm Springs Resource Area Office

MAPS: San Bernardino N.F. Map, San Gorgonio WIlderness Area Map

The San Bernardino Mountains rise like a fortress from the landscape, walling in the eastern edge of the Los Angeles Basin. This is the rooftop of southern California, with a number of ridges and peaks rising above treeline, including 10,806-foot Charlton Peak, 11,205-foot Jepson Peak, 10,624-foot San Bernardino Peak, 10,630-foot East San Bernardino Peak, and Mount San Gorgonio, at 11,502 feet the crowning height of southern California. From its broad summit on a clear day, exquisite views are possible, with the Sierra Nevada and much of the Mojave Desert visible. The peak is also the southern-most glaciated landscape in California, with Dollar Lake, Dry Lake, and Poopout Hill, all glacial landforms.

The San Bernardino Mountains are geologically younger than the San Gabriel Mountains and have a smoother, less eroded appearance. Like the San Gabriels, they are a fault-blocked range and are defined by very active faults, including the San Andreas, located along the southern edge of the mountains. The Mill Creek Fault slices through the range, providing an easy target for erosion, hence the deep canyon of Mill Creek. A mix of rocks, including granitic, gneiss, and limestone, can be found in the range.

The San Bernardinos have one of the most diverse floras of any southern California mountain range. At lower elevations on eastern slopes, there are Joshua Tree along with pinyon pine and juniper, while western low elevation slopes are dominated by chaparral. Higher up, magnificent forests of Coulter pine, ponderosa pine, Jeffrey pine, white fir, incense cedar, sugar pine, black oak, California dogwood, and bigleaf maple are found. At the highest elevations grow lodgepole pine and ancient limber pine, often forming open forests of barely alive, gnarled, twisted snags. Quaking aspen reaches its southernmost distribution in the United States here in the Fish Creek drainage and Arrastre Creek, while narrowleaf cottonwood, a Rocky Mountain species, is found in Holcomb Creek. A few meadows dot the range here and there, adding to the attractive mix. Wildlife includes bighorn sheep, mule deer, mountain lion, and black bear.

Mormon settlers from nearby San Bernardino were the first whites to exploit the mountains. They cut timber on the slopes and crest, building their first sawmills in Mill Creek, which is how it derived its name. By 1854 there were six sawmills operating in the mountains. In 1859, William Holcomb discovered gold in his namesake valley, which set off a minor rush to the area. More of the precious ore was discovered in nearby Bear Valley, and by 1860, several goldrush communities with as many as 2,000 residents dotted the crest of the San Bernardino Mountains. Eventually, the placer deposits gave out and most of the miners moved away, but hard rock mining continued well into this century.

In the 1880s, water was the new lure of these mountains. Several major dams were constructed, including Big Bear Lake and Lake Arrowhead. Roads were built to bring supplies, and, in turn, to bring people to build the reservoirs and, later, to enjoy the lakes. The Rim of the World Highway was completed in 1915, setting the stage for the latest and last major rush—recreation. Several ski areas were proposed for development in what eventually became the San Gorgonio Wilderness, and fortunately, the wilderness proponents won out. Although heavily used by hikers, their impact is very concentrated and minor—nothing more than cosmetic compared to the effects of logging, mining, and housing development that have influenced the rest of the range.

The area now encompassed by the San Gorgonio Wilderness was first part of the San Bernardino Forest Reserve that was set aside in 1893. Its special qualities were recognized when the Forest Service chief designated the high country around San Gorgonio a primitive area in 1931. Its name changed to San Gorgonio Wild Area in 1956, then again in 1964 when it was officially designated the San Gorgonio Wilderness. In 1984, the wilderness was enlarged by 23,720 acres, then the 1994 California Desert bill added another 37,980 acres, managed by the BLM, to the southeast corner in the Whitewater drainage. Today, the San Gorgonio Wilderness encompasses 94,702 acres and more than 100 miles of trails, allowing for everything from day hikes to extensive multi-day treks. Yet, much of the wilderness remains trailless, particularly the upper Whitewater and Hell For Sure drainages, offering potential solitude for the more intrepid hiker.

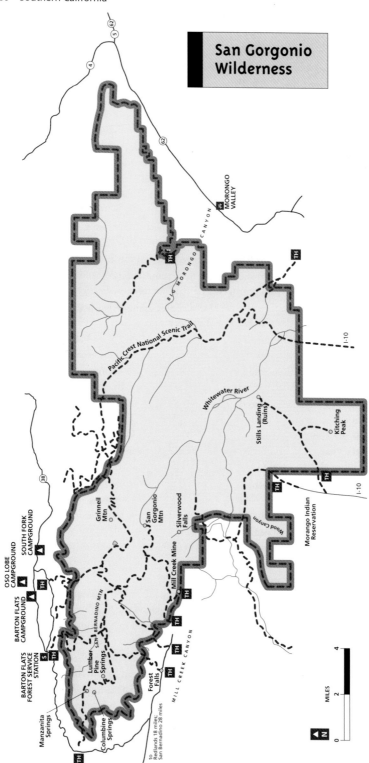

San Gorgonio Wilderness

> **DAY HIKE: SAN BERNARDINO PEAK**
> One-way length: 8 miles
> Low and high elevations: 6,000 to 10,624 feet
> Difficulty: moderate

This hike is long and climbs more than 4,600 feet, making a strenuous day hike, but the views from the summit of San Bernardino Peak are tremendous. To find the trailhead from I–10 in Redlands, follow Highway 38, 20.0 miles, then drive to the end of a short spur road; the trailhead is located by Camp Angelus.

The first part of the hike follows switchbacks up through a lovely forest of fir and pine, coming to the wilderness boundary 2.0 miles from the trailhead. Although the grade moderates occasionally, most of the time you are hiking uphill, passing campsites at Columbine Spring and Limber Pine Bench—both with active springs. The trail continues its climb to a short spur trail that will take you to the final summit at 10,624 feet.

> **DAY HIKE: VIVIAN CREEK–SAN GORGONIO PEAK**
> One-way length: 7 miles
> Low and high elevations: 7,200 to 11,502 feet
> Difficulty: moderate

San Gorgonio Peak, also known as Old Grayback, is the highest in the wilderness, and—like the center of a wheel—more than a half-dozen trails converge on its lofty summit. The Vivian Creek Trail, however, is considered by many to be the best to the top. Be ready for some climbing, as you must ascend more than a mile between the trailhead and summit. To reach the trailhead, take Highway 38 from Redlands east to Forest Home Road, which you follow for another 5.0 miles to the parking lot.

The first part of the hike follows Vivian Creek to Vivian Creek Trail Camp, where lovely pine and fir shade the stream. The route then passes through small meadows and open pine forests to High Creek Camp at 9,000 feet, a good potential overnight campsite. The trail continues, climbing with increasingly better views as you pass ancient limber pine and lodgepole pine, finally reaching timberline at 11,000 feet. You pass two more trail junctions before you reach the summit, where on clear days expansive views—south to Mexico and north to the Sierra Nevada—are possible. Mount San Jacinto, just to the south, seems so close you can almost reach out and touch it.

DAY HIKE: KITCHING PEAK
One-way length: 4.7 miles
Low and high elevations: 4,400 to 6,598 feet
Difficulty: moderate

Kitching Peak lies at the headwaters of Whitewater Creek on the southern edge of the San Gorgonio Wilderness, accessible from I–10 in Banning Pass. The peak offers great views of both Mount San Gorgonio and Mount San Jacinto. To reach the trailhead, leave I–10 in Banning Pass via Fields Road and drive north through the Morongo Indian Reservation, taking Morongo Road into Millard Canyon. Drive to Forest Road 2S05; take the first intersection right, then the next left, until you reach the parking area.

The hike follows Little Kitching Creek up the East Branch of Millard Canyon through oak and Douglas fir. After 2.0 miles, the trail leaves the creek and climbs to a ridge where a signed junction is located. Keep your eyes open for bighorn sheep. Turn right and take trail 2E24 south along the ridgeline through chaparral and occasional fir and sugar pine to the summit, where exceptional views of the surrounding countryside await you.

San Jacinto Wilderness 58

From desert to pine-covered peaks, the San Jacinto Wilderness is a cool haven lying above Palm Springs.

Granite outcrops on Tahquitz Peak, San Jacinto Wilderness.

Banning Pass separates the San Bernardino Mountains, part of the Transverse Ranges, from the San Jacinto Mountains, the highest portion of the Peninsula Ranges that run southward into Mexico. As dramatic as the San Bernardino Mountains may be, the San Jacinto Mountains are even more precipitous. In the space of six horizontal miles, these stupendous mountains rise in a rocky escarpment from less than 1,100 feet to the summit of 10,804-foot San Jacinto Peak, providing some of the greatest vertical relief anywhere in the nation. The contrast of desert cactus framing snow-capped peaks is one of the pleasures of living in Palm Springs, located near the base of the mountains. Despite the rugged nature of the slopes, the sky island of the San Jacinto Mountains levels off into a rolling plateau that is forested and dotted with small meadows.

LOCATION: 10 miles west of Palm Springs

SIZE: 32,851 acres

ELEVATION RANGE: 6,000 to 10,000 feet

MILES OF TRAILS: 80

ECOSYSTEMS: mixed conifer, chaparral

ADMINISTRATION: San Bernardino N.F., California State Parks

MAPS: San Bernardino N.F. Map, San Jacinto Wilderness Area Map

Mount San Jacinto, as well as the highest ridges and peaks, are protected as part of the San Jacinto State Wilderness, which is managed by California State Parks. The summit—the highest point in the state parks system—was climbed by John Muir in 1896, who called its view "…one of the most sublime spectacles to be found anywhere on earth!" Few would argue with his assessment. On a clear day, the entire Los Angeles Basin spreads out to the west, Mount San Gorgonio lies to the north, and, to the east, the Mojave Desert reaches beyond the horizon.

The state park, surrounded by the San Bernardino National Forest, is bordered on the north and south by the federally designated 32,040-acre San Jacinto Wilderness. Taken together, they provide a large wilderness unit that protects the entire top of the range.

The resemblance of these mountains to the Sierra Nevada is striking. The granitic-ribbed San Jacinto Mountains are a fault-block range with a westward tilt. Bounded on the west by the San Jacinto Fault and on the north and east by the San Andreas Fault, the entire region is seismically active: The range is still rising.

The 8,828-foot Tahquitz Peak, a granite dome in the federally protected San Jacinto Wilderness, is reminiscent of the granite outcrops of the Sierra Nevada. A favorite with climbers, the vistas from the summit are nearly as spectacular as those from Mount San Jacinto.

Granite ridges and domes forested with sugar pine, ponderosa, Jeffrey pine, incense cedar, white fir, lodgepole pine, limber pine, chinquapin, and black oak gives the entire range a mini-Sierra feel. Dozens of springs nurture cascading streams that provide a cacophony of splashing, cooling sounds along the trails.

The development history of the San Jacinto Mountains is similar to that of the San Bernardinos. The hunters were first, coming to the high country to kill the abundant deer and an occasional grizzly or bighorn sheep. Then loggers began to strip the ridges of their large, old-growth pine, while thousands of domestic sheep and cattle were grazed on the mountain meadows. Finally, President Grover Cleveland created the San Jacinto Forest Reserve in 1897 to control the abuses and to afford limited protection to the uplands. In 1907, the name was changed to the San Jacinto National Forest, then it was joined with the Trabuco Forest to become the Cleveland National Forest. Later, in 1925, the San Jacinto was attached to the San Bernardino National Forest, where it has remained since.

As early as 1919, proposals were put forth advocating that the higher parts of the range be set aside as a wilderness park. When the California State Parks system was set up in 1927, establishment of a San Jacinto State Park became one of the first priorities. In 1929, formal acquisition of private lands that dotted the mountain uplands began, and by 1935, the state controlled a core area of 12,695 acres that was designated in 1937 as a new unit in the state park system. The area was renamed San Jacinto State Park in 1963.

At the same time the state was working to acquire land for a state park on the mountain, the federal government designated the land south of the park as the San Jacinto Primitive Area. In 1964, it was renamed the San Jacinto Wilderness and was expanded in 1984 to 32,040 acres.

Just after the state park and federal primitive area became realities, a bitter fight ensued between developers in Palm Springs who wanted to build a tramway to the top of the mountain and conservationists who wanted to keep the area as it was. Several bills were introduced into the California legislature authorizing construction of the tram, and one finally passed in 1945. Attempts to thwart construction continued, however, and the tramway was not completed until 1963. Visitors are now whisked up 8,516 feet on a gondola where they merely look around, have a meal at the Mountain Station restaurant, or hike trails in the Long Valley area. The Pacific Crest Trail also crosses 36 miles of the wilderness.

DAY HIKE: MARION MOUNTAIN–MOUNT SAN JACINTO
One-way length: 5.6 miles
Low and high elevations: 6,560 to 10,804 feet
Difficulty: strenuous

This is the shortest and one of the steepest ways to the top of Mount San Jacinto. The trailhead lies at Marion Mountain Campground. To reach it, take Highway 243 to Idyllwild from I–10 in Banning Pass. At the Alandale Ranger Station, turn east by Stone Creek Campground and go another 3.0 miles to the Marion Mountain Campground. The first part of the trail steeply climbs a forested ridge to its junction with the Pacific Crest Trail. Follow the Pacific Crest Trail about 1.0 mile to the Deer Springs Trail, which takes you to the summit via Little Round Valley Camp — a good overnight site for those who want to make this more than a day hike.

DAY HIKE: SPITLER PEAK TRAIL–DESERT DIVIDE
One-way length: 5 miles
Low and high elevations: 5,000 to 7,200 feet
Difficulty: moderate

The Spitler Peak Trail accesses the rarely visited southern end of the San Jacinto Wilderness and provides great views of the Mojave Desert from the Desert Divide. To reach the trailhead, find your way to Idyllwild and proceed south on Highway 243 to the intersection with Highway 74. Turn south on Highway 74 to Apple Canyon Road, where you'll turn east (left) and reach the signed trailhead parking in less than 2.0 miles. The hike starts in oak woodland and chaparral, then climbs higher to Jeffrey pine and Coulter pine forest. The trail steepens the last 1.0 mile before the divide, climbing rapidly by switchback to the Pacific Crest Trail, which follows the rocky ridgeline north and south. The views are good from boulders that dot the divide.

DAY HIKE: SOUTH RIDGE TRAIL–TAHQUITZ PEAK
One-way length: 3.6 miles
Low and high elevations: 6,400 to 8,846 feet
Difficulty: moderate

The granite dome of Tahquitz Peak, the site of a fire lookout, offers a variety of views: the rocky spine of the San Jacinto Range running south toward the Santa Rosa Range, and those west into the Los Angeles Basin, sometimes visible through the smog. The shortest route to the peak is via the South Ridge Trail. To access its trailhead, drive south of Idyllwild and take Saunders Meadow Road. When you reach Pine Avenue, turn left, then right on Tahquitz Drive. As the name implies, this trail basically follows a ridge up to the granite summit of Tahquitz Peak.

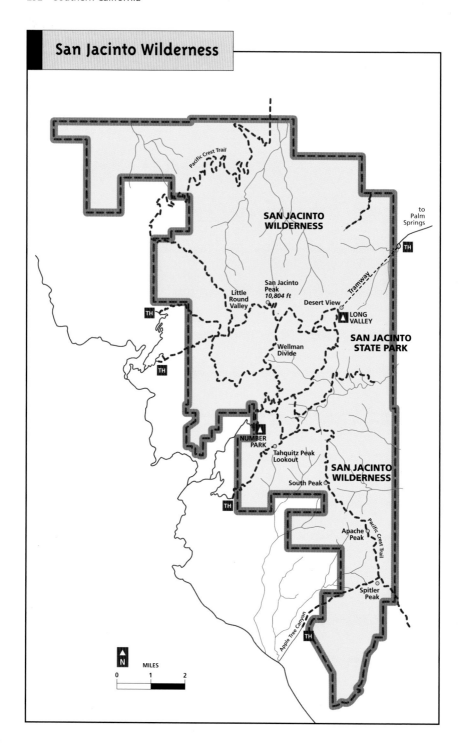

San Jacinto Wilderness

San Mateo Canyon Wilderness

*The San Mateo offers rugged chaparral-covered hills and
a perennial stream, all within sight of the Pacific Ocean.*

San Mateo Creek Canyon, San Mateo Wilderness.

The Santa Ana Mountains, which lie south of Los Angeles
and northeast of San Diego, make up the eastern perimeter
of Orange County. Most of the range has a granite core, but
it is overlain with sediments. Its highest parts lie in the north
at Mount Santiago (5,860), but San Mateo Canyon, lying to
the south of this region, is considered by many to be the pret-
tiest part of the entire range. Located west of Lake Elsinore
and only 20 miles inland from the coast, cool ocean breezes
and even fog are often funnelled up San Mateo Canyon, a
westward-flowing creek that eventually reaches the ocean at
Camp Pendleton Marine Base. The riparian vegetation is
delightful and includes 200-year-old oaks, large California
sycamores, cottonwood, and poison oak. Outside of the

LOCATION: 5 miles
east of Camp Pendleton

SIZE: 39,540 acres

ELEVATION RANGE:
200 to 3,500 feet

MILES OF TRAILS: 25

ECOSYSTEMS:
chaparral, riparian
woodland

ADMINISTRATION:
Cleveland National
Forest

MAP: Cleveland
National Forest Map

drainage bottoms, chaparral dominates in a thick blanket of shrubs that makes off-trail travel almost impossible. At one time, San Mateo Creek was a major steelhead fishery. The campsite known as "Fisherman's Camp" honors this past tradition, but the run is nearly extinct.

The area came under federal management when the Trabuco Canyon Forest Reserve was established in 1893. Later, in 1906, it was renamed the Trabuco National Forest, only to become the Cleveland National Forest in 1908. The 39,500-acre San Mateo Canyon Wilderness is the largest wildlands in the Cleveland National Forest and was designated in 1984 as part of the California Wilderness Act.

DAY HIKE: SAN MATEO CANYON
One-way length: 4 miles
Low and high elevations: 1,500 to 2,000 feet
Difficulty: moderate

San Mateo Canyon, with its delightful riparian vegetation and cool waters, is the most used access into its namesake wilderness, but despite its close proximity to millions of people, the area is hardly overrun with hikers. To reach the trailhead, exit I–15 by Wildomar onto Clinton Keith Road, then continue to Tenaja Road, passing the Tenaja Fire Station and campground to the intersection with Forest Road 7S02; park there. The first part of the hike follows an old fire road to Fisherman's Camp, where there are campsites along Tenaja Creek. From there, the trail switchbacks down to San Mateo Creek, offering views of the canyon along the way. Once at the creek, continue downstream—watching out for poison oak—and linger along the occasional sandy beach or boulder-lined pool. If you wish, it is possible to continue downstream 9.0 miles to the border of Camp Pendleton.

San Mateo Canyon Wilderness

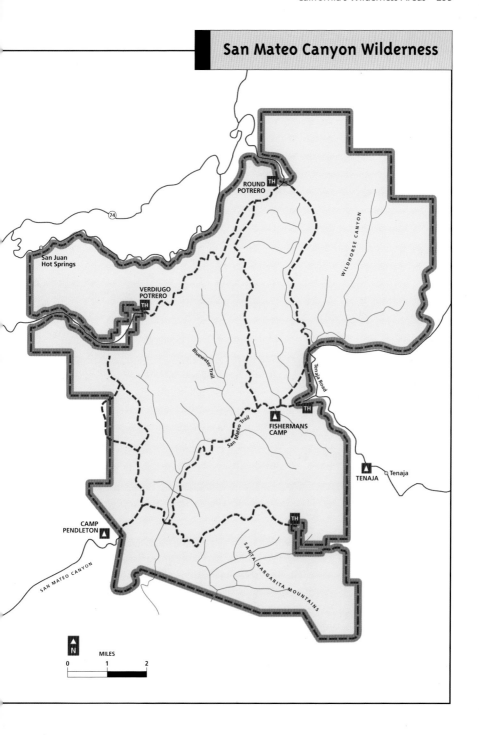

60 Santa Rosa Wilderness

The Santa Rose offers rugged desert washes to pine-clad peaks—the meeting of the Transverse Ranges and deserts.

Yucca in bloom frame Toro Peak, Santa Rosa Wilderness.

LOCATION: 7 miles south of Palm Springs

SIZE: 84,500 acres

ELEVATION RANGE: sea level to 8,700 feet

MILES OF TRAILS: 18

ECOSYSTEMS: desert shrub, chaparral, mixed conifer

ADMINISTRATION: San Bernardino N.F., BLM Palm Springs Resource Area Office

MAPS: San Bernardino N.F. Map, Santa Rosa Wilderness Area Map

South of Mount San Jacinto and Palm Springs to the Pines Highway lies the sky island of the Santa Rosa Range. Toro Peak, just outside of the wilderness, rises to 8,716 feet and is cloaked by magnificent forests of pine and fir. This is a striking contrast to most of the wilderness, which is largely desert plateau vegetated with ocotillo, agave, creosote bush, cactus, and scattered stands of pinyon and juniper.

Besides the usual southern California wildlife of coyote, ringtail, mountain lion, and mule deer, the Santa Rosa Wilderness is home to the largest Peninsula bighorn sheep herd in the state. Good places to see these wild mountaineers are the aptly named Sheep Mountain as well as Martinez Mountain.

The area was originally set aside as part of the San Jacinto Forest Reserve and was later combined with the Trabuco Reserve to form the Cleveland National Forest. In 1925, it was reassigned to the San Bernardino National Forest. The 20,160-acre Santa Rosa Wilderness was created in 1984 with the passage of the California Wilderness Act; in 1994, it was expanded with the addition of 64,340 BLM acres in the passage of the California Desert bill. The formally protected lands, totaling 84,500 acres, are immediately adjacent to some 87,000 acres of state wilderness in the Anza Borrego State Park to the south. However, more than 140,000 additional BLM and Forest Service acres are roadless and—if protected and combined with the adjacent state lands—could create a huge desert ecotone wildlands of nearly 300,000 acres.

Unlike most of the existing wildlands in California, this is primarily a desert uplands with few permanent water sources. Most of the access is via the Cactus Spring Trail, an old Native American route that crosses several perennial streams. You will enjoy this hike's lush, green riparian vegetation and the songs of the birds, which create a stark contrast to the surrounding desert. If you bother to wander far off the trail, you'll likely not encounter anyone else in this rarely used wildlands.

DAY HIKE: CACTUS SPRINGS TRAIL
One-way length: 5 miles
Low and high elevations: 4,000 to 4,200 feet
Difficulty: moderate

The Cactus Springs Trail, the only official route in the wilderness, extends 18 miles between Pinyon Flat on Highway 74 and Martinez Canyon in the Coachella Valley. The most popular hike is the section between Pinyon Flat and Cactus Spring. To locate the trailhead, drive Highway 74 southwest from Palm Springs Pass toward the Pinyon Flat Campground just beyond the California Department of Forestry Fire Station. The trailhead is located on the south side of the road between these two landmarks.

The first part of the hike follows a confusing knot of old mining roads, so you need to keep in mind that the trail heads southeast and bear in that direction. You'll pass an old dolomite mine and a sign indicating the way to the trail. Eventually, you will pass an official wilderness boundary sign and know you're on the right path. The trail works its way up and down along a draw to Horsethief Creek, a refreshing perennial stream lined by cottonwoods. After leaving the stream, the trail is sometimes difficult to locate as it follows washes to Little Pinyon Flat, eventually reaching Cactus Spring, which is usually dry. Look for cairns to mark the way beyond Horsethief Creek.

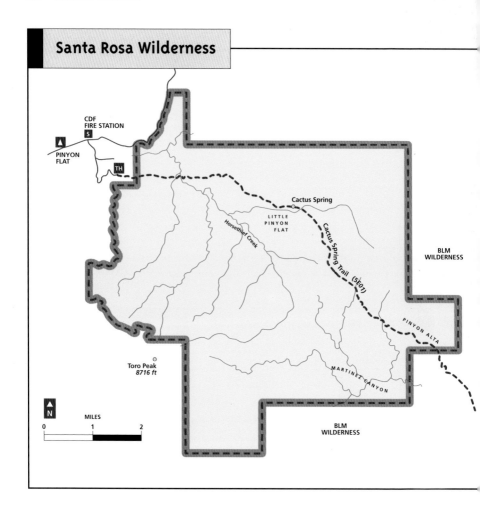

Santa Rosa Wilderness

CDF
FIRE STATION
PINYON
FLAT

Cactus Spring

LITTLE
PINYON
FLAT

Horsethief Creek

Cactus Spring Trail (5E01)

BLM
WILDERNESS

PINYON ALTA

Toro Peak
8716 ft

MARTINEZ CANYON

N

MILES
0   1   2

BLM
WILDERNESS

Sheep Mountain Wilderness **61**

*The Sheep Mountain Wilderness contains extremely
rugged terrain reaching to 10,000 feet.*

Snow covers San Antonio Ridge in Sheep Mountain Wilderness.

Named for the Nelson bighorn sheep that still roam the
canyons, the 43,600-acre Sheep Mountain Wilderness lies
14 miles northeast of Los Angeles in the San Gabriel Mountains.
Like the San Gabriel Wilderness, Sheep Mountain is dominated
by narrow crests and precipitous canyons with a majority of
the slopes exceeding 60 degrees. There is tremendous elevation
change, ranging from 2,100 feet in the canyon bottoms to
10,064 feet on top of Mount Baldy, also known as Mount
San Antonio.

With such an elevation difference, one would expect
quite a range of temperatures. Record highs exceed 110 degrees,
while lows of zero degrees or less have been recorded. Above
5,000 feet, snow depths of up to three feet occur in the winter,
and at higher elevations overall annual precipitation exceeds

LOCATION: 10 miles
north of Claremont

SIZE: 43,600 acres

ELEVATION RANGE:
2,100 to 10,064 feet

MILES OF TRAILS: 40

ECOSYSTEMS:
chaparral, mixed
conifer

ADMINISTRATION:
Angles N.F., San
Bernardino National
Forest

MAPS: Angeles N.F.
Map, San Bernardino
N.F. Map, Sheep
Mountain Wilderness
Area Map

20 inches. Vegetation is similar to that found throughout the region, but it also includes some ancient, twisted limber pine on some of the higher peaks, such as Mount Baden Powell and Mount Baldy.

At one time, there was a minor gold rush to the East Fork of the San Gabriel, and even today there are mining operations within the wilderness that predate its establishment in 1984. The largest operation is the Bighorn Mine below Mount Baden Powell.

There are 40 miles of trails within the wilderness. The Pacific Crest Trail wanders along Sheep Mountain's northern border, but the most popular trail ascends Mount Baden Powell. The peak, notable for its wide-ranging views, was named for a British army officer who founded the Boy Scouts.

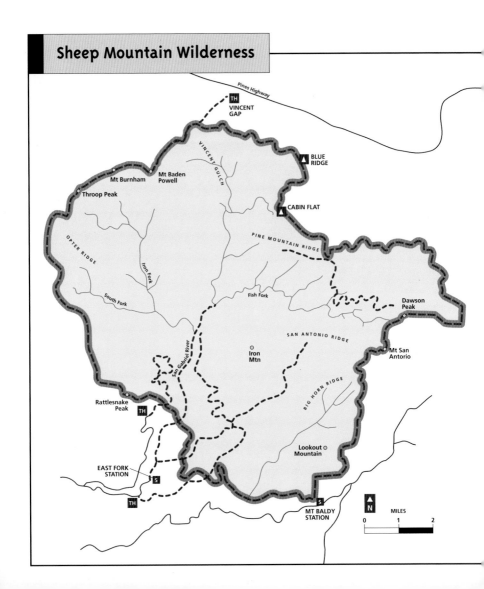

Sheep Mountain Wilderness

DAY HIKE: EAST FORK SAN GABRIEL RIVER
One-way distance: 4.5 miles
Low and high elevations: 2,000 to 2,800 feet
Difficulty: strenuous because of numerous
stream crossings

This trail follows the East Fork of the San Gabriel River, once the sight of a minor gold rush. It's one of the steepest river gorges in California. The trail requires quite a bit of boulder-hopping and wading of the stream, but this can be a pleasant experience during the warmer months of the year. Find the trailhead by driving I-10 to the Azusa Avenue exit and take Highway 39 north to East Fork Road; take this to Heaton Flat parking area, located just beyond the East Fork Ranger Station.

Back in the 1930s, a route through this canyon and over the mountains to the desert was envisioned and its construction begun. However, the giant flood of 1938 dampened enthusiasm for the road, and it was never completed. A bridge from the construction, now dubbed the "Bridge to Nowhere," is found isolated far up the canyon. The trail follows the old road, crossing and recrossing the stream, so be prepared to have wet feet. Just beyond the bridge lies the narrows where the river squeezes through a dramatic granite gorge. Here, the mountains rise from 2,800 feet at the river to 8,007 feet on Iron Mountain, some 5,200 feet in 1.7 miles. Narrows Trail Camp lies at the beginning of the gorge, a potential overnight campsite.

It's possible to continue beyond this point and hike all the way to Cabin Flat—14 miles from the trailhead—but that requires quite a bit of commitment and a previously arranged shuttle. You must wade the river for several miles, then climb the trail to the ridge and to your car. Most people choose to turn around at the bridge or just beyond.

DAY HIKE: MOUNT BADEN POWELL
One-way distance: 4 miles
Low and high elevations: 6,600 to 9,399 feet
Difficulty: moderate

This trail climbs 41 switchbacks from its start at Vincent Gap to the top of Mount Baden Powell, one of the highest peaks in the wilderness that overlooks the deep canyons of the East Fork of the San Gabriel and Iron Fork drainages. The peak, originally known as North Baldy, was changed to honor the founder of the Boy Scouts. Great views and the 2,000-year-old twisted limber pine on the summit make this a popular trail, despite its numerous switchbacks. To find the trailhead, drive the Angeles Crest Highway to Vincent Gap parking area, 5.5 miles west of Big Pines.

DAY HIKE: EAST FORK SAN GABRIEL RIVER
One-way distance: 4.5 miles
Low and high elevations: 2,000 to 2,800 feet
Difficulty: strenuous because of numerous
stream crossings

This trail follows the East Fork of the San Gabriel River, once the sight of a minor gold rush. It's one of the steepest river gorges in California. The trail requires quite a bit of boulder-hopping and wading of the stream, but this can be a pleasant experience during the warmer months of the year. Find the trailhead by driving I–10 to the Azusa Avenue exit and take Highway 39 north to East Fork Road; take this to Heaton Flat parking area, located just beyond the East Fork Ranger Station.

Back in the 1930s, a route through this canyon and over the mountains to the desert was envisioned and its construction begun. However, the giant flood of 1938 dampened enthusiasm for the road, and it was never completed. A bridge from the construction, now dubbed the "Bridge to Nowhere," is found isolated far up the canyon. The trail follows the old road, crossing and recrossing the stream, so be prepared to have wet feet. Just beyond the bridge lies the narrows where the river squeezes through a dramatic granite gorge. Here, the mountains rise from 2,800 feet at the river to 8,007 feet on Iron Mountain, some 5,200 feet in 1.7 miles. Narrows Trail Camp lies at the beginning of the gorge, a potential overnight campsite.

It's possible to continue beyond this point and hike all the way to Cabin Flat—14 miles from the trailhead—but that requires quite a bit of commitment and a previously arranged shuttle. You must wade the river for several miles, then climb the trail to the ridge and to your car. Most people choose to turn around at the bridge or just beyond.

DAY HIKE: MOUNT BADEN POWELL
One-way distance: 4 miles
Low and high elevations: 6,600 to 9,399 feet
Difficulty: moderate

This trail climbs 41 switchbacks from its start at Vincent Gap to the top of Mount Baden Powell, one of the highest peaks in the wilderness that overlooks the deep canyons of the East Fork of the San Gabriel and Iron Fork drainages. The peak, originally known as North Baldy, was changed to honor the founder of the Boy Scouts. Great views and the 2,000-year-old twisted limber pine on the summit make this a popular trail, despite its numerous switchbacks. To find the trailhead, drive the Angeles Crest Highway to Vincent Gap parking area, 5.5 miles west of Big Pines.

DAY HIKE: EAST FORK SAN GABRIEL RIVER
One-way distance: 4.5 miles
Low and high elevations: 2,000 to 2,800 feet
Difficulty: strenuous because of numerous
stream crossings

This trail follows the East Fork of the San Gabriel River, once the sight of a minor gold rush. It's one of the steepest river gorges in California. The trail requires quite a bit of boulder-hopping and wading of the stream, but this can be a pleasant experience during the warmer months of the year. Find the trailhead by driving I–10 to the Azusa Avenue exit and take Highway 39 north to East Fork Road; take this to Heaton Flat parking area, located just beyond the East Fork Ranger Station.

Back in the 1930s, a route through this canyon and over the mountains to the desert was envisioned and its construction begun. However, the giant flood of 1938 dampened enthusiasm for the road, and it was never completed. A bridge from the construction, now dubbed the "Bridge to Nowhere," is found isolated far up the canyon. The trail follows the old road, crossing and recrossing the stream, so be prepared to have wet feet. Just beyond the bridge lies the narrows where the river squeezes through a dramatic granite gorge. Here, the mountains rise from 2,800 feet at the river to 8,007 feet on Iron Mountain, some 5,200 feet in 1.7 miles. Narrows Trail Camp lies at the beginning of the gorge, a potential overnight campsite.

It's possible to continue beyond this point and hike all the way to Cabin Flat—14 miles from the trailhead—but that requires quite a bit of commitment and a previously arranged shuttle. You must wade the river for several miles, then climb the trail to the ridge and to your car. Most people choose to turn around at the bridge or just beyond.

DAY HIKE: MOUNT BADEN POWELL
One-way distance: 4 miles
Low and high elevations: 6,600 to 9,399 feet
Difficulty: moderate

This trail climbs 41 switchbacks from its start at Vincent Gap to the top of Mount Baden Powell, one of the highest peaks in the wilderness that overlooks the deep canyons of the East Fork of the San Gabriel and Iron Fork drainages. The peak, originally known as North Baldy, was changed to honor the founder of the Boy Scouts. Great views and the 2,000-year-old twisted limber pine on the summit make this a popular trail, despite its numerous switchbacks. To find the trailhead, drive the Angeles Crest Highway to Vincent Gap parking area, 5.5 miles west of Big Pines.

One Man's Opinion

by George Wuerthner

Livestock Grazing

Since the days when John Muir first coined the phrase "hooved locust" to describe the effects of domestic livestock on California's backcountry, the grazing of cattle and sheep on public lands has been controversial. Even though other compromising commercial activities such as logging, mining, and even motorized vehicle use are banned within designated wilderness, commercial domestic livestock grazing continues. I will dwell most on this activity, because it's an impact that most people don't recognize or appreciate, yet it is one of the most significant factors that is destroying biodiversity and degrading ecosystems in the West.

One of the major concessions made by wilderness proponents to gain passage of the 1964 Wilderness Act was a clause that permitted existing livestock grazing to continue, even if an area was designated as wilderness. The exception was designed to defuse opposition to the Wilderness Act from western lawmakers and livestock interests—who, in far too many instances, are one and the same person. The end result of this concession is that the integrity of wildlands throughout the West have been greatly compromised wherever livestock grazing remains.

Although the Wilderness Act states that grazing cannot be terminated merely because an area has been designated wilderness, it does explicitly say that grazing can be reduced or terminated for natural resource protection. In other words, though the simple designation of an area as wilderness is not considered justification for termination of grazing privileges, if grazing is compromising other natural resource values—recreation, wildlife, water quality, plant communities, and soils—then managing agencies not only have a legal right, but an obligation to remove grazing from the area. Unfortunately, few agencies are living up to their responsibility of managing public lands for the people's benefit, allowing livestock to significantly degrade resource values not only in wilderness, but on all public lands.

Grazing in California's wilderness areas is not insignificant. Except for wildlands so heavily forested they offer little forage or so rugged as to be impenetrable by domestic animals, most wilderness areas have some degree of domestic livestock grazing. Some of the California Wilderness Areas that allow livestock grazing are the John Muir, Desolation, Granite Chief, Bucks Lake, South Sierra, Golden Trout, Domeland, Emigrant, Ansel Adams, Hoover, Mokelumne, South Warner, Ishi, Carson–Iceberg, Ventana, Santa Rosa, Pine Creek, Marble Mountain, and Snow Mountain.

To most recreationalists, the presence of livestock may not be more than a nuisance. However, such a view is changing as a growing number of people realize the tremendous ecological toll that the animals have on the landscape. For example, in 1992 the Sierra Now Task Force noted, "Poor livestock grazing practices are the most overlooked and least addressed of the environmental problems on public lands…" While the Task Force was only addressing the Sierra Nevada, the statement is true for all public lands.

Livestock production impacts are ubiquitous. West-wide, nearly all suitable public lands are leased for domestic livestock production, including 90 percent of

Camping at Summit Lake, Hoover Wilderness.

the lands administered by the BLM and 70 percent of all Forest Service lands. Even some wildlife refuges and national parks are grazed. According to Eric Gerstrung, Endangered Species Biologist with the California Department of Fish and Game, nearly 80 percent of the Sierra Nevada is open to some form of livestock grazing. The only places in this mountain range that are not grazed are its national parks and some of the higher elevation alpine areas, which is more or less typical of the situation on most federal public lands in the state.

Wilderness areas are becoming increasingly important as scientific controls, where natural processes and native species are given priority. As such, they become a baseline against which the human manipulation that characterizes most private and public lands are measured. While it's important to recognize that human influences such as the use of fire by Native Americans in pre-Columbian forests did affect ecosystem function, the overall impact of modern civilization on much of the developed landscape is far greater. Thus the "naturalness" of, say, the John Muir Wilderness is still much closer to a pristine ecological condition than a manicured lawn in Sacramento or even a tree farm in the northern Sierra and, as such, is a useful model for comparison. The usefulness of wildlands as models of normality, however, is severely compromised not only by the presence of domestic livestock, but by their manipulation and impact.

Part of the problem is that unlike timber harvesting, off-road vehicle use, and other public lands resource practices, no attempt to determine land suitability for livestock has ever been conducted. This may be because most public lands grazing allotments recognized long-standing use by certain ranchers, and therefore made no effort to determine whether the lands could sustain grazing. In many instances, however, the lands are too steep, arid, or otherwise unsuitable for livestock production without incurring serious environmental degradation.

Even where livestock is well managed to minimize the more obvious problems, such as trampling of riparian zones or overgrazing of vegetation, their presence still compromises native biological diversity; that is, an area's indigenous plant life is being processed through exotic, alien animals. An analogous situation might be the planting of eucalyptus in place of native trees such as redwood, aspen, and ponderosa pine to favor the timber industry. Fortunately, this does not occur—at least not on public lands. With timber harvest, the native tree species are maintained, but not so with the livestock issue.

The problems associated with livestock production have more to do with fundamental structural issues that can't easily be resolved by "better livestock grazing" or "range reform." They are inherent with the attempt to raise a water-loving, slow-moving animal species that evolved in moist woodlands in Eurasia in an arid, rugged western landscape once full of predators. While it may be possible to reduce a few impacts—reducing cattle numbers might leave slightly more grass for other herbivores, for example—it is difficult, if not impossible, to eliminate the *cumulative* impacts that arise from the foolhardy efforts to "grow" cows in the West.

The nature of livestock *production* creates more problems. To produce livestock in the arid West means dewatering of streams for irrigation and pasture, the extirpation of large predators such as grizzlies and wolves, the transmission of disease from livestock to wildlife, water pollution, loss of riparian habitat due to trampling, the introduction of weeds, and competition with wild game for forage, water, and space. Most of these real ecological impacts are externalized—in other words, they are transferred to the land and the public at large, including those of us visiting wildlands. If these "costs" were internalized, it would no longer be profitable to raise livestock in the West!

The most obvious impact from domestic livestock grazing is the effect upon plant communities. Cattle and sheep have destroyed numerous mountain meadows, stripping away vegetation, compacting soils, and turning them into deserts. Loss of vegetative cover increases erosion, with 85 percent of the top soil loss in the western United States attributed to livestock grazing. Even where plant communities have not been destroyed, putting grass into the belly of a domestic sheep or cow means there's that much less for native herbivores, whether we are talking about grasshoppers, ground squirrels, marmots, or bighorn sheep. The consumption of forage also reduces cover for small rodents and ground-nesting birds, resulting in higher predation losses, hence fewer of these animals survive than they might otherwise.

The presence of domestic livestock has also contributed to the spread of cowbirds, which lays its eggs in the nests of other songbirds. The host bird is unable to distinguish between its own young and the often larger, more aggressive cowbird nestling. The baby cowbird gets the lion's share of food, and often pushes the other baby birds from the nest. Cowbirds follow stock, eating the seeds out of manure. Having followed domestic animals into the mountains, cowbirds now pose a serious threat to neo-tropical migratory birds—the warblers, thrushes, and other songsters associated with mountain riparian habitats.

Even more disastrous are the impacts to riparian zones. These fragile, thin lines of water-dependent vegetation bordering our waterways are critical habitat to nearly 75 percent of the species found in the arid West. Unfortunately, livestock grazing, more than any other factor, has destroyed much of this habitat. According to the Sierra Now Task Force, some 3,000 miles of riparian habitat in the Sierra Nevada alone are damaged by domestic livestock. The Inyo National Forest Plan concedes that "90 percent of its wet meadows were damaged or threatened with damage by accelerated erosion." Most of this is the result of domestic livestock use. Of 320 stream reaches in the Golden Trout Wilderness being evaluated for stream channel stability, only 10 percent were in good condition and 85 percent were considered to be in unsatisfactory condition—which is a nice way of saying that stream function is seriously impaired! The Sierra Now Task Force has gone so far as to suggest that riparian damage from livestock exceeds the damage caused by mining, water development, and logging combined. Riparian-dependent species, as divergent as the willow flycatcher to the Paiute trout, are endangered due to livestock-caused riparian damage.

In many instances, loss of streamside vegetation and bank breakage has lead to accelerated streambed erosion, resulting in arroyo cutting, a subsequent drop in water tables, and greater flooding. One solution is to fence cattle out of these fragile habitats, but fencing—besides intruding upon the sense of wilderness—costs thousands of dollars, an expense often borne by taxpayers, not the rancher using the public land. Furthermore, as endangered species biologist Eric Gerstrung points out, such attempts at mitigation merely transfer the impact to other parts of the landscape, such as first-order seeps and springs, which are usually just as sensitive.

According to Jim Carlson, a former Forest Service hydrologist from Truckee, it becomes impossible to entirely mitigate livestock impacts. The mere displacement of livestock by fencing from heavily damaged streams will not always bring about recovery in any kind of reasonable timetable. In some areas, such as Monache Meadows in the southern Sierra, the damage is so extensive that the Forest Service is actually proposing to use bulldozers to reconstruct stream channels and function.

Introduction of disease is another problem. The loss of bighorn sheep from many of the mountain ranges of California can be attributed to diseases transmitted from domestic animals to their wild cousins—a loss not restricted to the distant past. Disease from domestic livestock is thought to be the cause of a major 1980's bighorn sheep die off at Lava Beds National Monument, and another later on in the South Warner Wilderness.

In addition, the presence of domestic animals prevents the reestablishment of native species. A recent attempt to reintroduce sheep to Forest Service land in Lee Vining Canyon in the high country just east of Yosemite National Park had to wait. Wildlife officials didn't want to place wild sheep in the area until private parties were able to buy out a rancher who ran domestic sheep on public rangelands adjacent to the park.

The need for predator and pest control adds to the ecological cost associated with livestock production, resulting in the extinction of predators such as the grizzly and wolf. The livestock industry still thwarts the reintroduction of such species, even though there are areas of California that could sustain populations of both carnivores.

Other "non-target" species have suffered as well. Poisoning programs, aimed at reducing rodents and predators such as coyotes, also indirectly poisoned animals such as the San Joaquin kit fox and the California condor, who fed upon the targeted animals. Both the fox and condor are now listed under the Endangered Species Act, in part because of population reductions resulting from poisoning programs.

Livestock production not only includes the impacts associated with grazing, but also the growth of hay and pasture—most of it produced with irrigated water. The water used to produce livestock forage in California is equal to the domestic water use of 46 million urban dwellers! Dewatering of rivers means lower flows, and therefore less habitat for fish. To meet the demand for irrigated livestock forage, dams are constructed to create water storage reservoirs. Dams and reservoirs fragment aquatic habitats and disrupt the migration of fish such as salmon. In a very real sense, cattle are eating the habitat of Sacramento spring chinook salmon and Sacramento River delta smelt.

Finally, while backpackers and hikers are admonished, and in some cases even fined, if they camp too close to a lake or trample a meadow, domestic livestock do far more extensive damage with complete immunity. People are warned to go several hundred feet away from water sources to defecate, while domestic animals *can* and *do* foul directly into water courses! Not surprisingly, the Environmental Protection Agency has determined that domestic livestock are among the largest sources of non-point pollution in the West.

The impact on recreation must be considered, as well. No one likes to hike or camp in a place that smells and looks like a stock feed lot or drink from streams that are nothing more than open sewers.

All this damage benefits a very small minority of livestock producers, since most domestic animals are raised entirely on private lands. In the United States as a whole, only two percent of the forage comes from public lands, and—according to the General Accounting Office—nearly 80 percent of this public lands forage goes to *less* than 10 percent of the largest livestock operators! In other words, the public (us) is subsidizing, both economically as well as ecologically, the operations of a handful of corporations or wealthy family ranches. Due to the limited forage produced on public lands, it plays a relatively minor economic role in most communities, although to any individual rancher, it may be significant.

As the benefits of preservation of biodiversity and functioning ecosystems has grown, more and more citizens have begun to demand that domestic livestock grazing be phased out on public lands, particularly in national parks, wildlife refuges, and wilderness areas that are set aside specifically to protect and preserve native wildlife and natural landscapes. This position has been endorsed by an increasing number of regional environmental groups. For example, the California Wilderness Coalition recently voted to oppose livestock grazing in new wilderness areas and to work for its eventual termination in all existing wildernesses in California. Similar measures have been adopted by regional wilderness groups in Oregon, Idaho, New Mexico, and elsewhere. Perhaps like mining, domestic livestock grazing will eventually be phased out of the wilderness, and these lands will come closer to their full potential as biological preserves where native species, not alien animals, dominate ecosystem function and processes.

I don't want to leave the impression that I believe livestock production is only inappropriate in designated wilderness. Most of the problems that are noted for wilderness areas occur on *all* public lands and are unacceptable anywhere they occur. After a trip into Wyoming's Wind River Range, where extensive damage from livestock was observed, former Supreme Court Judge William O. Douglas noted that what he saw would be called "vandalism or worse" if it had occurred on anyone's private land. The ongoing vandalism of our public lands by the livestock industry should be terminated—and if not in wilderness, then where?

Pack Stock Use

As recreational use of California's wildlands grows, the impacts of pack stock use is under increasing criticism. Most of the original trails built in the mountains of the West were constructed to accommodate the use of these animals. Even Sierra Club outings relied upon pack stocks to carry food and supplies to base camps. But as equipment has improved, and more and more people have joined the growing ranks of outdoor enthusiasts, the percentage of people using pack stock has declined dramatically. Today, approximately 10 percent of the visitors to the Sierra Nevada wilderness rely on horses, while that percentage is even less in some of the other wildlands in the state.

Because stock use causes excessive trail and campsite damage, as well as increased dust and smell on the trail, a growing number of recreationalists are calling for their elimination from popular trails or an outright ban on stock. As a former horse packer who still enjoys riding horses, I know first-hand the kind of damage these animals can wreak on trails and campsites. A careful, conscientious packer can reduce the impacts, but not eliminate them.

Arguments against stock use include the fact that on a per capita basis, horses and mules have a much larger impact on that land than backpackers or hikers. The concentrated weight of a thousand-pound animal on each hoof has far more significant effect on a trail than lug sole boots. When talking about impacts to trails and campsites and compaction of soils and meadows, research has shown that each horse is equal to 10 to 50 backpackers, depending on the area and vegetation type. Thus, using the lower figure, a typical pack train of 20 to 25 horses and mules has the equivalent impact of 200 to 250 hikers. If we use the higher number, then one pack train may do the same amount of damage as 1,000 hikers. This has several implications.

The need for much of the trail maintenance results from stock-created impacts. Furthermore, since much of the justification for trailhead quotas on hikers and backpackers is to lessen ecological impacts in our wilderness areas, a reduction in stock use might allow more visitors to access our wildlands. In addition, in some wilderness areas commercial packers are *exempt* from trailhead quota limits, according to the High Sierra Hikers Association (HSHA).

Another negative impact associated with pack stock use is the grazing of meadows, resulting in changes in plant community structure—the same effect that domestic livestock create. Pack stock introduce weeds into backcountry areas through their feces, causing the kinds of disturbed conditions that weeds thrive in. They also trample stream banks, pollute waterways, and defecate on trails and around campsites, decreasing the area's suitability for other users. Finally, pack stock, along with domestic livestock, help spread cowbirds, a nest parasite that is a major factor in the decrease of many songbirds.

The National Park Service in its pack stock wilderness management plan admits that "many meadows along popular trails (are) severely impacted by pack and saddle stock, and their recovery denied by continued intense use." The management plan goes on to say that "past and on-going ecological studies in these Parks clearly indicate that overgrazing, not drought cycles and floods, has been the primary cause of meadow deterioration." Yet 50 percent of the meadows in both Sequoia and Kings Canyon National Parks are accessible and available to grazing by horses and mules.

Most of the pack stock use is by commercial outfitters, not individual horse users, and the largest groups tend to be commercial users. Thus, public lands are being jeopardized and compromised by commercial profit-oriented use. This, perhaps more than any other thing, is the reason some believe stock use, particularly commercial use, should be discontinued. This probably won't happen soon, since many agency personnel are stock users as well. For example, 20 percent of the horse use in Yosemite National Park is by the agency itself, while hikers and backpackers are admonished about low-impact camping and "loving wilderness to death." The truth is that backpackers using Leave No Trace Camping techniques have a minimal impact upon our wilderness areas.

Most federal agencies claim pack stock use is "traditional" (the same argument is used to justify livestock grazing), but many other practices that were considered traditional, including the cutting of bough beds and market hunting, are no longer allowed. As the HSHA points out in an editorial on pack stock use, "a destructive tradition is only destructive; it does not become benign because it is a tradition."

The other major argument used to justify stock use is that it provides wilderness access to many who are physically unable to enter wildlands on their own power. One could, of course, use this argument to justify cars, planes, snowmobiles, trail bikes, and mountain bikes. The point is that no one is denied access to wilderness: What *is* denied access are cars, snowmobiles, bikes, and perhaps, as HSHA argues, it's time that pack stock join this list, at least where it's obvious that conflict occurs and damage to the landscape is excessive. You don't have to be an Olympic runner to walk a wilderness trail. Some are steep and long, but there are also short, gentle hikes negotiable by almost everyone. I have met people as young as two years old and as old as 90 hiking the wilderness. I met an 80-year-old woman on Kearsarge Pass, huffing under a heavy pack. When I asked her where she was headed, she replied with a grin, "Mount Whitney." It was more than 50 miles away! It has been my observation that most people who say they require horses for access are crippled more by a lack of motivation rather than by any physical defect.

Admittedly, compared to the ecological impacts of domestic livestock, pack stock effects are far less damaging, mostly because they are concentrated and focused, while those of domestic livestock are far more widespread. Nevertheless, if wilderness regulations and quotas are to be taken seriously, it stands to reason that if a single kind of usage is responsible for the majority of the impacts, then that use should be eliminated or reduced *first* before everyone else is asked to sacrifice access to the wilderness. Quite likely, quotas on backpackers could be decreased or eliminated entirely if the numbers of pack stock were reduced. There is a surprising amount of support for such a change in regulations: A recent study conducted in the Trinity Alps Wilderness found that 87 percent of all users supported reductions or elimination of pack stock use.

The use of pack stock need not be curtailed everywhere, but the practice should be restricted or eliminated in high-use recreation areas, fragile environments, or at seasons when the animals may create significant damage, such as when trails are still wet in the spring. And anyplace trailhead quotas are found, commercial stock operations should be the first use to be eliminated.

Fish Stocking

Fishing is one of the most popular backcountry activities, yet in many ways it is one that has been artificially created. Originally, many of the higher elevation lakes and streams in California's wilderness areas were devoid of fish prior to the implementation of stocking programs at the turn of the century. As the concept of using wilderness areas as benchmarks of biological integrity has grown, an increasing number of people are questioning whether artificial stocking of lakes and streams can be justified.

There are two arguments against fish stocking. Studies have demonstrated that fish-stocked lakes and streams receive far more visitation than unstocked waters. One of the fastest ways to create a wilderness management overuse problem is by stocking fish in a previously fishless lake. Admittedly, this is an aesthetic issue—how pristine looking do we want our wildlands to be?

But an even more important question concerns the effect of introduced fish upon ecosystem function. Recent declines of frogs in the High Sierra are thought to be related, in part, to the presence of fish in many previously fishless lakes. Fish eat tadpoles, reducing the reproductive success of amphibians. And the fact is, few studies have looked at the impact of fish introduction on invertebrate populations in previously fishless lakes.

Of course, careful stocking of only waters that had native fish is one way to avoid these problems, but there are drawbacks to this. Stocked fish compete with native wild fish for food and shelter. Even though wild fish are better competitors, the higher fish numbers still stress native fish populations. Furthermore, sometimes stocked fish hybridize with existing native fish, creating genetic problems.

For all of the above reasons, a careful assessment of fish stocking policies should be part of any wilderness management plan.

Wilderness Management

One continuously hears how we are "loving wilderness to death." The threat of hordes of backpackers overrunning and destroying our wild areas is used to justify many restrictive management policies, such as permits, trailhead quotas, designated campsites, and—most recently—fees to pay for the growing bureaucracy necessary to operate such a program. I would argue that backpackers and hikers aren't the major threat to wilderness, and with only a few exceptions, we don't need any management of backcountry foot users. The fact is that most regulatory agencies purposefully or unconsciously avoid dealing with activities that cause far more damage and degradation to our wildlands than any number of backpackers ever could.

From my perspective, even if growing numbers of hikers and backpackers were a real physical threat, I would still object to using restrictive management techniques, such as trailhead quotas, reservations, permits, designated campsites, and other controlling policies. This type of regulation destroys one of the most cherished values of wilderness—the opportunity to explore unimpeded. I want my activity dictated by the landscape, weather, and my personal mood, rather than by a bureaucracy.

Restrictive wilderness management policies are justified because of the presumed impacts of backpackers and hikers, yet these result in nothing more than minor cosmetic blemishes. A few campfire rings, trampled campsites, deep trails, and hacked-up trees—the common maladies usually ascribed to "overuse"—are an almost negligible ecological impact when viewed within the context of a wilderness that is thousands or millions of acres in size. Most of these impacts are concentrated on a very small amount of land, and their effect in the big scheme of things is hardly worth worrying about, much less spending scarce resources to regulate. Educating and encouraging the use of low-impact camping techniques can go a long way toward reducing these negative effects further.

Low-impact camping won't reduce all human imprint to zero, but our wildlands can easily accommodate some minor human presence. Afterall, the modern backpacker is far lighter on the land (I am speaking specifically of the immediate land-

scape, rather than the cumulative impact of our resource consumption) than was the average Native American community. There is no comparison between the effect on the landscape from today's low-impact backpacker with that of an entire community of people hunting wildlife, digging up roots, burning firewood, and building shelters from local materials. I think native people actually did influence California's landscape considerably, especially as a consequence of hunting and the setting of wildfires. Nevertheless, their long-term effect upon the country was still negligible. And if hundreds of thousands of non-technological people living in California's backcountry had no noticeable long-term effect on the land, it is difficult to envision how modern wilderness recreational use does anything serious enough to warrant major management effort.

Many of the so-called impacts agencies are trying to reduce or eliminate aren't impacts at all. Take, for example, the often cited argument against burning wood because "we are destroying nutrients or soil." The same agencies that suggest a few campfires are destroying the ecological balance of a million-acre wilderness will promote the idea that wildfires are a perfectly acceptable and necessary part of the landscape. The truth is that campfires have no significant impact, and indeed, the problem facing most western ecosystems is the slow process of organic decay. Fire is one of the natural recycling agents, and whether wood is burned up in a campfire or in a wildfire is of little consequence to the ecosystem. Both have the same positive effect of releasing nutrients to the environment.

If one really thought overuse was causing serious ecological damage, there are other, more creative ways to reduce or manipulate people than by use of permits and other restrictive measures. Removing bridges from river crossings, closing access roads further away from trailheads, eliminating trail upkeep, and other less intrusive measures can all lead to reduced use of fragile landscapes. Such "rewilding" allows the land, rather than a bureaucracy, to dictate where and when one can or will travel. This is far more in keeping with the spirit of wilderness than quotas and permits. I am not necessarily suggesting we get rid of all trails, bridges, and other features that ease travel. I would, however, prefer to have no trail, no bridges, and no road access than have an agency tell me whether or not I can take a walk in the woods.

At the same time that most agencies are spending the majority of their wilderness funds to manipulate the land's use by hikers and backpackers, they ignore many more serious effects that do need attention. For instance, the ecological impacts of air pollution, livestock grazing, fish stocking, fire suppression, habitat fragmentation, loss of evolutionary processes such as major predators, and the introduction and spread of weedy exotic species—all these are the real threats to the ecological health of our wildlands, yet they get little attention from management agencies. Think how many times, for instance, you have read signs that admonished you to camp 200 feet away from a lake to reduce "impact" on "fragile" shoreline vegetation, while no mention is made, much less effort to restrict, the far more serious impacts from a thousand-pound cow, stomping and chomping the same vegetation. Management agencies either neglect these impacts, or perhaps because scarce resources are used to issue permits and deal with other aspects of managing wilderness users, the personnel and funds just aren't available to deal with these other, more important issues. It's a matter of priorities: Spending money and personnel time to manage backpackers while ecologically destructive activities continue unabated is like swatting mosquitoes to minimize blood loss in a person dying from a severed artery.

Finally, when biological considerations can't be utilized to justify wilderness management policies, social issues such as trail crowding are used to implement restrictive measures. Yet, research has demonstrated over and over what most of us know from experience—that the majority of use is concentrated in a few popular areas. Most trails receive almost no use at all; crowding and other perceived negative social impacts are actually quite restricted and easily avoided. Indeed, in researching this book, I hiked and backpacked into every designated wildlands in the state. Many of these areas I visited repeatedly, and in more than 50, I never encountered a single other party. Even in so-called "overused and popular" wildernesses such as Yosemite, I seldom met another person once I was a few miles down the trail. Hiking popular trails on weekdays or during the off-season, avoiding the easiest, shortest route access point, camping off trail—these and many other choices are available to anyone who wishes to avoid crowding or congestion.

The point is simple: If solitude is what you desire, it is easily obtained with a minimum of effort. I prefer to "earn" my solitude by my own effort rather than have it guaranteed by bureaucratic decree, and I believe such an approach is far more in keeping with the spirit of the Wilderness Act.

Furthermore, I personally believe that more people need to get out to experience and enjoy our wildlands. Removing or minimizing the obstacles to this enjoyment is critical to gaining the political and social power necessary to slow and, perhaps, reverse the continual chipping away at our wildlands heritage. Logging, road building, exotic plant invasion, fire suppression, livestock grazing—all of these are far more destructive to our wildlands than a few campfire rings or a rutted trail. Most people will only defend something they perceive as personally important, and without direct and repeated experience with our wildlands, people can't be expected to rally around the need to protect them.

No one should have to plan a year in advance to be able to take a walk in the woods, an activity not to be controlled by anyone, much less a government agency. At some level, access to natural landscapes is a birthright, not a privilege or something reserved for special occasions—or for those with sufficient funds to buy access. I fear the trend toward greater wilderness management, fees, and other measures threatens our collective wildlands heritage as much as logging roads, subdivisions, and cows.

Wilderness needs less management and more protection from outside forces. It needs fewer wilderness rangers, firefighters, and cows, and more biologists, fire ecologists, and supporters.

Appendix I: Wilderness Areas

California federal wilderness areas located outside of the California desert region.

BLM WILDERNESSES	Acreage	Year Designated
Ishi	240	1984
Machesna Mountain	120	1984
Santa Lucia	1,733	1978
Trinty Alps	4,623	1984
Yolla Bolly–Middle Eel	8,500	1964, 1984

These wildernesses are small parcels of BLM lands that are adjacent to existing Forest Service Wilderness areas.

FISH AND WILDLIFE SERVICE WILDERNESSES		
Farallon	141	1974

NATIONAL PARK SERVICE WILDERNESSES		
Ansel Adams	665	1984
Lassen Volcanic	78,982	1972
Lava Beds	28,460	1972
Pinnacles	12,952	1976
Point Reyes	25,370	1976
Sequoia–Kings Canyon	736,980	1984
Yosemite	677,600	1984

FOREST SERVICE WILDERNESSES		
Agua Tibia	15,933	1974
Ansel Adams	228,669	1964, 1984
Bucks Lake	21,000	1984
Caribou	20,625	1964, 1984
Carson–Iceberg	160,000	1984
Castle Crags	7,300	1984
Chanchelulla	8,200	1984
Chumash	38,150	1992
Cucamonga	12,981	1964, 1984
Desolation	63,475	1969
Dick Smith	64,700	1984
Dinkey Lakes	30,000	1984
Domeland	130,986	1964, 1984, 1994
Emigrant	112,191	1974, 1984
Garcia	14,100	1992
Golden Trout	303,287	1978
Granite Chief	25,000	1984
Hauser	8,000	1984
Hoover	48,601	1964
Ishi	41,600	1984
Jennie Lakes	10,500	1984

Appendix I: continued

FOREST SERVICE WILDERNESSES

	Acreage	Year Designated
John Muir	580,675	1964, 1984
Kaiser	22,700	1976
Machesna Mountain	19,880	1984
Mantilija	29,600	1992
Marble Mountain	241,744	1964, 1984
Mokelumne	104,461	1964, 1984
Monarch	45,000	1984
Mount Shasta	37,000	1984
North Fork	8,100	1984
Pine Creek	13,100	1984
Red Buttes	16,150	1984
Russian	12,000	1984
San Gabriel	36,118	1968
San Gorgonio	94,702	1964, 1984, 1994
San Jacinto	32,040	1964, 1984
San Mateo Canyon	39,540	1984
San Rafael	151,040	1968, 1984
Santa Lucia	18,666	1978
Santa Rosa	84,500	1984, 1994
Sespe	219,700	1992
Sheep Mountain	43,600	1984
Silver Peak	14,000	1992
Siskiyou	153,000	1984
Snow Mountain	37,000	1984
South Sierra	63,000	1984
South Warner	70,385	1964, 1984
Thousand Lakes	16,335	1964
Trinity Alps	495,377	1984
Ventana	219,000	1964, 1992
Yolla Bolly–Middle Eel	145,404	1964, 1984

STATE PARKS WITH STATE DESIGNATED WILDERNESS AREAS

Big Basin State Park (Waddell Creek Wilderness)
Cuyamca Rancho State Park
Henry Coe State Park (Orestimba Wilderness)
Mount San Jacinto State Park
Muro Point State Park (Boney Mt. Wilderness)
Sinkyone Wilderness State Park

Appendix 2: Addresses

The addresses listed below can be useful as contacts for specific information on hiking trails, access, permits, and other up-to-date materials.

AGUA TIBIA WILDERNESS
Palomar RD, Cleveland NF
1634 Black Canyon Road
Ramona, CA 92065

ANSEL ADAMS WILDERNESS
Mono Lake RD, Inyo NF
PO Box 429
Lee Vining, CA 93541

BUCKS LAKE WILDERNESS
Quincy RD, Plumas, NF
39696 Highway 70
Quincy, CA 95971

**CACHE CREEK
PROPOSED WILDERNESS**
Clear Lake Resource Area Office
2550 North State Street
Ukiah, CA 95482-3023

CARIBOU WILDERNESS
Almanor RD, Lassen NF
PO Box 767
Chester, CA 96020

CARSON–ICEBERG WILDERNESS
Carson RD, Toiyabe NF
1536 South Carson Street
Carson City, NV 89701

CASTLE CRAGS WILDERNESS
Mount Shasta RD, Shasta–Trinity NF
204 West Alma Street
Mount Shasta City, CA 96067

CHANCHELULLA WILDERNESS
Yolla Bolly RD, Shasta–Trinity NF
Platina, CA 96076

CHUMASH WILDERNESS
Mount Pinos RD, Los Padres NF
HC1 Box 400
Frazier Park, CA 93225

CUCAMONGA WILDERNESS
Cajon RD, San Bernardino NF
1209 Lytle Creek Road
Lytle Creek, CA 92358

DESOLATION WILDERNESS
Eldorado NF
3070 Camino Heights Drive
Camino, CA 95709

DICK SMITH WILDERNESS
Santa Barbara RD, Los Padres NF
Los Prietos Station, Star Route
Santa Barbara, CA 93105

DINKEY LAKES WILDERNESS
Pineridge RD, Sierra NF
PO Box 559
Prather, CA 93651

DOMELAND WILDERNESS
Cannell Meadow RD, Sequoia NF
PO Box 6
Kernville, CA 93238

EMIGRANT WILDERNESS
Summit RD, Stanislaus NF
Pinecrest Lake Road
Pinecrest, CA 95364

GARCIA WILDERNESS
Santa Lucia RD, Los Padres NF
1616 North Carlotti Drive
Santa Maria, CA 93454

GOLDEN GATE NATIONAL REC AREA
Fort Mason, Building 201
San Francisco, CA 94123

GOLDEN TROUT WILDERNESS
Mount Whitney RD, Inyo NF
PO Box 8
Lone Pine, CA 93545

GRANITE CHIEF WILDERNESS
Truckee RD, Tahoe NF
10342 Highway 89
North Truckee, CA 96161

HAUSER WILDERNESS
Descanso RD, Cleveland NF
3348 Alpine Blvd.
Alpine, CA 91901

HENRY COE WILDERNESS
Henry Coe State Park
PO Box 846
Morgan Hill, CA 95038

HOOVER WILDERNESS
Bridgeport RD, Toiyabe NF
PO Box 595
Bridgeport, CA 93517

ISHI WILDERNESS
Almanor RD, Lassen NF
Box 767
Chester, CA 96020

JENNIE LAKES WILDERNESS
Hume Lake RD, Sequoia NF
35860 East Kings Canyon Road
Dunlap, CA 93621

Appendix 2: continued

JOHN MUIR WILDERNESS
Mount Whitney RD, Inyo NF
PO Box 8
Lone Pine, CA 93545

KAISER WILDERNESS
Pineridge RD, Sierra NF
PO Box 300
Shaver Lake, CA 93664

LASSEN WILDERNESS
Lassen NP
PO Box 100
Mineral, CA 96063

LAVA BEDS WILDERNESS
Lava Beds NM
PO Box 867
Tulelake, CA 96134

MACHESNA MOUNTAIN WILDERNESS
Santa Lucia RD, Los Padres NF
1616 Carlotti Drive
Santa Barbara, CA 93454

MARBLE MOUNTAIN WILDERNESS
salmon River RD, Klamath NF
P O Box 280
Etna, CA 96027

MATILIJA WILDERNESS
Ojai RD, Los Padres NF
1190 East Ojai Avenue
Ojai, CA 93023

MOKELUMNE WILDERNESS
Eldorado NF
3070 Camino Heights Drive
Camino, CA 95709

MONARCH WILDERNESS
Hume Lake RD, Sequoia NF
35860 East Kings Canyon Road
Dunlap, CA 93621

MOUNT SAN JACINTO WILDERNESS
Mount San Jacinto State Park
PO Box 308
Idyllwild, CA 92549

MOUNT SHASTA WILDERNESS
Mount Shasta RD, Shasta–Trinity NF
204 West Alma Street
Mount Shasta, CA 96067

NORTH FORK WILDERNESS
Mad River RD, Six Rivers NF
Star Route, Box 300
Bridgeville, CA 95526

**PHILLIP BURTON WILDERNESS
(POINT REYES NS)**
Point Reyes National Seashore
Point Reyes Station, CA 94956

PINE CREEK WILDERNESS
Descanso RD, Cleveland NF
3348 Alpine Blvd.
Alpine, CA 91901

PINNACLES WILDERNESS
Pinnacles National Monument
Paicines, CA 95043

RED BUTTES WILDERNESS
Applegate RD, Rogue River NF
6941 Upper Applegate Road
Jacksonville, Oregon 97530

RUSSIAN WILDERNESS
Salmon River RD, Klamath NF
PO Box 280
Enta, CA 96027

SAN GABRIEL WILDERNESS
Mount Baldy RD, Angeles NF
110 North Wabash Avenue
Glendora, CA 91764

SAN GORGONIO WILDERNESS
San Gorgonio RD, San Bernardino NF
34701 Mill Creek Road
Mentone, CA 92359

SAN JACINTO WILDERNESS
Idyllwild RD, San Bernardino NF
PO Box 518
Idyllwild, CA 92549

SAN MATEO CANYON WILDERNESS
Trabuco RD, Cleveland NF
1147 East Sixth Street
Corona, CA 91719

SAN RAFAEL WILDERNESS
Santa Lucia RD, Los Padrea NF
1616 Carlotti Drive
Santa Maria, CA 93454

SANTA LUCIA WILDERNESS
Santa Lucia RD, Los Padres NF
1616 Carlotti Drive
Santa Barbara, CA 93454

SANTA ROSA WILDERNESS
Idyllwild RD, San Bernardino NF
PO Box 518
Idyllwild, CA 92549

**SEQUOIA–KINGS CANYON
WILDERNESS**
Sequoia and Kings Canyon NP
Three Rivers, CA 93271

SESPE WILDERNESS
Ojai RD, Los PAdres NF
1190 East Ojai Avenue
Ojai, CA 93023

SHEEP MOUNTAIN WILDERNESS
Mount Baldy Road, Angles NF
110 North Wabash Avenue
Glendora, CA 91741

SILVER PEAK WILDERNESS
Monterey RD, Los Padres NF
406 South Mildred
King City, CA 93930

SISKIYOU WILDERNESS
Happy Camp RD, Klamath NF
Box 377
Happy Camp, CA 96039

SNOW MOUNTAIN WILDERNESS
Stonyford RD, Mendocino NF
5080 Lodoga–Stonyford Road
Stonyford, CA 95979

SOUTH SIERRA WILDERNESS
Mt Whitney RD, Inyo NF
PO Box 8
Lone Pine, CA 93545

SOUTH WARNER WILDERNESS
Warner Mt RD, Modoc NF
PO Box 220
Cedarville, CA 96104

THOUSAND LAKES WILDERNESS
Hat Creek RD, Lassen NF
PO Box 220
Fall River Mills, CA 96028

TRINITY ALPS WILDERNESS
Big Bar RD, Shasta–Trinity NF
Star Route 1, Box 10
Big Bar, CA 96010

VENTANA WILDERNESS
Monterey RD, Los Padres NF
406 South Mildred
King City, CA 93930

YOLLA BOLLY–MIDDLE EEL WILDERNESS
Covelo RD, Mendocino NF
78150 Covelo Road
Covelo, CA 95428

YOSEMITE WILDERNESS
Yosemite NP, Box 577
Yosemite NP, CA 95389

YUKI PROPOSED WILDERNESS
Covelo RD, Mendocino NF
78150 Covelo Road
Covelo, CA 95428

Appendix 3: Wilderness Areas by Region

NORTHEAST
Caribou
Ishi
Lassen Volcanic
Lava Beds
Mount Shasta
South Warner
Thousand Lakes

NORTHWEST
Cache Creek (proposed)
Castle Crags
Chanchelulla
Golden Gate NRA
King Range-Chemise
Mt Sinkyone (proposed)
Marble Mountain
North Fork

Point Reyes/ Phillip Burton
Red Buttes
Russian
Siskiyou
Snow Mountain
Trinty Alps
Yolla Bolly–Middle Eel
Yuki (proposed)

SIERRA NEVADA
Ansel Adams
Bucks Lake
Carson–Iceberg
Desolation
Dinkey Lakes
Domeland
Emigrant
Golden Trout
Granite Chief

Hoover
Jennie Lakes
John Muir
Kaiser
Mokelumne
Monarch
Sequoia–Kings Canyon
South Sierra
Yosemite

SOUTH COAST
Chumash
Dick Smith
Garcia
Henry Coe State Park–Orestimba Wilderness
Machesna Mountain

Matilija
Pinnacles
San Rafael
Santa Lucia
Sespe
Silver Peak
Ventana

SOUTHERN
Agua Tibia
Cucamonga
Pine Creek–Hauser
San Gabriel
San Gorgonio
San Jacinto
San Mateo Canyon
Santa Rosa
Sheep Mountain

Appendix 4: Maps

Most California wilderness areas have a specific map that covers the entire wilderness. Also each national forest and national park has its own map that shows the entire forest or park, including wilderness areas. Recommended maps for each wilderness are:

AGUA TIBIA WILDERNESS: Cleveland National Forest Map

ANSEL ADAMS WILDERNESS: Sierra National Forest Map, Inyo National Forest Map, Ansel Adams Wilderness Area Map

BUCKS LAKE WILDERNESS: Plumas National Forest Map, Bucks Lake Wilderness Area Map

CACHE CREEK PROPOSED WILDERNESS: Cache Creek Visitor's Map

CARIBOU WILDERNESS: Lassen National Forest Map

CARSON–ICEBERG WILDERNESS: Toiyabe National Forest/Bridgeport Ranger District Map, Stanislaus National Forest Map, Carson–Iceberg Wilderness Area Map

CASTLE CRAGS WILDERNESS: Shasta–Trinity National Forest Map, Mount Shasta/Castle Crags Wilderness Areas Map

CHANCHELULLA WILDERNESS: Shasta–Trinity National Forest Map

CHUMASH WILDERNESS: Los Padres National Forest Map/Ojai Ranger District

CUCAMONGA WILDERNESS: Angeles National Forest Map, San Bernardino National Forest Map, Cucamonga Wilderness Area Map

DESOLATION WILDERNESS: Eldorado National Forest Map, Tahoe Basin National Forest Map, Desolation Wilderness Area Map

DICK SMITH WILDERNESS: Los Padres National Forest/Santa Barbara Ranger District Map, Dick Smith Wilderness Map

DINKEY LAKES WILDERNESS: Sierra National Forest Map, Dinkey Lakes Wilderness Area Map

DOMELAND WILDERNESS: Sequoia National Forest Map, Domeland Wilderness Area Map

EMIGRANT WILDERNESS: Stanislaus National Forest Map, Emigrant Wilderness Area Map

GARCIA WILDERNESS: Los Padres National Forest/Santa Lucia District Map

GOLDEN GATE NATIONAL RECREATION AREA: Golden Gate National Recreation Area Map

GOLDEN TROUT WILDERNESS: Sequoia National Forest Map, Golden Trout/South Sierra Wilderness Areas Map

GRANITE CHIEF WILDERNESS: Tahoe Basin National Forest Map, Granite Chief and Wentworth Springs 7.5' USGS Topo Maps

HAUSER WILDERNESS: Cleveland National Forest Map, Pine Creek/Hauser Wilderness Areas Map

HENRY COE STATE PARK–ORESTIMBA WILDERNESS: Henry Coe State Park Map

HOOVER WILDERNESS: Toiyabe National Forest/Bridgeport Ranger District Map, Inyo National Forest Map, Hoover Wilderness Area Map

ISHI WILDERNESS: Lassen National Forest Map

JENNIE LAKES WILDERNESS: Sequoia National Forest Map, Monarch/Jennie Lakes Wilderness Areas Map

JOHN MUIR WILDERNESS: Sierra National Forest Map, Inyo National Forest Map, John Muir/Sequoia/Kings Canyon Wilderness Areas Map

KAISER WILDERNESS: Sierra National Forest Map, Kaiser Wilderness Area Map

KING RANGE PROPOSED WILDERNESS: King Range Conservation Area Map

LASSEN VOLCANIC WILDERNESS: Lassen National Park Map

LAVA BEDS WILDERNESS: Lava Beds National Monument Map

MACHESNA MOUNTAIN WILDERNESS: Los Padres National Forest/Santa Lucia District Map

MARBLE MOUNTAIN WILDERNESS: Klamath National Forest Map, Marble Mountain Wilderness Area Map

MATILIJA WILDERNESS: Los Padres National Forest/Ojai Ranger District Map

MOKELUMNE WILDERNESS: Eldorado National Forest Map, Stanislaus National Forest Map, Toiyabe National Forest Map/Carson Ranger District, Mokelumne Wilderness Area Map

MONARCH WILDERNESS: Sierra National Forest Map, Sequoia National Forest Map, Monarch Wilderness/Jennie Lakes Wilderness Areas Map

MOUNT SHASTA WILDERNESS: Shasta–Trinity National Forest Map, Mount Shasta/Castle Crags Wilderness Areas Map

NORTH FORK WILDERNESS: Six Rivers National Forest Map

PINE CREEK AND HAUSER WILDERNESSES: Cleveland National Forest Map, Pine Creek/Hauser Wilderness Areas Map

PINNACLES WILDERNESS: Pinnacles National Monument Map

POINT REYES/PHILLIP BURTON WILDERNESS: Point Reyes National Seashore Map

RED BUTTES WILDERNESS: Klamath National Forest Map

RUSSIAN WILDERNESS: Klamath National Forest Map, Marble Mountains/Russian Wilderness Areas Map

SAN GABRIEL WILDERNESS: Angeles National Forest Map

SAN GORGONIO WILDERNESS: San Bernardino National Forest Map, San Gorgonio Wilderness Area Map

SAN JACINTO WILDERNESS: San Bernardino National Forest Map, San Jacinto Wilderness Area Map

SAN MATEO CANYON WILDERNESS: Cleveland National Forest Map

SAN RAPHAEL WILDERNESS: Los Padres National Forest/Santa Barbara Ranger District Map

SANTA LUCIA WILDERNESS: Los Padres National Forest/Santa Lucia Ranger District Map

SANTA ROSA WILDERNESS: San Bernardino National Forest Map, Santa Rosa Wilderness Area Map

SEQUOIA–KINGS CANYON WILDERNESS: Sequoia–Kings Canyon National Park Map, John Muir/Sequoia/Kings Canyon Wilderness Areas Map

SESPE WILDERNESS: Los Padres National Forest/Ojai Ranger District Map

SHEEP MOUNTAIN WILDERNESS: Angeles National Forest Map, San Bernardino National Forest Map, Sheep Mountain Wilderness Area Map

SILVER PEAK WILDERNESS: Los Padres National Forest/Santa Lucia Ranger District Map

SISKIYOU WILDERNESS: Six Rivers National Forest Map, Klamath National Forest Map

SNOW MOUNTAIN WILDERNESS: Mendocino National Forest Map, Snow Mountain Wilderness Area Map

SOUTH SIERRA WILDERNESS: Inyo National Forest Map, Golden Trout/South Sierra Wilderness Areas Map

SOUTH WARNER WILDERNESS: Modoc National Forest Map, South Warner Wilderness Area Map

Appendix 4: continued

THOUSAND LAKES WILDERNESS: Lassen National Forest Map
TRINITY ALPS WILDERNESS: Shasta–Trinity National Forest Map, Klamath
National Forest Map, Trinity Alps Wilderness Area Map
VENTANA WILDERNESS: Los Padres National Forest/Monterey Ranger District Map,
Ventana Wilderness Area Map
YOLLA BOLLY–MIDDLE EEL WILDERNESS: Mendocino National Forest Map,
Six Rivers National Forest Map, Shasta–Trinity National Forest Map, Yolla
Bolly–Middle Eel Wilderness Area Map
YOSEMITE WILDERNESS: Yosemite National Park Map, Yosemite National Park
Topo Map
YUKI PROPOSED WILDERNESS: Mendocino National Forest Map

Appendix 5: Map Sources

Most wilderness area, topographical, Forest Service, and Park Service maps can be
obtained locally in sporting goods and outdoor stores. However, you can also obtain them
in advance for planning purposes by contacting the following appropriate source agency:

FOREST SERVICE
USDA Forest Service
630 Sansome Street
San Francisco, CA 94111

You can also obtain an order form by
visiting the USFS Pacific Southwest
Region Web Page at:

www.r5.pswfs.gove/visctr/maporder.html

The Web Site is also a source for other
information on wilderness permits,
phone numbers, and brief descriptions
of each national forest in California.

NATIONAL PARK SERVICE
National Park Service, California Office
Fort Mason Building 201
San Francisco, CA 94123

Additional information about each
California national park can be obtained
by visiting the National Park Service
Web Site at:

www.nps.gov/park_ph.html#ca

**BUREAU OF LAND MANAGEMENT
(BLM)**
California State Office
2800 Cottage Way, E-2841
Sacramento, CA 95825
(916) 978-4754

CALIFORNIA STATE PARKS
California Dept. of Parks and Recreation
PO Box 942896
Sacramento, CA 94296-0001
(916) 653-6995

TOPOGRAPHICAL MAPS
For a FREE index to topographical maps
in California contact:

U.S. Geological Survey
345 Middlefield Road MS-532
Menlo Park, CA 94025
(415) 329-4390

The California office of the USGS does
not sell maps by mail. To order by mail,
you must contact the Denver office.

USGS Western Distribution Branch
PO Box 25286
Federal Center
Denver, CO 80225
(800) USA-MAPS

Appendix 6: Selected References

Barbour, Michael, Bruce Pavlik, Frank Drysdale, and Susan Lindstrom. 1993. *California's Changing Landscape—Diversity and Conservation of California Vegetation.* California Native Plant Society, Sacramento, CA.

Bernstein, Art. 1991. *The Best Day Hikes of the California Northwest.* Mountain N'Air Books, La Crescenta, CA.

Centers for Water and Wildlands Resources. 1996. *Status of the Sierra Nevada—Sierra Nevada Ecosystem Project.* Wildland Resources Center Report 37. UC Davis, Davis, CA.

Douglas, William O. 1961. *My Wilderness: East to Katahdin.* Doubleday, Garden City, NJ.

Evens, Jules. 1988. *The Natural History of the Point Reyes Peninsula.* Point Reyes National Seashore Association, Point Reyes, CA.

Hart, John. 1975. *Hiking Bigfoot Country.* The Wildlands of Northern California and Southern Oregon. Sierra Club Books, San Francisco, CA.

Hill, Mary. 1984. *California Landscape—Origin and Evolution.* University of California Press, Berkeley, CA.

Irwin, Sue. 1991. *California's Eastern Sierra—A Visitor's Guide.* Cachuma Press, Los Olivos, CA.

Jenkins, J. C. 1978. *Self Propelled in the Southern Sierra. Vol. 1: The Sierra Crest and Kern Plateau.* Wilderness Press, Berkeley, CA.

Johnston, Verna. 1994. *California Forests and Woodlands—A Natural History.* University of California Press, Berkeley, CA.

Linkhart, Luther, and Michael White. 1994. *The Trinity Alps—A Hiking and Backpacking Guide.* Wilderness Press, Berkeley, CA.

McKinney, John. 1994. *Walking the California Coast.* Harper Collins West, New York, NY.

McKinney, John. 1994. *Walking Southern California—A Day Hiker's Guide.* Harper Collins West, New York, NY.

Muir, John. 1961. *The Mountains of California.* The Natural History Library, Garden City, NY.

Ostertag, Rhonda and George. 1995. *California State Parks—A Complete Recreation Guide.* The Mountaineers, Seattle, WA.

Palmer, Tim. 1988. *The Sierra Nevada—A Mountain Journey.* Island Press, Covelo, CA.

Pavlik, Bruce, Pamela Muick, Sharon Johnson, and Marjorie Popper. 1991. *Oaks of California.* Cachuma Press, Los Olivos, CA.

Robinson, John. 1984. *San Bernardino Mountain Trails—100 Hikes in Southern California.* Wilderness Press, Berkeley, CA.

Robinson, John. 1984. *Trails of the Angeles—100 Hikes in the San Gabriels.* Wilderness Press, Berkeley, CA.

Schaffer, Jeffrey. 1990. *Lassen Volcanic National Park and Vicinity.* Wilderness Press, Berkeley, CA.

Schaffer, Jeffrey. 1988. *Hiking the Big Sur Country.* Wilderness Press, Berkeley, CA.

Schaffer, Jeffrey. 1987. *Desolation Wilderness and South Lake Tahoe Basin.* Wilderness Press, Berkeley, CA.

Schaffer, Jeffrey. 1986. *Yosemite National Park—A Natural History Guide and Trails.* Wilderness Press, Berkeley, CA.

Schinfrin, Ben. 1992. *Emigrant Wilderness and Northwest Yosemite.* Wilderness Press, Berkeley, CA.

Appendix 6 : continued

Schoenherr, Allan. 1992. *A Natural History of California.* UC Berkeley Press, Berkeley, CA.

Soares, John, and Marc Soares. 1994. *100 Hikes in Northern California.* The Mountaineers, Seattle, WA.

Stienstra, Tom, and Michael Hodgson. *The Complete Guide to California Hiking.* Foghorn Press, San Francisco, CA.

Thelander, Carl. (ed.) 1994. *Life on the Edge—A Guide to California's Endangered Natural Resources: Wildlife.* BioSystems Books, Santa Cruz, CA.

Thoreau, Henry David. 1992. *Walden, or Life in the Woods.* Knopf: Distributed by Random House, New York, NY.

Whitehill, Karen and Terry. 1991. *Best Short Hikes in the Southern Sierra.* The Mountaineers, Seattle, WA.

Whitney, Stephen. 1981. *The Sierra Nevada—A Sierra Club Naturalist's Guide.* Sierra Club Books, San Francisco, CA.

Wuerthner, George. 1994. *California's Sierra Nevada.* American Geographic Publishing, Helena, MT.

Wuerthner, George. 1994. *Yosemite—A Visitor's Companion.* Stackpole Books, Mechanicsburg, PA.

Appendix 7: Environmental Groups

CALIFORNIA WILDERNESS COALITION
2655 Portage Bay East
Davis, CA 95616
(805) 963-1622

**CENTRAL SIERRA
ENVIRONMENTAL CENTER**
PO Box 396
Twain Harte, CA 95383

HIGH SIERRA HIKERS ASSOCIATION
PO Box 8920
South Lake Tahoe, CA 96158

KLAMATH FOREST ALLIANCE
PO Box 820
Etna, CA 96027

SIERRA CLUB
85 Second Street
San Francisco, CA 94105

FAWN
PO Box 603
Georgetown, CA 95634

FRIENDS OF THE INYO
Drawer D
Lone Pine, CA 93545

FRIENDS OF THE RIVER
128 J Street
Sacramento, CA 95814

FRIENDS OF THE PLUMAS
PO Box 584
Quincy, CA 95971

KEEP THE SESPE WILD
PO Box 715
Ojai, CA 93023

**MENDOCINO
ENVIRONMENTAL CENTER**
106 West Stanley Street
Ukiah, CA 95482

**NORTH COAST
ENVIRONMENTAL CENTER**
879 9th Street
Arcata, CA 95521

SEQUOIA FOREST ALLIANCE
182 Reid Avenue
Porterville, CA 93257

THE WILDERNESS SOCIETY
PO Box 29241
San Francisco, CA 94129

Index

NOTE: Bolded entries denote trail descriptions; citations followed by the letter "p" denote photos; citations followed by the letter "m" denote maps.

Index

328

George Wuerthner

George Wuerthner is a freelance writer, photographer, and ecologist with 20 published books and hundreds of magazine articles and calendar publications to his credit. Previously published books include *Forever Wild—The Adirondacks, Maine Coast, Vermont—Portrait of the Land and Its People, Southern Appalachian Country, Yellowstone—A Visitor's Companion, Yellowstone and the Fires of Change, Rocky Mountain National Park—Rooftop of the Rockies, Nevada Mountain Ranges, Oregon Mountain Ranges, Idaho Mountain Ranges, Montana—Magnificent Wilderness, Alaska Mountain Ranges, Alaska, Texas' Big Bend Country, California's Sierra Nevada, Yosemite—A Visitor's Companion* and, soon to be released, *Grand Canyon—A Visitor's Companion.*

Previous to becoming a full-time freelance writer and photographer, Wuerthner worked as a biologist, botanist, river ranger, and wilderness ranger with various federal agencies and also instructed at several universities and colleges.

Wuerthner currently resides in Eugene, Oregon.